Parent–Infant Interaction

The Ciba Foundation for the promotion of international cooperation in medical and chemical research is a scientific and educational charity established by CIBA Limited – now CIBA-GEIGY Limited – of Basle. The Foundation operates independently in London under English trust law.

Ciba Foundation Symposia are published in collaboration with Associated Scientific Publishers (Elsevier Scientific Publishing Company, Excerpta Medica, North-Holland Publishing Company) in Amsterdam.

Associated Scientific Publishers, P.O. Box 211, Amsterdam

Parent-Infant Interaction

Ciba Foundation Symposium 33 (new series)

1975

Elsevier · Excerpta Medica · North-Holland

Associated Scientific Publishers · Amsterdam · Oxford · New York

ISBN Excerpta Medica 90 219 4037 x
ISBN American Elsevier 0-444-15181-8

Published in August 1975 by Associated Scientific Publishers, P.O. Box 211, Amsterdam, and American Elsevier, 52 Vanderbilt Avenue, New York, N.Y. 10017.

Suggested series entry for library catalogues: Ciba Foundation Symposia.
Suggested publisher's entry for library catalogues: Associated Scientific Publishers.

Ciba Foundation Symposium 33 (new series)

Printed in The Netherlands by Mouton, The Hague

Contents

Participants

Symposium on The Parent–Infant Relationship held at the Ciba Foundation, London, 5th–7th November, 1974

M. A. HOFER (*Chairman*) Albert Einstein College of Medicine and Montefiore Hospital and Medical Center, 111 East 210th Street, Bronx, New York, USA

*R. Q. BELL Child Research Branch, National Institute of Mental Health, Bethesda, Maryland 20014, USA

A. BENTOVIM Department of Psychological Medicine, The Hospital for Sick Children, Great Ormond Street, London WC1N 1EH, UK

J. BOWLBY School of Family Psychiatry and Community Mental Health, The Tavistock Institute of Human Relations, Belsize Lane, London NW3 5BA, UK

T. B. BRAZELTON The Children's Hospital Medical Center, 300 Longwood Avenue, Boston, Mass. 02115, USA

GENEVIEVE CARPENTER Psychology Department, Belmont Hospital, Brighton Road, Sutton, Surrey, UK

CHRISTINE E. COOPER Children's Department, The Royal Victoria Infirmary, Queen Victoria Road, Newcastle upon Tyne NE1 4LP, UK

G. H. CURTIS-JENKINS 50 Church Road, Ashford, Middlesex, UK

COLETTE DREYFUS-BRISAC Centre de Recherches Biologiques Néonatales, Hôpital Port-Royal, Université René Descartes, 123 Boulevard de Port-Royal, 75674 Paris Cedex 14, France

FRANCES D'SOUZA Wellcome Institute of Comparative Physiology, The Zoological Society of London, Regent's Park, London NW1 4RY, UK

**Present address:* Department of Psychology, University of Virginia, Charlottesville, Virginia 22901, USA

JUDY DUNN MRC Unit on the Development and Integration of Behaviour, University Sub-Department of Animal Behaviour, Madingley, Cambridge CB3 8AA, UK

J. HESS-HAESER Zoological Department, University of Basel, Rheinsprung 9, CH-Basel-4000, Switzerland

R. A. HINDE MRC Unit on the Development and Integration of Behaviour, University Sub-Department of Animal Behaviour, Madingley, Cambridge CB3 8AA, UK

J. H. KENNELL Department of Pediatrics, Case Western Reserve University, 2103 Adelbert Road, Cleveland, Ohio 44106, USA

M. H. KLAUS Department of Pediatrics, Case Western Reserve University, 2103 Adelbert Road, Cleveland, Ohio 44106, USA

P. H. LEIDERMAN Department of Psychiatry, Stanford University School of Medicine, Stanford, Calif. 94305, USA

J. A. MACFARLANE Department of Experimental Psychology, University of Oxford, South Parks Road, Oxford OX1 3PS, UK

T. E. OPPÉ Paediatric Unit, St Mary's Hospital Medical School, Praed Street, London W2 1PG, UK

H. PAPOUŠEK Max-Planck-Institut für Psychiatrie, Kraspelinstrasse 2 und 10, D-München 22, German Federal Republic

M. P. M. RICHARDS Unit for Research on Medical Applications of Psychology, 5 Salisbury Villas, Station Road, Cambridge CB1 2JQ, UK

J. S. ROSENBLATT Institute of Animal Behaviour, Rutgers University, 101 Warren Street, Newark, New Jersey 07102, USA

D. M. SALISBURY Department of Paediatrics, University of Oxford, John Radcliffe Hospital, Headington, Oxford OX3 9DU, UK

M. J. A. SIMPSON MRC Unit on the Development and Integration of Behaviour, University Sub-Department of Animal Behaviour, Madingley, Cambridge CB3 8AA, UK

ANN L. STEWART Department of Paediatrics, University College Hospital, Huntley Street, London WC1E 6JJ, UK

EVELYN B. THOMAN Department of Biobehavioral Sciences, The College of Liberal Arts and Sciences, The University of Connecticut, Storrs, Conn. 06268, USA

Editors: RUTH PORTER (organizer) and MAEVE O'CONNOR

Introduction

M. A. HOFER

Albert Einstein College of Medicine and Montefiore Hospital and Medical Center, Bronx, New York

The area of research that we are going to be discussing at this meeting is in a very exciting phase. We are beginning to see a kind of cross-pollination between research in animal behaviour and human neonatal studies which has injected vigorous new ideas into both fields. Probably as a part of the environmental or ecological movement, which is now worldwide, man is beginning to consider himself part of the living organic matrix of nature. The fact that social relationships have been demonstrated to be vital to the development of most other primates and some other infra-human mammals has in a peculiar way helped us to accept our *own* dependency on our first experiences with our parents. During my medical school years, it was Harlow's work with monkeys that convinced me and many of my colleagues that Spitz and Bowlby were right about the importance of the early human mother–infant relationship.

Over the past decade, we have come to recognize that the early parent–infant relationship has a profound impact on the development of emotional behaviour, cognitive faculties, even biological organization and resistance to illness.

Most recently, our views of the infant as a passive beneficiary, or victim, of the parents' influence has been successfully challenged by data from both animal and human studies. The infant turns out to be immensely powerful in his own special field—that of promoting and regulating the behaviour of his parents. This has had the good effect of making us think, design studies, and interpret those studies in terms of an *evolving interaction*. Such a complex model presents methodological problems which we must solve as soon as possible.

Much fo the work I have just described was done by people in this room, and with rats and monkeys as well as humans. So we can be sure that we are dealing with something absolutely fundamental to the life of mammals, but we must also admit how little we know about how it all works. Fortunately, ignorance arouses curiosity, and there are some interesting new developments in data, in methods and in theory which are the reason for this conference.

We are also learning more about the differences between species and beginning to know at what level of abstraction we can hope to apply principles across species. This particular point should come up early in the conference and probably will not be settled by us here, even in the limited area of the processes underlying early parent–infant interaction. Specifically, several recent lines of evidence have suggested that small differences in the timing, duration and setting of early mother–infant contact have a surprisingly powerful effect on the quality and intensity of that relationship, months and even years later. This phenomenon reminds one immediately of the ethological work on 'imprinting' and the concept of critical periods. However, these concepts are by no means settled issues in the field of animal behaviour, despite the 35 or 40 years since the words were first applied to the formation of early social relationships. In this field, enquiry has shifted to the next underlying level, namely to the patterns of sensory, hormonal and other influences which together determine the earliest behavioural interactions and the subsequent course of development. Our conference seems to indicate that this shift in the area of animal behaviour has also taken place in human studies.

We are concerned now with whether the infant has a period of special receptivity for the mother immediately after birth, and with the processes acting on parent and infant which make that period of life special.

These research issues have become enmeshed, at least in the United States, in a social movement which provides exciting energy and a sense of urgency to people working in this field. We are asked, should human birth be a very different experience from what it is now? Should medical and nursing practice, hospital design and obstetric and paediatric procedures be substantially altered on the basis of the research evidence now available? Equally important, we must be careful that research findings are not misinterpreted and exploited by vocal pressure groups forcing changes which we will all regret later.

The usefulness of international conferences like this one is that we have a chance to learn from others in widely different areas, with different methods and different theoretical bases. Our group represents a wide range of disciplines: animal behaviour, neonatal physiology, development psychology, paediatrics, psychiatry and social psychology. Usually in such a heterogeneous group there is an initial phase of defining one's discipline and drawing distinctions—a kind of 'territorial marking', to use the ethologists' term—a phase which can be prolonged and which delays transition to the next two stages: information transfer and eventually some kind of synthesis or shared understanding. I hope we can keep this first phase of territorial marking to a healthy minimum by indicating what we do not know as well as what we do know, and by not hesitating to ask questions of each other.

The programme begins with basic animal studies which give an evolutionary perspective and provide results from experiments which cannot be done with humans. This work will be used to illustrate theoretical issues and to frame principles which may govern the early human mother–infant interaction. We will move on to studies of the very earliest moments of the human mother–infant interaction, describe some of the unique behavioural events which take place at this time, and present evidence that different contexts and different interactions in those early hours and days may have long-term consequences for the relationship. We will then consider studies of the changing mother–infant interaction throughout the first year of life, dealing with processes stemming either from the infant or the mother, processes which shape the relationship over time. Finally, we will be dealing with the cognitive and emotional impacts of the developing relationship on both mother and child, and with how these impacts result in disturbances of health and in frank paediatric illness.

In our final discussion, the group may want to ask whether we are ready to try to apply some of our findings to health care practices, whether we can make any specific recommendations, and how such recommendations might be used to bring about change.

Mothers' and infants' roles: distinguishing the questions to be asked

R. A. HINDE

MRC Unit on the Development and Integration of Behaviour, Madingley, Cambridge

Abstract The mother–infant relationship consists of interaction sequences, each of which is in some measure unique. We must therefore study pooled data from interactions of the same 'type' occurring within a limited time period. Changes in the relationship must be assessed by comparing data from different time periods. To understand the dynamics of the interaction, it is essential to formulate sharply the questions being asked. In particular, the following questions must not be confused: 'Which partner is primarily responsible for determining the course of this type of interaction in a particular time period?', 'Changes in which partner are responsible for changes in the pattern of interaction between time periods?' and 'Are differences between mothers or between infants primarily responsible for inter-dyad differences in any one time period?' The argument is illustrated with data from rhesus monkeys.

That the mother–infant relationship depends on interactions in which the behaviour of each partner affects and is affected by that of the other no longer needs to be emphasized (e.g. Bell 1968). That the interactions themselves, even those involving very young babies, can be of considerable complexity, is becoming progressively more widely recognized. By analogy with interactional sequences that have been studied in non-human species (e.g. Baerends *et al.* 1955; Hinde 1970; Nelson 1964; Simpson 1968, 1973), we must expect each response of each individual to be determined not only by the preceding behaviour of the partner, but also by earlier behavioural events, the individual's current state, the environmental context, and so on.

Because the determinants are multiple, susceptible to mutual influence, and complex, each interaction sequence is in some measure unique. But science has no techniques for coping with unique events: we can ask questions only about populations of events judged to be, by some criterion, similar. We must therefore study categories of individually unique interaction sequences, regarding the component events as having probabilistic relations to each other. In practice we usually collect data on interaction sequences over limited and arbitrary time periods, pooling the data within each period and asking questions about the courses of the interactions within that period. For instance, we may ask how many of the attempts by an infant rhesus monkey to gain contact with his mother during his tenth week of life were rejected by her. Here we are abstracting data on events surrounding a point where the sequence of behaviour has two possible courses (infant approaches mother, mother rejects infant or mother receives infant), and asking not about the factors determining the course of the interaction in a particular case, but about the probability of its going one way or the other. On the basis of such data, we can better predict the next event the more preceding events we take into account (e.g. Altmann 1965); if we use enough data we should be able to predict with certainty, but in practice this is rarely possible, in part because the determinants of present events may lie in the fairly remote past (Simpson 1973).

To be of practical value, studies of the mother–infant relationship must not only bring understanding of the interactions within a limited time period, but must relate the course of those interactions to their immediate and long-term effects on the relationship. One issue here is that the effects of particular interactions on the course of a relationship may not be visible in their immediate consequences, but may be subtle and cumulative (Simpson 1973). It is partly for this reason that the questions one wishes to ask often concern overall probabilities of events and their patterning. Furthermore, it is often important to study not only the probability that one event will be followed by another but also the time relations between them. To take an example from a lower vertebrate, Simpson (1968) has presented convincing evidence that, in an aggressive encounter between two Siamese fighting fish (*Betta splendens*), the issues most crucial for predicting the outcome of the encounter concern the temporal relationships between the gill-raising display of one fish, the tail-beating display of the other fish, and the lowering of the gills of the first fish. Time relations between events are equally crucial in many of the interaction sequences between mother and child.

Both to assess the effects of interaction sequences on the long-term development of the relationship, and to elucidate their determinants within particular time periods, we must compare data from different time periods. In the first case we may examine sets of data on the same mother–infant pair in successive time periods. In the second we may for instance examine sets of data on the same mother–infant pair in different contexts, or different mother–infant pairs in the same context. The point to be emphasized here is that, if we are to understand the dynamics of a relationship over time, these questions must be recognized as distinct. To illustrate this point, we shall consider three questions, one concerned with data on one mother–infant pair within one time period, one with data in succeeding time periods, and one with otherwise comparable data on different individuals.

The issues will be discussed with reference to two measures. One is the time that infant and mother rhesus monkey spend in ventral-ventral contact. The other is a measure of the infant's role in the amount of contact observed. In our data collection we recorded each time that contact was made or broken, and whether the make or break was due to mother or infant. The difference between the percentage of makes due to the infant (% Mk_I) and the percentage of breaks due to the infant (% Bk_I) provides a measure of the infant's role in contact (Hinde & Atkinson 1970; Hinde & White 1974). The changes in these two measures with age are shown in Fig. 1. In each case the measures depend on data taken during watches totalling six hours either every week or every other week according to the age of the infant.

We may now consider these questions in turn.

(1) Is infant or mother primarily responsible for determining the lengths of contacts during each period? As indicated above, the difference between the proportion of contact-makes due to the infant and the proportion of contact-breaks due to the infant is an index of this. If the infant is responsible for a higher percentage of makes than of breaks, so that he has the greater role, the index will be positive; if he is responsible for more breaks than makes the index will be negative, the mother having the major role. Fig. 1 shows that in the early weeks it is the mother who is primarily responsible for ventral-ventral contacts, whilst later it is the infant.

Four points must be made. First, there are of course practical difficulties in telling who was responsible: the individual who actually breaks contact may be responding to inconspicuous signals from the partner. In practice, with rhesus monkeys this is probably not a major issue. Second, the value of the index depends to a limited extent on the number of observations: this is discussed elsewhere (Hinde & White 1974). Third, the index is concerned only with the *relative* role of the two partners: there are of course differences between, for instance, mother–infant dyads in which the infant is responsible for all the contacts and half of the breaks in contact and those in which he is responsible for half the contacts and none of the breaks in contact, yet both give a similar index. Finally, and perhaps most important in the present context, the index is only a summary of events during the time period in question; it tells us nothing about any individual sequence.

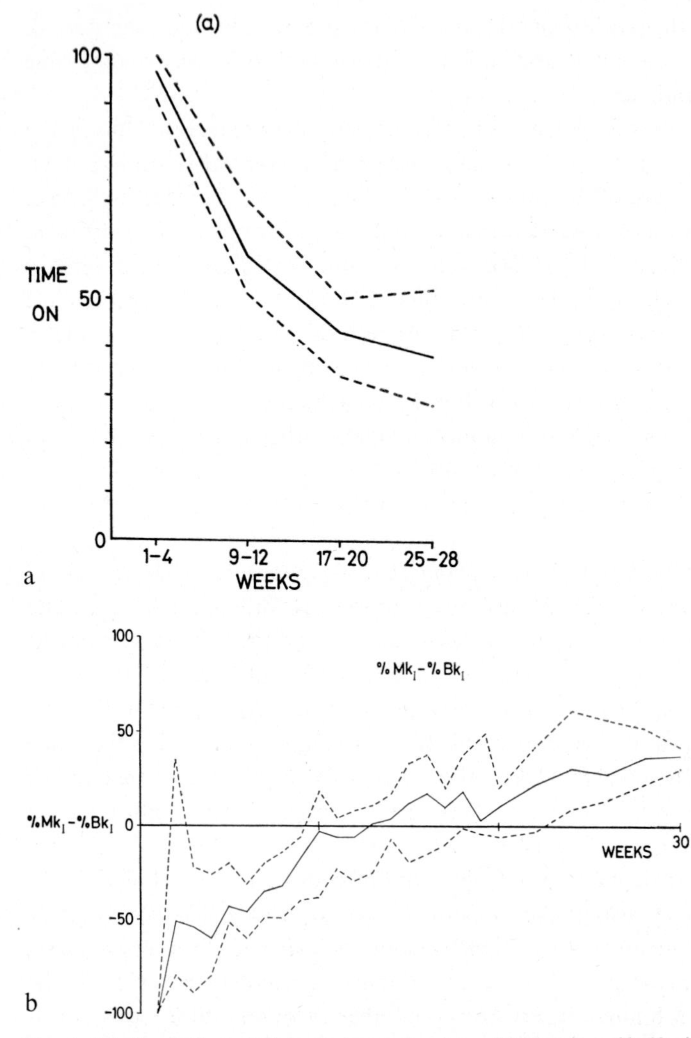

FIG. 1. Mother–infant relations in rhesus monkeys. (*a*) Number of half minutes in which infant was in ventral-ventral contact with mother as a percentage of the number observed. (*b*) Number of occasions on which infant was responsible for making contact, as a percentage of the total number of contact-makes (% Mk_I), minus the number of times infant was responsible for breaking contact, as a percentage of the total number of contact-breaks (% Bk_I).
Weeks: weeks of age of infant.
Continuous line: median. Discontinuous lines: interquartile range. (From Hinde & White 1974).

(2) Are the age-changes in the amount of ventral-ventral contact due more immediately to changes in the mother or to changes in the infant? This can be approached by looking at the relations between the changes in the two measures.

If the time in contact decreased due to a change in the behaviour of the infant, we should expect the index of the infant's role to decrease, but if it decreased due to a change in the behaviour of the mother, we should expect the index to increase. In general, a negative correlation between the two measures indicates that the mother's role is primary, whilst a positive correlation indicates that the infant's role is primary. Fig. 1 shows a negative correlation, and thus it is changes in the mother that are immediately responsible for the increasing independence of the infant. This is at first sight a surprising finding, since the increase in independence is correlated with, and seems at first sight to be due to, the infant's physical growth and increased tendency to explore his environment and seek for solid food. Nevertheless it is in harmony with the finding that infants reared on inanimate surrogate mothers, and infants reared without mothers but in pairs, maintain a considerable amount of ventral contact to a greater age than do infants reared on natural mothers (Hansen 1966; Harlow & Harlow 1965); the explanation in both cases no doubt lies in the rejecting behaviour of the natural mother.

This emphasis on the importance of changes in the mother's behaviour in promoting the increasing independence of the infant does not imply that the infant could not achieve independence on its own in the end: infants reared on inanimate mother surrogates do in fact leave them more and more as they grow older. Nor does it imply that the changes in the mother arise endogenously: they may be initiated by the infant's increasing demand for milk or its more vigorous locomotor play. But these activities in turn depend on maternal care, which in turn depends on communication with the infant, and so on. Development involves a constant interaction between mother and infant which, to be understood, must be gradually teased apart. This study is only a first stage to that end. But the present analysis demonstrates the importance of changes in the mother's behaviour in permitting and promoting the increasing independence of the infant, and shows that it is the changes in her behaviour that immediately regulate the speed with which independence is achieved.

The importance of this conclusion in the present context is this. During the first twelve weeks or so it is the *mother who is primarily responsible for ventral-ventral contact* ($\% \, Mk_I - \% \, Bk_I$ is negative) (Fig. 1). Nevertheless during this period it is changes in the mother that are immediately responsible for *promoting the increasing independence of the infant*. Thus the questions of who is responsible for the amount of contact at any one age, and that of changes in whom are primarily responsible for changes with age, are separate questions, not to be confused.

(3) At any one age, are the differences between mother–infant pairs primarily due to differences between mothers or to differences between infants? Here again, an examination of the correlations between measures can be valuable, using an argument similar to that used in the previous section. If, at any one age, those infants who have contact with their mothers are the ones who play the greatest role in contact (that is, in whom $\% \ Mk_I - \% \ Bk_I$ is highest), the differences in the amount of contact would be primarily due to the infants. If the correlation was significantly negative, the differences would be primarily due to mothers. In practice the correlations are near zero, indicating that differences between both mothers and infants are responsible. This question, it will be noted, is also independent of either of the two preceding ones.

Although these issues have been discussed before, they are repeated here in the hope that they may be relevant to some of the issues in this symposium. In fact, the questions are not infrequently confused in the literature. One example will suffice. Rosenblum (1971) has given careful consideration to the evidence that the rejecting responses of the mother contribute to the growth of independence in the infant, and tentatively suggests that their importance may have been overestimated. Of the cases he cites, three refer to the immediate determination of the amount of contact: Kaufmann's (1966) data on the role of play in promoting independence in rhesus monkeys; Harlow & Harlow's (1965) observations on the persistence with which the infants of primiparous 'motherless-mother' rhesus monkeys attempt to establish contact; and Rosenblum & Harlow's (1963) studies of the behaviour of rhesus infants on mother surrogates. One case concerns the determination of age-changes—Rosenblum's interpretation of Hinde & Spencer-Booth's (1968) data on rhesus infants. And four cases cited by Rosenblum concern the source of differences between mother–infant dyads at one age: Lindburg's (1969) comparison of normal and thalidomide-treated infant rhesus; Spencer-Booth's (1968) comparison between twin and singleton rhesus; Harlow & Harlow's (1965) comparison of rhesus infants reared by 'motherless' and by feral mothers; and Rosenblum's interpretation of some aspects of Hinde & Spencer-Booth's (1968) data on rhesus infants. Rosenblum also uses data relevant to two other questions: 'Are differences in mother–infant interaction between species due primarily to differences between the mothers or to differences between the infants' (Rosenblum's own data, Rosenblum & Kaufmann 1968); and 'Are differences in mother–infant interaction between dyads of the same species in different environments due primarily to differences between mothers or between infants' (Jensen *et al.*'s [1968] studies of pigtailed macaques)? My quarrel here is not with the particulars of Rosenblum's careful argument, but with the manner in which he confused these questions: they are logically distinct and must be treated as such. Comparable difficulties arise in some discussions of the human case (e.g. Rheingold & Eckerman 1971).

Having emphasized that the questions are distinct, I must also say that the first two are related, but to a limited extent. The mother–infant relationship is dynamic, and it must be assumed that each interaction may affect the subsequent course of the relationship—that is the subsequent pattern of interactions. Indeed potential change is inherent in every relationship—if a given interaction occurs, the subsequent relationship will be affected, but so also will it be affected if the interaction does not occur. (Both stability and change are to be understood in terms of the dynamic interrelations between participants [Hinde, unpublished] whose nature can in some cases be understood in terms of natural selection [Trivers 1974]). Since each interaction can be regarded as affecting the subsequent course of the relationship, the partner who determines the pattern of interactions in one time period must thereby affect the pattern in a later period. The nature of the effect, however, may depend on how much later that period is. Thus Rosenblum (1971) emphasizes that punishment by the mother can cause the infant to cling to her more tightly. However, while this may be an immediate effect of punishment, it is by no means clear that it is a longer-term one. Furthermore, the consequences of punishment for approaching the mother are known to depend on what alternatives are open to the infant (Jensen *et al.* 1969), and must also depend on the age of the infant.

But while an influence on the course of an ongoing interaction must be regarded as an influence on the course of subsequent ones, two further complications arise. First, it does not necessarily follow that the individual who primarily determines the course of an interaction is any less changed by that interaction than is his or her partner. Second, in a multiplex relationship (i.e. one in which the partners interact in more than one way), the course of any one type of interaction may be affected by previous interactions of other types. Thus a mother's propensity to reject her infant's attempts to cuddle against her may be affected by how much he has previously swung on her tail. The changes in the relationship reflect changes in the partners which are the result of the effects of diverse previous interactions within and outside the relationship. For these two reasons, understanding the role of the partners in a particular type of interaction in one time period may be no guide to understanding the nature of changes between time periods.

In conclusion, then, it is argued that full understanding of the dynamics of a relationship demands that the questions asked be framed in rather specific terms, and in particular that questions concerning the roles of the partners within a limited time period, questions concerning changes in the relationship over time, and questions concerning differences between relationships, should not be confused.

ACKNOWLEDGEMENTS

This work was supported by the Royal Society and by the Medical Research Council.

References

ALTMANN, S.A. (1965) Sociobiology of rhesus monkeys. II: Stochastics of communication. *J. Theor. Biol. 8*, 490–522

BAERENDS, G.P., BROUWER, R. & WATERBOLK, H.TJ. (1955) Ethological studies on *Lebistes reticulatus* (Peters): I. An analysis of the male courtship pattern. *Behaviour 8*, 249–334

BELL, R.Q. (1968) A reinterpretation of the direction of effects in studies of socialization. *Psychol. Rev. 75*, 81–95

HANSEN, E.W. (1966) The development of maternal and infant behavior in the rhesus monkey. *Behaviour 27*, 107–149

HARLOW, H.F. & HARLOW, M.K. (1965) The affectional systems, in *Behavior of Nonhuman Primates* (Schrier, A.M., Harlow, H.F., & Stollnitz, F., eds.) vol. 2, pp. 287–334, Academic Press, New York and London

HINDE, R.A. (1970) *Animal Behaviour: A Synthesis of Ethology and Comparative Psychology*, 2nd ed., McGraw-Hill, New York

HINDE, R.A. & ATKINSON, S. (1970) Assessing the roles of social partners in maintaining mutual proximity, as exemplified by mother-infant relations in monkeys. *Anim. Behav. 18*, 169–176

HINDE, R.A. & SPENCER-BOOTH, Y. (1968) The study of mother–infant interaction in captive group-living rhesus monkeys. *Proc. Roy. Soc. Lond. B*, *169*, 177–201

HINDE, R.A. & WHITE, L. (1974) The dynamics of a relationship—rhesus monkey ventro-ventral contact. *J. Comp. Physiol. Psychol. 86*, 8–23

JENSEN, G.D., BOBBITT, R.A. & GORDON, B.N. (1968) Effects of environment on the relationship between mother and infant pigtailed monkeys (*Macaca nemestrina*). *J. Comp. Physiol. Psychol. 66*, 259–263

JENSEN, G.D., BOBBITT, R.A. & GORDON, B.N. (1969) Patterns and sequences of hitting behavior in mother and infant monkeys (*Macaca nemestrina*). *Proc. 8th Int. Congr. Primatology*, Karger, Basle

KAUFMANN, J.H. (1966) Behavior of infant rhesus monkeys and their mothers in a free-ranging band. *Zoologica (N.Y.) 51*, 17–27

LINDBURG, D.G. (1969) Behavior of infant rhesus monkeys with thalidomide-induced malformations: a pilot study. *Psychonomic Sci. Anim. Physiol. Psychol. 15*, 55–56

NELSON, K. (1964) The temporal patterning of courtship behaviour in the glandulocaudine fishes (Ostariophysi, Characidae). *Behaviour 24*, 90–146

RHEINGOLD, H. & ECKERMAN, C.O. (1971) Departures from the mother, in *The Origins of Human Social Relations* (Schaffer, H.R., ed.), Academic Press, London and New York

ROSENBLUM, L.A. (1971) The ontogeny of mother–infant relations in macaques, in *The Ontogeny of Vertebrate Behavior* (Moltz, H., ed.), ch. 8, Academic Press, New York

ROSENBLUM, L.A. & HARLOW, H.F. (1963) Generalization of affectional responses in rhesus monkeys. *Percept. Mot. Skills*, *16*, 561–564

ROSENBLUM, L.A. & KAUFMANN, I.C. (1968) Variations in infant development and response to maternal loss in monkeys. *Am. J. Orthopsychiatr. 38*, 418–426

SIMPSON, M.J.A. (1968) The display of the Siamese fighting fish, *Betta splendens. Anim. Behav. Monogr. 1*, 1
SIMPSON, M.J.A. (1973) Social displays and the recognition of individuals, in *Perspectives in Ethology* (Bateson, P.P.G. & Klopfer, P.H., eds.), Plenum Press, New York-London
SPENCER-BOOTH, Y. (1968) The behaviour of twin rhesus monkeys and comparisons with the behaviour of single infants. *Primates, 9*, 75–84
TRIVERS, R.L. (1974) Parent offspring conflict. *Am. Zool., 14*, 249–264

Discussion

Hofer: How difficult is it to distinguish whether it is the mother or the infant rhesus monkey which is responsible for making or breaking contact, Professor Hinde?

Hinde: It is not difficult to see which it is, but it is difficult to be certain that, when the infant breaks contact, he isn't responding to slight signals from the mother. Similarly, when he makes contact the infant could be responding to distant signals that we don't detect. But we are watching animals with whom we are very familiar from close range, and we don't believe that this is an important issue in the early weeks of an infant's life. It may become progressively more important later on.

Macfarlane: After similar studies of human pairs we showed the mothers some of the videotape sequences and often they told us that they had picked up a clue to an infant's behaviour before we had observed anything—for example, just before a child vomits, the mother may feel the muscles at the back of the child's neck contract. Are you missing anything by your mothers not being able to tell you things like that?

Hinde: I don't think the picture that we abstract is qualitatively falsified. I deliberately talked here about only two measures, but the overall conclusions are based on a large number of measures.

Simpson: We can now record more detail about these moments of making and breaking, including any sharp jerks by the infant or the mother. We are surprised at how reliably we can record such tactile events.

Hofer: In the course of the developing relationship, certain kinds of behaviour which may be almost unobservable become cues for a subsequent kind of behaviour. We all learn that in certain people a twitch of an eye or ear means that pretty soon they are going to get angry, so we respond to the twitch before we are actually rejected. We make an 'I quit, you haven't fired me' statement. There must be quite a problem in trying to make such distinctions in animals and I suppose that all we can do is to look, as you suggest, more and more closely at those moments. Are you saying that the earlier you look at this, the less likely it is that the tiny cues are important?

Hinde: Later we shall present data showing that those cues become more important as the infant gets older.

Curtis-Jenkins: Surely the important thing is that the cues are there perhaps from the earliest days?

Hinde: Yes, I made this reservation in my paper.

Rosenblatt: Although there are differences between different dyads, can you detect a general pattern of changes likely to occur at, say, two months in all dyads?

Hinde: Yes, there are consistent age changes, as Fig. 1 shows.

Rosenblatt: Do these findings reflect basic features of the infant's development and of maternal behaviour?

Hinde: Yes, and these consistencies stand whether or not we miss subtle cues. But it must be added that every measure of the interactions between two members of a dyad depends on both of them. The changes with age shown in Fig. 1 depend on changes in both partners. What we are concerned about in Fig. 1*b* is which of the two partners is determining the rate of change.

Bowlby: Some light may be thrown on this by observations on animals brought up on dummy 'mothers', where the mother role is not being played at all (Harlow & Harlow 1969).

Hinde: An infant brought up on a surrogate mother as in those studies is different from the infant brought up on a real mother. If one is going to tease apart what is happening in a social situation, model experiments in which a large chunk of the social situation is missing can only be a guide. At the same time you have to observe the social interaction in terms of real life and tease that apart. This is terribly important for the whole approach to the development of early relationships. In the present context our data show that changes in the mother control the rate at which the infant becomes independent. How soon he would become independent if the mother did not change is another issue.

Hess-Haeser: My observations on mother–infant interactions in captive gorillas show that social and environmental factors strongly affect the contact situation (in terms of contact-making and contact-breaking rates) for both mother and infant. Do you find similar results in rhesus monkeys?

Hinde: Mother–infant pairs living alone have a different sort of relationship from mother–infant pairs living in a group. With segregated pairs, the infants spend more time off their mother than they do when living with a group. One can show that this is due to a difference between mothers. The mothers living in groups reject their infants less and appear more possessive than the mother–infant pairs living alone, at least in the cages that we use (Hinde & Spencer-

Booth 1967). Similarly, Jensen *et al.* (1968) have shown that the physical environment influences the nature of the mother–infant relationship.

Thoman: Do the infants of mothers who took a lot of initiative in making or breaking contact earlier on show much initiative later? That is, is the mother's behaviour earlier related to the infant's behaviour later on?

Hinde: We can't answer that, but those mothers who take a high initiative earlier continue to rank high on the same measure. In other words, the measures of the relationship are consistent, which argues against what you imply.

Rosenblatt: In our studies of cats we took a measure of what might be considered to be a lessening of maternal responsiveness in animals with litters of between one and four kittens (Schneirla *et al.* 1963). In the first week of their kittens' lives, the mothers jumped often to a shelf out of reach of the young. Then, if the litter consisted of two or more kittens, the mothers didn't do this again until the young were 35 days of age, after the young began to play. At first we thought this observation was a sampling error, but then it appeared in every record in which the mother had two or more kittens. Cats which had only one kitten also jumped to the shelf in the first week of their kittens' lives, but then the mothers continued to go to the shelf regularly; at 35 days the increase in jumping to the shelf was less than in the mothers with more kittens. It seemed that in the first week the mother showed a lessening of her tie to the young, then the young—depending upon their number and activity—brought her back to themselves and she remained tied to them until they became active at 35 days, which we think is what loosens the bond. It is possible that maternal behaviour is set in the first week, and that it is set at a greater intensity when the mother has more young than when she has fewer. Then maternal behaviour is reduced again at 35 days but its reduction depends on the number in the litter. A single kitten plays much less than many kittens but the mother doesn't let her own behaviour become very intense in the first place. Something happens in the first week which really determines a long period of mother–young interaction and which then relates to something happening later.

D'Souza: Could this pattern have anything to do with the changing quantity and/or quality of the maternal milk during the lactation period?

Rosenblatt: We haven't looked at that in the cat. In the rat lactation doesn't play much of a role in maternal behaviour (Moltz *et al.* 1967).

References

HARLOW, H.F. & HARLOW, M.K. (1969) Effects of various mother–infant relationships on rhesus monkey behaviors, in *Determinants of Infant Behaviour* (Foss, B.M., ed.), vol. 4, Methuen, London

HINDE, R.A. & SPENCER-BOOTH, Y. (1967) The effect of social companions on mother–infant relations in rhesus monkeys, in *Primate Ethology* (Morris, D., ed.), Weidenfeld & Nicolson, London

JENSEN, G.D., BOBBITT, R.A. & GORDON, B.N. (1968) Effects of environment on the relationship between mother and infant pigtailed monkeys *(Macaca nemestrina)*. *J. Comp. Physiol. Psychol. 66*, 259–263

MOLTZ, H., GELLER, D. & LEVIN, R. (1967) Maternal behaviour in the totally mammectomized rat. *J. Comp. Physiol. Psychol. 64*, 225–229

SCHNEIRLA, T.C., ROSENBLATT, J.S. & TOBACH, E. (1963) in *Maternal Behavior in Mammals* (Rheingold, H.L., ed.), pp. 122–168, Wiley, New York

Prepartum and postpartum regulation of maternal behaviour in the rat

J. S. ROSENBLATT

Institute of Animal Behavior, Rutgers University, Newark, New Jersey

Abstract Maternal behaviour in the rat consists of four principal components: nursing or crouching over the young, retrieving pups to the nest, body and genital licking of pups, and nest-building. Normally the onset of maternal behaviour occurs at parturition but studies reveal that the true onset is somewhat earlier, around 24 hours *pre partum*. The onset of maternal behaviour is hormonally determined and it is most likely that the ovarian hormone oestradiol plays a major role under the specific conditions that exist *pre partum*. The onset of maternal behaviour requires the resolution of tendencies of fear-avoidance of pups, based on their olfactory characteristics, and attraction to them and response to the pup stimuli that elicit maternal behaviour. In most animals this resolution occurs almost immediately but in some animals several hours of contact with the pups is required for maternal behaviour to be firmly established. After parturition, maternal behaviour appears to be regulated chiefly by stimuli from the pups, and hormones do not play a role apart from their role in lactogenesis. Size of litter, age of pups, amount of externally induced stress and other factors can affect the mother–young interaction: there is a period of special vulnerability to disruption of the mother–young interrelationship shortly after parturition which corresponds, we believe, to the period of transition from hormonal to non-hormonal regulation of maternal behaviour. Weaning and the decline of maternal behaviour is a specific phase of maternal care. Maternal behaviours gradually decline as avoidance behaviours increase.

Among all mammals the onset of maternal behaviour after parturition is rapid. Because this allows the mother and her newborn to form a behavioural bond that has important consequences for the young, this period has been referred to as a 'critical period'. Without the formation of such a bond the young suffer in their development. However in what sense this period is critical for the mother is not clear, since failure to form such a relationship has less serious consequences for her. Nevertheless mothers form a relationship with their newborn in all mammals that have been studied. This suggests that the formation of a relationship with the newborn is an important feature of the maternal behaviour cycle and that our understanding of this phenomenon should be sought within the context of an understanding of the factors which regulate maternal behaviour in the female.

The present article is an attempt to deal with this problem by the analysis of maternal behaviour in the rat. My aim will be to show that during certain phases of the cycle of maternal behaviour in the female the mother's relationship with her young plays an important role which can only be understood with reference to the prepartum and postpartum factors that regulate the female's maternal behaviour.

The major thesis that I shall present is that different phases of the maternal behaviour cycle are regulated by different kinds of processes. I shall present evidence, mainly from our own studies on Sprague-Dawley rats, that the onset of maternal behaviour during the normal reproductive cycle is based on hormonal secretions and that the postpartum maintenance, and probably the decline, of maternal behaviour depend chiefly on stimulation which the female receives from her young.

This conception of the regulation of maternal behaviour is based on an earlier formulation by Leblond (1938, 1940), who found that lactating female mice continued to exhibit maternal behaviour after hypophysectomy. He proposed therefore that maternal behaviour in mice was initiated by hormones but was maintained by stimulation from the pups. Koller (1956) proposed a similar interpretation for his finding that maternal nest-building in the pregnant mouse was stimulated by progesterone but could be maintained after parturition by pup stimulation alone. Richards (1967) more recently has reviewed the results of a large number of studies on maternal behaviour in small mammals along these lines.

I shall discuss first the onset of maternal behaviour in rats, then the maintenance and decline of maternal behaviour and finally the period of transition from prepartum to postpartum regulation of maternal behaviour.

In the rat, maternal behaviour consists of four major components: nursing, retrieving or carrying the young back to the nest when they have strayed from it, nest-building, and licking the pups to stimulate elimination. Normally only females that have given birth perform these actions, but by employing various experimental procedures we can stimulate females to perform them under other circumstances. Although I shall often refer to retrieving as a measure of maternal behaviour, retrieving is almost always accompanied by the other three components.

ONSET OF MATERNAL BEHAVIOUR IN RATS

Although females normally begin to show maternal behaviour after parturition, Wiesner & Sheard (1933) were able to show that they would begin earlier if Caesarean-section deliveries were performed three days before parturition (see also Labriola 1953). Whatever causes maternal behaviour in the female can be speeded by terminating pregnancy earlier than normally. We have used the same procedure in our studies but because we terminate pregnancy earlier than the 19th day it is necessary to remove the uteruses as well as the fetuses and placentas by performing hysterectomies. Our first study showed that we could speed the onset of maternal behaviour by performing hysterectomies as early as the eighth day of pregnancy (Lott & Rosenblatt 1969; Rosenblatt & Siegel 1975). However, we were concerned with how rapidly after hysterectomy females would begin to show maternal behaviour when they were presented with pups 24 h after the operation.

Earlier we had found that non-pregnant females could be stimulated to show maternal behaviour if they were simply exposed to pups continuously. Four to seven days of exposure were required, however, before these females began to show maternal behaviour (Rosenblatt 1967; Fleming & Rosenblatt 1974*b*). Under these conditions, maternal behaviour is not based on the secretion of hormones, as we shall show later.

Hysterectomies were performed during pregnancy to determine whether the time these females took before beginning maternal behaviour was shorter than for non-pregnant females. Our first study (Fig. 1) showed that this in fact was the case: females hysterectomized between the 10th and 19th day of pregnancy (i.e. until three-and-a-half to four days before parturition) had shorter latencies to maternal behaviour than non-pregnant females and non-pregnant hysterectomized females (Lott & Rosenblatt 1969; Rosenblatt & Siegel 1975). Moreover, females hysterectomized on the 19th day of pregnancy had shorter latencies than those hysterectomized on the 10th day (median latencies = 1 day and 3 days, respectively).

Females were hysterectomized on a given day of pregnancy in the first experiment, then given pups 24 h later. They were given new pups each day and were tested until they began to show maternal behaviour. In our next study hysterectomized females were first given pups either immediately after surgery, or 24 h, 48 h and 72 h after surgery. Also, in several groups the ovaries were removed at the same time as the females were hysterectomized. By testing females for the first time at different intervals after hysterectomy we could observe the effect of the hysterectomy on maternal behaviour when there had been no previous stimulation by pups, and by ovariectomizing females we could

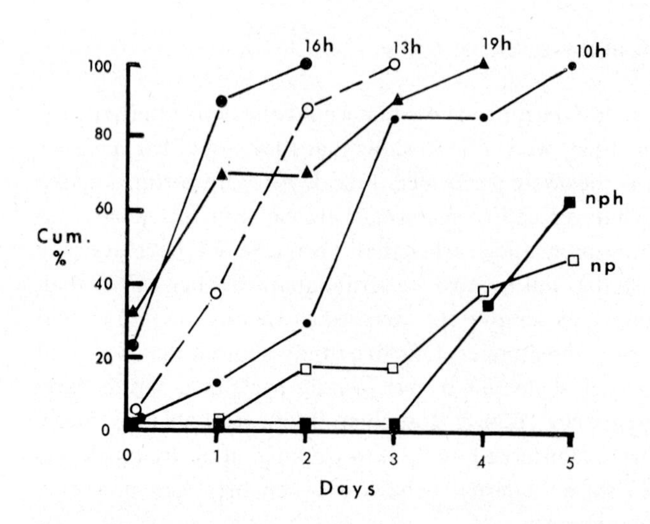

FIG. 1. Cumulative percentage (Cum. %) of retrieving latencies in groups of pregnant females hysterectomized (h) on the 10th (7 animals), 13th (8), 16th (10) and 19th (10) days, and of non-pregnant (np, 10) and non-pregnant–hysterectomized (nph, 8) females all exhibiting retrieving for the first time. Pups presented at 48 h after surgery; latencies measured from beginning of pup presentation.

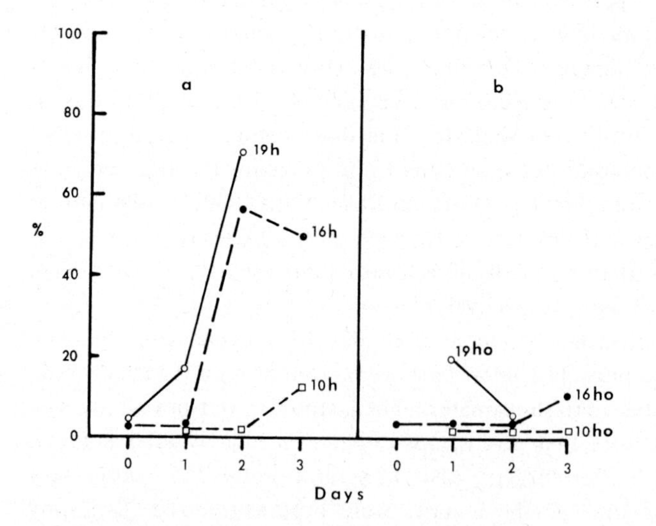

FIG. 2. Percentage of 10-, 16-, and 19-day pregnant females of each group exhibiting retrieving in the first test after (*a*) hysterectomy (h), and (*b*) hysterectomy and ovariectomy (ho), at intervals of 0, 1, 2, 3 days after surgery. Each point represents a different group and there were 5 to 17 females per group.

determine whether the shortened latencies before maternal behaviour began after hysterectomy were based on hormones secreted by the ovaries. It took 48 h for maternal behaviour to begin in females that were only hysterectomized; however females that had also had their ovaries removed had not yet begun to show maternal behaviour at this time (Fig. 2). Females hysterectomized during pregnancy could therefore begin maternal behaviour without prior stimulation by pups, provided that they retained their ovaries.

During pregnancy females normally do not undergo sexual or oestrous cycles; instead the ovaries secrete large amounts of progesterone and only small amounts of oestrogen. Just before the female gives birth the ovaries begin to secrete smaller amounts of progesterone; eventually they stop secreting this hormone (Hashimoto *et al.* 1968; Csapo & Wiest 1969; Morishige *et al.* 1973) and begin to secrete large amounts of oestrogen (Shaikh 1971). It is generally believed that this change in the pattern of secretion of these hormones by the ovaries and, in addition, the secretion of prolactin by the pituitary gland at this time, causes maternal behaviour. Maternal behaviour has in fact been stimulated in non-pregnant ovariectomized females by two groups of investigators (Moltz *et al.* 1970; Zarrow *et al.* 1971) who imitated this pattern of hormone secretion during pregnancy by injecting hormones for two to three weeks.

Our studies with hysterectomized females showed that the female requires only 48 h of hormone secretion by the ovaries to begin maternal behaviour. We suspected that the important hormone was oestrogen, on the basis of studies by Pepe & Rothchild (1972), Rothchild *et al.* (1973), Takayama & Greenwald (1973), Waynforth & Robertson (1972) and particularly, Morishige & Rothchild (1974) and Johnson (1972). These studies showed that progesterone secretion decreases rapidly after hysterectomy during pregnancy, and that oestrogen secretion increases. We compared the latencies we obtained before maternal behaviour began after hysterectomy with those before an oestrous cycle began (indicated by the appearance of a pro-oestrous vaginal smear, as reported by Morishige & Rothchild (1974) and Johnson (1972), and found a remarkably close correlation between the behavioural and the hormonal events. As Fig. 3 shows, females begin to show maternal behaviour and their first oestrous cycle five days after hysterectomy on the 10th day of pregnancy; as pregnancy advances maternal behaviour begins more rapidly after hysterectomy and so does the change in the secretion of hormones by the ovaries. The important point is that the ovaries begin to secrete increasing amounts of oestrogen during the 24 h that precedes pro-oestrus, as shown in Fig. 3, and this could be the cause of the maternal behaviour which begins 24 h later.

To study the effect of oestrogen on maternal behaviour we used pregnant females that were hysterectomized and ovariectomized (HO) at various times

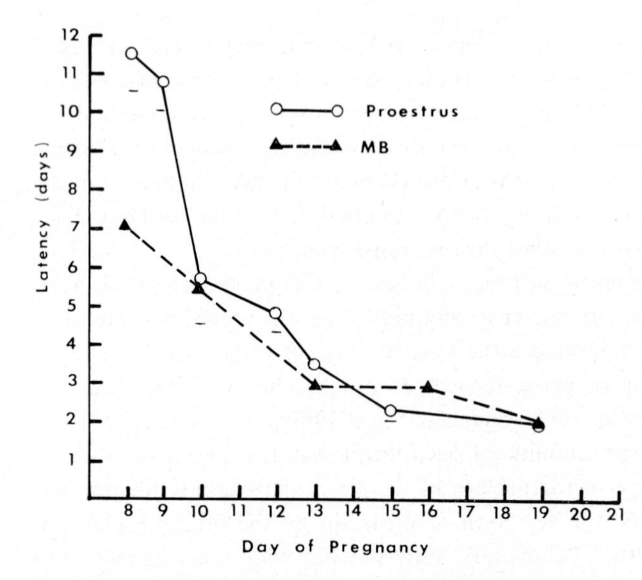

FIG. 3. Comparison of latencies from surgery for the onset of maternal behaviour and for the appearance of pro-oestrus in females hysterectomized on the day of pregnancy shown. Median latencies for maternal behaviour (MB) and mean latencies and standard error (dash below mean) for pro-oestrus. Pro-oestrus latencies taken from Morishige & Rothchild (1974).

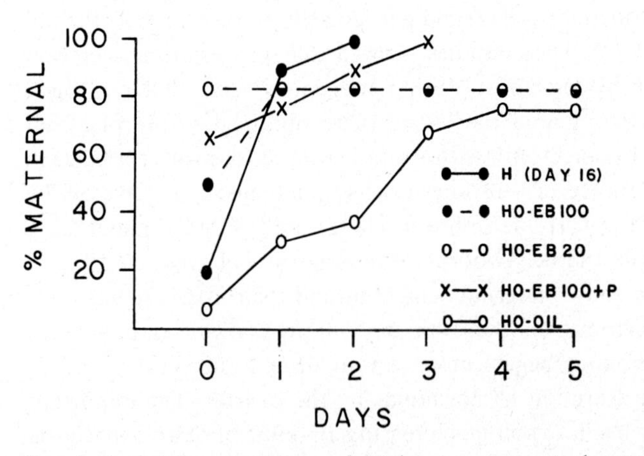

FIG. 4. Cumulative percentage of 16-day pregnant rats becoming maternal after either hysterectomy (H: 10 animals) or hysterectomy–ovariectomy (HO) plus either 100 μg/kg oestradiol benzoate (EB 100; 6), 20 μg/kg EB (EB 20; 6), 100 μg/kg EB and 0.5 mg progesterone (EB 100 + P, 9), or oil (13). EB injected at surgery and progesterone 44 h later. Pups presented 48 h postoperatively on Day 0.

during pregnancy and injected them with oestradiol benzoate at the time of surgery (Siegel & Rosenblatt 1975*a*). They were given either a high dose of oestradiol benzoate (100 μg/kg) or a low dose (20 μg/kg) and one group was given progesterone 44 h later. The results for the 16th day HO pregnant females are shown in Fig. 4 and are representative of groups that were treated similarly on the 10th, 13th, and 19th days of pregnancy. Females given either a high or a low dose of oestradiol benzoate began to show, at 48 h or shortly thereafter, maternal behaviour similar to that of females that were only hysterectomized and were not treated with the hormone. Progesterone did not affect maternal behaviour at all.

To test whether oestradiol benzoate would also stimulate maternal behaviour in non-pregnant HO females we followed the same procedure, using both high and low doses of the hormone (Siegel & Rosenblatt 1975*b*). The low dose of oestradiol benzoate proved ineffective but with the high dose females responded as rapidly as the pregnant HO females. Oestradiol benzoate can therefore stimulate maternal behaviour in pregnant and in non-pregnant hysterectomized–ovariectomized females equally well but the pregnant females are more sensitive to the hormone.

These studies do not rule out the possibility that prolactin may play a role in stimulating maternal behaviour. Oestradiol benzoate causes the secretion of prolactin by the pituitary. However Zarrow *et al.* (1971) have shown that blocking the secretion of prolactin during the last six to seven days of pregnancy does not interfere with the beginning of maternal behaviour after parturition.

How do these findings relate to the normal beginning of maternal behaviour at the end of pregnancy? From the time-relations between the decrease in progesterone and the rise in oestradiol at the end of pregnancy we predicted that maternal behaviour really begins before parturition if oestradiol is responsible for its onset. To test this prediction, pregnant females were given young pups at 2 h intervals starting 40 h before parturition. They began to exhibit nest-building at 34 h before parturition (mean $= 19.8 \pm 7.1$ h *pre partum*) and retrieving at 28 h *pre partum* (mean $= 13.6 \pm 7.6$ h: Rosenblatt & Siegel 1975). Slotnick *et al.* (1973) have also reported the beginning of maternal behaviour before parturition in rats.

It is likely that the oestradiol secreted around the 20th day of pregnancy stimulates the prepartum onset of maternal behaviour in our strain of rats. Females that have been ovariectomized from the 20th day of pregnancy onwards are not prevented from beginning maternal behaviour after parturition (Terkel 1970; Catalá & Deis 1973).

POSTPARTUM REGULATION OF MATERNAL BEHAVIOUR IN RATS

Our present ideas about the regulation of postpartum maternal behaviour in rats were arrived at through studies of the stimulation of maternal behaviour in non-pregnant female animals by prolonged exposure to young pups (i.e. sensitization) (Rosenblatt 1967; Cosnier & Couturier 1966; Wiesner & Sheard 1933). The evidence for the non-hormonal basis of this maternal behaviour is derived from several sources: (1) ovariectomy and hypophysectomy do not prevent sensitization and onset latencies are not significantly different, (2) oestrous cycles are not altered during sensitization and the onset of maternal behaviour is not associated with any particular phase of the oestrous cycle, (3) cross-transfusion of blood between sensitized and non-maternal females does not induce maternal behaviour, although maternal behaviour is induced when newly parturient mothers are cross-transfused with virgins (Terkel & Rosenblatt 1971, 1972), (4) the maternal behaviour of 'spontaneous retrievers'—those animals who retrieve pups upon their first exposure and often show other components of maternal behaviour—is not interrupted by the hormonal changes of pregnancy (Terkel & Rosenblatt 1971). In addition, (5) cross-transfusion of blood between spontaneous retrievers and non-maternal virgins does not accelerate the onset of maternal behaviour in the virgins (Terkel & Rosenblatt 1971). Recently Leon *et al.* (1973) have provided evidence that ovariectomy reduces the latencies for sensitization in non-pregnant females after eight weeks and oestradiol benzoate increases it, but we have not been able to confirm this in our strain of rats (Siegel & Rosenblatt 1975*b*).

Certain findings also suggest that postpartum maternal behaviour may not depend on hormones during the normal maternal behaviour cycle. Maternal behaviour is not affected by prepartum or postpartum absence of the pituitary gland (i.e. from the 12th day of pregnancy onwards) (Obias 1957; Bintarningsih *et al.* 1958), except of course for the interference with lactation, nor is it affected by ovariectomy during the first 12 h *post partum* (Rosenblatt, unpublished). Numan *et al.* (1971) found that preventing the release of prolactin with ergocornine hydrogen maleate did not prevent the display of postpartum maternal behaviour, and earlier Moltz *et al.* (1969) showed that progesterone injected during the four days *post partum* did not interfere with maternal behaviour. We have found that the effectiveness of blood cross-transfused between a recently parturient mother and a non-pregnant female in inducing maternal behaviour falls rapidly after delivery and is absent 24 h *post partum* (Terkel & Rosenblatt 1972).

It appears, therefore, that shortly after parturition maternal behaviour is not dependent on the hormonal conditions which have stimulated its onset—

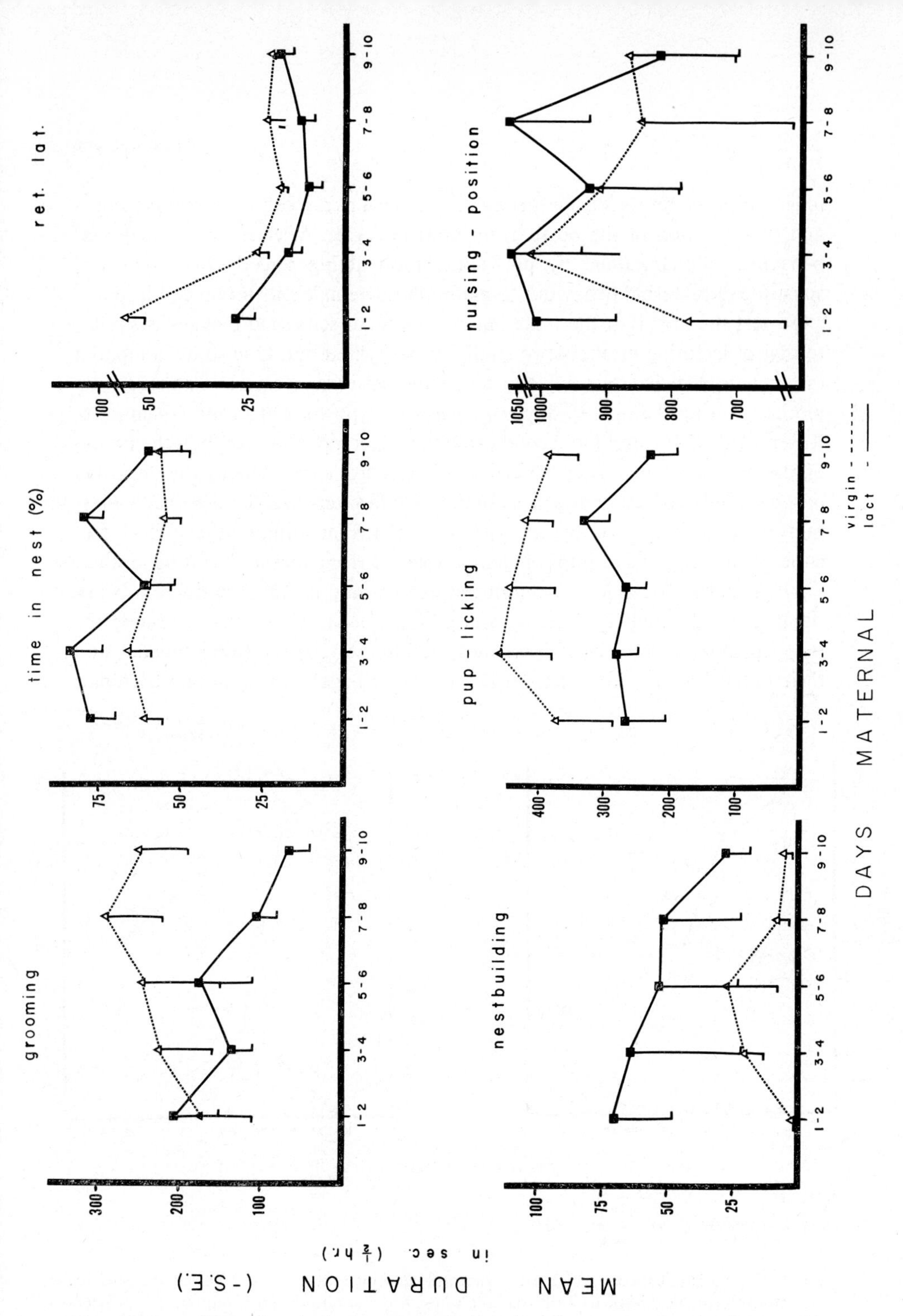

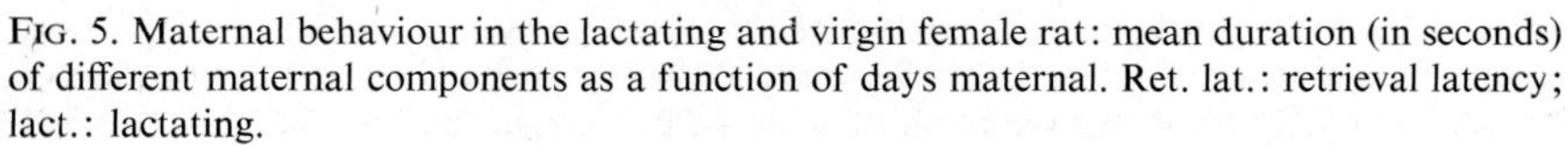

FIG. 5. Maternal behaviour in the lactating and virgin female rat: mean duration (in seconds) of different maternal components as a function of days maternal. Ret. lat.: retrieval latency; lact.: lactating.

indeed these conditions have themselves changed as a result of loss of placentas and the initiation of the postpartum oestrous cycle. After its onset, maternal behaviour is maintained by pup stimulation acting directly on the neural substrate of maternal behaviour to maintain the female's maternal condition.

To test the idea that the maternal behaviour of sensitized females is similar to that of lactating mothers two studies were carried out. One study compared the maternal behaviour of non-pregnant sensitized females and lactating mothers during the first 10 days *post partum* or post-sensitization (Fleming & Rosenblatt 1974*b*), and the second extended the comparison through the period of the decline of maternal behaviour, that is from the 10th to the 28th day *post partum* (Reisbick *et al.* 1975). In both studies sensitized females had foster-pups matched in age day by day with those of the lactating mothers which had either their own pups or pups of comparable age from another lactating mother.

The maternal behaviour of sensitized females and lactating mothers was not significantly different in most measures (Fig. 5) during the first 10 days; the only differences were the reduced nest-building of the sensitized females and their initially longer latencies before retrieving began (Fleming & Rosenblatt

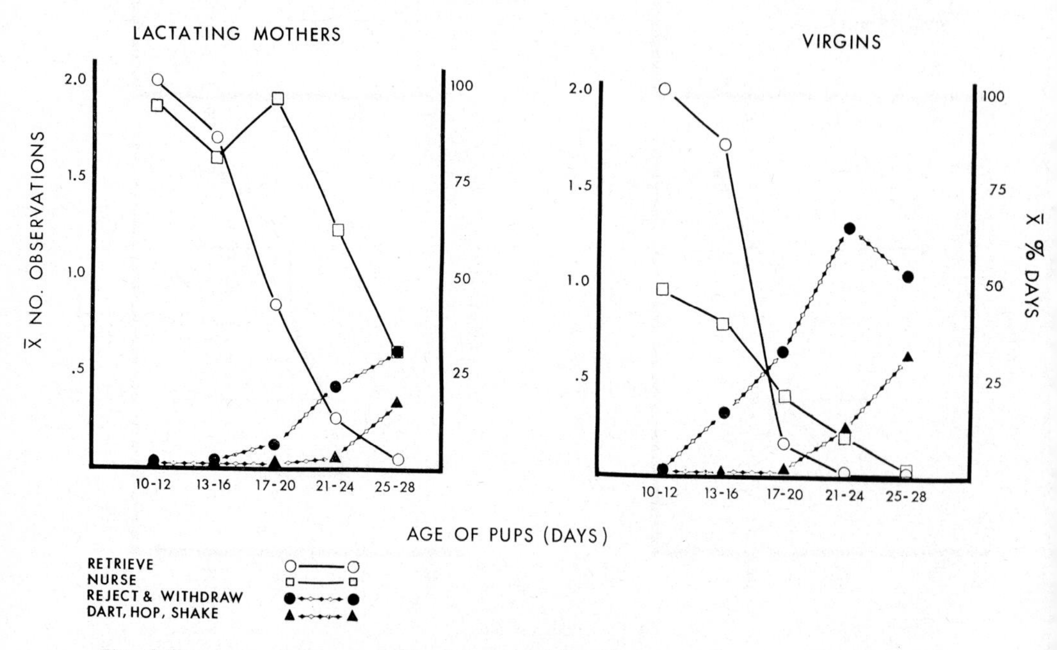

FIG. 6. Comparison between sensitized virgins and lactating mothers in the decline of maternal behaviour during tests with 10- to 28-day old pups. Abscissa shows age of pups and days after onset of maternal behaviour for females. Retrieving and nursing shown as percentage of group; reject and withdraw, and dart, hop, shake, shown as mean number of observations scored. Each point represents the mean of 3- or 4-day averages for 9 females.

1974*b*). From the 10th day on, sensitized females and lactating mothers showed a decline in maternal *care* and a rise in maternal *rejection*, *withdrawal* and *avoidance of nursing*. The decline in maternal care was somewhat earlier among sensitized females than lactating mothers (Fig. 6) and the rise in negative responses to the pups was also somewhat earlier (Reisbick *et al.* 1975). The similarities between sensitized females and lactating mothers far outweigh the differences and they provide further support for the conception that postpartum maternal behaviour is normally *independent of hormone stimulation* and is *dependent on pup stimulation* for both the maintenance and the decline. The differences suggest that the mode of onset, whether hormonal, as during the normal maternal behaviour cycle, or non-hormonal, as in the sensitized non-pregnant female, plays an important role even after the transition to non-hormonally based maternal behaviour has occurred. The intensity of maternal motivation is apparently stronger when it has been induced hormonally and this results in a more complete pattern of behaviour (i.e. including nest-building), with longer maintenance of maternal *care* and a greater resistance to those stimuli from the pups that might otherwise lead to maternal rejection and avoidance.

TRANSITION FROM PREPARTUM TO POSTPARTUM REGULATION OF MATERNAL BEHAVIOUR

The behaviour of the mother immediately *post partum* does not reveal that regulation of her behaviour is changing from the hormonal basis *pre partum* to dependence on pup stimulation. However, if a mother is separated from her litter during parturition, after the young have been licked clean and the afterbirths have been removed and eaten, but before retrieving and nursing have taken place, and if she is without young for four days, then on the fifth day, when a litter is returned to her, she is unresponsive to the pups (Rosenblatt & Lehrman 1963). A four-day separation from the litter after the period of transition has been completed (i.e. on the fourth day *post partum*) does not have the same drastic effect on maternal responsiveness, and nearly 80% of the mothers are immediately responsive to pups when litters are returned to them. In the absence of pup stimulation maternal responsiveness wanes rapidly, but as little as 12 hours' contact with pups *post partum* maintains maternal responsiveness, in 30% of a group of mothers, until the eighth day *post partum* (Rosenblatt, unpublished).

Hormonal factors may also affect the transition from prepartum to postpartum regulation of maternal behaviour. Slotnick *et al.* (1973) reported that a large number of females of the Wistar strain of rats do not show maternal behaviour before parturition. This may be due to a slower prepartum rate of increase in oestradiol secretion than in our strain of Sprague-Dawley rats, nearly all of whom begin their maternal behaviour before parturition. If the Wistar rats are not allowed continuous contact with pups after parturition those that have not begun to show maternal behaviour before parturition show a rapid loss of maternal behaviour. Those females that do begin maternal behaviour before parturition are able to maintain it with only small amounts of contact with pups after parturition.

Studies of sensitized non-pregnant females have contributed to our understanding of the nature of the transition from prepartum to postpartum regulation of maternal behaviour in lactating mothers. In analysing the factors responsible for the long latency required for sensitization we showed that the size of the cage has an important influence (Terkel & Rosenblatt 1971). Non-maternal virgins confined with pups in small cages which forced the female to be in continuous contact with the pups had reduced latencies that averaged only two days, and as cage size was increased latencies became proportionately longer.

It was also noted that these females initially avoided the young, presumably because non-maternal females dislike the smell of the pups. As a test of this idea, a group of non-maternal virgins were given intranasal infusions of zinc sulphate to reduce or eliminate olfaction temporarily, and in a second group the olfactory tracts were lesioned bilaterally to accomplish the same end of eliminating olfaction, but permanently in this case (Fleming & Rosenblatt 1974*a*). Both groups of females exhibited maternal behaviour very rapidly within 24 h of their first exposure to young pups, and they showed none of the initial avoidance of the pups characteristic of females with intact olfaction. Olfactory discrimination tests showed that in both groups olfaction was either absent or reduced during the period in which they initiated maternal behaviour. Later (Mayer & Rosenblatt 1975) we studied what would happen to the females treated with zinc sulphate, who had become maternal so rapidly when olfaction was reduced, once they regained the sense of smell, several weeks later. When the animals, which had been permitted only 1.5 days' contact with pups after exhibiting maternal behaviour under zinc sulphate treatment, regained olfaction and were presented with pups once again, their latencies increased (all but their retrieving latencies) to more than 2.5 days and in some animals latencies were as long as 4.0 days.

Although these studies were done with non-pregnant females and involve sensitization there is no reason to believe that the postparturient female is not faced with the same problem of adapting to the odours of the pups. Since such females usually exhibit maternal behaviour within a short time of giving birth, any aversion they may have to pup odours is not apparent, but one study showed that they require some time, perhaps a day and a half, to fully establish their maternal behaviour towards the newborn. In this study (Fleming & Rosenblatt 1974*b*) we sensitized non-pregnant females and permitted them 1.5 days' contact with the young before removing the pups. A group of post-parturient females were also permitted only 1.5 days' contact with their litters before the young were removed. Two weeks later both groups were presented with pups once again *for sensitization*, to see whether the non-hormonal (sensitization) and hormonal (parturition) inductions of maternal behaviour were equivalent in their effects on subsequent reinduction of maternal behaviour by sensitization. In fact, the sensitized females had shorter latencies upon reinduction than during the initial induction and lactating females had equally short latencies when given the opportunity to be sensitized.

More important for our present discussion is the study by Fleming (1973) in which lactating and sensitized mothers were *not* permitted 1.5 days' contact with pups after the onset of maternal behaviour and whose pups were removed at the first sign of retrieving. These two groups of females were also reinduced two weeks later and both had latencies for the onset of maternal behaviour that were no shorter than the original virgin induction. The improvement found in the first experiment was therefore based, not on the induction process—either pup exposure or hormonal induction—but on the 1.5 days of additional contact after the onset of maternal behaviour. In both lactating females *and* sensitized females, therefore, a period after the onset is needed during which maternal behaviour is 'fixed' so that it is more easily elicited at a later time. We suspect that some degree of adaptation to the odours of the pups is achieved which initiates maternal behaviour but that further adaptation occurs over the first 1.5 days, and that once the mother is adapted, and can approach and remain in contact with the pups for a period of time, then other stimuli from the pups (e.g. contact, ultrasonic vocalization, suckling, etc.) which elicit maternal care begin to play an important role in regulating the female's maternal behaviour.

SIGNIFICANCE

The importance of the female rat's first contact with the newborn pups after parturition can now be understood in the context of her cycle of maternal behaviour: she depends on this contact for establishing a relationship which enables her to make the transition from the prepartum hormonal to postpartum non-hormonal regulation of her maternal behaviour. The sense in which this period is 'critical' for the mother is therefore quite different from the way it is critical for the young. There is a danger in viewing the transition period as a 'critical period'. Many factors contribute to the outcome of the transition from prepartum to postpartum regulation of maternal behaviour, not all of which make their contribution solely within this period. The danger is that the critical period concept will lead to developments during the transition period being isolated from those that precede it and those that follow. As further research gives us a better understanding of the various factors, prepartum and postpartum, which influence the transition it will become apparent that we are dealing with a developmental sequence of interdependent phases, each of which is critical for one or another aspect of the pattern of maternal behaviour.

ACKNOWLEDGEMENTS

The research reported here was supported by United States Public Health Service Grant MH-08604, a Biomedical Grant, and a grant from the Alfred P. Sloan Foundation. I am indebted to a large number of students and associates who did the research to which I refer in the report, including Drs Joseph Terkel, Alison S. Fleming, Harold I. Siegel, Sydney Reisbick and Anne B. Mayer, and to research assistants Alice Trattner, Donna Wade and Marylin Dotegowski. I wish to thank Drs Michael Numan and Pat Bateson for a critical reading of the manuscript, which is publication number 203 of the Institute of Animal Behavior, Rutgers University.

References

Bintarningsih, Lyons, Wm.R., Johnson, R.E. & Li, C.H. (1958) Hormonally-induced lactation in hypophysectomized rats. *Endocrinology 63*, 540–547

Catalá, S. & Deis, R.P. (1973) Effects of oestrogen upon parturition, maternal behaviour and lactation in ovariectomized pregnant rats. *J. Endocrinol. 86*, 503–505

Cosnier, J. & Couturier, C. (1966) Comportement maternel provoqué chez les rattes adultes castrées. *C. R. Séances Soc. Biol. Fil. 160*, 789–791

Csapo, A.I. & Wiest, W.G. (1969) An examination of the quantitative relationship between progesterone and the maintenance of pregnancy. *Endocrinology 85*, 735–746

Fleming, A.S. (1973) Olfactory and experiential factors underlying maternal behavior in the lactating and cycling female rat. Unpublished doctoral thesis, Rutgers University, Newark, N.J.

Fleming, A.S. & Rosenblatt, J.S. (1974*a*) Olfactory regulation of maternal behavior in rats: II. Effects of peripherally induced anosmia and lesions of the lateral olfactory tract in pup-induced virgins. *J. Comp. Physiol. Psychol. 86*, 233–246

Fleming, A.S. & Rosenblatt, J.S. (1947*b*) Maternal behavior in the virgin and lactating rat. *J. Comp. Physiol. Psychol. 86*, 957–972

Hashimoto, I., Hendricks, D.M., Anderson, L.L. & Melampy, R.M. (1968) Progesterone and pregn-4-en-20α-ol-3-one in ovarian venous blood during various reproductive states in the rat. *Endocrinology 82*, 333–341

Johnson, N.P. (1972) Postpartum ovulation in the rat. Unpublished doctoral thesis, Purdue University, Lafayette, Indiana

Koller, G. (1956) Hormonale und psychische Steuerung beim Nestbau weiser Mäuse. *Zool. Anz. 19*, 123–132

Labriola, J. (1953) Effects of caesarian delivery upon maternal behavior in rats. *Proc. Soc. Exp. Biol. Med. 83*, 556–557

LEBLOND, C.P. (1938) Extra-hormonal factors in maternal behavior. *Proc. Soc. Exp. Biol. Med. 38*, 66–70

LEBLOND, C.P. (1940) Nervous and hormonal factors in the maternal behavior of the mouse. *J. Genet. Psychol. 57*, 327–344

LEON, M., NUMAN, M. & MOLTZ, H. (1973) Maternal behavior in the rat: facilitation through gonadectomy. *Science (Wash. D.C.) 179*, 1018–1019

LOTT, D.F. & ROSENBLATT, J.S. (1969) in *Determinants of Infant Behaviour* (Foss, B.M., ed.), vol. 4, pp. 61–67, Methuen, London

MAYER, A.B. & ROSENBLATT, J.S. (1975) Olfactory basis for the delayed onset of maternal behavior in virgin female rats. Experiential effects. *J. Comp. Physiol. Psychol*, in press

MOLTZ, H., LEVIN, R. & LEON, M. (1969) Differential effects of progesterone on the maternal behavior of primiparous and multiparous rats. *J. Comp. Physiol. Psychol. 67*, 36–40

MOLTZ, H., LUBIN, M., LEON, M. & NUMAN, M. (1970) Hormonal induction of maternal behavior in the ovariectomized nulliparous rat. *Physiol. Behav. 5*, 1373–1377

MORISHIGE, W.K., PEPE, G.J. & ROTHCHILD, I. (1973) Serum luteinizing hormone, prolactin and progesterone levels during pregnancy in the rat. *Endocrinology 92*, 1527–1530

MORISHIGE, W.K. & ROTHCHILD, I. (1974) Temporal aspects of the regulation of corpus luteum function by luteinizing hormone, prolactin, and placental luteotrophin during the first half of pregnancy in the rat. *Endocrinology 95*, 260–274

NUMAN, M., LEON, M. & MOLTZ, H. (1972) Interference with prolactin release and the maternal behavior of female rats. *Horm. Behav. 3*, 29–38

OBIAS, M.D. (1957) Maternal behavior of hypophysectomized gravid albino rats and the development and performance of their progeny. *J. Comp. Physiol. Psychol. 50*, 120–124

PEPE, G. & ROTHCHILD, I. (1972) The effect of hypophysectomy on day 12 of pregnancy on the serum progesterone level and the time of parturition in the rat. *Endocrinology 91*, 1380–1385

REISBICK, S., ROSENBLATT, J.S. & MAYER, A.B. (1975) Decline of maternal behavior in the virgin and lactating rat. *J. Comp. Physiol. Psychol.*, in press

RICHARDS, M.P.M. (1967) in *Advances in Reproductive Physiology* (McLaren, A., ed.), vol. 2, Academic Press/Logos Press, London

ROSENBLATT, J.S. (1967) Nonhormonal basis of maternal behavior in the rat. *Science (Wash. D.C.) 156*, 1512–1514

ROSENBLATT, J.S. (1970) in *Development and Evolution of Behavior: Essays in Memory of T.C. Schneirla* (Aronson, L.R., Tobach, E., Lehrman, D.S. & Rosenblatt, J.S., eds.), pp. 489–511, Freeman, San Francisco

ROSENBLATT, J.S. & LEHRMAN, D.S. (1963) in *Maternal Behavior in Mammals* (Rheingold, H.L., ed.), pp. 8–57, Wiley, New York

ROSENBLATT, J.S. & SIEGEL, H.I. (1975) Hysterectomy-induced maternal behavior during pregnancy in the rat. *J. Comp. Physiol. Psychol*, in press

ROTHCHILD, I., BILLIAR, R.B., KLINE, I.T. & PEPE, G. (1973) The persistence of progesterone secretion in pregnant rats after hypophysectomy and hysterectomy: A comparison with pseudopregnant, deciduomata-bearing pseudopregnant, and lactating rats. *J. Endocrinol. 57*, 63–74

SHAIKH, A.A. (1971) Estrone and estradiol levels in the ovarian venous blood from rats during the estrous cycle and pregnancy. *Biol. Reprod. 5*, 297–307

SIEGEL, H.I. & ROSENBLATT, J.S. (1975*a*) Hormonal basis of hysterectomy-induced maternal behavior during pregnancy in the rat. *Horm. Behav*, in press

SIEGEL, H.I. & ROSENBLATT, J.S. (1975*b*) Estrogen-induced maternal behavior in hysterectomized-ovariectomized virgin rats. *Physiol. Behav*, in press

SLOTNICK, B.M., CARPENTER, M.L. & FUSCO, R. (1973) Initiation of maternal behavior in pregnant nulliparous rats. *Horm. Behav. 4*, 53–59

TAKAYAMA, M. & GREENWALD, G.S. (1973) Direct luteotropic action of estrogen in the hypophysectomized-hysterectomized rat. *Endocrinology 92*, 1405–1413

TERKEL, J. (1970) Aspects of maternal behavior in the rat with special reference to humoral factors underlying maternal behavior at parturition. Unpublished doctoral thesis, Rutgers University, Newark, N.J.

TERKEL, J. & ROSENBLATT, J.S. (1971) Aspects of non-hormonal maternal behavior in the rat. *Horm. Behav. 2*, 161–171

TERKEL, J. & ROSENBLATT, J.S. (1972) Humoral factors underlying maternal behavior at parturition: Cross transfusion between freely moving rats. *J. Comp. Physiol. Psychol. 80*, 365–371

WAYNFORTH, H.B. & ROBERTSON, D.M. (1972) Oestradiol content of ovarian venous blood and ovarian tissue in hypophysectomized rats during late pregnancy. *J. Endocrinol. 54*, 79–85

WIESNER, B.P. & SHEARD, N.M. (1933) *Maternal Behaviour in the Rat.* Oliver and Boyd, London

ZARROW, M.X., GANDELMAN, R. & DENENBERG, V.H. (1971) Prolactin: Is it an essential hormone for maternal behavior in the mammal? *Horm. Behav. 2*, 343–354

Discussion

Bell: Does the smell of the pups increase other kinds of maternal behaviour at the same time as it produces the effect on latency? That is, does the mother try to get the pups under her where she can't smell them as much, or lick them more, or something?

Rosenblatt: The mother sniffs the pups and runs away from them. She covers them with sawdust and hops over them when she comes close to them.

Richards: What is the hormonal basis for the short latency in rodents that don't have a postpartum oestrus, for example the hamster?

Rosenblatt: I am not prepared to guess.

Richards: Have you any evidence that the hormonal process you described has differential effects on various aspects of maternal behaviour? You implied that all these types of behaviour run together, which would be unlike what has been reported in other rodents (Richards 1967) which differ from the rat in various aspects of maternal behaviour.

Rosenblatt: I think that in the rat the different components of maternal behaviour depend on different hormones. However, blood from a mother contains a substance which induces all kinds of maternal behaviour, except nest-building, when it is cross-transfused at the right time into virgin rats. This suggests that there is something common to all the behavioural components that are related to the pups (Terkel & Rosenblatt 1972). Nest-building seems to segregate itself, and in fact we know that its regulation differs from that of the other components.

I would not generalize the picture of hormonal regulation in the rat to that in any other animal, although the rabbit is quite similar to the rat. The hamster is different and some of the techniques we used in the rat do not work in the hamster. The fall in progesterone and the rise in oestrogen which occur in the rat do not happen in human pregnancies, where concentrations of oestrogen and progesterone remain high until labour begins, when both decrease very rapidly. The hormone picture is different and the behavioural picture in humans has not been studied in detail.

Klaus: Could prolactin be responsible for any of these aspects of maternal behaviour?

Rosenblatt: Prolactin certainly affects maternal behaviour but attempts to induce maternal behaviour with prolactin alone have not been successful (Lott & Fuchs 1962; Beach & Wilson 1963). On the other hand, in studies in two separate laboratories, carefully timed doses of three hormones in series (oestrogen, progesterone and prolactin) induced maternal behaviour in ovariectomized virgin rats. Twelve days of hormone treatment were needed in one study and 22 days in the other (Moltz *et al.* 1970; Zarrow *et al.* 1971), whereas we gave one injection of oestrogen. However, when the release of prolactin is inhibited during the last six days of pregnancy in the rat, the onset of maternal behaviour is not prevented (Zarrow *et al.* 1971). Apparently prolactin is not a necessary component for the onset of maternal behaviour, but it is a necessary component for the onset of lactogenesis and lactation.

D'Souza: Maternal behaviour is not a unitary phenomenon and I assume that you are correlating all your measurements of behaviour with the hormonal pattern that you talked about. I take it that you are not simply equating this sort of increased activity with raised oestrogen levels; rats in oestrus are more active than at other times and would probably show more retrieval behaviour as a result of this hyperactivity.

Rosenblatt: No, being more active doesn't mean that a female will retrieve more. Rats in oestrus run away from the pups, while the oestrogen-treated rats I have described show more maternal behaviour. What we see is a more specific activity than oestrous activity alone.

Brazelton: Is there any proof that the effect could be due to a change in the level of stress hormones rather than to specific female hormones?

Rosenblatt: We haven't tested all possible hormones but we have tried to narrow it down, as I indicated. I really don't know how we can show that the effect is due specifically to oestrogen. I have used other hormones, including prolactin, and not shown this effect.

Brazelton: I think of behaviour around the birth process as being in response to stress, with initial mothering behaviour perhaps being part of a general response to stress, with a protective response to an immature, helpless organism as part of this generalized response towards survival.

Rosenblatt: I think the question we have come to is what causes the shortening of latency if pregnancy continues rather than being interrupted by hysterectomy. After hysterectomy we see a more rapid onset later in pregnancy than we see earlier. There are two possibilities to examine. One is whether the rate at which oestrogen builds up to a certain level is more rapid later in pregnancy than earlier in pregnancy. Or has the nervous system become more sensitive to the effect of oestrogen so that the same amount of oestrogen has a greater effect later in pregnancy than it has earlier? The only evidence we have is that if we give the same amount of hormone to pregnant hysterectomized animals from the 13th to the 19th days, we get the same rate of onset with the same level of hormone. On the other hand, we have to give pregnant females and non-hysterectomized virgins different amounts of hormones to get the same degree of responsiveness (Siegel & Rosenblatt 1975*a,b*). That suggests that during pregnancy the differences at different stages are based on the rate at which oestrogen reaches a certain level, whereas there is a different basic level of responsiveness in pregnant and virgin animals.

Curtis-Jenkins: I have seen four human mothers in the last ten years who had considerable difficulty in accepting a child after birth. They said that the child 'didn't smell right'. In your rats, did maternal behaviour vary according to the sex of the pups, Dr Rosenblatt?

Rosenblatt: There is some indication that female rats can differentiate between female and male pups but we don't know that the responsiveness is different.

Oppé: Are there any big differences between rats having first pregnancies and subsequent ones? In other words, do they 'learn' anything by indulging in maternal behaviour?

Rosenblatt: After only 1.5 days of postpartum contact with their pups, lactating mothers show a much reduced latency of three days, instead of six days, in the test of induction. Work by Cosnier & Couturier (1966) indicates that once the virgin female has been maternal and reared a litter she is always maternal. Maternal behaviour is close to the surface and the non-pregnant animal needs only a short period of subsequent contact to show the full pattern.

Leiderman: Have you any data on whether the mother who has had previous experience 'pushes' the non-hormonal phase to the prepartum situation?

Rosenblatt: I have no data but Cosnier & Couturier (1966) have shown that the female who has given birth and reared her young will show maternal behaviour just on being exposed to young. Between the two episodes of maternal behaviour they ovariectomized the female, so there was no contribution from the ovaries.

Leiderman: Would the 'hormonal' state of the mother who has had previous experience be different?

Rosenblatt: The fact that this behaviour appears after removal of the ovaries suggests that the hormones are not involved.

Macfarlane: Is there any interplay between hormonal levels and olfaction?

Rosenblatt: That is one of the possibilities. The work I described on the role of olfaction was done mainly on virgin animals. I want to put that into the context of what happens to the lactating mother when she gives birth. It has been suggested that the hormones—particularly oestrogen, which induces maternal behaviour—may either affect the ability of the female to smell the young, or affect her responsiveness to the smell of the young. We have no evidence on that yet.

Klaus: What is known about the hormonal basis for attachment in animals that form an early strong bond to a specific infant?

Rosenblatt: The goat is a paradigm of rapid bonding of mother to infant (Klopfer & Klopfer 1968). That is largely on the basis of taste or smell. There is some indication that the mother goat is responsive *pre partum*, when she tries to steal other young, but once she gives birth that behaviour wanes rapidly. The young must get to her very quickly for maternal behaviour to be established. In the first couple of minutes when she licks them she accepts all young, not differentiating her own from others, but after another two minutes of licking she identifies her own young. In the goat and sheep the transition period is very rapid, and it is differentiated into phases, rising and declining sharply.

Hofer: You also mentioned some work on the strength of the potential for mothering *pre partum* between two species and between individuals, and the fate of that potential according to different postpartum experiences.

Rosenblatt: One can estimate how well the hormonal phase has developed by observing different strains of rats in which the strength of mothering is different. In our Sprague-Dawley rats about 75% of females retrieve before parturition, but only 25% of Wistar strain rats retrieve before parturition (Slotnick *et al.* 1973). The difference between these strains may be due to the different time of release of oestrogen—that is, to the rate of secretion of hormones. The consequences are significant, in that the Wistar strain females may need an additional period *post partum* to build up the hormonal basis, whereas the Sprague-Dawley strain females apparently build it up *pre partum*. In certain strains of rabbits, too, nest-building appears after parturition, while in others it appears before parturition. It is simply due to the timing of the secretion of oestrogen and progesterone. If one pulls their young away from females whose hormonally based maternal behaviour is weakly developed, that behaviour declines rapidly. Animals of the same strain which have built up their prepartum maternal behaviour fairly substantially may need only ten minutes of contact with the pups each day to maintain their maternal behaviour.

One of the factors which may determine the success of transition is how well this prepartum phase has been elaborated, and that is different in different individuals and in different strains.

Hofer: Some individual mothers may be more susceptible to periods of separation in the postpartum relationship than others. This may be relevant to the clinical observations we shall be hearing about later in the meeting.

Rosenblatt: Separation is not the natural thing. The mothers may depend differentially upon contact with the young whilst building up both phases—the final stages of the hormonal phase and the beginning of the non-hormonal phase.

Cooper: In human mothers there is a wide variation in behaviour. What is the degree of variation in latency in rats?

Rosenblatt: The latency of the virgin rat may range from three to nine days, the average being five or six days. In the animals treated with zinc sulphate perhaps 40–60% show maternal behaviour immediately on being presented with young, but the remainder show it in the next 24 hours. The variability is slight.

Cooper: Have studies like those on olfaction been done on how visual and auditory stimuli also affect maternal behaviour?

Rosenblatt: Working on the mouse, Noirot (1972) has been able to specify in general which stimuli elicit which components of maternal behaviour. In rodents ultrasonic sounds made by the young seem effective in eliciting retrieval and perhaps nest-building by the mothers. Olfaction and tactile stimuli are more likely to elicit nursing and licking. Also, if the primary behaviour to be elicited is not permitted, the animal shifts over to a secondary one in relation to the same stimulus. Analysis has only just begun, but different sensory stimuli are apparently mainly responsible for different components of maternal behaviour.

Cooper: What about the visual stimuli?

Hinde: Vision is less important for rodents. In nearly all primates young infants look different in some more or less conspicuous way from the adult. This is circumstantial evidence that they have a particular visual attractiveness.

References

BEACH, F.A. & WILSON, J.R. (1963) Effects of prolactin, progesterone, and estrogen on reactions of nonpregnant rats to foster young. *Psychol. Rep. 13*, 231–239

COSNIER, J. & COUTURIER, C. (1966) Comportement maternel provoqué chez les rattes adults castrées. *C.R. Séances Soc. Biol. Fil. 160*, 789–791

KLOPFER, P.H. & KLOPFER, M.S. (1968) Maternal 'imprinting' in goats: fostering of alien young. *Z. Tierpsychol. 25*, 862–866

LOTT, D.F. & FUCHS, S.S. (1962) Failure to induce retrieving by sensitization or the injection of prolactin. *J. Comp. Physiol. Psychol. 55*, 1111–1113

MOLTZ, H., LUBIN, M., LEON, M. & NUMAN, M. (1970) Hormonal induction of maternal behaviour in the ovariectomized nulliparous rat. *Physiol. Behav. 5*, 1373–1377

NOIROT, E. (1972) in *Advances in the Study of Behavior* (Lehrman, D.S., Hinde, R.A. & Shaw, E., eds.), vol. 4, pp. 107–145, Academic Press, New York

RICHARDS, M.P.M. (1967) Maternal behaviour in rodents and hagomorphs, in *Advances in Reproductive Physiology* (McLaren, A., ed.), vol. 2, Academic Press/Logos Press, London

SIEGEL, H.I. & ROSENBLATT, J.S. (1975*a*) Hormonal basis of hysterectomy-induced maternal behaviour during pregnancy in the rat. *Horm. Behav.*, in press

SIEGEL, H.I. & ROSENBLATT, J.S. (1975*b*) Estrogen-induced maternal behaviour in hysterectomized–ovariectomized virgin rats. *Physiol. Behav.*, in press

SLOTNICK, B.M., CARPENTER, M.L. & FUSCO, R. (1973) Initiation of maternal behaviour in pregnant nulliparous rats. *Horm. Behav. 4*, 53–59

TERKEL, J. & ROSENBLATT, J.S. (1972) Humoral factors underlying maternal behaviour at parturition: cross transfusion between freely moving rats. *J. Comp. Physiol. Psychol. 80*, 365–371

ZARROW, M.X., GANDELMAN, R. & DENENBERG, V.H. (1971) Prolactin: is it an essential hormone for maternal behaviour in the mammal? *Horm. Behav. 2*, 343–354

Qualities of mother – infant relationships in monkeys

R. A. HINDE and M. J. A. SIMPSON

MRC Unit for the Development and Integration of Behaviour, Madingley, Cambridge

Abstract We habitually use qualitative terms to describe relationships. This paper is concerned with methods for describing, assessing and classifying these qualities objectively.

Some judgements about qualities depend on which interactions occur, some concern qualities of the interactions themselves, and some depend on the way in which the different interactions within a relationship are patterned. In addition some judgements depend on diverse criteria which are not necessarily correlated with each other and need not all be satisfied. Limitations of everyday concepts of quality are discussed.

Our attempts to assess qualities of the mother–infant relationship in rhesus monkeys in a quantitative fashion are described. Special attention is paid to groups of measures which appear to refer to qualities which could be described as 'maternal warmth', 'maternal rejectingness', 'maternal control', and 'meshing/dissonance' (i.e. the extent to which the goals of each partner coincide with those of the other). A type of interaction which could be called 'a game' is described. The extent to which such assessments have predictive value is discussed.

In studying relationships, we tend to label them in the first instance in terms of the nature of the individuals involved and what they do together. Mother–infant relationships are classified as such in part because of the age/sex categories of the participants, and in part because the interactions upon which the relationship depends consist of nursing/suckling, crying/succouring, and so on. But all mother–infant dyads participate in interactions of these sorts: if we are to compare mother–infant relationships, we must do so on the basis of their 'qualities'.

This paper is addressed to the problems of what is meant by the 'qualities' of a relationship and how those qualities can be studied objectively. In any study of social behaviour, it quickly becomes apparent that an infinite number of things could be measured, and one could soon wallow in a morass of detail.

One solution would be to accept that difficulty, measure a large number of aspects of the interactions, and rely on computer-based factor or cluster analysis to assess their meaning. This solution would have the important advantage of showing which measures co-vary, and thus of determining which are redundant, or which may be related to a common underlying mechanism. It would have the disadvantage that, however many measures are used, *some* selection must operate, and the factors extracted are inevitably determined by the data that are fed in. Furthermore, qualities may depend not on the presence or absence of particular features of interactions, but on properties of sequencing and reciprocity, and the inclusion of all possible measures would be impossible.

Therefore, since we must be selective in the measures we take, it seems reasonable not to discard as guidelines the qualities that we notice in everyday life —is this couple rough or gentle with each other, responsive to each other, are they affectionate or competitive? Then the questions remain, how can we translate these terms into objectively measurable criteria, and how can we determine which measures are important—i.e., which relate to the immediate or long-term course of the relationship? Of course the use of everyday qualities as guidelines does not necessarily diminish the need for mathematical analysis, which can be invaluable for showing which measures are redundant and for suggesting, supporting or exploding hypotheses.

THE NATURE OF THE QUALITIES OF RELATIONSHIPS

As a start, we may note that the judgements we make about relationships tend to fall into several categories. First, some judgements depend on which types of interaction occur. Thus we are more likely to describe a mother–infant relationship as distant if play never occurs than if it is frequent, though of course other criteria also contribute to our judgement. And the frequent occurrence of the sequence 'infant rhesus approaches mother and attempts to take nipple, mother denies it' gives the mother–infant relationship a quality of 'rejectingness'.

Second, some judgements concern the qualities of the interactions themselves. The mother may reject the infant roughly, by hitting it or pushing it away; or gently, by crossing her arms over her nipples but remaining available for the infant to cuddle against; or she may move away. And if she permits access to the nipple she may or may not embrace the infant as it cuddles to her. Another important quality, to be discussed in more detail later, concerns the extent to which the behaviour of infant and mother mesh with each other, or whether they are dissonant—that is, are the goals of each aligned with the ongoing behaviour of the other? Such qualities may concern some or all types of interaction within the relationship, or even interactions of one type in some contexts but not in others.

Third, some judgements depend not on the course of particular types of interaction, but on how interactions are patterned. Thus if a rhesus mother frequently rejects her infant's attempts to gain ventral-ventral contact and never initiates them, we might describe her as rejecting. If she never rejects the infant and frequently initiates contact herself, we might describe her as possessive. But if she often rejects and often initiates, or seldom does either, we would describe her respectively as controlling or permissive. These judgements could not be based solely on one type of interaction, and must depend on both.

Finally, many everyday judgements about relationships turn out on analysis to depend on many properties which may not be related to each other, and which need not all be present in any one case. For example, we would be more prone to describe a relationship as affectionate if:

(*a*) It involves interactions of a number of different types (i.e. is multiplex);
(*b*) It is of long duration;
(*c*) In the absence of the other each partner shows special types of behaviour adapted to or tending to restore proximity;
(*d*) The anxiety induced by strange objects or situations is alleviated by the presence of the partner;
(*e*) The behaviour of each partner is organized in relation to the ongoing behaviour of the other (i.e. they mesh).

It is not suggested that these are all the properties on which the designation 'affectionate' may depend, nor that all these are always necessary; those listed, however, can all be identified and studied with moderate rigour, even in the rhesus monkey mother–infant relationship.

In referring to the qualities of a relationship, it is usually necessary to specify their range of applicability. On the one hand, a quality of one of the constituent interactions of a relationship may not be applicable to others. For example a mother may be rejecting of her infant's nursing requests but not his requests to be groomed: indeed chimpanzees and rhesus mothers often comfort infants who are distressed because access to the nipple has been denied them with other types of attention. Furthermore the quality even of one type of interaction may vary with the context: rhesus monkey mothers reject their infants less when living alone than when in a group (Hinde & Spencer-Booth 1967), and pigtailed monkey mothers hit their infants more when living in a poor laboratory environment than when in a so-called rich laboratory environment (Jensen *et al.* 1968).

On the other hand, qualities can be valid not only for all types of interaction within a relationship, but for all or most of the relationships of a given individual. In so far as one individual behaves consistently to diverse others, but differently from the way in which they behave to each other, he may be labelled as rejecting, cold, affectionate and so on.

Qualities which apply to reciprocal interactions (i.e. those in which the two partners take similar parts, either at the same time or alternately, as in peer–peer play) may apply either to one *or* to both partners. Thus it is possible for both partners to show sensitivity, or for one to behave with sensitivity and the other not. But where the qualities imply complementarity (i.e. two partners take different parts, as in male–female sexual behaviour), they tend to apply to the interaction more readily than to either partner independently: if one partner controls, the other must be controlled; if one rejects, the other must be rejected. Of course qualities that apply to the patterning of interactions, and qualities that are multidimensional, necessarily apply to substantial areas of the relationship rather than to particular interactions: whilst an isolated interaction might be described as involving gentleness or sensitivity, it hardly makes sense, in the absence of other information, to call it affectionate or loving.

Where a quality depends on both partners, it is likely to do so in complex ways. For example, how often a rhesus monkey mother rejects an infant's attempts to gain the nipple depends in part on how often he makes them; the same mother might never reject an undemanding infant but frequently reject a demanding one. Conversely, how often the infant attempts to make contact will depend in part on how often the mother rejects him, as well as on other factors such as his changing requirements for milk, the availability of playmates, and so forth.

At this point it may be as well to stress that our emphasis on behavioural criteria for qualities in no way denies the importance of the subjective aspects of a relationship. But as observers looking in from the outside, we can tackle these only in so far as they are revealed in behaviour. For example, our emphasis on 'meshing' can be regarded as an attempt to come to grips with some aspects of 'intersubjectivity' (Asch 1952).

SOME QUALITIES OF RHESUS MONKEY MOTHER–INFANT INTERACTIONS

We may now consider some attempts at measuring these qualities in rhesus monkey mother–infant pairs.

(1) 'Warmth' in mothering

Rhesus monkey mothers vary in how much they take the initiative in making ventral-ventral contact with their infants, and those who rank high on this

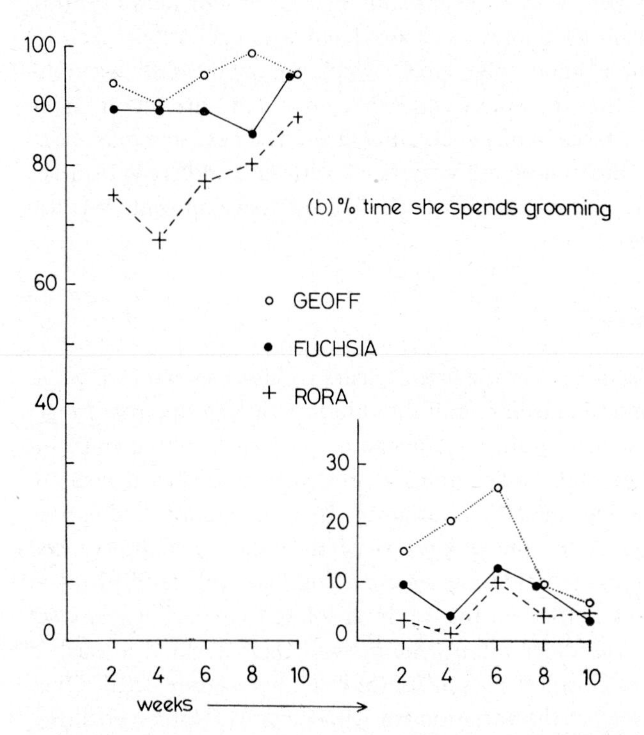

FIG. 1. The percentage of time spent by rhesus monkey mothers (*a*) with their arms round, and (*b*) grooming their infants through 10 weeks. Only the times when the mothers were in ventral-ventral contact with their infants were examined.

measure are also those who groom their infants more than others (Hinde & Spencer-Booth 1971*a*). Fig. 1 shows some related measures. It examines first what proportion of the time that mothers spend in ventral-ventral contact with their infants they have their arms around them. The figure refers to the mothers of only three infants, but shows that the mothers were consistently different through the five weeks shown. The proportion of ventral-ventral contact-time spent by these mothers in grooming their infants is also shown. Again, the mothers were consistently different, and the mothers who spent longer with their arms around their infants also groomed them for longer. This finding was slightly surprising, because it seems easier for a rhesus monkey mother not to hold her arm round an infant while she grooms it.

Two points can be made from these observations, assuming that they continue to hold when we have completed our study. First, if the three measures of mothering—role in making ventral-ventral contact in the first place, proportion of ventral-ventral time spent with arm round infant, and proportion of ventral-ventral contact-time spent grooming—are correlated with each other, then we could subsume the three under one label, which we might call 'warmth'. Secondly, Fig. 1 shows that the differences, while consistent, are rather small. Studies of this kind may reveal many such differences. The next step must be to discover whether such differences are correlated with later differences in the infants, or whether they are irrelevant to the infants' development. We will return to this issue later.

(2) *Maternal 'rejectingness'*

The frequency of rejections over the first $2\frac{1}{2}$ years of life is shown in Fig. 2*a*. The thick line represents the median, and the thin line the interquartile range, of between eight and sixteen mother–infant pairs. The median frequency increased to about two per 100 half-minutes at one year, and then decreased, but there was considerable individual variation. It is of interest to compare these findings with figures for the *proportion* of the infant's ventral-ventral contacts or attempted contacts that are rejected (Fig. 2*b*): this levelled off at about a year. Presumably, although the fall in absolute frequency was a facet of decreasing demand, the older infants maintained their demand at such a level that a more or less constant proportion of attempts were rejected. Once again, however, the extent of the variation was conspicuous. Not surprisingly, at any one age these two measures tend to be positively correlated with each other: the greater the absolute, the greater the relative frequency of rejections (Table 1). However the correlation is far from absolute in older age groups: some individuals suffer a much higher absolute frequency of rejections in

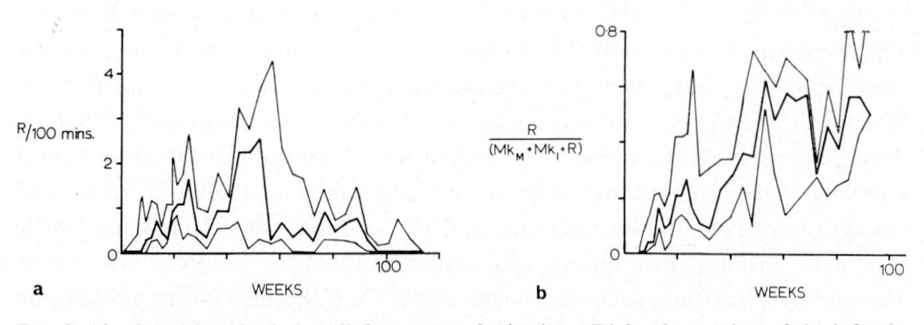

FIG. 2. Absolute (*a*) and relative (*b*) frequency of rejections (R) by the mother of the infant's attempts to gain ventral-ventral contact. (The continuous line represents the median and the discontinuous line the interquartile range for the 19 infants observed. Mk_M = maternal make, Mk_I = infant make.)

TABLE 1

Spearman rank order correlation coefficients between individual mean scores of four measures. (From Hinde & Spencer-Booth 1971*a*.)

	$R/(Mk_I+Mk_M+R)$	$\%Ap_I-\%L_I$	$Mk_M/(Mk_I+Mk_M)$
R	0.98^b	0.63^b	-0.29
	0.98^b	0.77^b	-0.40^a
	0.90^b	0.36^a	-0.21
	0.67^b	0.30	-0.15
$R/(Mk_I+Mk_M+R)$		0.62^b	-0.34
		0.82^b	-0.44^a
		0.56^b	-0.31
		0.55^b	-0.41^a
$\%Ap_I-\%L_I$			-0.40^a
			-0.36^a
			-0.10
			0.19

Upper left to bottom right, weeks 4–6, 7–12, 13–18 and 19–24 in each case. R: frequency of rejections. Mk_I and Mk_M: no. of ventral-ventral contacts initiated by infant and mother respectively. $\%Ap_I$ and $\%L_I$: percentage of approaches and leaves initiated by the infant. ^{a} $P<0.05$ ^{b} $P<0.01$

maintaining a given relative frequency than do others. Not surprisingly again, these measures are positively correlated with the infant's role in maintaining proximity ($\%\ Ap_I - \%\ L_I$; see Hinde & Atkinson 1970) and less strongly negatively correlated with the proportion of ventral-ventral contacts or 'makes' initiated by the mother (Mk_M/Mk_I+Mk_M) (Table 1). These correlations strongly suggest that the first three measures are related to a factor which could be described as 'maternal rejectingness' (or 'absence of maternal warmth') in the relationship. However the lower correlations with the proportion of contacts initiated by the mother suggest a less close relationship with the measures discussed in the preceding section.

(3) Maternal Control

As suggested earlier, the relative frequency of rejections and the proportion of ventral-ventral contacts initiated by the mother tend to be negatively correlated with each other. Fig. 3 shows actual data for 16-week old rhesus infants; dyads whose points lie high on and close to the ordinate would be described as having a relationship involving a rejecting mother, those (two) lying far out and close to the abscissa as possessive. The dimension of control/permissiveness might be judged by the distance from the line. Those points

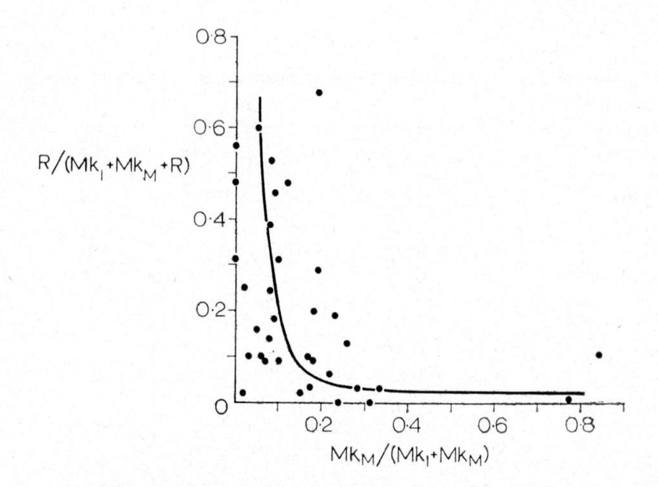

FIG. 3. Relation between proportion of occasions on which infant gained or attempted to gain nipple contact ($R/(Mk_I + Mk_M + R)$) and proportion of nipple contacts initiated by mother ($Mk_M/(Mk_I + Mk_M)$). Results for 16-week-old infant rhesus monkey. Curve drawn by hand.

lying further from the axes than the line involve more maternal control than those lying between the line and the axes. A dyad may have a rejecting (or possessive) relationship, and yet vary along the dimension of maternal control.

(4) Meshing

A quality of special interest concerns the degree of meshing versus dissonance between mother and infant. We have approached this in two ways. First, in the course of the mother–infant relationship, this quality appears to change to a considerable extent with age. Some evidence in this direction is provided by Figs. 2*a* and 2*b*: the very fact that the frequency of rejections falls while the relative frequency remains constant indicates that the infant is becoming less likely to attempt to gain the nipple when the mother is unwilling to let him have it. Further evidence comes from observations of the type shown in Fig. 4, which shows the probability that bouts of ventral-ventral contact will be terminated by mother (discontinuous line) or infant (continuous line) in successive time intervals after their initiation. The bouts have been divided into those initiated by the infant and those initiated by the mother. In constructing Fig. 4, we treated each contact started by each baby as a life insurance firm would treat a life: into which time interval did it survive, and what brought it to an end—the infant or the mother breaking contact? Each curve in the figure was based on a population of such lives, and could be called a 'hazard function', describing the probability of a contact that has lasted a particular length of

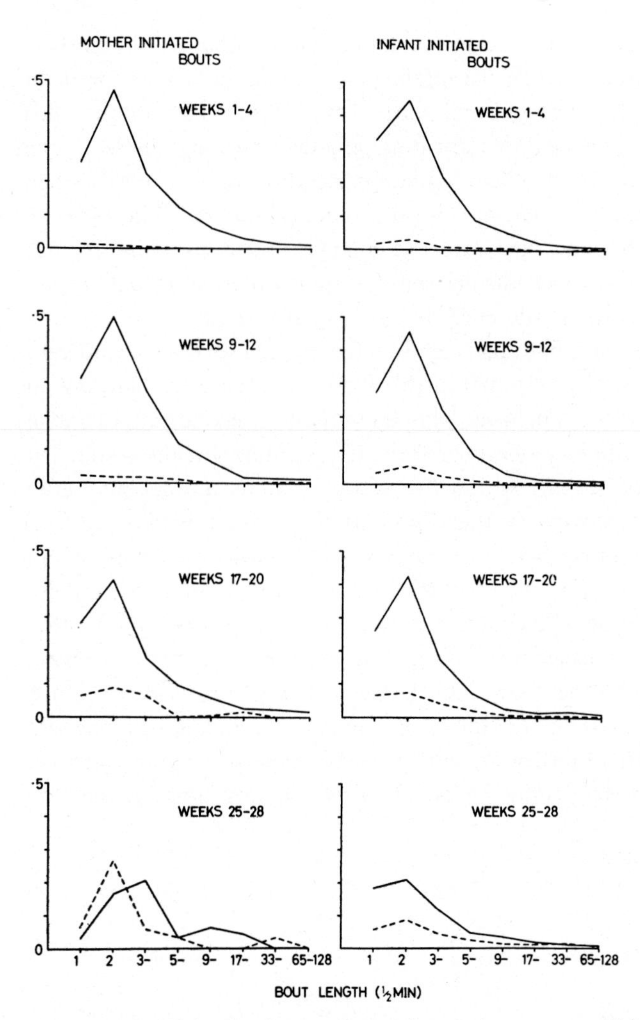

FIG. 4. Probabilities that bouts of ventral-ventral contact would be terminated by mother or infant during successive intervals after initiation of contact. The four graphs on the left show bouts initiated by the mother, the four on the right those initiated by the infant. Continuous lines indicate bouts terminated by the infant, discontinuous lines those terminated by the mother (Hinde & White 1974).

time being brought to an end in the interval in question in one of the two ways shown. (See Simpson 1968 for details of this method, and Slater 1973 for a review of methods of sequence analysis.) Comparison between the two sides of Fig. 4 shows that with infants of 1–4 and 9–12 weeks old contact is more likely to be terminated by the infant at any point after its initiation if it was initiated by the mother, and contact is more likely to be terminated by the mother if it was initiated by the infant than if she initiated it herself. In other words, mothers are likely to initiate contact when the infant is not 'ready' and therefore subsequently terminates the contact, and vice versa. With older infants this difference disappears, presumably indicating greater 'meshing' between the behaviour of the infant and mother. Similar principles apply to bouts when infant and mother were *not* in ventral-ventral contact (Hinde & White 1974).

But these findings are concerned with age-changes in groups of infants. Of much greater interest here are results derived by a quite different technique, and suggesting marked individual differences in meshing at one age.

We will illustrate this with findings from two female infants born to different mothers in the same social group within two weeks of each other. During an infant's first 12 weeks of life, much can happen in the few seconds after contact between infant and mother has been broken. If the infant breaks contact, it may or may not regain contact within five seconds, or its mother may grab it and restrain it from moving further away. If the mother breaks contact, the infant may quickly grasp her, or even jerk and squeak, or it may accept the situation and start to play. We will first consider two measures of mother–infant harmony at the time when contact is broken. First, if it was the mother who broke contact, do mother and infant differ in their readiness to regain contact? When Becky's mother, Sarah, broke contact (Fig. 5*a*), *Becky* regained contact within five seconds on 13 out of 100 occasions, and her *mother* did so nine times. With Ari's mother, by contrast, the respective figures were 50 and zero. (Both infants were eight weeks old.) It would seem that, at the time

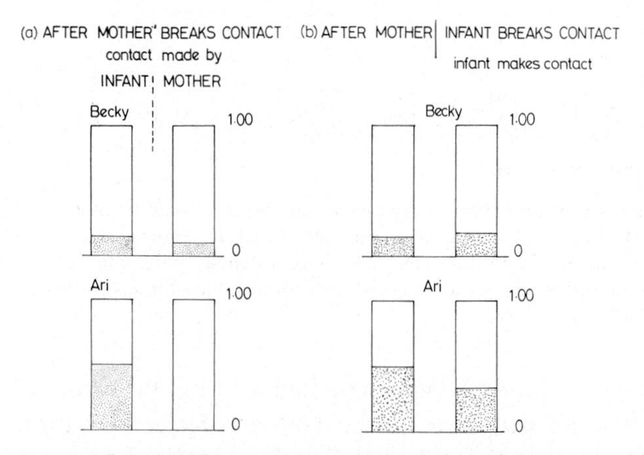

FIG. 5. (*a*) Probabilities of infant and mother making contact within 5 s of mother breaking contact, in two mother–infant pairs, when the infants were 8 weeks old.
(*b*) Probability of infant making contact with mother within 5 s of contact being broken by mother (left-hand column) and infant (right-hand column), in two mother–infant pairs when the infants were 8 weeks old.

when Ari's mother breaks contact, mother and infant are less equal in readiness to stay together than are Becky and her mother. But Ari's high value could stem from the fact that she was generally more active than Becky. Therefore, we used a second method to look at mother–infant harmony, namely comparison of the infant's readiness to regain contact when the infant herself had just broken it, with the infant's readiness for contact when the mother had just broken it. Fig. 5*b* shows that, whether it is Becky or her mother that has broken contact, Becky is about equally likely to regain contact. In contrast, when Ari's mother has broken contact, Ari is more likely to regain it than when it was Ari herself who had broken it. We could say that Becky's mother manages better than Ari's at breaking contact when Becky does not want to retain it.

Fig. 6 shows similar findings from the 4th to the 24th weeks, comparing the effect of mother and infant breaking contact on the infant's readiness to regain contact in the next five seconds. Whilst in weeks 8 and 12 Ari is more likely to regain contact if it was her mother who had broken contact than if she herself had, by 20 weeks Ari and her mother seem to have achieved some harmony.

Any quality is more meaningful if we can study it in several aspects of a relationship and find correlations between them. So far we have assessed

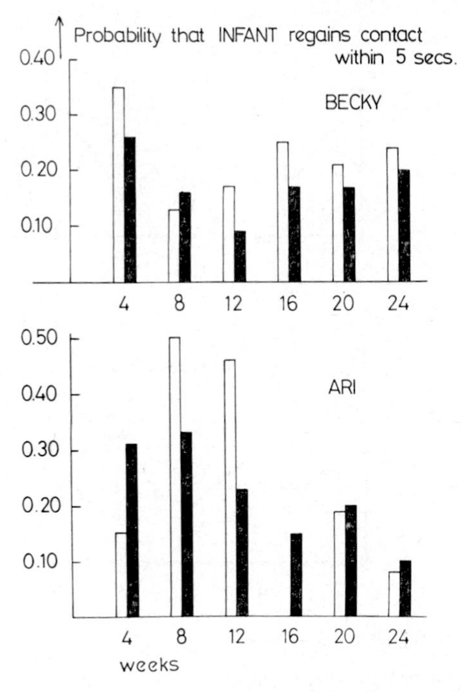

Fig. 6. Probability of infant making contact with mother within 5 s of contact being broken by mother (□) and infant (■), in two mother–infant pairs, through the infants' first 24 weeks.

'meshing versus dissonance' by whether the mother or infant were equally ready to regain a ventral-ventral contact which had been broken. Our next measure concerns mothers' and infants' readiness to move apart when they are together.

Even at four weeks of age, rhesus monkey infants often leave their mothers to explore and play. The return visits between the excursions are rather short, and these visits are of interest, both because the probability of an infant ending such a visit by going off again is not constant, and because the mother is sometimes responsible for the end of a visit. The question thus arises: on those occasions when the *mother* brings a visit to an end by leaving, does she do so at a time when the infant was likely to leave anyway? Fig. 7 compares Ari and

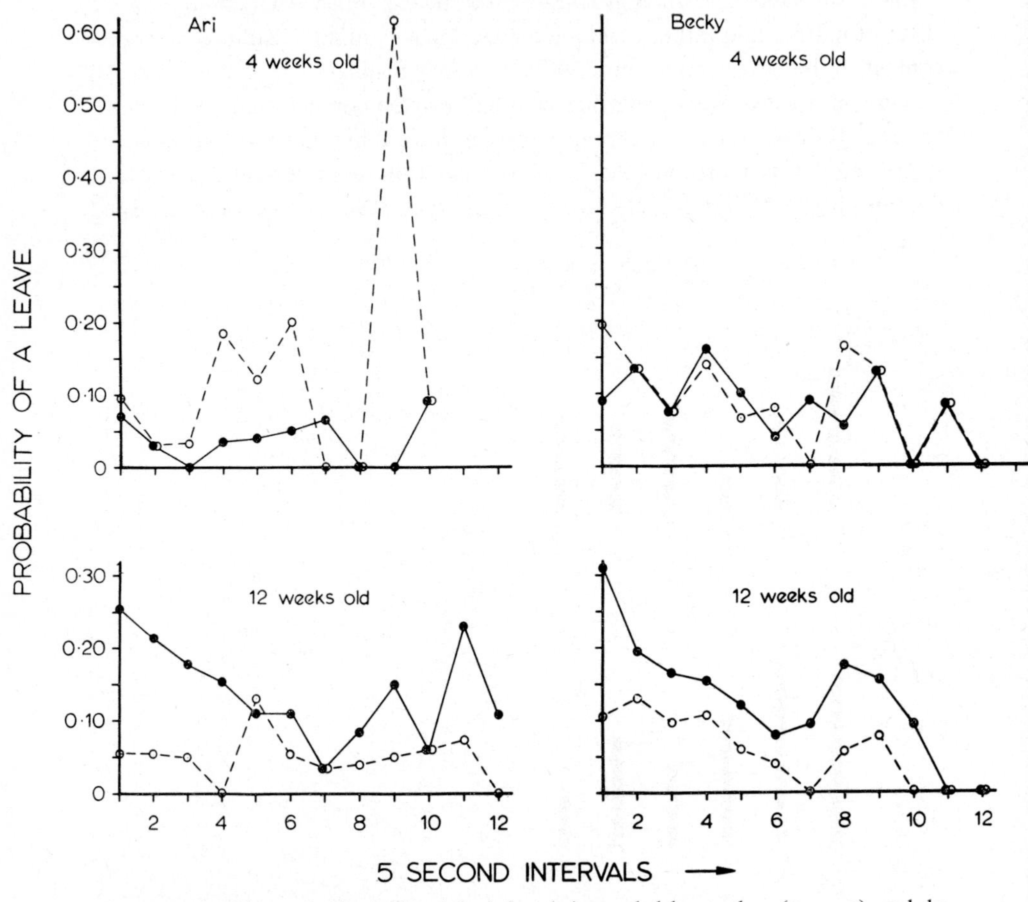

FIG. 7. Probabilities of visits initiated by infant being ended by mother (○---○) and by infant (●——●) when the visits have lasted between 0 and 5 s, 5 and 10 s (i.e. lasted into the second 5-s interval), 10 and 15 s, and so on (ordinate). See text.

Becky at 4 and 12 weeks. This figure was constructed in a similar way to Fig. 4. At both ages, Becky's mother's curve follows Becky's curve more closely than Ari's mother's curve follows Ari's. When Becky is unlikely to leave, Becky's mother is also less likely to leave.

If Ari's mother were less adept at leaving when Ari was ready to be apart than Becky's mother is, we would expect that Ari would be more ready than Becky to rejoin her mother. At four weeks of age, we do not find a difference, but by 12 weeks Ari approaches her mother within five seconds on 43% of the occasions when her mother leaves, while Becky does so only on 18% of the occasions.

If Becky's mother is better than Ari's at breaking contact when her daughter is ready to stay out of contact, it could be because she is more sensitive to Becky's protests—jerks and sometimes squeaks—at mistimed maternal actions, or because Becky protests more vigorously at such actions. In general, closely meshed relationships could be the result (1) of partners being sensitive (i.e. responding vigorously) to the other's 'mistakes', or (2) of partners being sensitive to the other's protests about such mistakes, or (3) of both these factors. Thus an understanding of the mechanisms of meshing will require a further stage of analysis (cf. Ainsworth & Bell 1970).

(5) Mother–infant 'games'

When their infants are between two and eight weeks of age, a few of our monkey mothers, including Sarah, mother of Becky, leave them frequently; this

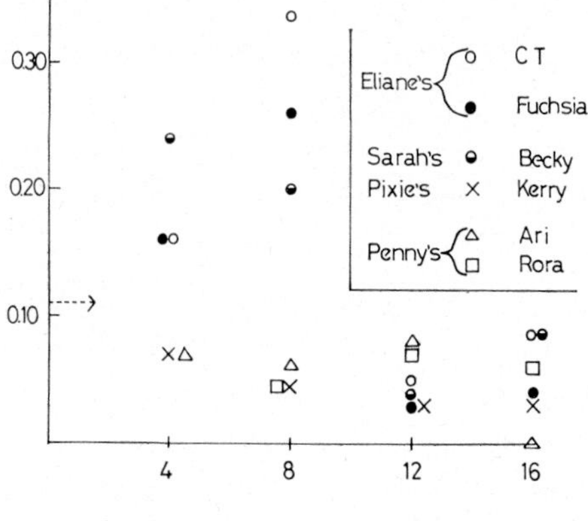

FIG. 8. Mothers repeating their departures within 10 s of a parting: probabilities of four mothers doing this at four ages of their infants. 0.11 is the probability that the mother with the highest leaving score was expected to have by chance. Rora is not shown at 4 weeks, because mother left her less than 10 times.

is long before the time when rejections increase in frequency. Such mothers also often approach their infants, so that one sees sequences like this: mother leaves, pauses two or three seconds, approaches, perhaps lets infant make contact, then leaves again. Sometimes the infant approaches after such a departure by its mother, and then the mother leaves again. The departures of such mothers are bunched in time: with her eight-week-old son C-T, Eliane left 163 times in six hours of watching, and 54 of those occurred within 10 seconds of one of her previous departures (Fig. 8). If those departures had been randomly spread through the six hours, only about 11% should have followed within 10 seconds of another departure, rather than the 33% shown for C-T in Fig. 8. This criterion of temporal bunching distinguishes three of the mothers we have studied from the others, of which three are shown.

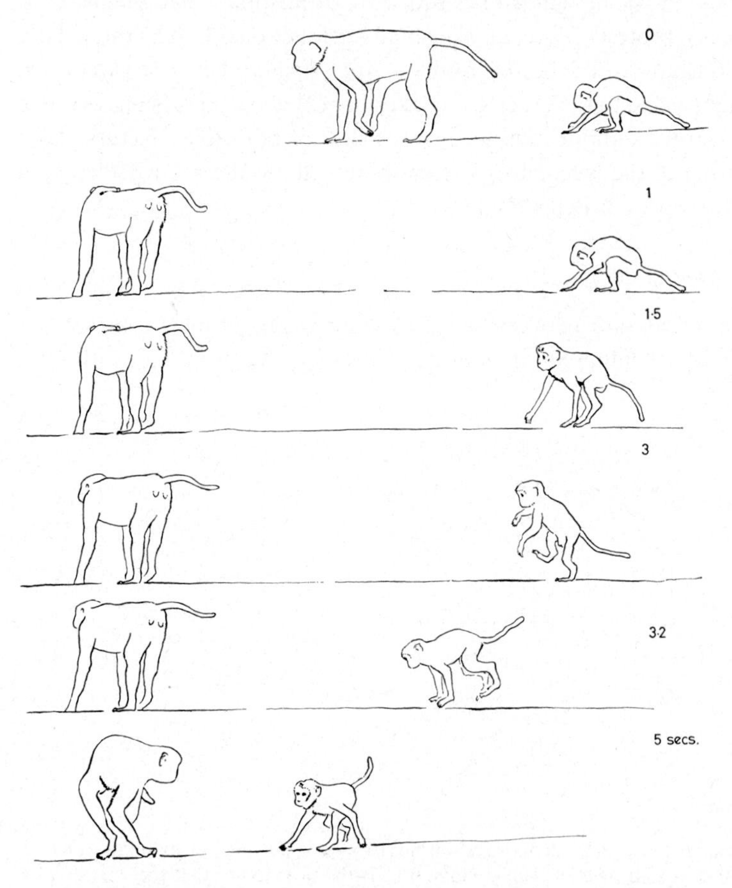

FIG. 9. A 5-s sequence of a mother–infant leaving game, based on film. The approximate times of the frames are shown on the right. Explanation in text.

This is a colourless way of describing what seems to be a game between mother and infant. Fig. 9 illustrates five seconds of such a game. Sarah walks firmly and smoothly away from Titus (her second infant), who is rubbing food along the ground. About 0.75 s later she pauses. As she walks away, and at the moment of her pause, her tail is below the horizontal, but during the next quarter of a second (six frames of film) her tail is raised above the horizontal, and she looks round at Titus. The tail-raising, pausing and looking round are parts of what Hansen (1966) would call an 'affectional' present, albeit rather a low intensity one. Such presents can be seen when mothers attempt to entice their infants out of some place inaccessible to them, and can include head-lowering, even to looking through the legs, lip-smacking at the baby and scratching the thigh. In this particular case, Sarah held her position for more than two seconds, and Titus approached her as she was turning to approach him. Sarah then left Titus almost at once. Had Titus not approached she might have returned to him, but, having done so, she would probably have left him again.

We give in to the temptation to call this kind of interaction a 'game' because it seems, intuitively, to have the qualities of human mother–infant looking–looking-away games. The Tinbergens' 'taming procedure' by which a strange adult can initiate interaction with human children, including autistic ones (Tinbergen & Tinbergen 1974), includes looking (Tinbergen 1972) and touch games which have much in common with our rhesus monkey approach–leave games. The approach–withdrawal behaviour of the rhesus mother is also very similar to that of a three-year-old female child attempting to engage a small infant in play. Moreover, there is an element of 'as if' in the interaction: the mother leaves, but she is quick to show that she does not really 'want' to be apart, by making friendly gestures like lip-smacking, presenting, etc., and by returning anyway if the infant does not catch up with her. Moreover, the infant shows the relaxed movements he would show in infant–infant play: he may hop and handstand as he approaches.

We would like to make the following points out of this pattern of interaction. First, here is a kind of interaction which is not shown by all mothers. It is interesting that the few who have shown it are also the ones who have relatively well-'meshed' relationships with their infants—Becky's mother in contrast to Ari's, for example. Second, although we know that some mother–infant pairs play this game and others do not, as yet we know nothing of its longer-term consequences. We suspect that, through this game, the mother could discover when her infant first becomes quick to follow her when she leaves, and when he first follows her after a delay. Fig. 10 refers to the infant C-T with his mother at five ages. Each column shows the probability that, after his mother leaves, the two will come together again if they have been apart as long as between

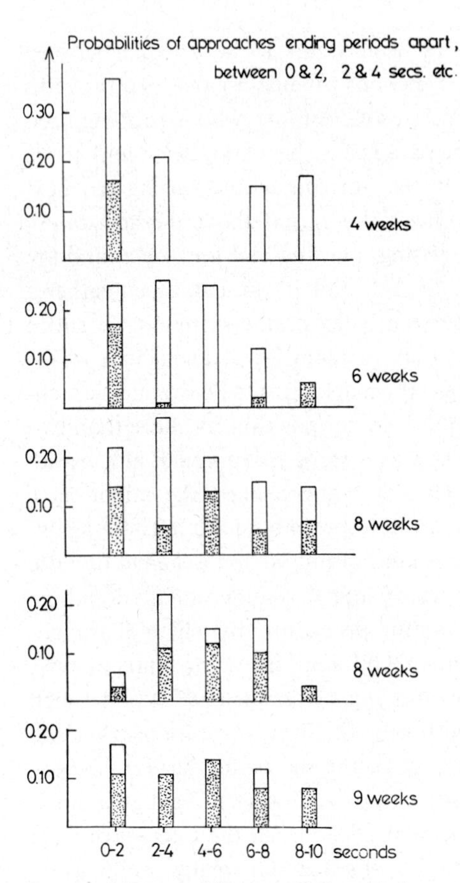

FIG. 10. Eliane and her son C-T: periods apart started by mother leaving. Probabilities of approaches by mother (□) and infant (▦) ending periods apart that have lasted between 0 and 2 s, 2 and 4 s and so on, at five different ages of the infant.

0 and 2 s, 2 and 4 s, and so on. The stippled part of each column shows the proportion of the returning due to the infant. At four weeks, the infant is already approaching his mother within two seconds, but after they have been apart for two seconds, she is responsible for all the returns. In those periods apart that last between two and four seconds (i.e. the second column in Fig. 10), we see that with age the infant gradually becomes responsible for a greater proportion of the returns that bring the two together. (As the infant does this, the female comes to play the game less often: Fig. 8.)

LONG-TERM CONSEQUENCES OF THE QUALITY OF THE MOTHER–INFANT RELATIONSHIP

Reports of animal behaviour include many studies of the long-term effects of the disruption of early social relationships (e.g. Harlow & Harlow 1965, 1969; Sackett 1968). However, we know of few studies in which the consequences of variations in the mother–infant relationship within the normal range were assessed (but see, e.g., Lagerspetz 1964; Southwick 1968). This is largely because ethologists tend to examine the outcome of experimental treatments without examining how those treatments affect the mother–infant relationship.

However, two sorts of data indicate that the measures of 'maternal rejectingness' that we mentioned earlier have considerably more predictive value than measures of how much time infant and mother spend together. First, they tend to be somewhat more consistent over successive age spans. This is shown in Table 2. Second, in experiments on the effects of separating infants from their mothers for 13 days, it was found that these measures correlated significantly with a measure of the distress shown by the infant during the period after reunion. The latter was measured (not wholly satisfactorily: L. McGinnis & R. A. Hinde, unpublished work) by summing the ranks of the infants on three measures of behaviour affected by the separation experience —'whoo calling', sitting in the hunched depressed posture, and depressed locomotor activity. The relative frequency of rejections and the infant's role in the maintenance of proximity, whether measured before separation or contemporaneously, were positively correlated with the distress index. The actual time that infant and mother spent together or in proximity showed much lower correlations (Table 3).

TABLE 2

Spearman rank order correlation coefficients between various measures of mother–infant interactions for individuals at different ages. (From Hinde & Spencer-Booth 1971*a*.)

	Weeks		
	4–6 with 7–12	*7–12 with 13–18*	*13–18 with 19–24*
Time off	0.35[a]	0.45[a]	0.34
Time more than 60 cm from mother	0.53[b]	0.58[b]	0.33
R	0.54[b]	0.63[b]	0.02
$R/(Mk_I + Mk_M + R)$	0.65[b]	0.63[b]	0.47[a]
$Mk_M/(Mk_I + Mk_M)$	0.62[b]	0.60[b]	0.64[b]
$\%Ap_I - \%L_I$	0.61[b]	0.51[b]	0.58[b]

See Table 1 (p. 45) for explanation of symbols and abbreviations.

TABLE 3

Spearman rank order correlation coefficients between index of distress shown by rhesus monkey infants reunited with their mothers after a six-day separation period, and measures of the mother–infant relationship before separation (mother and infant were reunited on Day 10, and coefficients calculated separately for data obtained in the periods Days 11–16 and 23–37). (From Hinde & Spencer-Booth 1971*b*.)

Measure of mother–infant relationship	*Correlation coefficient*	
	Days 11–16	*Days 23–37*
Time off	−0.07	−0.13
Time more than 60 cm from mother	−0.28	−0.18
$R/(Mk_I + Mk_M + R)$	0.59[a]	0.43[a]
$\%Ap_I - \%L_I$	0.64[b]	0.41

See Table 1 (p. 45) for explanation of symbols and abbreviations.

CONCLUSION

We would like to emphasize that, while those who work with animals are forced to focus on behaviour, the approach need not be so reductionist as it might seem at first glance. We cannot ask the monkey mothers how they feel, and so we must focus on what they do. But we believe, for instance, that monkey mothers enjoy seeing their infants move, and the game we have described permits them to do so. Again, while we have specified certain behavioural characteristics of affectionate relationships, we are not suggesting for a moment that such relationships involve nothing but the symptoms we describe.

Students of human mother–infant relationships can both enquire and empathize. However, such procedures can be scientifically dangerous, and the need to focus on fine behavioural details in order to study the qualities of relationships has been stressed by a number of workers (e.g. Stern 1971, 1974; Richards, 1974). We hope that studies of the relatively simple mother–infant relationships of rhesus monkeys will aid both conceptual clarity and methodology in this field. But we would stress that the final test of the usefulness of such descriptions lies in the degree to which they enable us to predict future social behaviour, and for that long-term studies are essential.

ACKNOWLEDGEMENTS

This work was supported by the Medical Research Council and by the Royal Society. We would like to thank a number of colleagues, especially Anne Simpson and Lilyan White for help with data collection and analysis, Jock Jolley for his care of the monkeys, and Judy Dunn for her comments on the manuscript.

References

AINSWORTH, M.D.S. & BELL, S.M. (1970) Attachment, exploration and interaction. *Child Dev. 41*, 49

ASCH, S.E. (1952) *Social Psychology*. Prentice-Hall, New York

HANSEN, E.W. (1966) The development of maternal and infant behavior in the rhesus monkey. *Behaviour 27*, 107–149

HARLOW, H.F. & HARLOW, M.K. (1965) The affectional systems, in *Behavior of Nonhuman Primates* (Schrier, A.M., Harlow, H.F. & Stollnitz, F., eds.), vol. 2, Academic Press, New York and London

HARLOW, H.F. & HARLOW, M.K. (1969) Effects of various mother–infant relationships on rhesus monkey behaviors, in *Determinants of Infant Behaviour* (Foss, B.M., ed.), vol. 4, Methuen, London

HINDE, R.A. & ATKINSON, S. (1970) Assessing the roles of social partners in maintaining mutual proximity, as exemplified by mother–infant relations in monkeys. *Anim. Behav. 18*, 169–176

HINDE, R.A. & SPENCER-BOOTH, Y. (1967) The effect of social companions on mother–infant relations in rhesus monkeys, in *Primate Ethology* (Morris, D., ed.) Weidenfeld & Nicolson, London

HINDE, R.A. & SPENCER-BOOTH, Y. (1971*a*) Towards understanding individual differences in rhesus mother–infant interaction. *Anim. Behav. 19*, 165–173

HINDE, R.A. & SPENCER-BOOTH, Y. (1971*b*) Effects of brief separation from mother on rhesus monkeys. *Science (Wash. D.C.) 173*, 111–118

HINDE, R.A. & WHITE, L. (1974) The dynamics of a relationship—rhesus monkey ventro-ventral contact. *J. Comp. Physiol. Psychol. 86*, 8–23

JENSEN, G.D., BOBBITT, R.A. & GORDON, B.N. (1968) Effects of environment on the relationship between mother and infant pigtailed monkeys *(Macaca nemestrina)*. *J. Comp. Physiol. Psychol. 66*, 259–263

LAGERSPETZ, K. (1964) Studies on the aggressive behaviour of mice. *Suom. Tiedeakat. Toim.* [*Ann. Acad. Sci. Fenn. B*] *131*, 1–131

RICHARDS, M.P.M. (ed.) (1974) *The Integration of a Child into a Social World*. Cambridge University Press, London

SACKETT, G.P. (1968) The persistence of abnormal behaviour in monkeys following isolation rearing, in *The Role of Learning in Psychotherapy* (*Ciba Found. Symp.*, Porter, R., ed.) Churchill, London

SIMPSON, M.J.A. (1968) The display of the Siamese fighting fish, *Betta splendens*. *Anim. Behav. Monogr. 1*, 18–22

SLATER, P.J.B. (1973) Describing sequences of behavior, in *Perspectives in Ethology* (Bateson, P.P.G. and Klopfer, P.H., eds.), Plenum Press, New York

SOUTHWICK, C.H. (1968) Effect of maternal environment on aggressive behavior of inbred mice. *Commun. Behav. Biol. A 1*, 129–132

STERN, D.N. (1971) A micro-analysis of mother–infant interaction: behavior regulating social contact between a mother and her 3½ month-old twins. *J. Am. Acad. Child Psychiatr. 10*, 501–517

STERN, D.N. (1974) Mother and infant at play: the dyadic interaction involving facial, vocal, and gaze behaviors, in *The Effect of the Infant on its Caregiver* (Lewis, M. & Rosenblum, L.A., eds.), Wiley, New York

TINBERGEN, E.A. & TINBERGEN, N. (1972) Early childhood autism: an ethological approach. *Z. Tierpsychol. Beih. 10*, 1–53

TINBERGEN, N. (1974) Ethology and stress diseases. *Science (Wash. D.C.) 185*, 20–27

Discussion

Richards: Which animal is the one that initiates contact seems to make remarkably little difference to the length of contact. In human relationships the issue of power is extremely important and, although I can't produce results comparable to yours, I think one would find, at least early on, enormous differences according to whether contact was initiated by the baby or the mother. The mother monkey appears not to mind, if I can put it that way, that the baby is responsible for what is happening, whereas human mothers do mind.

Hinde: I think that is true. The differences are small and because they are given as probabilities I think they seem even smaller than they really are. Many human mothers who look at monkey mothers are impressed by the tolerance of the monkeys.

Simpson: What we showed in Fig. 4 is an average picture; individuals may show big differences either way.

Bell: I was interested that you decided to call one kind of interaction a 'game'. I agree that it is. In some mother–infant interaction sequences we looked at, during which the babies were smiling and vocalizing and the mothers were stimulating the babies in various ways, the defining characteristic seemed to be that the actions were repeated over and over again, whereas in earlier interactions, in the first month, there was a chain or branch sequence. Was the playing something that was repeated?

Simpson: The most stringent criterion we can find is its repetition. In addition, it looks like play: the mother leaves the infant, yet she will come back soon if he does not follow; she will lip-smack, which is a way of making him follow, and she will present to him, which is a gesture monkeys use to call other monkeys out of a place inaccessible to them. Tinbergen & Tinbergen (1972) have used the same kind of timing as our monkey mothers in trying to elicit and initiate interaction with children who are strangers to them. But the Tinbergens' game involves looking at and looking away, rather than approaching and leaving.

Brazelton: We see babies use a game of looking, then looking away, as a way of dominating their mothers' behaviour.

Bell: Watson (1966) tried to condition his own infant and he mentions what he calls contingency games. After he had established the learning contingencies they then had a 'game', each behaving as though they wanted to increase or maintain the frequency of the behaviour in the other individual, just as in an adult card game. The interesting problem is how to define play in infants. There has been a lot of discussion about this amongst those studying adult play and games.

Dunn: What was the relationship between the qualities of warmth and controlling?

Hinde: We have only recently started to look at the 'arm round infant' measure with this new technique for collecting information and cannot yet answer this question.

Bentovim: You stated that the effects of early separation were related to the quality of the interaction beforehand. What other factors do you think might affect the quality of meshing? Is the quality something to do with the temperament of a particular infant, or previous experiences of the mother? These are important factors when the quality of human mother–infant interaction is being considered.

Hinde: Meshing is something we have only just begun to study by this new technique. We have recently analysed all our findings on the other measures for about 60 infants. Nearly every possible independent variable that we could look at affected the nature of the mother–infant relationship—maternal dominance in the group, whether the mother was born in or out of the colony, whether peers were present or not, and sex of infant. Furthermore there are quite complicated interactions between these variables, and the nature of the effect varies with age (White & Hinde 1975).

Brazelton: Measuring contact alone may be too simple as a measure of interaction or bonding. In human mother–infant interactions we feel that touching or holding is only one of the behaviours which are demonstrated. In fact, separating behaviours into proximal and distal may help us to differentiate between pairs and their individual modes. Timing of the shift from distal to proximal may be another way of differentiating maternal behaviours. A shift to proximal may even come earlier in those who touch a lot at the beginning. Do you have any way of looking at these modalities in monkeys?

Simpson: We have the results, and it is just a matter of following enough individual histories. Are you suggesting that those who touch a lot early in life may develop the relationship differently?

Brazelton: Early proximal contact (such as looking a lot at the baby) may maintain an affectional bond just as well as touching.

Hinde: Where a large amount of early touching is due to infant demand, the demand might continue for a long time. But if this activity is due to high maternal responsiveness, it might enable the infant to become more independent. So perhaps one can't make predictions unless one knows which of the two partners is responsible, at each age.

Brazelton: That makes sense. Leonard Rosenblum's two groups of macaques behave very differently with their newborns (Rosenblum & Cooper 1968). One group waits for the infants to do all the clinging to and approaching the breast after delivery, and the other group picks the infants up and puts them to the breast. I wondered about the difference in the infant monkeys themselves, and what role their behaviour played in generating these different maternal behaviours. The mother does everything for an infant who is more passive and who lies at the mother's feet after birth waiting for her to take care of him. The more active babies engender a passive response in their mothers and it looks as if the mothers are responding to that behaviour.

Hinde: Again you are making the dangerous jump from the question of species differences to the question of what happens at different ages within one species.

Hofer: The ratios or probability measurements that you use have great descriptive power, Professor Hinde. How did you arrive at them? Did you use your own subjective response to the situation to give you the questions, which you then answered by proposing these ratios? Or did you begin with the observations and try various analytic procedures? In other words, do you have an empirical or a subjective approach? To what extent do you say that the mother must be 'feeling' something, or that the infant must be 'demanding', and so on? How useful is that kind of thinking in this kind of research?

Hinde: We started with what we believed to be a number of objective measures. We thought that the most important would be the time that the mother and infant spent in proximity or in ventral-ventral contact. That proved to be a wrong presupposition. We also recorded things like rejection and the initiation of contact, and they turned out to be more important—that is, to have more predictive power. I am sure that our subjective feelings about monkeys guided us in our choice of measures. Thelma Rowell and the late Yvette Spencer-Booth, with whom I was fortunate to work in earlier stages of this study, both had great sensitivity about the monkeys, and I think that played an important part in the way we thought.

Simpson: It was my wife who first described the activity as a game and noticed that they kept repeating this sequence. We had all been recording data about the sequence on the machine for about two years by then, but not calling it a 'game'. When we looked at our findings again, the game sequence was clear. It is a kind of a two-way process; in recording events second by second, one bypasses any conscious formulation of what is going on and just records the observations, which are then available for use. At least this example seemed to show that we had got something even though we didn't know we were getting it.

Bell: Your experience of what behaviours and parameters go together in the monkeys must explain why you feel comfortable with those ratios, Professor Hinde. Most of us are afraid of ratios, because of how many things can affect them.

Hinde: Of course we have the absolute values as well.

Cooper: Can you match up what happened to the mother when she was an infant with what she does to her own infant?

Hinde: It is too soon for us to say anything about that.

Cooper: What about the rats, who breed more frequently?

Rosenblatt: We haven't looked at that either.

Simpson: Our monkey mother Eliane played approaching and leaving games with her infant, and Eliane's daughter also played such games with her own infants. At least in that one example the tradition has gone through.

Hess-Haeser: We observed a primiparous gorilla mother (Goma) raising her infant without any special difficulties.* In her infancy, 36 hours after birth, this mother had been separated from her own mother and had then been raised exclusively by humans during the first year of life. However, most of the captive primiparous gorilla mothers (wild-caught animals) do not act normally towards their newborn infants. These females, most of them caught in early infancy, also suffered from early separation from their own mothers. The only difference between those mothers and Goma is that Goma's separation took place in the earliest days of her life and without any stress. In addition she was cared for immediately after separation.

Cooper: I suppose this might depend a little on the quality of the substitute care when they are separated.

Hinde: Another issue is whether the primiparous mothers with whom you are comparing this animal have been able to observe mother–infant pairs during their own adolescence.

Hess-Haeser: The hand-raised gorilla infant Goma had a partner of the same age by the end of her first year of life. Later Goma lived in a group of juvenile gorillas. During her infancy and adolescence Goma had sometimes been able to see her own mother raising other newborn infants, but Goma was unable to have direct contact with her mother or with the infant her mother was rearing.

Hofer: Is there good evidence, from animals, on whether mothering qualities are learned mainly from the mother's own experiences as an infant, or mainly from her later experience in watching other mother–infant interactions? This is important in man, and people hold various opinions on it.

Hinde: There are many relevant observations but it is very complicated.

* During the meeting Mr Hess showed a 16 mm black and white film he has made, entitled 'Mother–infant behaviour of captive lowland gorillas, *Gorilla g. gorilla*', which shows Goma with her infant. [The film, by J. P. Hess—27 min, English commentary, optical sound—, was produced by and is available from the Swiss Scientific Film Association, Kapellenstrasse 33, CH-4000 Basle.]

When mice of one strain are reared by mice of another strain, the type of maternal care that they subsequently show is affected by the type of maternal care they had in their infancy. But the direction of the effect seems to be unpredictable. It may make them rougher or it may make them gentler, according to the interactions between their own 'temperament' and that of their foster-mothers (for references see Hinde 1974).

Hofer: And of course mice probably don't have the capacity to learn by imitation in the way some other species do.

Rosenblatt: We have been studying the ontogeny of maternal behaviour, and the word 'game' takes on a different connotation now. In rats, males and females begin to exhibit maternal behaviour at around 20 days of age, which is before their own weaning. When they are placed in a cage with rats aged one to two days, the 20-day-old rats will adopt a nursing position, lick the pups and show the ecstatic look of nursing. Shortly afterwards when they are put back with their own mothers they will suckle, becoming both mother and infant within a short time. When I tell people this, they say 'But they're just playing'. The games that children play among themselves may also not be games, any more than these activities are games. They are a lighter aspect of the relationship. Parental behaviour in both males and females can apparently be looked for very early in life, and not just in adulthood.

Hofer: These findings fit with the fact that female rhesus monkeys that are separated from their siblings at an early age may have severe defects in mothering behaviour (Harlow 1963).

Thoman: Rats which are isolated at birth later behave relatively normally as mothers, although there are some effects which are observable in their offspring. Rat pups of totally isolated mothers weigh less at weaning than pups of mothers who have been reared with a mother or with peers. The infants of animals reared in isolation were also slower to open their eyes (Thoman & Arnold 1968).

Hofer: Are those that show defects the ones that have a mother but don't have siblings?

Thoman: Absence of either siblings or the mother affects maternal behaviour. In both cases they can rear their young adequately, as indicated by direct measures of maternal behaviour. But as I just mentioned, their offspring reveal the effects of differential maternal behaviours. Contrary to the expectation that the animal reared as a singleton with the mother should show defects, we found that there was a much higher rate of survival among the offspring of the solitary animals reared with a mother (Thoman & Arnold 1968).

Rosenblatt: Evidence is emerging that hormones present immediately after birth, in the rat, can affect the pattern of parental behaviour. In one strain of rats in which males do not characteristically retrieve pups but show all the other components of maternal behaviour (without hormone treatment), one can make the males retrieve pups by castrating them in infancy; conversely, one can prevent females from retrieving pups by treating them with testosterone in infancy (Quadagno & Rockwell 1972; Quadagno *et al.* 1973).

Oppé: Is it possible to induce mothering behaviour in adult male animals?

Rosenblatt: Yes. Apart from lactation, male rats of our strain (Sprague-Dawley), and male mice, show maternal behaviour similar to that of females.

Hinde: Even in rodents, the ease with which males can be made maternal depends on the particular strain of animal. In primates it varies enormously between different species of monkeys; in some species the males are regularly maternal and in some they are virtually never so. In those species in which they are maternal, the bases of their 'maternity' are diverse. In some species the males use babies as passports with which to approach their seniors, so the males are manipulating the infants as well as behaving maternally (Deag 1974; Mitchell 1969; Ransom & Ransom 1971).

Leiderman: In an agricultural community in Kenya I observed that some human mothers get young males to help with the infants if no older females are available. These young boys, generally aged 7–12 years, seem to perform quite adequately, though it is not a task they particularly relish. The infants show no marked preference for female caretakers over males, as indicated by their reaction to recognition or response to separation. We have not studied the effect of infant caretaking on young males, though Professor Beatrice Whiting is in the process of collecting such observations.

Richards: These questions about roles and about the effects of previous experience are just the ones where human studies can never be helped by animal work, as social behaviour cannot be biologically determined. We have to study variation within and between human cultures if we are to find answers to these questions.

Brazelton: If the male monkey was the only parent available, would he become maternal more quickly? Margaret Mead (1973, personal communication) says that in cultures where the males are expected to do the hunting or gathering they are never allowed to imprint on the infants in the first month. There is always a ritual by which the male is pushed out of the way of the infant.

D'Souza: My preliminary observations (unpublished) of extended family groups in Borneo showed that the amount and kind of mothering by young boys correlated with both the age and sex of the baby. Young boys and men did not handle babies below the age of about three months but young girls and women other than the mother consistently did. Furthermore, after the first three months boys tended to carry and mother male babies only, but girls mothered both sexes.

Brazelton: We have been constructing a course on infant development for high schools in the USA (Educational Development Center, Cambridge, Mass.) and when we were pretesting films on adolescents aged 12–15 years, we found that if boys were startled while they were watching a film they returned to watching it much more quickly than the girls. The girls did not seem to be nearly as absorbed in the films about small infants and their behaviour as the boys were.

Hofer: Dr Rosenblatt talked about virgin females and about males repeatedly assuming nursing positions over the young. Since the nursing interaction cannot be completed, the persistence of this behaviour seems to violate our interactional hypothesis. Yet it happens. And it gets back to the relevance of animal work to humans. If it is possible for males to adopt so much 'maternal' behaviour, males must have a great deal of built-in flexibility.

Rosenblatt: E.W. Hansen (unpublished work, 1974) has reported that when young rhesus monkeys are deprived of their mothers, they will go to a sibling male and force that male into a parental position. Apparently the infant itself does not always distinguish male from female.

Hinde: Our observation is that adolescent female monkeys are much more interested in babies than adolescent males are (Spencer-Booth 1968).

Hess-Haeser: Whether we can say that males show mothering behaviour or not depends on how we define mothering. If we use the word in a general way, young male gorillas in play groups certainly show it. Juvenile gorillas of both sexes will even 'mother' substitute objects, such as pieces of wood or sacks. I have seen such behaviour in the gorillas in Bristol Zoo as well as in our own colony.

I think that comparison of the sexes reveals, not a difference of quality within these patterns, but a difference in frequency. Besides other reasons, this difference in frequency depends on the behaviour of the mother. Mothers probably do not provide young males with the same opportunities for caring for small infants as they provide for young females.

The interest of adult males in mothers and their offspring varies greatly. Recently I was able to compare two cases. In one case (male, Pepe; female Goma, with newborn male Tamtam), the male was early attracted by the female and the infant. This male often tried to make contact with both mother and infant, but the female wouldn't allow the infant to be touched before a certain time. In the other case (male Stefi; female Achilla, with newborn female Wimbi), the adult male showed no interest in touching or making direct contact. It was then the female who offered the infant to the male for touching.

Rosenblatt: The mother rat also keeps the male away in a corner for about nine days, but by seven days he has already been induced to show maternal behaviour and when she releases him he is already maternal from being exposed to the young.

Kennell: In Sweden, human fathers who had been asked to undress the babies twice within the first five days of life were compared with a group of fathers who did not have that experience. There was a significant difference in how much time the fathers spent playing with their babies three months later if they had had that early experience (J. Lind, unpublished work, 1974).

Stewart: We have been encouraging fathers to come into our intensive care unit to see their babies as soon after birth as possible and have been impressed by the good relationship which these fathers have developed with their infants. They are efficient at all aspects of caring; several fathers bring their children back to the clinic without the mothers! We even had one father who appeared to be in competition with the mother, to the extent that the mother became distressed.

Kennell: Some of the mothers in our premature nursery are unmarried so we have focused our studies on the mother and infant. In our Neonatal Intensive Care Unit we encourage fathers to visit, touch and care for their babies, particularly during the first few days when the mother is unable to visit. This has often resulted in strong father-to-infant attachments that have occasionally presented some problems to us with our studies. For example, one month after discharge we observe the mother with her baby during a physical examination. When we asked one father to wait until we had first seen his wife and baby, he became very upset, almost belligerent. Thus it is our impression that early contact strongly affects the attachment and role of the father.

Hinde: Can anyone suggest which measures we could select for studying the mother–infant relationship that would be relevant later on?

Bell: You said that we can't get anything more out of a factor analysis than we put in.

Hinde: No, I said that what one gets out is influenced by what is put in (see p. 40).

Bell: What you don't put into it, of course, you can't get out. But what you put into it can emerge in a number of ways. Concerning the selection of measures, my inclination is to look at the infants and make choices based on hypotheses about what is going on. The problems arise when one moves from single measures to sets of measures. I did a factorial study of infants a long time ago, as a training exercise. Once I got an idea about the many measures that emerged together in a factor analysis, I didn't do much more with factor analysis of infant behaviours.

We all differ in how we handle the results. I have never tried using ratios but you have good reasons for having used them, on the basis of what you saw the animals do, Professor Hinde. Variations in the ratio of the infant making and breaking contact can come about from several directions, so if one uses a ratio one has to look at other things too, to make sure of knowing which of several possibilities is determining the variation.

One needs to pay most attention to the clustering and grouping of measures when the changes in the organism with time are so great that qualitatively different behaviours appear in Time 2 compared with Time 1. If one keeps the same measure for a long time, one may be using the same label for very different things. For example, Kagan & Moss (1962) had a measure called 'achievement' which in the first few years happened primarily to involve persistence, but which in the later years primarily concerned how children wanted to succeed in school work. These are very unlikely to be the same things, despite the fact that the same label has been used.

One solution that I suggest for long-term changes, although perhaps it is not applicable to the work with monkeys, is that one could measure most of the salient parameters at the two periods of time, group them into the factors that they form at each time period, and then see how the factors relate between time periods. This approach has the advantage that one does not lose sight of metamorphic changes. This type of analysis is also appropriate when one doesn't even have an idea about the nature of relationships between the two time periods. Then it is best to measure comprehensively and carry out a factor analysis of the measures. There is also a statistical reason for grouping the measures into factors. If one relates a lot of measures from Time 1 to a lot of measures at Time 2, it may not be possible to tell whether there are more significant relations than would be expected by chance. Grouping the measures makes it possible to satisfy statistical criteria as to how many relations should be obtained. That is why I am still carrying out some factor and cluster analysis, though my work has most recently involved cross-stage comparisons between infancy and the preschool period.

References

DEAG, J. M. (1974) A study of the social behaviour and ecology of the wild Barbary macaque, *Macaca sylvanus*. Ph. D. thesis, Bristol University

HARLOW, H. K. (1963) The maternal affectional system, in *Determinants of Infant Behaviour* (Foss, B. M., ed.), vol. 2, Methuen, London

HINDE, R. A. (1974) *Biological Bases of Human Social Behavior*, McGraw-Hill, New York

KAGAN, J. & MOSS, H. (1962) *Birth to Maturity*, Wiley, New York

MITCHELL, G. D. (1969) Paternalistic behaviour in primates. *Psychol. Bull. 71*, 399–417

QUADAGNO, D. M & ROCKWELL, J. (1972) The effect of gonadal hormones in infancy on maternal behavior in the adult rat. *Horm. Behav. 3*, 55–62

QUADAGNO, D.M., MCCOLLOUGH, J., HO, G.K. & SPEVAK, H.M. (1973) Neonatal gonadal hormones: effect on maternal behavior and sexual behavior in the female rat. *Physiol. Behav. 11*, 251–254

RANSOM, T.W. & RANSOM, B.S. (1971) Adult male-infant relations among baboons *(Papio anubis)*. *Folia Primatol. 16*, 179–195

ROSENBLUM, L.A. & COOPER, R.W. (eds.) (1968) in *The Squirrel Monkey*, p. 209ff., Academic Press, London

SPENCER-BOOTH, Y. (1968) The behaviour of group companions towards rhesus monkey infants. *Anim. Behav. 16*, 541–557

THOMAN, E. & ARNOLD, W. (1968) Effects of incubator rearing with social deprivation on maternal behavior in rats. *J. Comp. Physiol. Psychol. 65*, 441–446

TINBERGEN, E.A. & TINBERGEN, N. (1972) Early childhood autism: an ethological approach. *Z. Tierpsychol. Beih. 10*, 1–53

WATSON, J.S. (1966) The development and generalization of 'contingency awareness' in early infancy: some hypotheses. *Merrill-Palmer Q. 12*, 123–135

WHITE, L.E. & HINDE, R.A. (1975) Some factors affecting mother–infant relations in rhesus monkeys. *Anim. Behav. 23*, in press

Does human maternal behaviour after delivery show a characteristic pattern?

MARSHALL H. KLAUS, MARY ANNE TRAUSE and JOHN H. KENNELL

Department of Pediatrics, Case Western Reserve University, Cleveland

Abstract Specific kinds of maternal behaviour such as nesting, retrieving, grooming and exploring, are seen in non-human mammalian mothers immediately before, during and after delivery. In this study 22 human mothers were filmed during the first 10 minutes of contact with their normal nude full-term infants, who were placed beside them in private rooms in hospitals in Guatemala and the US; and nine mothers of premature infants were filmed on their first three visits to the nursery. Another 10 Guatemalan mothers and infants were observed for 10 minutes almost immediately after delivery in hospital. These observations were compared to maternal behaviour after home deliveries in California. After hospital delivery all US mothers, but only half of the Guatemalans, began touching their infants' extremities with their fingertips and proceeded within a few minutes to palm contact on the trunk. US mothers had an intense interest in eye-to-eye contact. Mothers of premature infants showed only fragments of this behaviour. In home births when the mothers are active participants in delivery, they pick up the infant immediately after birth, stroke its face with their fingertips and start breast-feeding within the first minutes after delivery. Initially the infant only licks the nipples. There is a striking elevation in mood in the parents. These observations focus attention on reciprocal behaviour patterns that develop early between mother and infant and which serve to unite them.

Detailed and precise observations of many species have shown that adaptive species-specific patterns of behaviour—including nesting, exploring, grooming and retrieving—before, during and after parturition, have evolved to meet the needs of the young in the animal's usual environment.

For example, the domestic cat, whether in Russia, the United States or England, behaves in a characteristic way at the time of the birth of her kittens. Towards the end of her pregnancy, she is less active and agile than usual, doing markedly less jumping and climbing. She finds a warm dark place, preferably with a soft surface, in which to give birth. Through labour and delivery, she spends increasingly more time licking her genital region. After delivery, she continues licking, but with the newborn kitten as her object. The placenta is usually promptly eaten. After the birth of the last kitten, the mother lies down, encircling her kittens, and rests with them for about 12 hours. Nursing, which may begin as early as 30 minutes after birth, appears to be stimulated by her licking. For the first two days, she stays with her litter at the birth site (Schneirla *et al.* 1963).

We have searched for similarly specific behaviour in the human mother in the hope that close observation of very early interaction between mother and infant might provide us with clues or principles that might not be evident at other times. If humans exhibit such specific patterns of behaviour, knowledge of the sequence might be clinically applicable in situations where mothers and infants are at present separated early, such as in premature delivery or sickness during the neonatal period. A further reason for studying this period is our hypothesis that there is an immediate interlocking and a reciprocal set of behaviours for attachment which must quickly operate because of the infant's precarious state after delivery. The infant requires a devoted caretaker to provide warmth and protection. Feeding is also an early necessity.

An additional stimulus to exploring this area was the unusual behaviour we observed when we first invited mothers of premature infants into the nursery in the first days and weeks of life. On the first visit, mothers walked round the incubator rather warily. When shown how to put their hands into the incubator, they would only briefly and hesitantly poke the baby's extremities with their fingertips. They were frightened and often unable to take an active role (Barnett *et al.* 1970). After observing this many times, we decided to examine in detail the behaviour of mothers of full-term and premature infants during the first minutes and hours of their initial interactions.

HOSPITAL DELIVERIES IN THE UNITED STATES

In our first explorations several years ago (Klaus *et al.* 1970), we observed nine mothers of premature infants on their first three visits to the nursery and twelve mothers of full-term normal infants during the first contact after delivery (Table 1). Except for one mother of a premature infant who needed a Caesarean section, all the women were well at the time of labour and were delivered vaginally. Social and economic status of both groups covered a wide range. At the time of the study, all planned to keep their babies and all infants were free of anomalies. Behaviour of mother and infant was recorded by a time-lapse camera which took a picture every second. The mothers in both groups were aware that they were being photographed. Every fifth frame of the first 10 minutes of a 15-minute film was analysed in detail and the mother's remarks were recorded

TABLE 1

Clinical data from five studies of early mother–infant contact

	Premature infants: Incubator	*Full-term infants*			
		US hospital	*Guatemala delivery table*	*Guatemala private room*	*US home delivery*
Number	9	12	10	10	5
Mother's age range	19–42	17–39	14–33	17–33	–
Unmarried mothers	3	6	3	2	0
Primiparous mothers	4	5	5	2	3
Infants' mean birth weight (grams)	1660	3029	2787	3081	–

–: not recorded

on audiotape. The full-term infants were filmed by a camera at the foot of the bed from 30 minutes to 13 hours after delivery, with a mean of 5.3 hours. The bed was flattened, the infant was undressed and its head was placed about six to eight inches from its mother at the level of her shoulder, as shown in Fig. 1. Only the first contact was recorded for full-term infants. Mothers of

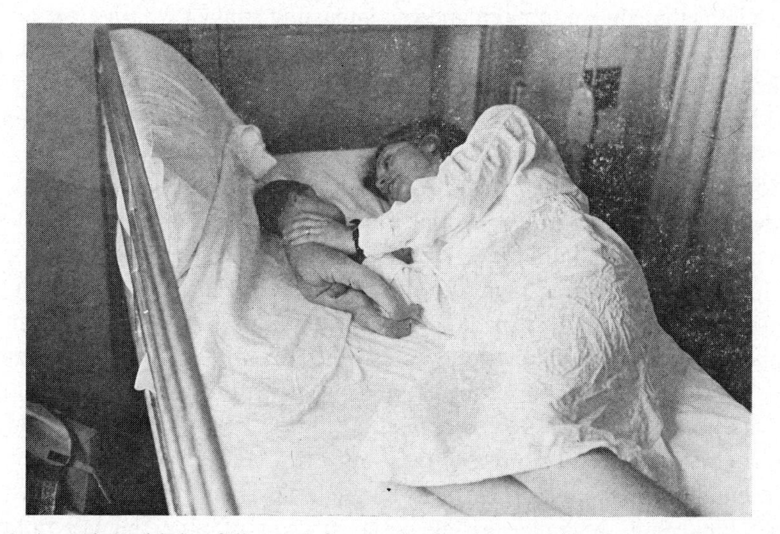

FIG. 1. A mother with her full-term infant in the first hours of life, in the *en face* position. *En face* is defined as occurring when the mother's face is rotated so that her eyes and those of the infant meet in the same vertical plane of rotation.

premature infants were first filmed one to three days after delivery, at an average of 1.2 days. The camera was placed inconspicuously outside the glass wall of the nursery. The nurse demonstrated how to enter the incubator, and stayed only to answer questions. The mean time of the second filming of the mothers of premature babies was 3.3 days, and that of the third, 5.1 days after delivery. The following activities were analysed: movement of the infant, position of the mother's fingertips and palms on the trunk, extremities or head of the infant, and maternal smiling, physical support and encompassment of the infant. Encompassment was defined as the mother's enclosing either the trunk or head with her entire hand. We measured the amount of time spent *en face*, a position defined by Robson (1967) as when the mother's face is rotated so that her eyes and those of the infants' meet fully in the same vertical plane of rotation. Fig. 1 also illustrates the *en face* position.

The same sequence of behaviour was observed in all the mothers of full-term infants when they first interacted with them. Every woman began with fingertip-touching on the infant's extremities and proceeded within the first four to eight minutes to massaging and encompassing palm contact on the trunk, often with her simultaneously showing progressively heightened excitement which continued for several minutes. Her activity then diminished to such a degree that sometimes she fell asleep. Fingertip contact decreased from 52% of the first three minutes of contact to 26% of the last three minutes, while palm contact increased from 28% to 62%. Every mother made this changeover.

The immediate move to palm and encompassing contact within a period of a few minutes does not concur with the observations of Rubin (1963) who studied mothers' interactions with infants wrapped in blankets on the second, third and fourth days of life. Rubin noted that palm touching and close contact only developed after several days.

Mothers of premature infants exhibited an attenuated sequence of this behaviour during the first visit, and the progression from more fingertip to more palm contact did not occur even during the first three visits. In fact, palm and fingertip contact both increased during the second and third visits (Fig. 2).

In both groups, interest in the eyes of the infants was measured from the number of comments about the eyes recorded on the audiotape. An intense desire to wake the infant in order to see its eyes was expressed by many of the mothers, and some even voiced a relationship between the condition of the baby and its eyes: for example, 'Open your eyes', and 'If you open your eyes I will know you are alive'. They said they felt closer to their babies when the babies looked at them. Surprisingly, the amount of time the US full-term mothers spent looking at the babies *en face* increased from 10% in the first three minutes to 23% in the last three minutes of a ten-minute session (Fig. 3).

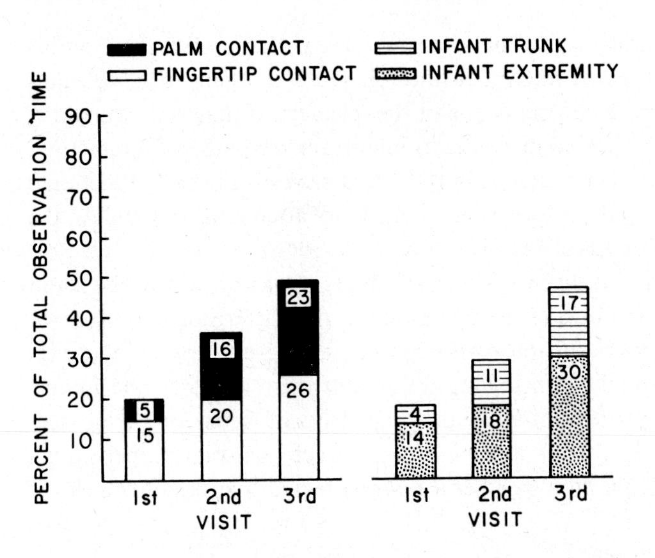

FIG. 2. Mothers' palm and fingertip contact on the trunk and extremities at the first three postnatal visits (9 mothers of premature infants). (From Klaus *et al.* 1970.)

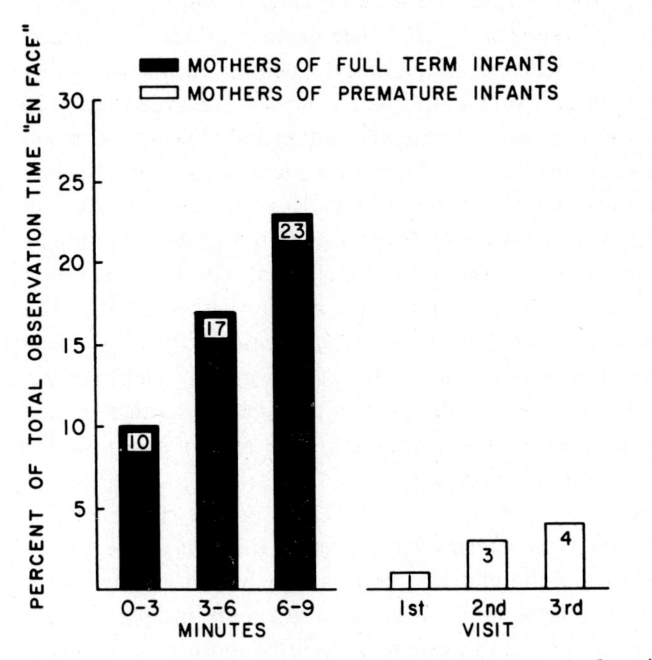

FIG. 3. Percentage of time spent *en face* recorded during the first visit of 12 mothers of full-term infants and the first three visits of 9 mothers of premature infants. (From Klaus *et al.* 1970.)

The large amount of time that mothers spent *en face* with their full-term infants and their verbally expressed interest in the infant's eyes agree with Robson's (1967) suggestion that eye contact is one of the releasers of maternal caretaking behaviour. The baby's eyes seem to be an important mediator of interaction. Complementing the mother's interest in the infant's eyes is the early functional development of its visual pathways, enabling it to attend to and follow the human face in the first hour of life (Brazelton *et al.* 1966).

It should be emphasized that whenever an observer was present in the room and privacy was violated during the first contact, the pattern of moving from fingertip to palm contact and the marked increase in eye-to-eye contact was distorted, and the mother often made only tentative overtures to the infant. We were surprised by the similarity and regularity of behaviour from one mother to the next, even though each one's experience, plans and expectations differed. This led us to question whether this was a regular pattern of behaviour after delivery.

HOSPITAL DELIVERIES IN GUATEMALA

To investigate this question further, we have observed additional groups of mothers. The first group consisted of 10 Guatemalan mothers of full-term infants who were studied immediately after a hospital delivery, while the mother and baby were still on the delivery table. Behaviour was recorded every 20 seconds for 10 minutes with a time-sampling technique, and the observer stood behind the mother in the delivery room. A physician and nurse were also present. Five of the 10 mothers began touching the baby's extremities or trunk with their fingertips and within one to four minutes proceeded to touching the infant's trunk with their palms. Two mothers immediately touched the baby's face with their fingertips. Two positioned their heads *en face* with the baby. The interactions were interrupted frequently by painful stimuli from suturing which sometimes completely diverted the mother's interest from the infant. An especially interesting observation was that 84% of the time the mothers talked to the infants in a high-pitched voice, although they always spoke to the physician and nurse in a natural voice.

Another 10 Guatemalan mothers were observed in a private room half-an-hour after delivery. A time-lapse camera was placed at the foot of the bed to photograph behaviour during the mother's first contact with her infant for a 10-minute period. The time-lapse film was exposed at one frame per second. We observed the same variables as in our first study of mothers in the US. Five of the 10 mothers showed a similar sequence of behaviour, starting with fingertip contact on the extremities and moving to palm contact on the trunk.

Three observations of the mothers were hindered because the mother's knees sometimes obscured the picture and we were unable to see the interaction. The brightness of the small light used to illuminate the room also seemed to bother some of the women and they would sometimes shield their own or their baby's eyes. The *en face* position was rarely observed on these films. Less excitement was noted in the 20 Guatemalan mothers than in the mothers in the US. Two appeared posed and inhibited by the camera. On other occasions when we attempted to observe the feeding methods of women from the same population in a maternity division, we were unsuccessful because they all stared at the female observer. This, plus the Indian belief in the evil eye, may render naturalistic observations impossible in this society.

HOME DELIVERIES IN CALIFORNIA

To explore this behaviour further, we have begun to study home deliveries in California. These observations have radically altered our ideas about this early period. Preliminary studies of home deliveries have been made from videotapes and 8 mm films and we have also had long discussions with a perceptive midwife (R. Lang, personal communication) who has made valuable naturalistic observations during 52 home deliveries of women who were members of the birth centre in Santa Cruz, California. In sharp contrast to the woman who gives birth in hospital, the woman who delivers at her own home appears to be in control of the process. She chooses the room in the house and the location within the room for her birth, as well as the guests who will be present. She is an active participant during her labour and delivery rather than a passive patient.

Thirty-seven per cent of the 52 deliveries observed by Lang (1972) were made in the hands and knees position. A few minutes after the birth but before delivery of the placenta, the mothers turned and picked up the infant and often assumed the *en face* position (Fig. 4). Other midwives deliver in a lateral position which allows the mother to watch the birth of her own infant. Immediately after delivery, the mothers appeared to be in a state of ecstasy. The observers were also extremely elated during the delivery and offered encouragement and support to the mother. Striking in the films is the observers' intense interest in the infant, especially in the first 15 to 20 minutes of life. This supports the observations of Eibl-Eibesfeldt (1971), who has emphasized the unique qualities of the human infant, such as the large forehead and small face, large eyes, chubby cheeks, small mouth and unequal physical proportions. These attractive and compelling properties of the infant tend to draw not only the mother and father but all those present to the infant. Raven Lang has observed that the infant quieted down when given to the mother. Almost always the mother

FIG. 4. A mother in the *en face* position shortly after a home delivery.

rubbed the baby's skin, starting with the face. Rubbing was done with the fingertips; it was always a gentle stroking motion. This occurred before the initial nursing and before delivery of the placenta. The baby was usually offered the breast but often did not suck right away. The most common action for the baby when given the mother's nipple was to lick it over and over again (Lang 1972).

Most of the mothers and fathers in the home deliveries used a high-pitched voice when talking to their infant, and there appeared to be a higher level of excitement than in the hospital deliveries. Many mothers who have delivered at home have reported they had sensations very similar to orgasm at the time of delivery. Before the placenta was delivered, the baby was put to the breast. The mother was also often groomed by one of her female friends.

Thus home deliveries in a select population show, in some aspects, a pattern of behaviour different to hospital deliveries, where we observe only fragments of these behaviours. Summarizing the findings in a home delivery:

(1) the mother is an active participant;
(2) she immediately picks up the infant after birth;
(3) she begins to stroke its face with her fingertips and moves to palm contact of the body and head within a few minutes;
(4) a striking elevation in mood is observed in association with great excitement of the other participants;
(5) everyone is drawn to look at the infant for prolonged periods;
(6) the mother is groomed;
(7) breast-feeding starts within five to six minutes, beginning with prolonged licking by the infant;
(8) the parents use a high-pitched voice when talking to the infant.

Brazelton *et al.* (1974) and Stern (1974) have started to decode the normal intricate mother–infant interchanges which occur continuously at three to four months of age, sometimes within periods of just a few seconds. Condon & Sander (1974) made the striking observation that at birth the normal neonate has a complex interaction system in which the organization of his motor behaviour can be entrained by and synchronized with adult speech (English or Chinese). From their work and our preliminary films and videotape recordings, we suggest that this neat synchronizing or dance of mother and infant begins in the first minutes of life. These intricate visual, tactile and auditory interactions focus our attention on the specific interlocking behaviour patterns that develop so early between mother and infant and which serve to unite them.

Although at present we are unable to identify species-specific behaviour, it is our hypothesis that the more natural setting of a home delivery may elicit more closely characteristic behaviour. Further exploration of this early period in the home may be especially fruitful since it might uncover further interlocking processes for bonding the mother and infant.

SUMMARY AND CONCLUSIONS

Five studies of maternal behaviour after delivery reveal the problems of attempting to study the behaviour of the human mother. At present, it is not possible to answer either the question of whether there are specific patterns of behaviour after delivery or of how one would go about determining whether or not the observed behaviour is characteristic. However, it is especially interesting to see the recurring patterns in these differing delivery situations: the high-pitched voice in both the Guatemalan hospital and the home delivery in the US; the movement from fingertips to palm contact and touching, first of the extremities and then of the trunk, compared to immediate stroking of the face in the home deliveries, and the special interest in eye-to-eye regard.

It is our hypothesis that for survival of the human infant, several powerful inducers of attachment must operate quickly to tie the mother to her infant. Clinical observations suggest that an order in the pattern of behaviour may be seen shortly after delivery which may mediate the formation of this special bond. Survival of the infant is not left to chance; complex mechanisms trigger maternal and infant behaviour and thus ensure immediate care of the young.

ACKNOWLEDGEMENTS

We are grateful to the Grant Foundation, the Educational Foundation of America and the Research Corporation for the support they have given for our work, and we owe special thanks to the many medical students who have worked on these projects.

References

BARNETT, D., LEIDERMAN, P.H., GROBSTEIN, R., & KLAUS, M.H. (1970) Neonatal separation: the maternal side of interactional deprivation. *Pediatrics 45*, 197–205

BRAZELTON, T.B., SCHOOL, M.L. & ROBEY, J.S. (1966) Visual responses in the newborn. *Pediatrics 37*, 284–290

BRAZELTON, T.B., KOSLOWSKI, B. & MAIN, M. (1974) in *The Effect of the Infant on its Caregiver* (Lewis, M. & Rosenblum, L., eds.), pp. 49–76, Wiley, New York

CONDON, W.S. & SANDER, L.W. (1974) Neonatal movement is synchronized with adult speech: interactional participation and language acquisition. *Science (Wash. D.C.) 183*, 99–101

EIBL-EIBESFELDT, I. (1971) *Love and Hate*, Holt, Rinehart & Winston, New York

KLAUS, M.H., KENNELL, J.H., PLUMB, N., & ZUEHLKE, S. (1970) Maternal behavior at the first contact with her young. *Pediatrics 46*, 187–192

LANG, R. (1972) *Birth Book*, Genesis Press, Ben Lomond, California

ROBSON, K. (1967) The role of eye-to-eye contact in maternal-infant attachment. *J. Child Psychol. Psychiatr. Allied Disciplines 8*, 13–25

RUBIN, R. (1963) Maternal touch. *Nurs. Outlook 11*, 828–831

SCHNEIRLA, T., ROSENBLATT, J. & TOBACH, E. (1963) in *Maternal Behavior in Mammals* (Rheingold, H., ed.), pp. 122–168, Wiley, New York

STERN, D. (1974) in *The Effect of the Infant on its Caregiver* (Lewis, M. & Rosenblum, L., eds.), pp. 187–213, Wiley, New York

Discussion

Macfarlane: In films taken in the labour ward immediately after birth, I have observed that mothers may refer verbally to the hands or face and so on of the child but they do not actually greet the child as a person until he opens his eyes. Have you seen anything like that?

Klaus: On the second or third day after delivery, many mothers have told us that they did not feel the baby was really theirs until he had looked into their eyes.

Brazelton: My profession of paediatrics, in addition to having negative effects on mothers and babies in the first few days, has upset young mothers in our culture by saying that babies don't see. When we show our neonatal behaviour assessment (Brazelton 1974) to mothers in our studies, one of the most important issues for them is that babies fix and follow on human faces immediately. Mothers are very excited by this and by our demonstration; they say 'It's great that you believe they see too!'

Curtis-Jenkins: I don't believe that doctors are responsible for that myth. It goes even deeper. We have other myths like 'Don't pick him up or you might spoil him' and I am sure these are cultural myths.

Brazelton: At many medical schools in the US, students are still being taught that babies don't see anything but blurs until they are four weeks old, that they don't hear because their ears are full of wax, and so on. Neither of these assertions is substantiated.

Bentovim: One mother I saw whose baby girl was born with congenital anophthalmia (without eyes) remarked spontaneously that she only regarded her baby as 'a person' when glass eye-prostheses had been implanted at the age of 18 months.

Klaus: In the US, most mothers first receive their baby several hours after birth, when the infant is asleep and is not as easily aroused to the quiet alert state as during the first hour of life. In addition, during the first meeting the eyelids are usually oedematous and partially closed from the instillation of silver nitrate. We usually miss getting the mother together with her infant when her neonate is especially alert and when she is most easily excited and interested in the infant's eyes. What significance could this excitement or special ecstasy, seen especially in home deliveries, suggest? Is it an important element in the attachment process?

Rosenblatt: Excitement is seen in all animals at parturition. Even birds seem to show a special excitement when eggs hatch. I would guess that this is an optimal time when the mother is receptive to the young, and of course we should take advantage of it.

Curtis-Jenkins: The excitement seems to be infectious, affecting everybody else involved with the labour. People who watch films of deliveries also get excited.

Rosenblatt: One of two photographers who came to film a birth in California said afterwards that he felt he loved the woman more than he loved his wife. Both photographers felt very involved with the family.

Leiderman: I interviewed several of the mothers who had home births near Stanford University and I can attest to the tremendous enthusiasm both mothers and fathers show towards even the idea of home birth. Because of this preparturition 'excitement', I want to remind you that, for human beings at least, ideology and belief systems have very powerful effects on experience; therefore the birth experience of animals cannot be simply compared to the more ideologically conditioned experience of humans. Because of this enthusiasm of the observer one must be especially cautious in drawing conclusions about the possible benefits of home birth. We have found that most women in this group are pleased, but a few are guarded in their praise. As in hospital births, I believe we should listen to the minority as well as to the majority.

We are currently following 22 cases from the group around Santa Cruz, California, to record their reactions and particularly to evaluate the effect of father's presence at home birth on the mother and the infant. We hypothesized that if the fathers were present at the birth there would be a closer relationship with the mother and newborn. Of the first four fathers we observed, two subsequently deserted the mother and two appeared much closer to their wives and infants when the families were assessed six weeks after the birth. We shall continue to record our observations, realizing that the first four cases may be atypical. However I should like to caution against premature enthusiasm for the Santa Cruz style of childbirth, or for any other style of childbirth that is conceptually divorced from the belief system and values of the culture.

Klaus: We agree with your precaution and we are not as yet recommending home delivery. However, in studying these mothers, we may become aware of significant behaviours that we might otherwise miss because they are only apparent in very subtle forms in other kinds of birth.

Brazelton: A study that we did 15 years ago, at about the same time as Greta Bibring was doing her important study on pregnancy (Bibring 1959), taught me something important that bears on what might be lost when we interfere with the excitement or euphoria of this initial perinatal period. We were studying young women weekly in psychoanalytic interviews, to try to understand what their personalities were like before they had their baby. We interviewed the fathers monthly. These were women who turned out to be normal mothers later on and who had already mothered a previous child successfully. Then we made predictions comparable to those suggested by Escalona & Heider (1959): that is, at the end of each stage one makes a prediction for the next stage, then also looks back at the previous prediction to see what was wrong with it. Seeing one's mistakes in prediction gives one a very powerful way of understanding observer bias. The predictions made by their therapists at the end of these women's pregnancies were that all of them were likely to be psychotic when they got their babies. As a paediatrician I could not agree with this and when the predictions indeed turned out to be wrong, we had to reorganize our thinking about the anxiety that normally occurs in pregnancy. It is something like this: anxiety and disruption of old concepts, through dreams, become part of a normal process, a kind of unwiring of all the old connections to be ready for the new role. As I began to look at what happened to these women as they assumed their new roles it became apparent that the mother's prenatal anxiety helped her to shape herself in a very powerful way around the individuality of the particular baby she had. I began to see this anxiety as very constructive for the women in coping with their new roles.

The mothers in this same study pointed out to us that if they could not see the baby right away, they were not sure whether it was really their baby. That was the first level of questioning of their own attachment. The second level was that they could not believe in the baby's individuality and it took them a longer time to see anything special about this baby if they weren't allowed to see him for the first 24 hours. What they told us seemed to indicate that we may be losing an important opportunity of fostering, in parents, their specific attempts to relate to the baby *early* as an individual, when the baby offers cues at the time of delivery.

Dreyfus-Brisac: Have you any kind of measure of whether the anxiety of the mothers affects their behaviour, Dr Klaus? Were the mothers of premature babies more anxious than the others?

Klaus: They were very concerned about the infant's health. Often they said they were afraid to touch the infant for fear they might hurt him.

Richards: We saw the same eye contact in mothers and infants in Cambridge as you did, but we have to remember that most of the drugs used during labour seem to delay eye-opening after delivery. In home deliveries in Cambridge we never noticed the licking of the breast that you mentioned, but the midwife there is concerned with getting the baby to suck and it is not the same free-choice situation as you saw.

I recently saw a delivery in a hospital in London where an epidural injection was given and various kinds of monitors were being used. There was no excitement at all. There is excitement during the home deliveries we have seen, although not as much ecstasy as you described. I have seen a midwife at a home delivery kiss a newborn baby and I just can't imagine that happening in a hospital delivery room.

Finally, I think a lot of the negative effects of hospitals have something to do with people's control over their own bodies and their babies' bodies. In general, mothers are able to maintain much more control at home than during hospital deliveries.

Klaus: I am glad you emphasize control. In the present system we expect the woman to do something active, that is to take on this baby, yet we make her passive and she has to adjust abruptly. What we saw in Guatemala was exaggerated because being in hospital was such an unusual experience for the women.

Of course the difficulty in studying interaction is that the environment is different for almost every delivery and we can't compare them properly. What a nurse says, what a doctor says, and all sorts of other things may change behaviour.

Papoušek: In connection with the mother's touching the infant with her fingertips or with her palms, it is important to know whether the pregnancy was wanted or unwanted. Mothers who do not want their pregnancy touch more and longer with the fingertips and this correlates with the amount of crying in their babies. Where everything is in order the mothers choose more palm contact and the babies are calmer in the first days. If premature infants are more often unwanted that of course explains the difference you saw between their mothers and the full-term mothers, Dr Klaus.

Brazelton: We know that women face a premature or damaged baby with ambivalence—both wanting him and being somewhat repelled by him. In addition, they suffer from a grief reaction like that first described by Cobb & Lindemann (1943) in the survivors of the Cocoanut Grove fire, which in these mothers' cases might be seen as grieving for the perfect baby of which they dreamed but had not produced. This grief is coupled with a serious amount of guilt at having damaged the baby by their ambivalent feelings, of which they were aware in pregnancy. Unless we are aware of our roles in supporting the positive side of a mother's ambivalence, and in helping her to work out her grief reaction, she may end up by rejecting the at-risk baby (cf. the high incidence of abused or 'failure to thrive' babies who have been premature infants), or she may continue to grieve for the idealized baby and be unable to relate in a healthy way to the baby she really has. Our role in helping her to overbalance her negative feelings (present in *all* women) is crucial, and every effort should be made to determine the critical times when she needs support (Solnit & Stark 1961). Kennell & Klaus's work (1971) points out how crucial early contact may be in this way.

Bentovim: I have been intrigued since the comment about ecstasy and excitement was first made. When Dr Klaus showed the film [during his presentation] of a birth in Santa Cruz, there was a moment of excitement in the group here. The boundaries between each of us seemed to dissolve with the shared feeling.

The potential for ecstasy therefore seems to be universally present, particularly in those with a vested interest in infancy!

Women expecting babies share such an interest, and the capacity for becoming excited may be an important component of the changes towards a state of 'motherhood' and mothering. During pregnancy a number of processes are going on. Positive expectations—ideals—develop about the infant having wished-for qualities or reaching unachieved goals, or through a new person creating, or re-creating, known or wished-for parents, brothers, sisters—friends and comforters. There are parallel fears of the worst, and at the same time there is the crisis of the mother realizing that previous identities, roles and relationships have in part to be relinquished so that she can make herself available for her new expected infant.

These processes of preparation for motherhood are accompanied by a variable amount of fears, conflicts, excitement and anxiety during the pregnancy, which can reach pathological degrees. Presumably at the time of birth itself, these psychological changes are given additional charge by the euphoriant effect of the hormonal state, so that a potential for excitement appears. This may have the effect of facilitating the birth of the infant not only in a physical sense but also in a psychological sense. The sense of excitement may well help the ideals and expectations that have been growing about the baby to become crystallized and realized on the actual person of the new baby. Perhaps the early presentation of the infant to the mother produces that feeling of recognition—the 'aha' experience and feeling that this is the infant expected, who is somehow going to fit the ideals that have grown up during the waiting period. Fathers and the rest of the family can share the moment of birth and identify the infant as a 'body' and a 'person'—the first moment of attachment and bonding.

Problems arise when separation at birth, a premature or deformed baby, or one of the 'wrong' sex, and so on, interfere with the process of externalization of an internal object that has been growing during nine months. For satisfactory attachment the infant has to be recognized as fitting in terms of the fantasy that has grown. The birth of handicapped infants, in particular, disturbs a parent's expectations (Bentovim 1972, 1975). Instead of gaining the infant expected, she gains one she feared she might have, and angry rejecting feelings follow.

Without such distortions, through excitement 'fulfilled', a mother sees the actualization of an ideal in the person of the infant, an experience which continues to enable her to meet his needs. Winnicott (1958) described an analogous 'abnormal–normal' state of mind which he called 'primary maternal preoccupation!' This heightened state of sensitivity in the first weeks enables the mother to respond to the infant as if his needs are her own. Thereby she not only feeds him with physical necessities, but nurtures the child that was part of her in fact and in fantasy.

Leiderman: We have termed this phenomenon 'creating psychic space'. Within the family unit there has to be an opening to include this new individual. Until that space has opened up, the individual is almost isolated, psychologically.

Curtis-Jenkins: Katherina Dalton (1971) showed that the only positive factor that correlated with puerperal depression was ecstasy or euphoria during pregnancy, and that progesterone given by injection or in pessary form to a mother with puerperal depression removed the depression more quickly than antidepressants or electroconvulsive therapy. I have treated six women who had puerperal depression with progesterone alone and their response was satisfactory enough for me not to have to use antidepressants or refer them to a psychiatrist. Puerperal depression is more likely to be correlated with euphoria during pregnancy than with a long or difficult labour, size of the baby, home delivery versus hospital, or anything else. The argument is that if progesterone at the time of delivery falls too fast it alters brain chemistry.

Leiderman: I should remind the group that progesterone also has some sedative properties.

D'Souza: Do women prone to puerperal depression have unusually high levels of progesterone during pregnancy?

Curtis-Jenkins: I don't know. One woman in my care had four children and had been admitted to hospital with puerperal depression four times. We were prepared for the fifth baby and I had just read Katherina Dalton's paper. The mother said she was getting the depression and instead of admitting her to hospital I gave her progesterone. Within a week the depression had lifted. Then she stopped taking progesterone and the depression returned. She started taking progesterone again and it lifted again. The effect seemed to last for as long as she lactated (she continued to breast-feed for about nine months).

Hofer: Is the implication that ecstasy is a result of a high progesterone level?

Curtis-Jenkins: I don't know.

Hofer: I should think that ecstasy probably has other origins, mainly psychological.

References

BENTOVIM, A. (1972) Handicapped pre-school children and their families—effects on the child's early emotional development and family attitudes. *Br. Med. J. 3*, 579–581; 634–663

BENTOVIM, A. (1975) Deformed children: emotional development and family responses, in *Applied Teratology* (Berry, C.J., ed.), Elsevier, Amsterdam

BIBRING, G.L. (1959) Some considerations of psychological processes in pregnancy. *Psychoanal. Study Child 14*, 113

BRAZELTON, T.B. (1974) *Neonatal Behavioural Assessment Scale* (Clinics in Developmental Medicine No. 50), Spastics International Medical Publications/Heinemann, London

COBB, S. & LINDEMANN, E. (1943) Neuropsychiatric observations after the Cocoanut Grove fire. *Ann. Surg.* June

DALTON, K. (1971) Puerperal and premenstrual depression. *Proc. R. Soc. Med. 64*, 1249–1251

ESCALONA, S. & HEIDER, G.M. (1959) *Prediction and Outcome*, Basic Books, New York

KENNELL, J.H. & KLAUS, M.H. (1971) Care of the mother of the high risk infant. *Clin. Obstet. Gynecol. 14*, 926

SOLNIT, A.J. & STARK, M.H. (1961) Mourning and the birth of a defective child. *Psychoanal. Study Child 16*, 523

WINNICOTT, D.W. (1958) Primary maternal preoccupation, in *Collected Papers: Through Paediatrics to Psycho-Analysis*, pp. 300–305, Tavistock, London; Basic Books, New York

Evidence for a sensitive period in the human mother

JOHN H. KENNELL, MARY ANNE TRAUSE and MARSHALL H. KLAUS

Department of Pediatrics, Case Western Reserve University, Cleveland

How long does the fire of love endure
If the eyes and touch are not there to kindle it.
Dante: *The Divine Comedy*

Abstract In certain animal species immediate separation of a mother from her young for a brief period after delivery (the sensitive period) may result in aberrant maternal behaviour.

In the human, disorders of mothering, including child abuse, increase disproportionately in situations associated with early neonatal separation of mother and infant, such as prematurity. Mothers in the United States who were offered early contact with their premature infants showed differences in attachment behaviour when compared with mothers whose first contact with their infants was three weeks after delivery. Mothers who had one hour of close physical contact with their nude full-term infants within the first two hours after delivery and who had 15 extra hours of contact in the first three days behaved significantly differently during a physical examination of the infant at one month and one year, and in their speech to their infants at two years, from a control group of mothers who had only routine contact. In a similar study in Guatemala, mothers who had 45 minutes of early extra contact showed significantly more attachment behaviour at the time of the first breast-feeding (12 hours). These and other studies in the human suggest that shortly after birth there is a sensitive period which appears to have long-lasting effects on maternal attachment and which may ultimately affect the development of the child.

Is there a unique period in the human mother soon after delivery when she is especially sensitive to her baby and most ready to become attached to it? Nursery practices in the modern hospital in the United States do not generally acknowledge this possibility and mother and infant are routinely separated immediately after birth, the mother to be monitored in an adult recovery area and the baby in a transitional care nursery. If there were convincing evidence of an early sensitive period in the human, major changes in hospital care practices would be necessary to ensure that mother and baby remain together.

There are many difficulties in systematically studying whether or not there is a sensitive period in the human. Human maternal behaviour is determined by a multitude of factors, including the woman's past experiences with her own mother, the patterns of her culture, whether or not the baby was planned, and the quality of her relationship with the baby's father. In some cases, the intellectual abilities of a mother may enable her to bridge potential difficulties such as an early separation from her infant. Because of these many influences, it is difficult to isolate and demonstrate the effects of the sensitive period on maternal attachment. Nonetheless, we believe that a number of observations fit together in such a way as to suggest that this period does have special importance for the development of the mother's bond to her child. This report presents these observations, speculates on their meaning, and suggests questions which need further study.

Valuable insights may be gained by examining animal behaviour, even though human behaviour is much more complex. The goat, for instance, provides an extreme example of a time-limited maternal sensitive period. If a goat mother and her kid are not kept together during the first five minutes after delivery, she does not develop a specific discriminant attachment to her kid. Without this bond, she treats the kid as an alien and in most cases refuses to care for it, butting or kicking it away as it approaches her (Klopfer 1971).

We use this example because we believe that there is a similar, although less fixed, period of heightened sensitivity in the human mother during which she interacts with her newborn infant and begins to form a special attachment to it. An attachment can be defined as a unique emotional relationship between two people which is specific and endures through time. Although it is difficult to define this enduring relationship operationally, we have taken as indicators of attachment those behaviours such as fondling, kissing, cuddling and prolonged gazing which serve to maintain contact with and show affection to a particular individual. 'Maternal sensitive period' refers to that time after delivery when the mother forms, or begins to form, a special attachment to her infant. Increased contact, or especially separation, during this period is likely to alter later maternal attachment. We hypothesize that during this early sensitive period a cascade of reciprocal interactions begins between the mother and baby which locks them together and mediates the further development of attachment.

The process that takes place during the maternal sensitive period differs from imprinting in that there is not a point beyond which the formation of an attachment is precluded. This period is the optimal but not the only one during which an attachment can develop. The process can occur at a later time, although it will be more difficult and take longer to achieve. This is similar to the finding of Hersher *et al.* (1963) that if drastic measures were taken to keep a mother goat in a small enclosure with her kid, starting within the first 12 hours after delivery, maternal attachment could still be achieved after the period of her heightened sensitivity. However, a process which takes but a few minutes immediately after delivery took an average of ten days once the sensitive period had passed.

Experimental studies that might yield well-defined answers are restricted by the inappropriateness of manipulating the human mother in the same way as the animal. For example, one could never justify presenting a woman with an alien infant immediately after birth to test whether specific attachments are best formed during that time. Thus, conclusions about the existence of specific attachments can only be tentatively drawn.

However, clinical observations have suggested that specific attachments are made during this early period. In a remarkable accident in an Israeli hospital, two mothers were inadvertently given the wrong babies, whom they took home and cared for. At the time of the two-week check-up, the error was discovered and efforts to return the babies to their own families were begun. Surprisingly, each mother had become so attached to the baby she had cared for during the first 14 days that she did not wish to give it up. Their husbands, on the other hand, strongly supported correcting the error because of facial and other characteristics that were unique to the individual families (L. Lothstein, personal communication). In other nursery accidents when the wrong baby has been presented to a mother for the first feeding or to hold for a brief period, we have been greatly impressed by the mother's lingering thoughts about that baby. Often months later, when her own child seems completely satisfactory in every respect, she will refer to that first infant and say, 'Oh that was such a lovely baby'.

These observations of the behaviour of mothers when the wrong baby was presented to them in the first minutes lead to the question of what happens when a baby is separated from his mother during the newborn period. In our clinical experiences, we have noted that a number of mothers who have been separated from their infants are hesitant and clumsy when they begin to care for their full-term or premature infants, taking several visits to learn the simple mothering tasks of feeding and changing that most women pick up rapidly. When the separation is prolonged, mothers report that they sometimes forget momentarily that they even have a baby. After a premature baby has gone home, it is striking to hear how often the mother reports that although she is fond of her baby, she still thinks of it as belonging to someone else—the head nurse in the nursery or the physician—rather than to her.

Even grosser distortions of mother–infant attachment are apparent in the mother of a child who is battered or the mother of an infant with no organic disease who has failed to thrive but who gains weight easily when his needs are more adequately met by another caretaker. Prematurity and low birth-weight often lead to prolonged mother–infant separation. Significantly, according to a number of studies, infants who had been premature constitute a disproportionately high number of both battered children (23–31%) and those with the 'failure to thrive' syndrome in which no organic cause is found (Fanaroff *et al.* 1972). Even with the shorter separation associated with delivery by Caesarean section, the incidence of child abuse is ten times greater than with vaginal deliveries (R. E. Helfer, personal communication).

The clinical observations of Rose *et al.* (1960) and Kennell & Rolnick (1960) have suggested that affectional ties can be disturbed easily and may be altered permanently during the immediate postpartum period. Relatively mild illness in the newborn appears to affect the relationship between mother and infant. Among these minor problems are mild jaundice, slow feeding, and the need for incubator care in the first 24 hours for mild respiratory distress. The mother's behaviour was often disturbed during the first year of the baby's life or longer, even though the infant's problems had been completely resolved before discharge, and often within a few hours.

Here we give results from eight studies in which the time of first contact between a mother and her neonate was varied and the outcome measured. As an example, in a carefully controlled investigation of 28 primiparous mothers and their normal full-term infants, 14 mothers were given their nude babies in bed for one hour in the first two hours after delivery and for five extra hours on each of the next three days of life. The other 14 mothers received the care that is routine in most hospitals in the United States: a glimpse of the baby at birth, a brief contact for identification at 6–8 hours and then visits of 20–30 minutes for feedings every four hours. The two groups were matched as to age and marital and socioeconomic status of the mothers, and were not significantly different in the sex and weight of the infants. Women were randomly assigned to a group, were all given the same explanation of the study and, to the best of our knowledge, were not aware that there were differences in mother–infant contact in the first three days. Those making the observations in this and the follow-up studies did not know to which group the subjects belonged.

When the mothers and babies returned to the hospital at one month, there were significant differences between the two groups (Klaus *et al.* 1972). The 'early contact' mothers usually stood near their infants and watched during the physical examination, showed significantly more soothing behaviour, engaged in more eye-to-eye contact and fondling during feeding, and were more reluctant to leave their infants with someone else than were mothers not given the early and extended experience of contact. At one year, the two groups were again significantly different (Kennell *et al.* 1974). 'Extended contact' mothers spent a greater percentage of time assisting the physician while he examined their babies and soothing the infants when they cried.

We wondered if just a few mothers in one or both groups had accounted for the persistence and consistency of the differences over the span of 11 months. However, the ranking of the mothers within each of the two groups showed no significant correlation for the measures at the one-month and one-year examinations.

At two years, five mothers were selected at random from each group, and the linguistic behaviours of the two groups while speaking to their children were compared. The extended contact mothers used twice as many questions, more words per proposition, fewer content words, more adjectives and fewer commands than did the controls (Ringler *et al.* 1975). This study will have to be repeated, because with so few subjects the differences could have been due to chance selection. However, these findings suggest that 16 extra hours of contact in the first three days of life appear to have affected maternal behaviour for one year and possibly longer, thus offering support for the hypothesis that there is a maternal sensitive period soon after delivery.

Notice that this study does not test for the specificity of attachment. Also, even the mothers in the experimental group were actually separated from their infants at delivery. The baby was not placed with the mother until 30 minutes to two hours after birth and did not remain with her constantly from birth as he would in a natural home delivery. Although the amount of anaesthesia and drugs given to the mothers in this study would be considered the minimum for primiparous mothers in a university hospital in the United States, the medication received by mothers and infants in both groups may have influenced the effects of this early contact. Thus, differences emerged in spite of a number of factors which could be expected to reduce differences between the groups.

During the past four years, five other studies of mothers and their full-term infants have either been completed or are under way.

In a carefully controlled study, Winters gave six mothers in one group their babies to suckle shortly after birth and contrasted these to six mothers who did not have contact with their babies until approximately 16 hours later. All had originally intended to breast-feed and none stopped because of physical problems. When checked two months later, all six mothers who had suckled their babies on the delivery table were still breast-feeding, whereas only one of the other six was still nursing her baby (N. Winters, unpublished work).

Recently, with Drs Mata, Sosa and Urrutia, we started a long-term study in Guatemala using an experimental design similar to that presented earlier. In the I.G.S.S. Hospital in Guatemala City one group of 19 mothers were given their babies on the delivery table during the episiotomy repair period, then allowed to stay with them in privacy for 45 minutes. Each mother–infant pair was nude, skin-to-skin, under a heat panel. The other group of 19 mothers were separated from their babies shortly after delivery, which is the usual routine in this hospital. Except for this difference in initial contact, the care of the two groups was identical. The infants were discharged with free milk at two days, which is the practice of the hospital. When the babies were checked 35 days after birth, the mean weight gain of the infants in the early contact group was 1208 g, or 203 g more than that of the control group (1005 g). The mothers in the two groups did not differ significantly in socioeconomic, marital, housing, or income status.

In a similar study at Roosevelt Hospital, Guatemala City, we found no significant differences in weight gain at 35 days. Information which might help to account for these discrepant findings is not yet available.

In Pelotis, Brazil, P. L. Sousa (unpublished work) recently compared the success of breast-feeding during the first two months of life in two groups of 100 women who delivered normal full-term babies in a 20-bed maternity ward. In the study group, the newborn baby was put to the breast immediately after birth and permanent contact between the mother and baby was sustained during the lying-in period, when the baby lay in a cot beside his mother's bed. The control group had the traditional contact with their infants—a glimpse shortly after birth and then visits for approximately 30 minutes every three hours, seven times a day, starting 12 to 14 hours after birth. The babies were kept in a separate nursery. Successful breast-feeding was defined as no complementary feedings other than tea, water, or small amounts of fruit juice being used until two months after birth. When the babies had reached two months of age, 77% of the early contact mothers were successfully breast-feeding, in contrast to only 27% of the controls. A weakness in this design which limits the strength of the findings is that during the experimental period a special nurse was working in the unit to stimulate and encourage breast-feeding. Although not definitive in itself, this study adds weight to our hypothesis.

In another study last summer at the Roosevelt Hospital in Guatemala, a different group of nine mothers were given their babies nude, skin-to-skin, under a heat panel, after they had left the delivery room. A second group of ten were separated, according to the usual routine. The babies in both groups were sent to the newborn nursery for the next 12 hours, after which they went to the mother in a seven-bed room for the first breast-feeding. At 12 hours, each mother's interactions with her infant were observed by D. Hales, who did not know to which group they belonged. Observations of the mother's fondling, kissing, looking 'en face', gazing at, and holding her baby close were made for 15 seconds in every minute for 15 minutes (Fig. 1). The group with early contact showed significantly increased attachment behaviours.

Two studies, one at Stanford and one at Case Western Reserve, of mothers

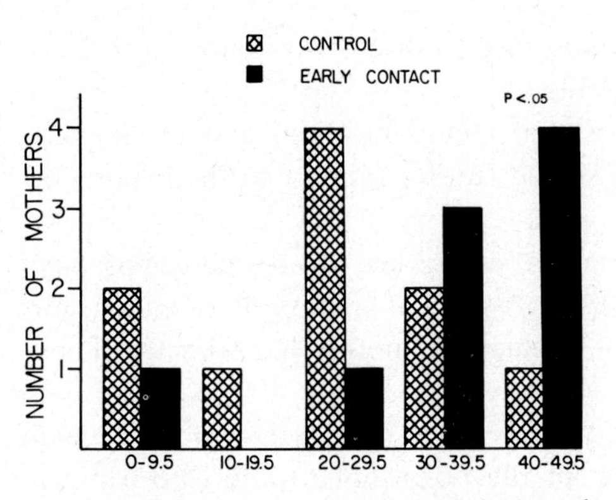

FIG. 1. Attachment scores at 12 hours in 9 mothers who had early contact with their babies and in 10 mothers who were separated from their babies after delivery in Roosevelt Hospital, Guatemala City.

of premature infants also have similar designs to those already described. In these investigations, half the mothers were permitted to come into the nursery as soon as they were able and the other half after three weeks. In the study at Stanford (Leifer *et al.* 1972; Leiderman *et al.* 1973) there were seven interviews with the parents while their babies were in the premature nursery. Thus, the mothers in both groups at Stanford received some attention, whereas in our study at Case Western Reserve, statements to the parents were limited.

In our study, significant differences between the early and late contact groups were found at the time of discharge on one measure of attachment behaviour: mothers given early contact looked at their infants more during a feeding which was filmed at that time. Also at discharge, mothers of girls in the early contact group held their infants close to their bodies for a greater percentage of time than mothers of girls in the late contact group. Strikingly, preliminary data on the Stanford Binet I.Q. levels of these two groups of children at 42 months indicate that those in the early contact group scored significantly higher than those in the late contact group (mean I.Q. 99 vs. 85). Furthermore, a significant correlation (correlation coefficient = 0.71) was found between the I.Q. at 42 months and the amount of time women spent looking at their babies during the filmed feeding at one month of age. This supports our hypothesis that early contact affects aspects of the mother's behaviour which may have significance for the child's later development.

At Stanford, the mothers who were separated from their premature babies for 3–12 weeks showed no significant differences in attachment behaviour at one month from those permitted early contact. However, there were more divorces (five compared to one) in the group of mothers with prolonged separation, and more infants were relinquished by them (two compared to zero) (Leifer *et al.* 1972; Leiderman *et al.* 1973).

Studies of fathers by J. Lind (personal communication) and of mothers rooming-in by Greenberg *et al.* (1973) lend further support to the hypothesis that there is an early sensitive period.

Further research is needed to determine exactly when this period begins, how long it lasts, and what events modify it. Also, it is important to study how attachment is affected by the type of contact the mother has with the infant during this period.

In summary, we hypothesize that there is a sensitive period in the human mother which is the optimal time for an affectional bond to develop between the mother and her infant. The suggestion that mother–infant contact and interaction in the early minutes and hours after delivery influence subsequent mothering behaviour is supported by the results in six of these eight controlled studies of mothers of premature infants and parents of full-term infants. The effects may persist in the mother of a full-term infant for as long as two years, affect the weight gain of the infants in Guatemala in the first month, and be manifest in the performance of premature infants 42 months later. These observations have obvious clinical implications for those caring for normal, premature or sick infants.

ACKNOWLEDGEMENTS

The work reported in the paper would never have been accomplished without the help of the many medical students who have been associated with us in our studies and the generous support of the Grant Foundation, The Educational Corporation of America, and The Research Corporation. The work in Guatemala is being done in collaboration with Drs L. Mata, R. Sosa and J. Urrutia.

References

FANAROFF, A., KENNELL, J. & KLAUS, M. (1972) Follow up of low birthweight infants—the predictive value of maternal visiting patterns. *Pediatrics 49*, 287–290

GREENBERG, M., ROSENBERG, I. & LIND, J. (1973) First mothers rooming-in with their newborns: its impact upon the mother. *Am. J. Orthopsychiatr. 43*, 783–788

HERSHER, L., RICHMOND, J.B. & MOORE, A.V. (1963) Modifiability of the critical period for the development of maternal behavior in sheep and goats. *Behaviour 20*, 311–320

KENNELL, J.H. & ROLNICK, A.R. (1960) Discussing problems in newborn babies with their parents. *Pediatrics 26*, 832–838

KENNELL, J., JERAULD, R., WOLFE, H., CHESLER, D., KREGER, N., MCALPINE, W., STEFFA, M. & KLAUS, M. (1974) Maternal behavior one year after early and extended post-partum contact. *Dev. Med. Child Neurol. 16*, 172–179

KLAUS, M., JERAULD, R., KREGER, N., MCALPINE, W., STEFFA, M. & KENNELL, J. (1972) Maternal attachment—importance of the first post-partum days. *New Engl. J. Med. 286*, 460–463

KLOPFER, P. (1971) Mother love: what turns it on? *Am. Sci. 59*, 404–407

LEIDERMAN, P.H., LEIFER, A., SEASHORE, M., BARNETT, C. & GROBSTEIN, R. (1973) Mother–infant interaction: effects of early deprivation, prior experience and sex of infant. *Early Dev. 51*, 154–175

LEIFER, A., LEIDERMAN, P.H., BARNETT, C. & WILLIAMS, J. (1972) Effects of mother–infant separation on maternal attachment behavior. *Child Dev. 43*, 1203–1218

RINGLER, N.M., KENNELL, J.H., JARVELLA, R., NAVOJOSKY, B.J. & KLAUS, M.H. (1975) Mother to child speech at two years—effects of early postnatal contact. *J. Pediatr. 86*, 141–144

ROSE, J., BOGGS, T., Jr. & ALDERSTEIN, A. (1960) The evidence for a syndrome of 'mothering disability' consequent to threats to the survival of neonates: a design for hypothesis testing including prevention in a prospective study. *Am. J. Dis. Child. 100*, 776

Discussion

Oppé: Is your definition of a premature infant based on birth weight or gestational age? In talking about the sensitive period it is important to know the duration of the pregnancy.

Kennell: We use the Amiel-Tison Neurological Evaluation of the Maturity of Newborn Infants to determine the gestational age, and then we plot the length, weight and head circumference on the Lubchenco Intrauterine Growth Curves (Amiel-Tison, 1968; Lubchenco *et al.* 1966). We only include healthy premature infants of 36 weeks or less, with weight appropriate for gestational age.

Rosenblatt: Does the mother of a premature infant go through the same hormonal changes as she would otherwise? In animals premature births can be induced by giving hormones.

Leiderman: I understand that three years ago these endocrinological studies had not been done. Can anyone add more recent information?

Macfarlane: There is some indication that in induced births the level of corticosteroids may be much lower than if they are not induced, but I don't know about the oestrogen–progesterone concentrations.

Bentovim: Dr Kennell, how 'normal' was the group of mothers who had additional contact with their infants whom you described previously (Kennell *et al.* 1974)? They were a lower social class group, often without husbands. Would there have been a lesser effect of such additional contact in a group more highly motivated towards wanting and being able to care for a baby.

Kennell: Whether legally married or not, all the mothers in our premature and full-term studies definitely wanted to keep their babies. Your question brings out some of the difficulties in carrying out studies of maternal attachment in the human. In the design of our studies it is essential that the control and experimental mothers should come from the same population. The 28 mothers in our full-term study were selected because they were healthy, primiparous, had made prenatal visits to the clinic, planned to keep their babies, and were willing to take part in the study. In our community we know that very few of the mothers seen by staff physicians will breast-feed. One of our measures of attachment was the mother's behaviour during a bottle feeding, so a breast-feeding mother would not have been selected. The group of lower-class staff mothers has both advantages and disadvantages for a study of maternal attachment. The mothers had not been to childbirth classes, so they did not know what to expect in the hospital. They had done little reading, so they were rather 'pure' for the purposes of this study. Almost all were black and their incomes and circumstances were similar in both groups. One difficulty with studies of maternal behaviour is that when people in the community begin to hear about it, their behaviour changes. Educated mothers may then behave in a special way because of what they have heard or read. We felt more secure about these results because one group did not know that another group was getting different attention.

Curtis-Jenkins: In my practice I visit the mothers and babies when they arrive home from hospital and carry out a full examination of the babies when they are between 9 and 20 days of age. I examine the naked baby in front of the mother and demonstrate to her that it can see, hear and has all the primitive reflexes. Some mothers respond in a very characteristic way: they giggle nervously and say 'Oo, I never knew he could do that', or 'Oo, I wouldn't do that myself'. I used to think this was idle chatter until a health visitor who came to see a mother at the same time said, as we came away from the house, that the woman would not be a good mother. When I asked why, she said that the health visitors had realized this when the girl went to their antenatal classes. Since then, I have observed that some mothers respond in this characteristically nervous way. It is a strange sort of 'one step away from their babies' act, which should relate, in a sense, to the behaviour of the mothers you described who were shown their babies late. But the mothers in our unit are allowed to have their babies on the first day, quite often on the labour bed, so there must be an additional factor.

Kennell: This is in agreement with a study by Katherine Barnard in Seattle, Washington (unpublished work, 1973). One group of mothers received routine care. The mothers in the experimental group were shown the Brazelton Neonatal Behaviour Assessment being performed on their babies just before discharge. One month later all the mothers were asked what they did when the baby cried. The mothers in the routine group said they gave the baby a bottle. The mothers in the experimental group said they looked to see whether the baby was comfortable, whether he wanted to be held or turned or rocked, and so on. We thought that the mothers and nurses in Guatemala might have had no exposure to some of the new neonatal assessment measures but then we found that Brazelton tests had been carried out in the nursery at the Roosevelt Hospital for three or four years! In our Cleveland nursery, when a baby cries the nurses almost immediately put a bottle in his or her mouth. In Guatemala the nurses tended to put their hands on a crying baby, hold the baby's arms at his or her side, and to carry out other soothing measures which are part of the Brazelton tests. I don't know whether this was a long-standing Guatemalan practice for breast-fed babies or whether it was the result of the Brazelton tests.

Two of the people who came from the United States to work with us told us that they did not particularly like babies, least of all newborn babies. These two students participated in a number of preliminary Brazelton assessments, often somewhat reluctantly, until the day when a baby first clearly followed their eyes. Then they were not only locked onto that particular baby but onto newborn babies in general. The visual and auditory response of these babies had a powerful effect on them.

Klaus: Mothers of premature infants have special difficulties. The baby is asleep for two hours, wakes up for three minutes and then goes back to sleep. When the mother comes into the nursery, the limp sleepy baby will not usually give her any special responses. We are now doing a study in which all the mothers of premature babies are permitted to come into the nursery but only half of them are given tasks such as touching the baby's skin or sending a message to the baby. Each of the mothers in the experimental group comes in six times in the first 14 days. During this time the researcher explains to the mother that her baby sees and hears and then asks her to watch for responses from him. For the first two or three visits, the mother may laugh about sending a message, then after several days she is usually able to make contact. She catches the baby at a period when he is awake and is able to soothe him and look at his eyes. She is very excited by this exchange.

Stewart: The babies of very low birth weight from our unit go home around 38 weeks of gestation at a stage when they are beginning to stare at faces. This is about the first positive sign of responsiveness that the mothers get and they find it most encouraging; it is often the thing that makes the parents begin to think of the baby as a real person.

Klaus: Where fluorescent light is used for treating hyperbilirubinaemia, mothers of full-term babies often become terribly panicky if the patches put on to protect the baby's eyes are not removed for feeding.

Kennell: In Guatemala City, even though the deliveries are all in the hospital, with the mother and baby separated and breast-feeding diminishing, there are certain features of the care of the babies that seem to be advantageous in a country where both mothers and babies are malnourished, and where it is crucial for the mother to care for the baby early. The mothers receive no drugs during their delivery, and the babies, due partly to the absence of drugs and anaesthesia, or to either a different variety of silver nitrate being applied to the eyes or to there being less adipose tissue around the eyes, have very bright eyes which are open more than those of babies in our hospital in Cleveland in the first two days. Not only at birth but even after silver nitrate drops have been applied, the babies have their eyes wide open when they come to their mothers.

Hofer: It seems as if the newborn baby has certain aversive or anxiety-producing qualities which have to be overcome. One of the main ways of overcoming that is through eye-to-eye contact, which may make the mother more comfortable for a variety of reasons. Dr Rosenblatt has reported that the rat mother has to overcome a certain olfactory aversion to the infants. Maybe the same kind of thing applies to other sensory systems in the human.

Brazelton: I think that is an important issue, particularly for an at-risk baby and a mother who is going through a grief reaction for having had such a baby. We have been so convinced by Kennell and Klaus's work that we have been using Brazelton neonatal behavioural assessments to try to lock mothers of damaged babies, or of babies who have been in an incubator for a long time, to their babies before discharge. Eye-to-eye contact is so fleeting and so difficult to get in some of these babies that we have looked at babies' responses to auditory stimulation, which seems to be easier to demonstrate in these stressed infants.

Even premature babies have a wonderful capacity for choosing a female voice rather than a male's, so we can demonstrate this difference very easily. As soon as he is captured with an auditory stimulus the baby quiets down, has a studied look on his face even when his eyes are closed, and turns towards his mother's voice. When he does, the mother begins to soften and gets locked onto the baby's face. Then we demonstrate his status to her and show her how far he has got. At this time we show her the good and the questionable things about him. We explain that in two or three weeks, when the baby goes home, he will have got even further. So, first the mother is given a channel through which she can attach to the baby, and then she is helped to adjust to whatever his pathological behaviour may be. When he does go home, we give her a goal for her work with him. We see this as training the mothers as part of a team to work with the babies. With this kind of approach, we have found that instead of the mothers having made the expected two weeks' progress when they come back for their first follow-up visit, they have made four weeks' progress with their babies. We have felt as if parents have in them the energy for nurturing at-risk babies and that this can be captured and entrained into the whole therapeutic process of bringing a disordered baby around.

Curtis-Jenkins: I agree absolutely. Even in grossly damaged children there are islands of normality or appropriate behaviour. If you can demonstrate that clearly to the mother, her whole attitude to her child changes dramatically.

Brazelton: It is partly her own self-image which is at stake, not just her image of the baby. By giving her an active therapeutic role, you are giving her credit for having the capacity to respond to and nurture even a damaged baby.

Kennell: Drastic things are done to mothers and healthy babies in hospitals. We put solutions in the baby's eyes that blur his vision and cause swelling of the lids, which sometimes closes the eyes. We wash and wipe the baby's skin and the mother's nipples, which probably changes the odours. Our procedures interfere with many parts of the mother's specific behaviour with her baby at this particular time. These interferences as well as the separation may drastically disturb the attachment process.

Macfarlane: Drugs given during labour might have exactly the same effect as separation. The woman is probably going to be under the effect of the drug for eight hours or so after she has delivered the child. In England, that is much more common than actual separation.

Kennell: I agree about drugs. It is interesting that the mother is given drugs that dull her perceptions and cause amnesia during a period when heightened responsiveness may be needed for attachment to occur. I was taught, a long time ago, that the drugs don't affect mother or baby in the doses used—and this is still the prevailing belief. But Dr Brazelton has shown that very small doses of drugs can have drastic effects on mother and baby (Brazelton 1961). They may dampen perceptions and responses that might be very crucial (at that time). Drugs may be one of the factors in hospital deliveries that eliminate some of the euphoria seen in home births.

Cooper: I have observed that when the mother handles her newborn baby in the earliest hours, he cries far less than when hospital staff handle him. A lot of the things like wiping, wrapping, flicking the feet to waken the baby to feed him, and so on, that the staff do are rather rough, whereas the mother is usually very gentle with her baby. Face-to-face contact of mother and baby, or kissing of the baby, hasn't been mentioned much. This is surprising, because if most mothers are left alone I think within a minute or two they will not only have palm contact, but kissing or face-to-face contact, or both, also soon follow.

Kennell: In Indian villages in Guatemala, where mothers deliver in their homes, the incidence of skin infections in small infants is reported to be extremely low. However, there is a high incidence of these infections, usually staphylococcal, in babies born in hospitals. A question that we are attempting to answer in our study in Guatemala is whether a mother who kisses her newborn baby gives him her own organisms, such as her types of staphylococci, so that the infant does not pick up the pathogenic hospital staphylococci. This can be compared to planting a lawn with fine grass seed (the mother's organisms) which will discourage the growth of weed seeds (hospital staphylococci) that arrive later. We suspect that there are physical and bacteriological benefits, as well as behavioural benefits, when mother–infant contact is maintained after birth.

Our first impressions in Guatemala were that mothers were not interacting with their infants. We made many observations and tried several techniques before we were able to obtain the observations 12 hours after delivery that I have reported here. The mothers stopped whatever they were doing when they noted that we were obviously looking at them. That dramatically demonstrated to us how inhibited these women were by all the people around them. We then discovered that if we kept our eyes open we could see a rich variety of greatly subdued interactions. In the hospitals in Guatemala City and in the Indian villages we were impressed with how little crying we heard. We questioned whether this was due to malnutrition. But the babies can cry loudly if they are hurt. The mothers seem to be very sensitive, feeding their babies often, soothing them frequently and keeping them on their bodies where there is always some movement. There is a quick response to the baby's needs. In one case, after just 15 minutes of privacy with her baby, one still-bleeding mother got out of bed and walked to the door to tell the investigator outside the door that her baby needed food, when the baby had just made a few soft cries. These mothers appeared to be worried that the cry was not being answered by an immediate source of breast milk.

Cooper: What about the problem of a mother needing to fuse the fantasy of the baby in her womb with the reality of the baby in her arms?

Kennell: This is an important question. My attention was drawn to this process by an excellent paediatrician in London who told me that she loved normal newborn babies so much that she had arranged in her training for three extra years of experience with normal healthy newborns. Then later on, when she looked at her own first baby, she could see that it was a perfectly healthy neonate with normal colour and respiration, and with arms, legs and so forth, and for the first 36 hours she considered it to be like many other normal healthy newborns. Then suddenly it became the most marvellous baby that had ever lived, the most beautiful, the most responsive and so forth. Many mothers describe similar experiences. It may be 12 hours, or two or three days, until the mother can fuse the image of her anticipated magazine-cover, curly-haired, perfect-complexioned, baby girl with the actual straight-haired bruised boy who is beside her.

Cooper: It is interesting to listen to mothers telling you why they took so long to adjust to a baby. Their reasons seem highly individual and a great variety are given. I suspect that the degree of fantasy affects the amount of time it takes them to attach, as well as all the other things we have been talking about.

Rosenblatt: The rat mother during pregnancy changes the pattern of her licking. Virgin rats generally do not lick far down on the body, but as pregnancy advances they increasingly lick more posterior regions, probably in response to developments of the mammary glands and so forth. When we prevented pregnant rats from reaching that part of the body, their mammary glands only developed to 50% of normal (Roth & Rosenblatt 1967, 1968). Licking plays an important role in developing the glands, and we found that either licking of the nipples or licking of the genital regions could contribute equally to their development (Whitworth 1972). Raven Lang also reports (unpublished findings, 1974) that human mothers often rub their own bellies and have long conversations with their unborn babies. So the baby is not fantasy, but apparently much more real than one might think. During pregnancy, rat mothers become increasingly maternal, physiologically, and the human female's dreams or fantasies about the baby may not be simply anticipation but sensitivity to her own physiological condition.

Curtis-Jenkins: Fantasy often arises from ignorance. Mothers are intensely curious, and gynaecologists and obstetricians often do nothing to satisfy that curiosity. But if you can show the mother where the head is, or let her listen to the heart, the fantasy goes. I am certain that then she knows that the baby inside her is a reality.

References

AMIEL-TISON, C. (1968) Neurological evaluation of the maturity of newborn infants. *Arch. Dis. Child. 43*, 89

BRAZELTON, T.B. (1961) Psychophysiologic reaction in the neonate, II: the effects of maternal medication on the neonate and his behavior. *J. Pediatr. 58*, 513–518

KENNELL, J., JERAULD, R., WOLFE, H., CHESLER, D., KREGER, N., MCALPINE, W., STEFFA, M. & KLAUS, M. (1974) Maternal behavior one year after early and extended post-partum contact. *Dev. Med. Child Neurol. 16*, 172–179

LUBCHENCO, L.O., HANSMAN, C. & BOYD, E. (1966) Intrauterine growth in length and head circumference as estimated from live births at gestational ages from 26–42 weeks. *Pediatrics 37*, 403–408

ROTH, L.L. & ROSENBLATT, J.S. (1967) Changes in self-licking during pregnancy in the rat. *J. Comp. Physiol. Psychol 63*, 397–400

ROTH, L.L. & ROSENBLATT, J.S. (1968) Self-licking and mammary development during pregnancy in the rat. *J. Endocrinol. 42*, 363–378

WHITWORTH, N. (1972) Relationship between patterns of grooming, endocrine function and mammary gland development in the pregnant rat. Doctoral dissertation, Rutgers University, New Brunswick, N.J.

Olfaction in the development of social preferences in the human neonate

AIDAN MACFARLANE

Department of Experimental Psychology, Oxford

Abstract Olfactory perception in the human neonate has been largely ignored. The present experiments examine the possibility that neonates can use smell to locate a food source and that they can differentiate between their own mother and another mother on the basis of smell. Head-turning to breast pads was used in preference tests. Although the neonate did not appear to be able to use smell to localize a food source, significantly more babies spent more time turning towards their own mother's breast pad than towards a clean breast pad at five days of age. By six days of age babies were showing a differential response between their own mother's breast pad and another mother's breast pad, although this differentiation was not present at two days of age.

Much research has been devoted to visual and auditory perception in the human neonate, but little to olfactory perception. This may be because in the human neonate, unlike some animals, olfaction does not appear to be a dominant sense. In those animals in which olfaction does play a more dominant role—as in the guinea pig (Carter 1972), rats (Marr & Lilliston 1969), and spiny mouse (Porter & Etscorn 1974)—studies have shown that olfactory imprinting occurs to both the natural smell of the mother and to an artificial olfactory stimulus such as ethyl benzoate and acetophenone. Many of these studies have entailed long exposures of the animals to the training odours, which then could have been associated with the reinforcers of food and warmth. Rosenblatt (1972) also found that smell appeared to be an important cue used by young kittens in the identification of particular preferred nipples on the mothering cat.

That human neonates do show differential reactions to different smells has been shown by Engen *et al.* (1963), though these workers used asafoetida and anise oil as olfactory stimuli. They also found that infants in the first days of life could apparently turn away from unpleasant odours after some experience of them. Bower (1974, p. 19) concludes that the capacity for localizing the positions of olfactory sources is innate. My interest in olfaction in the human neonate arose from watching mothers breastfeed and noting that the babies often seemed to turn their heads towards the breast before any eye movement towards the breast had been noted, and before a rooting reflex had been elicited by the nipple or breast against the cheek. There could be several explanations for this: for instance the baby may become conditioned so that when its right side is held against the mother it turns its head to the right to obtain food and vice versa, or the child may be using auditory clues, or it may be sensitive to the heat of the breast; indeed any of these are possible. An alternative explanation is that the baby is using smell to localize the side of the food source. If the child can in fact do this, then head-turning towards the smell of the breast or breast milk would be reinforced from birth (in breast-fed babies) with food as the reward. However, I have also wondered whether the experience of the fetus *in utero* of the mother could be used by the child after delivery to distinguish familiar and novel in some modalities. It seemed possible that the infant might be born with the ability to distinguish between its own mother and another mother on the basis of smell. If this was not so, then perhaps it could learn the discrimination over the first few days of life. I have therefore done two experiments which go a little way towards answering these problems.

Papoušek (1967) has shown the effectiveness of conditioning head-turning by using appetite reinforcement, and as this might occur naturally—if the child can localize smell—I decided to use head turning as an indication of preference between two breast pads. In the first experiment one breast pad was clean and the other had been in contact with mother's breast for three to four hours; in the second experiment one breast pad had been in contact with the breast of the child's own mother, and the other had been in contact with the breast of another mother.

EXPERIMENT 1

Procedure

Breast-fed babies were tested in a uniformly lit, quiet laboratory in the Paediatric Department at the John Radcliffe Maternity Hospital. Breast-feeding mothers with clinically normal babies were contacted on the ward and those who agreed to take part in the study came to the laboratory with their babies three to four hours after a feed. The mothers were requested not to put lanolin on their nipples after the feed (some mothers with sore nipples had been advised by the hospital staff to rub lanolin into their nipples after feeds). Mothers were also requested to wear the standard hospital breast pads (gauze pads of 9.5 cm^2). One pad was removed and put on a balance by experimenter I.

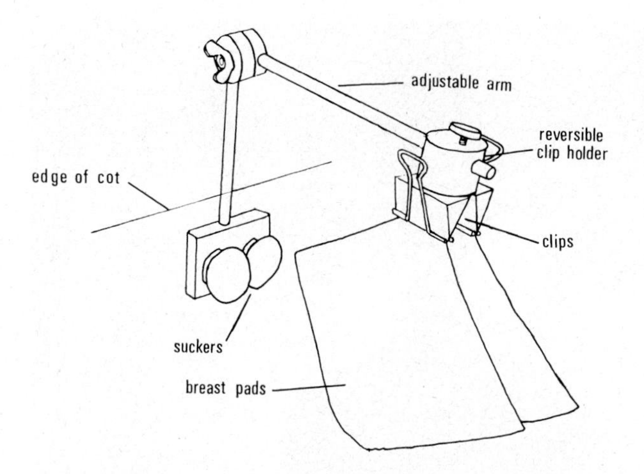

FIG. 1. Diagram showing adjustable arm with which breast pads could be lowered over the baby's face.

On the other side of the balance was a clean breast pad to which sterile water was added until both pads weighed the same. In fact most of the pads (18 out of 20) from the mothers were dry and it was not necessary to add water to the clean pad. Each pair of breast pads was then placed in clips mounted on a piece of Perspex in such a way that the pads hung side by side 1 cm apart, with the side of the mother's breast pad that had been against her breast hanging inwards. The piece of Perspex to which the clips were attached could be reversed so that the left pad hung on the right and vice versa. The Perspex was attached to the end of an adjustable arm secured to the top of the baby's cot (see Fig. 1).

For the experiment the baby was turned so that he was lying flat on his back. He was then played with until he reached an alert state (Prechtl state 4 or 5: Prechtl & Beintema 1964) by experimenter II, who held the baby's arms away from his mouth throughout the testing session. (Although experimenter II was theoretically ignorant of which side the mother's breast pad was on during this experiment, some bias may have occurred while the experimenter held the baby's hands, as a clean breast pad does not always look the same as a pad that has been in contact with a mother's breast for four hours.)

When the baby was ready, experimenter I lowered the adjustable arm attached to the cot so that the clips were 1 cm above the baby's nose and the pads hung down on each side, touching the baby's cheeks. The baby had to turn his head about 20 degrees from the midline for his nose to come into contact with the pad, and when his head was turned 45 degrees off the midline his nose was in the centre of the pad.

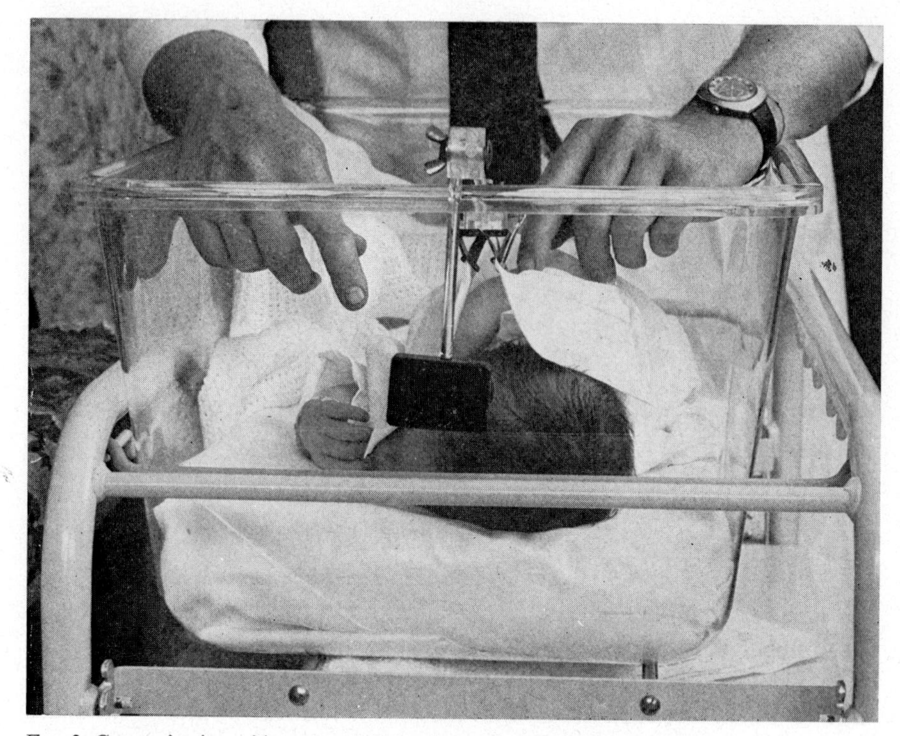

FIG. 2. Camera's view of breast pads being lowered over the baby's face.

Before each test session began, the baby's head was randomly turned 45 degrees into each pad by hand and then returned to the midline—care being taken not to elicit the rooting reflex with the fingers. Each baby was tested for two one-minute sessions, between which the pads were reversed so that the right pad hung on the left and the left hung on the right. This was to counteract any effects of laterality of head turning. The baby was videotaped throughout on a portable Sony AV 3400 with the camera mounted on a tripod three feet from the infant's head and along the baby's axis (the camera's view is shown in Fig. 2).

The videotapes were later analysed independently by two experimenters, a score being made of the total time within each minute spent turning towards each breast pad. A baby was judged to have turned towards a breast pad when his nose actually touched the pad and to be turning for all the time his nose was in contact with it. When a difference of more than one second arose between observers within a one-minute scoring session, the session was scored again. Interobserver reliability on the first scoring sessions was better than 90%. For each baby the scores for the two one-minute sessions were summed and a measure of the total time spent turning to own mother's and to the clean breast pad were obtained. Side of initial head turn (defined as the breast pad that the baby first touched with his nose in each session) was also recorded.

Calculations were made of:

(1) The percentage of the total time available (120 s) spent turned towards either breast pad.
(2) Time spent turned to the right as a percentage of (1). This was to see if the baby tended to turn his head significantly more often to one side than the other.
(3) Time spent turned to own mother's breast pad as a percentage of (1).
(4) The number of babies that turned more towards their own mother's breast pad than to the clean breast pad.
(5) The percentage of initial head turns of each session that were towards their own mother's breast pad.

Information was also recorded for the babies' gestation age, chronological age, sex, type of delivery, drugs used during labour, and drugs administered to mothers after delivery.

The sample

Twenty-three clinically normal babies were tested; three babies were dropped from the study, two because they were too drowsy and one who began the experiment screaming uncontrollably. Ten were male and ten female, all aged between two and seven days (mean 4.8 days, S.D. 1.44). Gestational age (calculated from last menstrual period) varied from 38 weeks to 42 weeks (mean 40 weeks).

Results (see Table 1)

If babies were indifferent to the two breast pads they should distribute their head-turning equally between them. However the mean time that the whole group spent turned to the mother's breast pad as a percentage of the total time that the baby spent turned to either breast pad was 70.9 % (S.D. 19) and 17 out of the 20 babies spent more time turned towards the mother's breast pad than to the clean pad (significant at $P < 0.001$ binomial test). This group of babies spent more than three-quarters of the time turned towards their own mother's breast pad. The distribution of initial head turns at the beginning of each session (40 sessions—two for each baby) was 21 (52 %) towards the mother's breast pad and 19 away. The amount of time spent turned towards the right was 52.9 % of the total time spent turning to either breast pad, which

TABLE 1

Experiment 1: clean breast pad compared with mother's breast pad ($N = 20$)

(1) Percentage of total time (120 s) spent turned to either breast pad	76.7%
(2) Time spent turning head to right as a percentage of (1)	52.9%
(3) Time spent turning head to mother's breast pad as percentage of (1)	70.9% (S.D. 19.4)
(4) Number of babies turning head more towards mother's breast pad than clean breast pad	17 out of 20 ($P < 0.001$ binomial)
(5) Number of sessions in which initial turn was toward stimulus side	21 out of 40

does not vary significantly from chance. The infants spent 76.7% of the total time available to them turning to one breast pad or the other. Thus we may conclude that a neonate is able to distinguish between the smell of a clean breast pad and a breast pad that has been in contact with mother's breast. We cannot yet conclude that he is able to distinguish between the smell of his own mother and another mother. To examine this possibility we conducted a second experiment.

EXPERIMENT 2

The equipment used was exactly the same as that in experiment 1. However this time two mothers at a time were brought with their babies to the laboratory and each removed one breast pad. Again, virtually all these breast pads were dry. The pads were placed in the clips so that the side that had been against the breast was hanging inwards, with a pad from one mother on one side and a pad from the other mother on the other side. The testing procedure was then exactly the same as in experiment 1, the person holding the baby being ignorant of which side the stimulus breast pad was on.

Testing was carried out on the second and sixth day after birth on one group of babies. The results of this experiment indicated the need to test an older group and the same experiment was carried out on a separate group of 8–10-day-old babies.

The sample

Forty-seven clinically normal babies delivered within two weeks of their expected date of delivery were tested on the second day after birth. Fifteen of these had to be removed from the test either because they went home before the sixth day or because they were too drowsy to test, and 32 babies were successfully tested on days two and six. Of the 33 babies tested at 8–10 days of age, one was omitted from the study because he was too sleepy.

Results

The total time spent turned to both breast pads (Table 2) increased from 72.3 % on the second day to 82.6 % on the sixth and 89.4 % at 8–10 days.

Total time spent turned to the right as a percentage of total time spent turned to either pad (Table 3) varied from 43.7 % to 53.4 %. The results did not differ significantly from chance for any of the age groups. Time spent turned towards their own mother's breast pad (Table 4) increased from 51.8 % (S.D. 29.6) at two days, to 60.3 % (S.D. 30.0) at six days, and 68.2 (S.D. 23.6) at 8–10 days. A Mann-Whitney U test showed that the eldest babies spent a significantly greater proportion of the time turned to their own mother's

TABLE 2

Experiment 2: Percentage of total time (120 s) spent turned to either breast pad ($N=32$)

Age (days)	*% total time*
2	72.3
6	82.6
8–10	89.4

TABLE 3

Experiment 2: time spent turning head to right as percentage of total time spent turned to either breast pad ($N=32$)

Age (days)	*% total time*
2	43.7
6	53.4
8–10	46.2

TABLE 4

Experiment 2: time spent turning head to own mother's breast pad as a percentage of total time spent turned to either breast pad ($N=32$)

Age (days)	*% total time*
2	51.8 (S.D. 29.6)
6	60.3 (S.D. 30.0)
8–10	68.2 (S.D. 23.6)

TABLE 5

Experiment 2: number of babies turning more toward their own mother's breast pad than other mother's breast pad ($N=32$)

Age (days)	*No./total no.*
2	17/32 (N.S.)
6	22/32 ($P<0.02$ binomial)
8–10	25/32 ($P<0.001$ binomial)

N.S.: not significant

breast pad than did the youngest group. At two days 17 out of 32 babies were turning more towards their own mother's breast pad (not significant binomial), at six days 22 out of the 32 were turning more towards their mother's breast pad ($P<0.02$ binomial) and by 8–10 days the figure had increased to 25 out of 32 ($P<0.001$ binomial). In this last group the 25 spent a mean of 79% of the total time turning to their own mother's breast pad.

Drugs given during labour, drugs administered to mothers after delivery, sex of the infant, and side of initial presentation of own mother's pad, were not found to be significant variables on an analysis of variance.

Two observations of interest were also noted during the testing sessions in both experiments. First, the usual pattern of head-turning between the pads was for the baby initially to turn backwards and forwards between the two, and then settle for an extended time on one—often mouthing and lifting the head of the mattress. After this period with the nose in one breast pad there were signs of increasing frustration (increased activity and crying), followed by a quick head turn to the other pad and back again. Secondly we noted (often by the smell) that many babies defaecated during the period of testing, and as this is a general observation we wondered whether smell released this behaviour—although it may simply be a function of the time from the previous feed.

DISCUSSION

The results of the first experiment suggest that the infant is capable of distinguishing breast pad only from breast pad plus mother's smell—and if head-turning is an indicator of preference, then the baby prefers the smell of mother's breast. However, as the initial turns were not significantly more towards the stimulus side it would appear that, in the conditions of this experiment, the baby was unable to use smell to locate the pad. One possible explanation is that the smell of the breast pad may not be strong enough to reach the baby's olfactory area when his nose is in the midline and he may not be able to smell it until he turns his nose to touch a pad. A second explanation is that although the baby may be able to smell the pad when his nose is in the midline and a smell gradient is present, he cannot use the gradient for discriminating between right and left and for turning his head towards the smell. That the baby can make this right/left discrimination using other senses, such as sound, has already been documented (Wertheimer 1961). If the baby could smell the breast or breast milk and was conditioned to expect food to follow smell on a contingent basis but was unable to locate the source, then one might expect to see the baby increase his head-turning in both directions so that he could locate the nipple. In our experiment it was impossible to test this as the breast pads were against the babies' cheeks and therefore tended to initiate a rooting reflex which could itself be responsible for the initiation of head-turning. This then might be a third explanation for the baby's failure to locate the source of the smell—the rooting reflex which was equal on both sides may overcome any propensity to head-turning to smell during the initial phase. A final possibility is that the baby can locate smells such as breast smell or clean breast pads and that he explores each. Preferences may operate only after turning, not before.

The second experiment was designed to test whether babies could distinguish between the smell of their own mother and the smell of a strange mother, shortly after birth, or whether they were able to learn this capacity during the first few days after birth. When head-turning is used as an indicator of discrimination, it appears that whereas babies aged two days cannot make the discrimination, by 8–10 days they can. However it can be argued that the babies are capable of making the discrimination at birth but that they don't demonstrate it by head-turning.

The experiment therefore neither proves nor disproves the hypothesis that experience *in utero* may influence what is familiar and what is novel—*ex utero*. What it does show is that babies can make a differential response to mother versus stranger on the basis of smell and that this response is present by 10 days of age.

However, certain hospital practices are likely to produce negative results in such experiments. For example, mothers are encouraged to wash their breasts before each feed, lanolin is frequently applied to the nipples to keep them soft, and mothers use deodorants. Experimentally, the first two are the worst. Lanolin has a fairly definite smell, and work by Marr & Lilliston (1969) indicates that stronger artificial smells were preferred by infant rats to their mother's natural smell if the infant rats had previously been exposed to both. Another question is whether the baby is smelling or tasting, or whether there is any value in discriminating between the two. Smell in adults is far more discriminative than taste, and although the babies in our experiment did attempt, and succeed, in bringing their lips into contact with the pad, it seems unlikely that any baby actually tasted with his tongue anything that was on the pad—which was usually dry anyhow. If a baby is using his sense of smell, what is he smelling? Is it the breast milk, the breast itself, or a combination of the two? Differential responses by the neonate have been found to different types of feed (see Johnson & Salisbury, this volume) but so far there is no clear evidence that infants respond differently to their own mother's breast milk and another mother's breast milk, although this may yet be found. That people have distinctive odours is an undisputed fact, and much of this smell is from the unusual lipids of sebum being acted on by the skin microflora. Nicolaides (1974) points out that because of the huge numbers of fatty acids that the skin can make, and because variations in enzyme concentrations, pH, body temperature, or cofactor concentrations can easily and markedly affect the final concentrations of each fatty acid, each individual has a chemical signature. It may be this signature that the baby is discriminating by the 10th day. It is interesting to speculate that this chemical signature may be influenced by genetic factors and that relatives may have related smells. And if this is so would a baby who had learnt to discriminate its own mother's smell show more preference for one of her close relatives than for a stranger?

However it is not only on the basis of smell that the infant can discriminate between his usual caretaker and a stranger. Carpenter (1974) found that the infant had clearly differentiated responses to mother's face versus stranger's face by two weeks of age. Sander (1969) also found that when one caretaker was housed with an infant on a self-demanding feeding schedule from the first 24 hours of its life, substitution of an unfamiliar though highly experienced caretaker when the baby was 10 days old was accompanied by certain very specific disturbances in neonatal regulation. It would therefore appear that by 10 to 14 days the child is able, using several senses, to show fine discrimination between his usual caretaker and a stranger, that in everyday life the infant is probably using all of these senses simultaneously to distinguish the familiar from the novel and that the more changes of caretaker there are at this period, the more neonatal behaviour will be upset. It may be that after birth (or perhaps before if mother and postnatal caretaker are the same person) the child develops an appreciation of its caretaker, which gradually becomes more specific the more the child is exposed to that person. Bateson (1973), referring to chicks, said 'It would be more appropriate to liken the development of social preferences to the painting of a portrait in which the broad outlines are sketched in first and the details gradually filled in afterwards'. However, in the same article Bateson points out the dangers of correlating animal work with human work, and it would seem that, unlike what is seen in chicks, if this process occurs in the human neonate it takes place over an extended period of time, and if it is interrupted it does not lead to immediate and severe perturbation. In a species where high infant and maternal mortality has existed until recently this is probably advantageous—for if the mother died in the puerperal period it would be disadvantageous to the survival of the child if it could not accept an alternative caretaker easily (Macfarlane 1974).

ACKNOWLEDGEMENTS

I am very grateful to Ian Barnes for his help with the experiments, to Ann Pledger for her help with the mothers and babies, and to the John Radcliffe Maternity Hospital, Oxford for providing testing facilities.

This work was supported by NIMH Grant No. MH 12623-07 and by the Oxford Regional Health Authority.

References

BATESON, P.P.G. (1973) The imprinting of birds, in *Ethology and Development* (Barnett, S.A., ed.) (Clinics in Developmental Medicine No. 47), Spastics International Medical Publications/Heinemann, London

BOWER, T. (1974) *Development in Infancy*, Freeman, San Francisco

CARPENTER, G. (1974) Mother's face and the newborn. *New Sci.*, 21st March, 742–744

CARTER, C.S. (1972) The effects of olfactory experience on the behaviour of the guinea pig *(Cavia parcellus)*. *Anim. Behav. 20*, 54–60

ENGEN, T., LIPSITT, L.P. & KAY, H. (1963) Olfactory responses and adaptation in human neonate. *J. Comp. Physiol. Psychol. 56*, 73–77

MACFARLANE, J.A. (1974) 'If a smile is so important...' *New Sci. 62*, No. 895, 164–166

MARR, J. & LILLISTON, L.G. (1969) Social attachment in rats by odor and age. *Behaviour 33*, 277–282

NICOLAIDES, N. (1974) Skin lipids: their biochemical uniqueness. *Science (Wash. D.C.) 186*, 19–27

PAPOUŠEK, H. (1967) Conditioning during early postnatal development, in *Behavior in Infancy and Early Childhood* (Brackbill, Y. & Thompson, G.G., eds.), Free Press, New York

PORTER, R.H. & ETSCORN, F.O. (1974) Olfactory imprinting resulting from brief exposure in *Acomys cahirinus*. *Nature (Lond.) 250*, 732–733

PRECHTL, H. & BEINTEMA, D. (1964) *The Neurological Examination of the Full Term Infant* (Clinics in Developmental Medicine No. 12), Spastics International Medical Publications/ Heinemann, London

ROSENBLATT, J.S. (1972) Learning in newborn kittens. *Sci. Am. 227*, 18–25

SANDER, L.W. (1969) Regulation and organization in the early infant–caretaker system, in *Brain and Early Behavior* (Robinson, R.J., ed.) Academic Press, New York, London

WERTHEIMER, M. (1961) Psychomotor coordination of auditory-visual space at birth. *Science (Wash. D.C.) 134*, 1692

Discussion

Salisbury: Once you had seen a positive recognition response in a baby aged 8–10 days, did you test the same baby again to see whether the response was the same?

Macfarlane: No.

Salisbury: Could you yourself smell the difference between the breast pads?

Macfarlane: No.

Curtis-Jenkins: Did you test babies of mothers who were not breast-feeding?

Macfarlane: No, but I would like to test whether babies who are bottle-fed prefer the smell of plastic and rubber.

Hinde: It would be interesting to put the mother's breast pad straight in front of the infant and see whether its head turns less. What you see in your experiments could be a straight kinesis, with movement reduced in the presence of the stimulus.

Macfarlane: Do you mean that the preference would only be shown after the baby has turned to both breast pads?

Hinde: No, the baby might stop turning when he got the smell he liked, so the nice smell would produce a decrease in turning.

Rosenblatt: Olfaction is peculiar in that it hasn't got a bilateral distribution with a space in between, like seeing and hearing. Infants and almost all mammals seem to compensate for that by swinging the head from side to side. By their movements they create asymmetry: at one end of the swing they receive the odour and at the other they don't.

Macfarlane: These infants initially turn their heads from side to side in a searching pattern before they settle on one pad.

Salisbury: The fact that you don't find any significance in the head turn at about two to four days of age may just indicate that the breast pads don't smell at all, because mothers may not be leaking any milk. It may tell you nothing about the baby's ability to discriminate between smells.

Macfarlane: I am not claiming that 'head-turning' results at two days mean that they cannot make the discrimination but that by ten days they can discriminate. I agree that it is more likely that the smell is not reaching the infants at the early age than that they are not making the discrimination.

Bell: The threshold differences Lipsitt *et al.* (1963) have reported for olfaction may be contributing to your results. For the first five days threshold drops steadily. The newborns they studied were initially relatively insensitive even to such things as asafoetida, but they became increasingly sensitive by the fifth day.

Brazelton: L.P. Lipsitt (personal communication, 1973) finds that they are sensitive to taste changes in the first 24 hours.

Bell: There is some sensitivity even on the first day but I was less interested in how early sensitivity was shown than in the change during the newborn period. Generally there is a gradient, which shows a steady increase in sensitivity each day.

Klaus: Can the mother identify her infant by odour? J. Lind has shown that mothers can identify their own infant's cry in the first days of life.

Macfarlane: It would be an easy experiment to do. We could blindfold a mother and get her to distinguish which of two babies is her own when both are placed under her nose.

Klaus: The baby does a lot of licking when he is first put to the breast. Were babies who had been with their mothers in the first few minutes of life quicker to select their mother's pad?

Macfarlane: It would be interesting to look at that. The other thing we should do is to see whether any other smell on the mother was more effective than the breast.

Klaus: The babies may become hooked on perfume.

Macfarlane: That is the trouble. And once we told the mothers that we were going to do a study on whether the babies could smell them, the mothers were apt to rush off and put deodorants on.

Papoušek: We must remember that the nasal passages are blocked with amniotic fluid before birth and in neonates. Prenatal stimulation would be trigeminal rather than olfactory. Similar to what happens in the auditory system, about which we know more, the slow disappearance of obstructing amniotic fluid can cause differences in thresholds and in the discrimination capacities during the first day of life.

Macfarlane: In some English obstetric units the nasal passages are sucked out after delivery. I was thinking of also testing whether babies could differentiate between their own mother's amniotic fluid and another mother's fluid on the basis of smell.

Dreyfus-Brisac: Were the babies hungry when you tested them, Dr Macfarlane?

Macfarlane: They were tested four hours after the previous feed, at just about the time they were due to be fed again. As the breast pads hung down each side of the face, the rooting reflex must have been initiated. This may play a part in the non-localization, or lack of initial turn towards the smell. Since the baby could smell, maybe the rooting reflex overcame the impulse to turn towards the mother's breast pad.

Rosenblatt: There is evidence that kittens can discriminate between the odours that define the home and which we think come primarily from the mother. They know where their home is within the cage by about three days of age. By about four or five days of age, they can move from outside the home back to the home, largely by olfaction. If they are placed in the cage of another mother whose own kittens of the same age can successfully find their way, the kittens from the other litter cannot find their way to the new litter. They begin to orient to the new litter after a day or two but they forget the odours of their original litter (Freeman, unpublished work, 1974). Clearly by four days kittens are olfactorily quite sophisticated.

Macfarlane: I have heard of newborn babies who were left at their mothers' feet immediately after delivery rather than being picked up and who then found their own way up to the breasts. I don't know whether this has been substantiated but perhaps it was the smell that led them there.

Rosenblatt: In several small mammals orientation to the mother is based on thermal stimulation. Certainly in the rat, the young orient to siblings on the basis of thermal stimulation for about the first eight or nine days. Then they begin to switch over and orient on the basis of olfactory characteristics which were previously paired with the thermal stimulation; so the olfactory stimulation becomes effective because it was paired with the thermal stimulation. The earliest responses of the kitten to the environment and to the mother are probably also on a thermal basis. The mother has a large thermal gradient with the highest temperatures at the nipples (Freeman, unpublished work, 1974). All the thermal gradients lead to the nipples, and all the kitten has to do is follow these to arrive at the nipples. The initial orientation seems to be thermal and then it gradually shifts over to olfactory.

Macfarlane: An infrared photograph of the human mother would probably show the breast as being warmer than the rest of the body.

Curtis-Jenkins: The mouth shows the same temperature as the breasts, on infrared photographs.

Hinde: Thermal gradients ought to be more important in animals living in nests than in animals where mother and infant have continuous contact, like man.

Brazelton: I have found that Dr Macfarlane's findings work clinically. Mothers tell me that when they are breast-feeding it becomes difficult to get the baby to take a bottle from them unless they introduce the bottle by the second or third week. They attribute this to his preference for the smell of her milk as well as its taste. I already knew that if a baby of four to five weeks was taking a bottle from the father, the baby would stop and would not go back to the bottle if he or she heard the mother's voice in the distance. But mothers say that the baby is responding to all of the stimuli around the feeding, and they have insisted that his capacity to smell their milk will also stop the baby feeding from a bottle. We watched what happens when the mother gets close enough for olfaction to become a competing stimulus when the father is holding the baby, comparing the effect with that produced by another female (who was not lactating). By eight weeks, olfaction stops the baby from going back to the bottle even if he can't see the mother. He alerts to the approach of anyone but goes back to the bottle if the person is not his mother.

Reference

LIPSITT, L. P., ENGEN, T. & KAYE, H. (1963) Developmental changes in the olfactory threshold of the neonate. *Child Dev. 34*, 371–376

Breathing and sucking during feeding in the newborn

P. JOHNSON and D. M. SALISBURY*

*The Nuffield Institute for Medical Research and *Department of Paediatrics, University of Oxford*

Abstract Eighteen normal full-time infants aged from 1–10 days were fed both normal saline and distilled water from a conventional feeding bottle. Fifty-four sets of observations were made when 44 infants were fed both cow's milk (Half Cream Cow & Gate) and expressed human milk. During feeding, measurements were made of breathing, sucking, and the flow of milk from a feeding bottle which incorporated an electromagnetic flowmeter transducer. Integration of the flow of milk measured the volume of milk swallowed by the baby. The results suggest that the patterns of feeding and breathing differ in some infants when different fluids are given to them.

If water is introduced into the upper airways of the newborn lamb, calf or rhesus monkey, breathing is arrested and usually, but not always, swallowing movements are induced (Johnson *et al.* 1972). This effect is due to stimulation of sensory receptors on the arytenoid processes and over the laryngeal surface of the epiglottis. It is abolished by bilateral section of the superior laryngeal nerves. Swallowing usually terminates the apnoea by removing the fluid from the neighbourhood of the sensory receptors. Otherwise the apnoea may end spontaneously or may continue for a long time, with or without intermittent gasping. If the apnoea is prolonged, the liquid may have to be removed from the upper airways and artificial ventilation carried out before breathing can be restored.

The sensory units have the characteristics of 'water receptors', a specialized form of taste receptor (Storey & Johnson 1975). Water, cow's milk, glucose (5 or 20% w/v) or 0.01 M-HCl solution induce apnoea when they are applied to the entry of the larynx in a lamb, while normal saline (0.9% w/v), amniotic fluid or sheep's milk do not.

We have therefore studied newborn human infants to determine whether changes in their pattern of breathing and swallowing during sucking suggest that they too can discriminate between water and saline solutions, or between cow's milk and human milk.

METHODS

Normal full-time infants were fed with sterile solutions, warmed to 37° C, from interchangeable bottles containing either normal saline or water, with a sterilized teat. A vinyl catheter (Portex No. 2) was attached to the infant's forehead and nose so that the tip of the catheter was in the air stream. The respired carbon dioxide (%) was measured continuously at a sampling rate of 400 ml/min (Beckman Medical Gas Analyzer LB1). An air-filled balloon of silicone rubber ($1 \times 1 \times 0.30$ cm) was fixed with adhesive tape to the skin of the infant's neck just above the larynx. Each elevation of the larynx caused a rise in pressure in the balloon which was detected by an AC-coupled crystal transducer (Cambridge Instruments). The heart rate was measured from the electrocardiogram (ECG). All the infants were observed about 30 minutes before their feed was due, at a time when they were awake and alert. They were lightly swaddled and held by an assistant in a normal feeding position.

We also compared the effects on breathing and swallowing of feeding infants with a preparation of cow's milk (Half Cream Cow & Gate milk—pre-packed Babymilk 1) or expressed human breast milk.

A feeding bottle was constructed with an electromagnetic flowmeter transducer (Clark & Wyatt 1969) between the reservoir and the teat (Fig. 1). A rubber valve in the reservoir opened when milk was withdrawn by the infant and so bubbles did not pass up through the transducer during feeding. The flow measurement was integrated to give the volume of milk swallowed. The infants were fed with each milk for at least one minute and they were fed with both kinds of milk in different sequence.

RESULTS

Eighteen infants, of which two had not been previously fed, were given saline solution or water. The gestational ages at birth (39.8 weeks $\pm$ 1.62 S.D.) and the weights (3316 g $\pm$ 565 S.D.) were within normal limits. All infants were offered water, which was always swallowed and never inhaled. Eight infants inhaled saline during feeding. This was recognized by the sound of fluid in the airway and the saline feed was immediately stopped. None of these infants had any residual signs when examined by auscultation.

Table 1 shows that the risk of inhalation of saline seemed greatest on the first and second days of life.

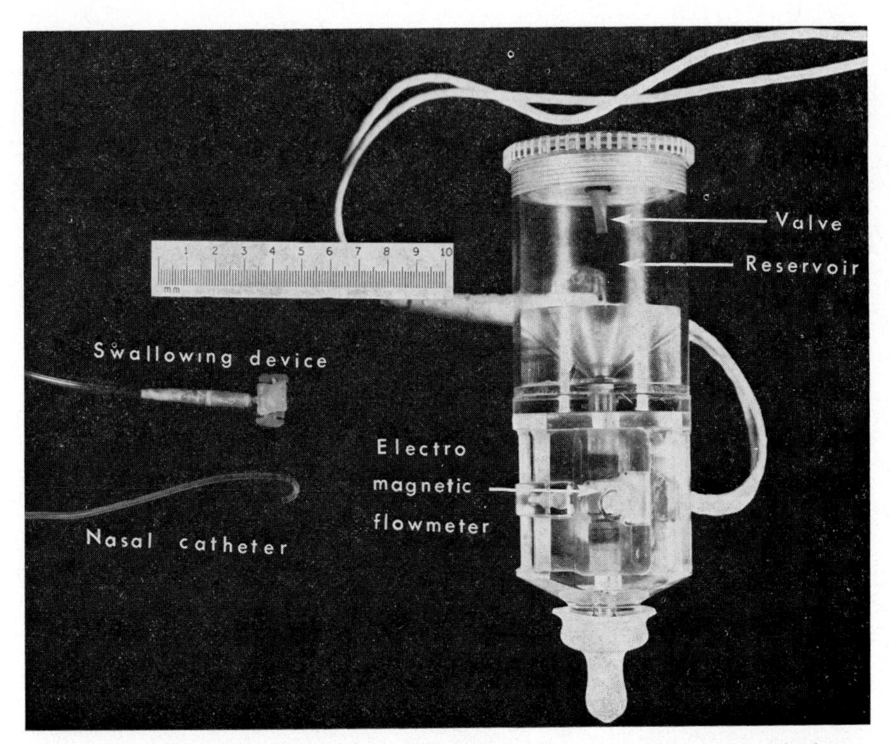

FIG. 1. The infant feeding bottle used in these studies is shown here with a standard teat. The milk reservoir has a detachable top in which there is a rubber valve. The electromagnetic flowmeter transducer is positioned between the reservoir and the teat. A nasal catheter and the device for measuring laryngeal movements are also shown.

Fifty-four sets of observations were made on 44 infants (25 female and 19 male) fed with expressed breast milk or the preparation of cow's milk. The infants were of normal gestational age (39.5 weeks $\pm$ 1.08 S.D.) and birth weight (3347 g $\pm$ 446 S.D.). They were fed with each milk for one minute or more. The number of breaths and sucks and the intervals between breaths and between sucks were counted from comparable periods of the records taken during feeding with each milk. Table 2 shows the total number of breaths and sucks

TABLE 1

Number of infants inhaling saline, out of total number, at different ages

Age (days)	*Inhalation of saline*
1– 2	7/10
6–15	0/7
18	1/1

TABLE 2

Frequency distribution of intervals between sucks or between breaths of infants during feeding with breast milk or cow's milk.

Interval length (seconds)	*Numbers of sucks*		*Numbers of breaths*	
	Breast milk	*Cow's milk*	*Breast milk*	*Cow's milk*
<0.5	115	44	71	17
0.5 < 1	2676	2651	1372	942
1 < 1.5	563	775	702	563
1.5 < 2	70	45	310	365
2 < 2.5	22	25	123	153
2.5 < 3	19	10	39	57
3 < 4	25	9	52	53
4 < 5	14	13	17	25
5 < 6	8	4	11	18
6 < 7	6	1	3	5
7 < 8	3	0	3	3
8 < 9	6	1	0	1
9 < 10	2	0	2	5
>10	9	1	8	14
Total	3538	3579	2713	2221

during feeding with each milk. The frequency distribution of the time intervais between breaths and sucks is also shown.

Table 2 shows that the total number of sucks is the same during feeding with each milk. Most of the intervals between sucks last less than 1.5 s and the distribution of these intervals is different during sucking with each milk. There are more very short intervals, of less than 0.5 s, during feeding with breast milk, and more intervals of 1.5 s between sucks during feeding with cow's milk. This table of the frequency distribution also shows that there are more intervals of longer duration between sucks during feeding with breast milk.

Table 2 also shows that the total number of breaths is reduced during feeding with cow's milk. There are more long intervals between breaths during feeding with cow's milk and more short intervals between breaths during feeding with breast milk.

The numbers of breaths during comparable periods of feeding have been expressed as breaths/min for each pair of observations. Fig. 2 shows the relationship between the number of breaths/min during feeding with each milk. The regression coefficient of this relationship is significantly different ($D = 5.36$, $P < 0.001$) from a regression coefficient of 1. Thus, the frequency of breathlng is reduced during feeding with cow's milk.

The total number of sucks is the same with breast milk or cow's milk but the frequency distribution is different.

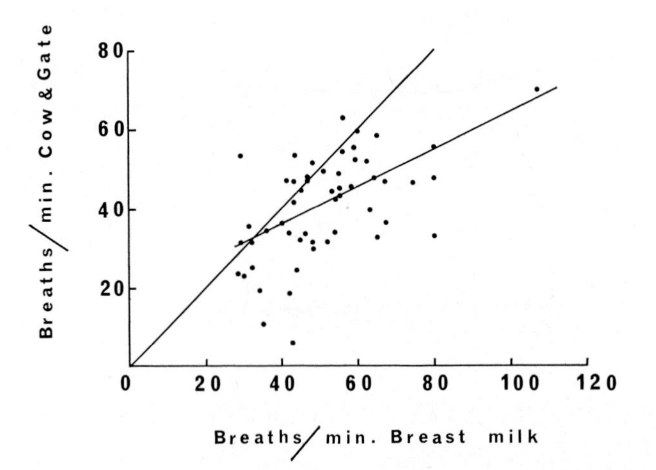

FIG. 2. The relationship of breathing frequencies (breaths/min) during feeding with either breast milk or cow's milk. The regression coefficient of this relationship is significantly different to the regression coefficient of the line of equality (D = 5.36, $P = <0.001$). Breathing frequency is slower during feeding with cow's milk than with breast milk.

Table 2 shows the frequency distribution of sucking and breathing intervals with breast milk or cow's milk in *all* the babies studied. However, whereas the pattern of sucking and breathing during feeding with cow's milk was the same in all the infants studied, the patterns of those feeding on breast milk showed considerable variation. At one extreme, the records of sucking and breathing during feeding with either milk are indistinguishable; the other extreme is illustrated by Figs. 3 and 4, recorded from one infant. Fig. 3 shows that during feeding with cow's milk the infant was sucking continuously and breathing was irregular; the heart rate fell. Fig. 4 shows that when the same infant was drinking breast milk there were pauses between episodes of sucking. This difference in sucking pattern in babies drinking breast milk is reflected in the different frequency distributions of sucking intervals shown in Table 2. Breathing was more regular during feeding with breast milk than the breathing recorded in Fig. 3, and the heart rate remained steady. Breathing of this regularity was never seen during feeding with cow's milk.

The infants who breathed more regularly during feeding with breast milk were not obviously different to the others. Their postnatal ages, sex, gestational ages, birth weights, types of feeding and types of delivery all matched, and their mothers received the same analgesics during labour.

In 10 infants, sucking was observed by recording movements of the larynx during breast-feeding. The pattern of sucking was of short episodes and pauses in eight of these infants; the other two infants sucked continuously for at

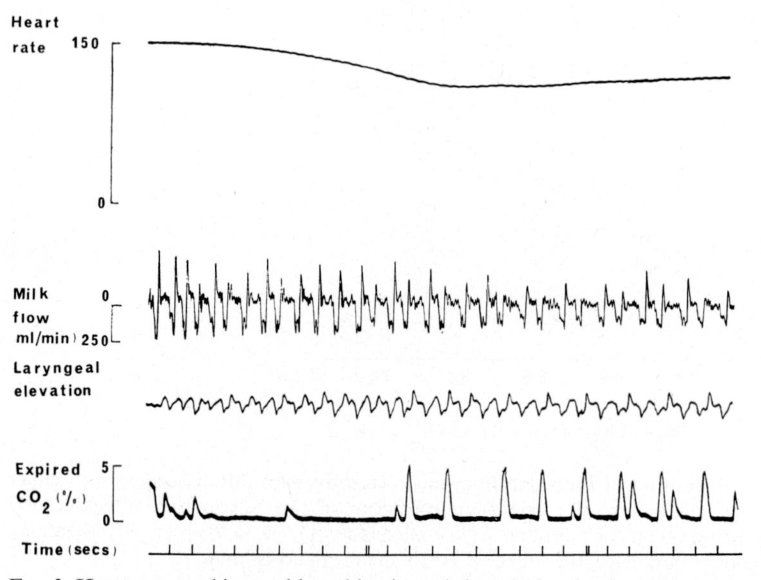

FIG. 3. Heart rate, sucking and breathing in an infant during feeding with cow's milk.

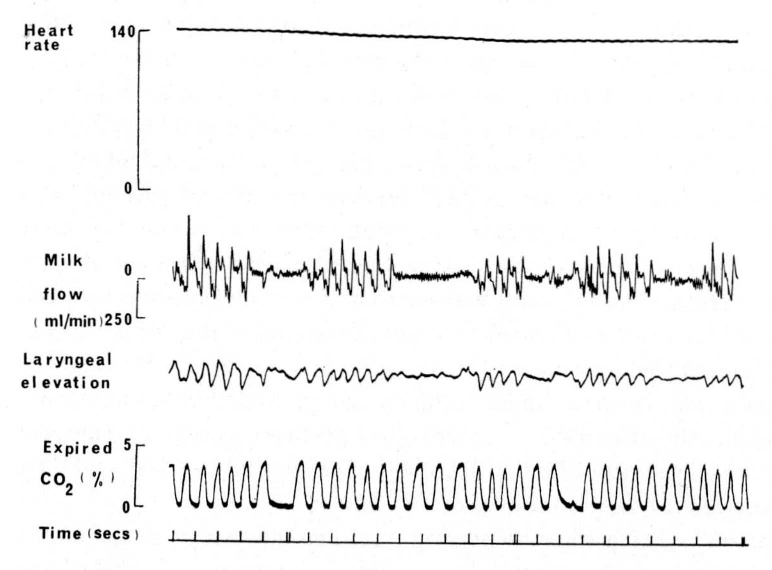

FIG. 4. Heart rate, sucking and breathing in the same infant as in Fig. 3, during feeding with breast milk.

least one minute. Observations were made on a further eight infants while they were sucking on a teat with no hole. The pattern of sucking was always of short episodes of sucking with pauses between episodes. The mean sucking frequency during 36 episodes was 110/min (± 18.6 S.D.) compared with 83/min (± 13.8 S.D.) during breast-feeding. This pattern of sucking episodes and pauses persisted in some infants when they were given breast milk from a bottle but was not seen in infants given cow's milk.

The volume of milk obtained at each suck during bottle-feeding has been calculated by dividing the integrated flow by the number of sucks when feeding was well established. This was 0.6 ml/suck ± 0.17 S.D.

DISCUSSION

The previous observations on newborn lambs already mentioned showed that the presence of water on receptors at the entrance to the larynx caused apnoea and swallowing, whilst the presence of saline did not. It was noted that prolonged apnoea was most easily induced in the newborn and became less prolonged with increasing age. Our results showed that newborn human infants swallow water and do not inhale it. However, saline solution (0.9% w/v) may be inhaled in the immediate newborn period. In 1932, Jensen recorded the patterns of sucking when infants were fed on saline solutions and water. Three of these records indicate that coughing occurred while infants were drinking saline solutions (0.9% w/v). This may have been caused by the inhalation of saline. However, coughing was not reported during feeding with water.

Previous studies of infant feeding have usually relied on measurements of sucking pressure or laryngeal movement. Although sucking causes a negative intra-oral pressure and elevation of the larynx, each suck is not necessarily associated with a nutritive swallow (G. Ardran, unpublished data). It is only the measurement of the net flow of milk that identifies which sucks are associated with the withdrawal of milk from the bottle. During feeding from a conventional bottle, a negative pressure is generated above the milk. In the feeding bottle used in these studies, a valve was inserted into the reservoir in order to prevent the development of a negative pressure and thus minimize the retrograde passage of air through the teat that occurs with each suck. The electromagnetic flowmeter then provides a faithful measurement of milk flow. Thus a coincident benefit of this technical modification of the feeding bottle is an appreciable reduction in the variation in the supply of milk. It therefore seems reasonable to assume that the differences in sucking behaviour were largely due to differences in the composition of the milks being fed. The mean volume of milk obtained per suck was observed to be 0.6 ml, the same as that calculated by

Süsswein in 1905 during his observations on breast-feeding. He had also noted more pauses between episodes of sucking during breast-feeding than during bottle-feeding.

The pattern of sucking during breast-feeding and during non-nutritive sucking in the human has been described by Luther *et al.* (1974) and Levin & Kaye (1964). Wolff (1968) in his studies on infant sucking suggests that it is only the human infant that exhibits this characteristic burst–pause pattern of sucking and that this only occurs during non-nutritive sucking either when an infant is awake with a blind teat in the mouth or asleep with no teat. In Wolff's studies the composition of fluid in the milk reservoir was changed, and its flow rate, but apparently he did not investigate the effects of milk of the same species. In our study, the episodic pattern of sucking persisted in some infants during feeding with human breast milk but did not persist during feeding with artificial milk. It would seem, then, that it is the nature of the fluid being sucked, and not the use of this feeding bottle, which modifies sucking behaviour.

The studies on breathing during feeding in infancy (Ardran *et al.* 1958; Barrie 1968; Russell & Feather 1970) have the same limitations as those on the pattern of sucking, as comparisons were not made during feeding with different milks. A deficiency of the present study is that the expressed breast milk used was not from the same mother. Thus the chemical composition (Hytten 1954) and the taste may have varied considerably. However, from Luther's observations it would seem that most infants suck in an episodic pattern from the breast and this rhythm is not influenced by the administration of oxytocic agents to the mother.

It is by no means certain that the chemo-sensory pathways which have been described in the lamb are involved during sucking in the human newborn. This is suggested at least partly by the fact that saline is aspirated into the lower airways during sucking. However, the episodic sucking pattern and regular breathing is not disturbed unless the baby coughs. It may be significant that extralingual taste buds have been observed to be concentrated in the epithelium of the additus to the larynx in both lamb and human newborns (Lalonde & Eglitis 1961, and our own observations). It would seem reasonable to conclude that one or more chemo-sensory afferent pathways exist in the upper airway of the human, the specific stimulation of which during feeding can modify sucking and breathing patterns. Whether the modifications of these patterns, as during feeding with artificial milk, have any subsequent influence on neurological development, particularly the neuroregulation of breathing, remains to be seen. It is for example currently thought that the sudden infant death syndrome (SIDS) may represent a failure of the regulation of breathing during a critical stage of maturation.

The interrelationship between sucking, swallowing and breathing during development is a complex one. The successful integration of these reflex events is not only essential to survival in infancy but may well provide a measure of development and well-being, when further elucidated. The value of assessing the effects of a natural 'challenge' to respiration, such as feeding, during development requires further observation.

Summary

An upper airway reflex mechanism has been previously described through which water and milk from different species may cause apnoea and stimulate swallowing. Saline, and milk from the same species, do not have this effect. The present results show that inhalation of saline into the airway may occur frequently in the human neonate in the first 48 hours of life. Water, however, was not inhaled. Different patterns of sucking and breathing have been demonstrated in newborn infants, depending on whether they were drinking artificial milk or human milk. The frequency of breathing during feeding with a cow's milk preparation was slower than the frequency during feeding with human milk. The nature and possible significance of these reflex events are discussed.

ACKNOWLEDGEMENTS

This work was carried out with the help of grants from the Cot Death Foundation (P.J.), the Spastics Foundation, and the Sir William Coxon Trust Fund (D.M.S.). Dr D. Wyatt of the Nuffield Institute for Medical Research designed and constructed the feeding bottle and the electromagnetic flowmeter. Miss A. Raines (supported by the Nuffield Foundation) provided valuable technical assistance. The advice and help of Professor G.S. Dawes and Professor J.P.M. Tizard is gratefully acknowledged.

References

Ardran, G.M., Kemp, F.H. & Lind, J. (1958) A cineradiographic study of bottle feeding. *Br. J. Radiol. 31*, 11–22

Barrie, H. (1968) Effect of feeding on gastric and oesophageal pressures in the newborn. *Lancet 2*, 1158–1160

Clark, D.M. & Wyatt, D.G. (1969) An improved perivascular electromagnetic flowmeter. *Med. Electron. Biol. Eng. 7*, 185–190

Hytten, F. (1954) Studies in human lactation. *Br. Med. J.* 176–182

Jensen, K. (1932) Differential reaction to taste and temperature stimuli in newborn infants. *Genet. Psychol. Monogr., 12*, 361–479

Johnson, P., Robinson, J.M. & Salisbury, D.M. (1972) in *Sir Joseph Barcroft Centenary Symposium on Foetal and Neonatal Physiology* (Comline, K.S. *et al.*, eds.) pp. 217–221, Cambridge University Press, London

Lalonde, E.R. & Eglitis, J.A. (1961) Number and distribution of taste buds on the epiglottis, pharynx, larynx, soft palate and uvula in a human newborn. *Anat. Rec. 140*, 91–93

LEVIN, G.R. & KAYE, H. (1964) Non-nutritive sucking by human neonates. *Child Dev. 35*, 749–758

LUTHER, E.C., ARBALLO, J.C., SALA, N.L. & CORDERO FUNES, J.C. (1974) Suckling pressure in humans: relationship to oxytocin-reproducing reflex milk ejection. *J. Appl. Physiol. 36*, 350–353

RUSSELL, G. & FEATHER, E.A. (1970) Effects of feeding on respiratory mechanics of healthy newborn infants. *Arch. Dis. Child. 45*, 325–327.

STOREY, A. & JOHNSON, P. (1975) Laryngeal water receptors initiating apnoea in the lamb. *Exp. Neurol. 47*, 42–55

SÜSSWEIN, J. (1905) Zur Physiologie des Trinkens beim Säugling. *Arch. Kinderheilkd. 40*, 68–80

WOLFF, P.H. (1968) Sucking patterns of infant mammals. *Brain Behav. Evol. 1*, 354–367

Discussion

Dreyfus-Brisac: What happens to heart rate during sucking in your observations?

Salisbury: I do not have enough observations of heart rate during feeding to make any feature of that. I found it difficult to get accurate and continuous records of heart rate while infants were being fed while held in an assistant's arms. There is a lot of interference and the records are poor.

Dreyfus-Brisac: Nobody understands the syndrome of sudden infant death and the data obtained in studies dealing with this problem are not very clear. Your studies could shed some light on it or lead to a new approach.

Salisbury: Our observations were made during feeding, and the circumstances surrounding the syndrome of sudden infant death are rather different. Our studies of animals where prolonged apnoea and death occurred are perhaps more relevant than the observations on the human infants. Some animals spontaneously began breathing again after apnoea had been induced, even if the stimulus was still present, whereas in other animals apnoea was prolonged. If we could discover why some are more susceptible than others, that might shed some light on the problem.

Hofer: The incidence of sudden infant deaths rises from birth to three months (Froggatt *et al.* 1968), whereas most of the sensitivity you described is much nearer to birth, Dr Salisbury.

Salisbury: Some reports have suggested a slight protective effect from breast-feeding (Camps & Carpenter 1972) but other studies have shown no difference between breast-fed and bottle-fed infants in this respect (Froggatt *et al.* 1971). In our newborn animals, although we were introducing fluids into the upper airway, we had cut the trachea so that the lower airway was clear. There was no blockage of the airway, because we were perfusing up the trachea into the larynx and into the upper airway.

Klaus: You showed a difference in respiratory rate but what about alveolar ventilation? Were there differences in alveolar CO_2?

Salisbury: The records are run too slowly to show a proper plateau at each expiration and we have no measurements of alveolar ventilation.

Hofer: Had all these infants been breast-feeding?

Salisbury: Some had been artificially fed, some had been breast-fed, and some had experienced both. Whether they changed their patterns of breathing or sucking did not relate to whether they had previously been breast-fed or bottle-fed. Nor did it relate to their birth weight, gestational age, postnatal age up to one week, or to drugs given to the mother during delivery.

Both milks came from the same bottle. We offered the bottle to an infant for one minute, then poured out one kind of milk and poured in the other one. It is the same bottle, the same teat and the same person giving it to the infant, with a short pause in between.

Hofer: So the reaction you are describing is not to something novel but one that is specific to the composition of the fluid itself.

Macfarlane: Adults find it difficult to breathe and swallow at the same time, yet infants seem to do this. Do neonates really swallow or do they jet the milk straight down the back of their throats?

Salisbury: The flow of milk at the transducer is very fast, so there must be a jet.

Macfarlane: Do they just hold the back of their throat open so that the milk goes straight down?

Salisbury: Most is probably going down the lateral food channels of the pharynx. We measure breathing below the nostrils, with the sampling catheter, so it may be an averaging technique in that one may not see very quick closures of the glottis on the record of breathing. The nipple is full of milk when we offer it to the infant. The infant often seems to vacillate when it first bites on the nipple, and we can see this from the flow signal: integration of the flow measurement shows that there is no net forward or backward flow. As soon as there is forward flow into the infant the integrator starts to show the volume of milk taken from the bottle.

Papoušek: According to Peiper (1936), newborn babies can drink and breathe at the same time because the entrance of the larynx protrudes higher in neonates, and the milk can flow around it when swallowed. He assumed that this was a morphological peculiarity of neonates; however, his radiological evidence for this assumption was not strong enough to eliminate a functional interpretation.

Salisbury: Peiper was citing the observations of Negus and these are not supported by the cine-radiological observations of Ardran *et al.* (1958).

Papoušek: Yes, that is what I mean. The protrusion of the larynx could just as well result from reflex responses of the tongue and throat muscles, which are known to play important differentiated adaptive roles in the neonate's adjustment to breast sucking.

My second point concerns the part played by breathing in response to novelty. We studied such changes and their habituation in neonates in different behavioural states. Neonates habituate during sleep, but only during quiet sleep when there are no rapid eye movements. The slow and rhythmical breathing becomes irregular for a few seconds in response to stimulation and this response habituates after the stimulus has been repeated eight or ten times. However, sometimes the pattern of breathing changes entirely; for example, regular breathing may be replaced by Cheyne-Stokes breathing with periodically increasing and decreasing amplitudes. Obviously, these changes are of a regulatory type. A change in the pattern of breathing may thus also be a response to novelty independent of other activities of the newborn.

Salisbury: We tried to feed all the infants just before their feed was due normally. We also tried to feed them all when they were awake, and as often as possible the observations were started when they were breathing regularly.

Curtis-Jenkins: I thought that when the baby sucked on the breast, it was not sucking milk out of the breast but stimulating the flow of milk into the mouth, so the sucking on the bottle is surely a totally different mechanism.

Salisbury: When the baby is on the breast one can certainly record rhythmic negative pressures in the mouth. Luther *et al.* (1974) have measured oxytocin-induced contractions in the breast and pressures in the infant's mouth at the gum, mid-oral cavity and the back of the mouth during breast-feeding. The changes of negative pressure in the mouth were episodic, with pauses, as were seen in some of the observations we made on infants feeding breast milk, either from a bottle or from the breast. Luther *et al.*'s description of the contractions within the breast do not appear to be in line with the observations of the infant's sucking efforts. It has been suggested that these contractions may fill terminal spaces in the breast and the infant then sucks the milk. During breast-feeding, stimulation by sucking on one breast causes contractions in the other non-feeding breast and although the non-feeding breast may leak somewhat, the milk is still in it when the infant is put to it. You were suggesting that the flow of milk into the infant's mouth is independent of its sucking movements and this seems unlikely.

Rosenblatt: Do the two kinds of milk differ in consistency?

Salisbury: Breast milk certainly looks more watery than the artificial milk used.

Thoman: If the thickness of the two kinds of milk differs, what you see may be due to a difference in the difficulty of pulling milk through the nipple hole rather than to a chemical difference in the milk.

Salisbury: But the volume of milk taken by the infants was usually the same.

Thoman: The effort to get it through the hole is certainly greater with artificial milk. During breast-feeding, milk flow is rapid at first and then becomes slower. Does the infant's respiration stay regular throughout breast-feeding?

Salisbury: We did not look at that throughout breast-feeding but recorded it when the infant was sucking after the mother reported let-down, which we hoped was when milk flow was rapid. I suspect that as feeding on the breast becomes less rewarding, as time goes on, there will be even less disturbance of breathing. During non-nutritive sucking on a blind teat, breathing is regular and, if anything, accelerated, not reduced in frequency.

Thoman: The sucking pattern is nearly continuous during the first two or three minutes of breast-feeding and then as the milk flow subsides the suck–pause pattern appears (Kaye 1972).

Salisbury: The interrupted pattern of sucking occurred within the first minute in our own infants of over three days of age. The problem with this technique is that we cannot measure the volume of milk obtained in breast-feeding. Observations of this kind are not really comparable unless the volumes of milk obtained are known.

Richards: From what you said about your initial experiment that did not work, do you think it makes a difference to breathing whether the baby is fed with the traditional glass or plastic bottle, or with the kind that has a plastic bag inside that collapses as the milk is withdrawn?

Salisbury: A few of the infants who were fed from the conventional rigid bottle without a valve did show two different patterns of sucking. There were much longer episodes of sucking during feeding with artifical milk, while the pattern of sucking was of bursts and pauses during feeding with breast milk. Infants fed with collapsible bottles containing liners are really being fed with something like the bottle with the valve that we used. During feeding with artificial milk preparations the infants perhaps would show a reduction in breathing frequency which may not have occurred with a rigid bottle, when they would not have continuous access to milk.

The prolonged apnoea and swallowing seen in animals when some fluids are introduced into the upper airway may be a protective reflex for the lower airway. In lambs, saline solution, ovine amniotic fluid and colostrum may not stimulate apnoea and swallowing, whereas milk from a different species often does. We do not have the evidence, in the human infant, to say that these observations result from the same response, because we are not introducing the milk or the fluids with the same technique. We don't know that we are perfusing exactly the area that we perfuse in animals. It is hard to discount the possibility that because the viscosity is different, this has modified access to the supply. The observations on saline inhalation, however, have direct counterparts with the animal experiments.

Thoman: If you increased the viscosity of breast milk would you see the same effect with both milks?

Salisbury: Perhaps we would then be comparing different formulae of artificial milk.

Curtis-Jenkins: Did you try manipulating the chloride, sodium or potassium level or the osmolarity of the breast milk? That would surely be the key.

Salisbury: The key would probably be to bottle-feed an infant with the mother's breast milk and compare that with the effect of artificial milk, another mother's milk, and feeding the baby on the mother's breast.

Hofer: You still have the problem of viscosity.

Salisbury: Yes, but these observations might help to answer why there is variation, and whether the variation is due to the baby, the milk or the type of feeding.

Dunn: Could you decrease the viscosity of the artificial milk?

Salisbury: Yes, but then any changes to the milk would still mean that we would be comparing differing types of milk.

Hofer: To compensate for the viscous flow resistance you could use a larger nipple opening for the more viscous fluid, thereby getting around the problem of effort.

Oppé: Did you select 'ideal' minutes during the time the babies were feeding?

Salisbury: No, we were taking the first minute of record on infants fed with the two milks given in different orders. The records were therefore comparable.

Oppé: I was wondering if there was a difference in settling down to the milk.

Salisbury: No. They were fed the milks in different orders, starting with one milk, then the other, then returning to the first. The records began when the integrator showed that milk had started to be taken by the baby from the bottle.

D'Souza: Have you any evidence that babies have to learn how to suck? I have heard a tape-recording of a baby sucking at the breast for the first time and thereafter at regular intervals during the first couple of weeks of life. The tape revealed clearly that the baby became increasingly competent at breathing and sucking, especially during the first few moments of feeding when the mother's milk was abundant.

Salisbury: The observations we made on babies feeding on the breast were not made in the first few days after birth. The non-nutritive sucking they do before the milk supply is established would not have provided a valid comparison with the effect of an *ad libitum* supply of breast milk from a bottle.

D'Souza: Have you any other observations on whether babies get better at sucking even later?

Salisbury: Perhaps a relevant observation is that they only inhaled saline during the first two days after birth, not later on. L. Lipsitt (personal communication) has also compared non-nutritive sucking with sucking for dextrose solution. During non-nutritive sucking he sees, as everyone does, short episodes of sucks and pauses, while during nutritive sucking for dextrose there are longer strings of sucks.

Bentovim: It would be helpful if you could relate your observations to the general theme of mother–infant interactions, Dr Salisbury. Is this work related to the way infants are genetically programmed to respond to mother's milk?

Salisbury: The work may be relevant to Dr Macfarlane's observations. Working in the same hospital and making similar observations we may have a lot of common ground, and there is scope for combined observations which could possibly go quite a way to saying something about a baby and its responses to some of the environmental conditions provided, perhaps unwittingly, by the mother.

Papoušek: We really cannot regard this experimental situation as anything like the mother–infant interaction in life. The mother is active in postnatal learning and a lot of adjustment goes on after birth, on both sides. It is an intriguing interlocking mechanism. The more we pay attention to it, the more we realize how little we understand it.

Hofer: We can relate this work to the broader framework of our meeting if we remember that the chemical senses have generally been neglected in trying to understand an interaction. They are hard to study. We don't think that we use them much so we don't look for them. We perhaps have innate prejudices and a lack of knowledge about the chemical senses, particularly in social interaction. I think this is one of the messages that we have to get across here, in order to understand how the infant is operating in this complex situation. He may be operating over sensory pathways that we would not be aware of if we had not been warned by Drs Macfarlane and Salisbury.

Dr Pauline Singh and I have been making young rats anosmic with intranasal zinc sulphate, a method which does not produce direct lesions of the central nervous system. Infant rats made anosmic at from two days up to about ten days of age depend so much on their olfactory sense that they do not survive. The defect seems to be in 'attachment', in the literal sense of not being able to orient to and make successful contact with the nipple. Once the nipple is put in their mouths they will suck, but if the mother is anaesthetized, these anosmic pups don't seem to find their way to any nipple. Also we have observed that when normal infant rats are put near their mother after they have been kept away for a time, they show something like the ecstasy Dr Klaus mentioned—we call it 'frantic scrambling'. Even the younger ones become very active, with frequent orienting and paddling movements. This crescendo and high intensity of activity is not seen in the anosmic pups, who instead treat the mother like an inanimate or neutral object in the cage. Pups which have been put back with their mother after being made anosmic show the same behavioural changes as infants separated from their mothers for a number of hours (Hofer 1975). We were surprised that one sensory system should be so crucial at this age. It is a warning that we should never take anything for granted.

Rosenblatt: The theme that has been running through our discussions is one of synchrony between mother and infant. We are seeing this at all levels, from behaviour interactions to biochemical interactions between the mother's milk and the infant. Some relevant observations we made (Sachs & Rosenblatt 1974) were almost accidental. We put five-day-old rats with adult female rats during the last few days of pregnancy in order to induce maternal behaviour. If these pups remained with the mother overnight when she gave birth, then the pups that the mother delivered all died in the next two days. They obviously died from lack of milk, yet the mother was lactating quite well and was also very maternal towards her own young. One experiment we did to find out why the younger pups died was to coat the mouths of the older pups so that they could not suck, although they induced maternal behaviour. In those conditions, the new pups survived. Finally we found that if the older pups sucked during a period of 12 to 18 hours just before birth it ruined the nipples for the younger ones. The ducts had collapsed because of the sucking by the older pups and no milk was coming through the ducts although there was plenty in the gland. If the older ones sucked earlier than that, the nipples were not affected. Five days later, the mother's nipples can tolerate sucking by her own five-day-old pups without being ruined. Apparently there is a period when the hormones which give rise to parturition and maternal behaviour make the nipples mouldable to the sucking efforts of the younger pups. Then as the pups get older they mould the nipples to their own sucking abilities, and this continues. The degree of synchrony between mother and infant is remarkable.

References

ARDRAN, G.M., KEMP, F.H. & LIND, J. (1958) A cine radiographic study of bottle-feeding. *Br. J. Radiol. 31*, 11–22

CAMPS, F.E. & CARPENTER, R.G. (eds.) (1972) in *Sudden and Unexpected Deaths in Infancy*, Wright, Bristol

FROGGATT, P., LYNAS, M.A. & MARSHALL, T.K. (1968) Sudden death in babies: epidemiology. *Am. J. Cardiol. 22*, 457–477

FROGGATT, P., LYNAS, M.A. & MARSHALL, T.K. (1971) Sudden unexpected death in infants: report of a collaborative study in Northern Ireland. *Ulster Med. J. 40*, 116–135

HOFER, M.A. (1975) Studies on how early maternal separation produces behavioral change in young rats. *Psychosom. Med.*, in press

KAYE, K. (1972) Milk pressure as a determinant of the burst–pause pattern in neonatal sucking. *Proc. Annu. Conv. Am. Psychol. Assoc. 80*

LUTHER, E.C., ARBALLO, J.C., SALA, N.L. & CORDERO FUNES, J.C. (1974) Suckling pressure in humans: relationship to oxytocin-reproducing reflex milk ejection. *J. Appl. Physiol. 36*, 350–353

PEIPER, A. (1936) Der Saugvorgang. *Erg. Inn. Med. Kinderheilkd. 50*, 527–567

SACHS, B.D. & ROSENBLATT, J.S. (1974) Prepartum suckling reduces survival of newborn in the rat. *Dev. Psychobiol. 7*, 399–406

Early mother-infant reciprocity

T. BERRY BRAZELTON, EDWARD TRONICK, LAUREN ADAMSON, HEIDELISE ALS and SUSAN WISE

Harvard Medical School and Children's Hospital Medical Center, Boston, Massachusetts

Abstract By three weeks of age, the human neonate demonstrates behaviours which are quite different with an object and with a human interactant. He also demonstrates an expectancy for interaction with his caregiver which has clearly defined limits, as demonstrated behaviourally. In microanalysis of videotape, we saw regularly a set of interactive behaviours which were demonstrable in optimal face-to-face interaction between infants and their mothers. All parts of the infant's body move in smooth circular patterns as he attends to her. His face-to-face attention to her is rhythmic with approach-withdrawal cycling of extremities. The attention phase and build-up to her cues are followed by turning away and a recovery phase in a rhythm of attention-non-attention which seems to define a cyclical homeostatic curve of attention, averaging several cycles per minute.

When she violates his expectancy for rhythmic interaction by presenting a still, unresponsive face to him, he becomes visibly concerned, his movements become jerky, he averts his face, then attempts to draw her into interaction. When repeated attempts fail, he finally withdraws into an attitude of helplessness, face averted, body curled up and motionless. If she returns to her usual interactive responses, he comes alive after an initial puzzled period, and returns to his rhythmic cyclical behaviour which has previously characterized their ongoing face-to-face interaction.

This attentional cycling may be diagnostic of optimal mother–infant interactions and seems not to be present in more disturbed interactions.

We have been interested in achieving a deeper understanding of the reciprocal social interactions between mothers and their young infants. It is through an early system of affective interaction that the development of the infant's identification with culture, family and other individuals will be fueled and supported. Our objective is to characterize the structure of this interaction, and its patterns, rhythms and behavioural components (Brazelton *et al.* 1974; Tronick *et al.* 1975).

We have chosen face-to-face interaction as our primary study. This event

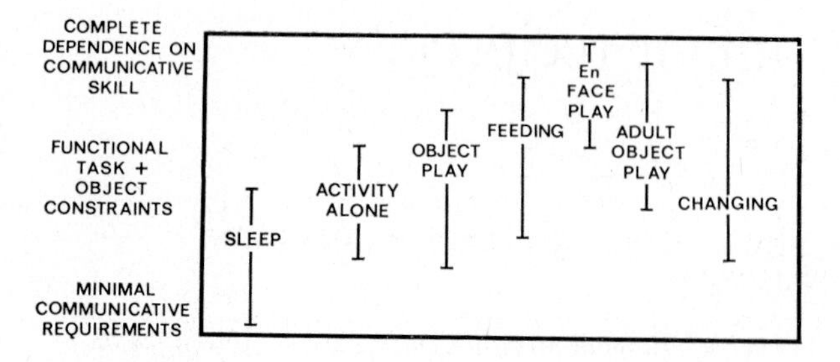

FIG. 1. Relative communicative requirements of different infant activities.

has the greatest communicative requirements and places the greatest demands on the communicative skill of the interactants (Fig. 1). Functional tasks, such as feeding or changing the infant, have a set of constraints which help to structure the interchange, while *en face* play demands complete reliance on communicative skills. Thus, it is an excellent situation in which to observe the underlying structure of dyadic communication and of each partner's social capabilities. Our studies indicate that it is, in fact, a reciprocally organized system in which the infant makes skilful adjustments of his action and manifests appropriate emotional expressions in response to the displays of his partner.

PROCEDURE

Our subjects are 12 mother–infant pairs who were seen repeatedly over the infant's first five months of life. We have known most of the mothers since the birth of their infants and our contact with them is relaxed and supportive. We explain that we are videotaping their behaviour so as to gain an understanding of the normal development of infant social capabilities, and we make an effort to inform them about our ongoing analyses.

During each session the infant, when alert and calm, is placed in an infant seat situated in a curtained alcove. The mother comes from behind the curtain and plays with him for three minutes. She then leaves and we continue to record the infant's behaviour for 30 seconds while he is alone. The mother then returns for a second three-minute period of interaction.

The videotape is made unobtrusively with two cameras, one focused on the infant and the other on the mother (Fig. 2). The camera outputs are fed simultaneously into a special effects generator that produces a frontal view of the mother and the baby. An electronic digital time display is also fed onto the image (Fig. 3).

The videotapes are reviewed several times so that we can characterize the

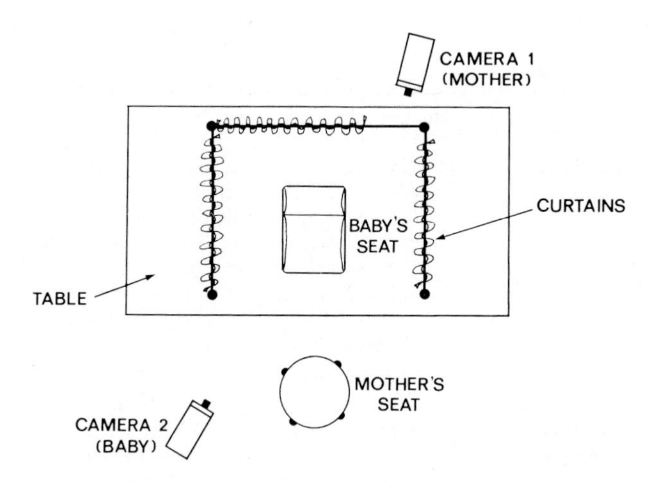

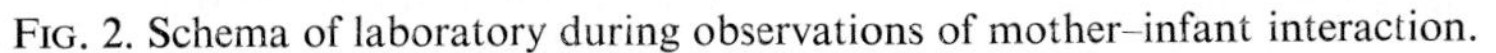
FIG. 2. Schema of laboratory during observations of mother–infant interaction.

type and quality of each interactor's behaviour. To aid this review, we have analysed many of the tapes by using a detailed microbehavioural descriptive system which divides the infant's behaviours into ten categories and the mother's into six (Table 1). This analysis is done by two trained observers as the videotape runs at one-seventh of normal speed. The behaviours are categorized according to their occurrence throughout a one-second interval, and not simply on still frames one second apart.

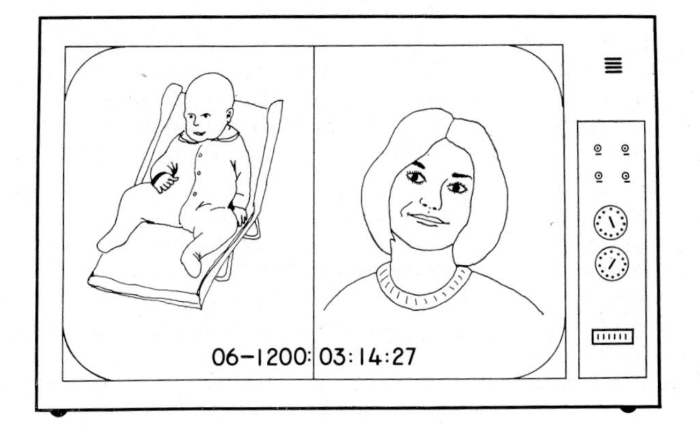

FIG. 3. Schema of picture on TV monitor.

TABLE 1

Behaviour scored for mother and infant

Infant	*Mother*
(1) *Vocalization*: 1. none; 2. isolated sound; 3. grunt; 4. coo; 5. cry; 6. fuss; 7. laugh	(1) *Vocalizing*: 1. abrupt shout; 2. stern, adult narrative; 3. rapid tense voice; 4. whispering; 5. little or no vocalizing; 6. rhythmic sounds with little modulation; 7. burst–pause talking; 8. single bursts in rapid succession with wide pitch range; 9. burst of sound that peaks with much change of modulation and pitch
(2) *Direction of Gaze*: 1. towards mother's face; 2. away from mother's face; 3. follows mother; 4. looking at toy or hand mother is using as part of interaction	(2) *Head Position*: 1. towards and down; 2. towards and up; 3. towards and level; 4. part side and down; 5. part side and up; 6. part side level; 7. towards and level; 8. towards and up; 9. towards and down; 10. thrusting; 11. nodding; 12. nuzzling; 13. cocked head
(3) *Head Orientation*: 1. head towards, nose level; 2. head towards, nose down; 3. head towards, nose up; 4. head part side, nose level; 5. head part side, nose down; 6. head part side, nose up; 7. head complete side, nose level; 8. head complete side, nose down; 9. head complete side, nose up	(3) *Body Position*: 1. turns body full away; 2. sits back and still; 3. slumping; 4. neutral–slightly forward; 5. sideways shifts; 6. slight rocking; 7. large sideways shifts into line of vision; 8. medium–close forwards; 9. going close and staying close; 10. large shifts forwards and back
(4) *Head Position*: 1. left; 2. right	(4) *Specific Handling of the Infant*: 1. abrupt shift of baby's position; 2. abrupt but no shift; 3. jerky movement of limbs; 4. no contact; 5. gently containing; 6. small rhythmic backing; 7. rhythmic movements of limbs; 8. intensive movement, fast rhythm
(5) *Facial Expression*: 1. cry face; 2. grimace; 3. pout; 4. wary/sober; 5. lidding; 6. yawn; 7. neutral; 8. sneeze; 9. softening; 10. brightening; 11. simple smile; 12. coo face; 13. broad smile	(5) *Direction of Gaze*: 1. towards infant's face; 2. towards infant's body; 3. away from infant but related to interaction; 4. away from infant and not related to interaction
(6) *Amount of Movement*: 1. 3/4 limbs, large movement; 2. 1/2 limbs, large movement; 3. 3/4 limbs, medium movement; 4. 1/2 limbs, medium movement; 5. 3/4 limbs, small movement; 6. 1/2 limbs, small movement; 7. no movement; 8. mother moving infant	(6) *Facial Expression*: 1. angry; 2. frown; 3. serious, sad, sober; 4. lidded; 5. neutral flat; 6. brightening; 7. animated; 8. simple smile; 9. imitative play face; 10. kisses; 11. exaggerated play face; 12. broad full smile; 13. 'ooh' face
(7) *Blinks*: 1. yes; 2. no	

TABLE 1, *conttnued*

Infant	*Mother*
(8) *Specific Hand Movements*: 1. eye-wiping; 2. hand to mouth; 3. swipe; 4. fidgets 5. all lower limbs extended forwards	
(9) *Specific Foot Movements*: 1. kick; 2. startle	
(10) *Tongue Placement*: 1. tongue slightly exposed; 2. tongue maximally exposed	

A TYPICAL INTERACTION

The following is a description of an interaction between a 60-day-old infant and his mother:

> Baby is looking off to side where mother will come in. He lies completely quiet, back in his baby seat, face serious, cheeks droopy, mouth half open, corners down, but there is an expectant look in his eyes as if he were waiting. His face and hands reach out in the same direction. As his mother comes in, saying, 'Hello' in a high-pitched but gentle voice, he follows her with his head and eyes as she approaches him. His body builds up with tension, his face and eyes open up with a real greeting which ends with a smile. His mouth opens wide and his whole body orients toward her. He subsides, mouths his tongue twice, his smile dies and he looks down briefly, while she continues to talk in an increasingly eliciting voice. During this, his voice and face are still but all parts of his body point toward her. After he looks down, she reaches for and begins to move his hips and legs in a gentle, containing movement. He looks up again, smiles widely, narrows his eyes, brings one hand up to his mouth, grunting, vocalizing, and begins to cycle his arms and legs out toward her. With this increasing activity, she begins to grin more widely, to talk more loudly and with higher-pitched accents, accentuating his vocalizations with hers and his activity with her movements of his legs. The grunting vocalizations and smiles, as well as the cycling activity of his arms and legs come and go in two-second bursts—making up small cycles of movement and attention toward her. She contains his hips with her hands as if to contain the peaks of his excitement.
>
> Meanwhile, with her voice and her face, as well as with her hands, she both subsides with and accentuates his behaviour with her own. He looks down again, gets sober at 40 seconds, makes a pouting face. She looks down at his feet at this point, then comes back to look into his face as he returns to look up at her. She lets go of his legs, and they draw up into his body. He bursts out with a broad smile and a staccato-like vocalization for three repetitions. Each time, his face broadens and opens wide, his legs and arms thrust out toward her. She seems to get caught up in his bursts, and smiles broadly, her voice getting brighter, too. After each burst, he subsides to a serious face, limbs quiet, and her quieting response follows his.
>
> At 70 seconds, he subsides completely, and looks down at his feet with a darkly serious face. She gets very still, her face becomes serious, her voice slows down and almost stops, the pitch becomes low. Her mouth is drawn down, reflecting his serious mouth. After three seconds, he begins to brighten again into a wide, tonguing smile. This time, he is more self-contained, holding back on the movement of his extremities and his excitement. She responds immediately, cocks her head coyly, smiles gently and her voice gently begins to build up again. He builds up to two more staccato vocalizations with smiles and

jerky, cycling movements of his legs out toward her. She contains his hips, and this time her voice doesn't build up to a peak of excitement with him. She looks down after 6 seconds to pick up his arms with her hands as if to keep control over his build-up. He follows her downward look about ten seconds later, by looking down, too. His movements subside and his face becomes serious. She is quite serious also, at 90 seconds.

He sneezes, she responds with a staccato 'God bless you!' and a brighter face, head nodding toward him. She begins to talk more insistently as he looks serious, studying her face. He finally brightens to a smile, and with it, she throws back her head to smile broadly and excitedly. After this broad smile, they both subside, he continues to look at her seriously and quietly. She talks seriously to him, holding his buttocks and legs between her hands. At prolonged intervals, he gives her two rather brief, tentative but encouraging smiles. After each, he returns to a quiet serious face, body entirely motionless. She smiles to his smiles, but doesn't get more insistent and continues to talk quietly. At 135 seconds, he looks down at his feet, then comes in with a longer smile—tongue showing at his lips. His legs also cycle out toward her. She looks down when he does, then begins to move his legs in cycles. As he smiles at her, she looks up, brightens, moves his legs more rapidly and her voice builds up. This smile decreases after 5 seconds and he looks away again. Then, they begin another period of serious looks, alternating with brief smiles in short cycles. She builds up with each of his cues, pumping his legs, smiling and vocalizing more herself, building up to a final peak. Each partner produces wide smiles, her voice becomes high-pitched, her hands pump his legs together. He subsides first to look down and serious. She loses her broad smile, gets up to leave, letting his legs go. At this, he looks beseechingly up into her face, his mouth turns down, his eyebrows arch, his legs and arms quiet, and he follows her with his eyes and head as she moves away.

This interaction can be conceptualized as a sequence of phases, each representing different states of the partner's mutual attentional and affective involvement. The dyadic phases in an interaction of a typical two-month-old infant and his mother are: (1) initiation, (2) mutual orientation, (3) greeting, (4) play-dialogue and (5) disengagement. The phases are not defined by a single piece of behaviour. *Initiation* may occur when the mother brightens and baby-talks to a sober baby, or a baby vocalizes and smiles to a caretaker who has paused too long. *Mutual orientation* may take place with neutral or bright faces, with the caretaker talking or the infant making single utterances. *Greetings* occur with smiles and 'ooh' faces, and *play-dialogues* with mother talking in a burst–pause pattern and the baby making grunts or continuous vocalizations. *Disengagement* may occur when the caretaker goes from neutral face to sober face, or keeps the neutral face but starts to talk to the infant in adult conversational terms, or starts looking away from the baby. In each case, behaviours can be substituted for one another.

A phase analysis of this interaction shows that it begins with a greeting phase and not an initiation phase (Fig. 4, point a). As soon as the mother enters the infant's visual field, the greeting phase starts. It continues through seconds 2 and 3. The interaction decelerates at second 5 to mutual orientation, but then the greeting is resumed (Fig. 4, point b). Both partners cycle again through

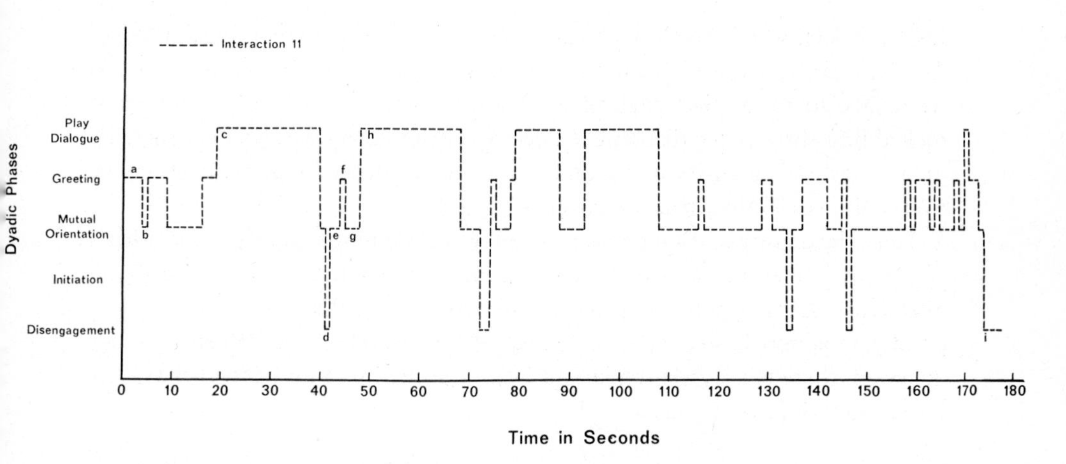

FIG. 4. Phase flow diagram for interaction.

the greeting–mutual orientation phase, and then go into prolonged play-dialogue (Fig. 4, point c). At the close of this phase, there is a momentary (2 seconds) disengagement (Fig. 4, point d). After this brief disengagement, the mutual attention–vocalizing–disengagement cycle (Fig. 4, points e, f, g, h) begins again and continues in much the same way until the interaction ends when the mother leaves (Fig. 4, point i).

The sequence of dyadic phases resulting from a phase analysis characterizes the attentional and affective involvement which occurs in a face-to-face interaction. It captures the build-up to greetings and the decelerations to disengagement. In this example, the analysis highlights one of the most striking qualities of successful interactions: the mutual cycling of attention and affectivity. The infant demonstrates his participation in this cycling by alternately attending and then withdrawing either partially or completely. The sensitive mother likewise regulates her own behaviours so that her affectivity cycles along with her infant's.

For us to expect to characterize the sequential or cyclic quality of an interaction by a single behaviour such as smiling or vocalization, or to define a particular phase by a set cluster of behaviours, would be missing the point. For example, in contrast to the above interaction a baby might start his cycle of activity by a slight frown. As he builds up, he slowly reaches out, coos, eyes widen, both arms jerk forward, head pulls back and his face brightens. At this point, he seems to have reached an upper limit and he begins to turn away. His eyes look past his mother's head, fix on the wall behind her, his hand grasps his shirt and 'place-holds' as he overtly tries to maintain this phase of non-attention to her cues. After several seconds, he looks slowly back at her, his hand lets go of the shirt and he begins his cycle of activity again, smiles faintly, then frowns and vocalizes, both arms withdraw up by his shoulders as he builds up to another peak of attention to her. Meanwhile, his mother is locked into these cyclic displays of affectivity. Her behaviours seem to increase in number and intensity as he builds up, and to decrease perceptively as he averts his eyes so that he can recover.

Thus, the quality of each partner's display relative to the quality of the other's display is a measure of the match existing between their intentionality and affectivity. When synchronization is achieved, we feel that we are observing a good interaction based on a mutuality of affect and intent. When it is not achieved, there is a dysrhythmia and lack of cyclic build-up of the behaviours into a smooth flow of phases.

THE INFANT'S ROLE IN AN INTERACTION

The achievement of affective synchrony, the substitutability of behaviours within a phase and the cyclic rhythm in the interaction all suggest that mother–infant interaction is a regulated homeostatic system. The mother's contribution to this system is quite apparent as she adapts and modifies her behaviours in response to the infant's display. A most dramatic example of this adaptation is her attempt to 'infantize' her adult behaviour to better fit the infant's limited capacities for processing information (Stern 1974). Less was previously known about the infant's contribution to the interaction. That he does possess capabilities for reciprocity is indicated in three of our observational studies.

Infant interactions with objects and people

In previous work we observed that infants produce qualitatively different patterns of attention, action and affectivity when interacting with an object than with a person (Brazelton *et al.* 1974). With an object the infant's attention is characterized by rapt attention followed by abrupt and brief turning away. His movements are jerky, come in bursts, and are often accompanied by short swipes out towards the object. This is a different pattern of affective attentional cycling and behaviour than we observe in his performance with people. With people, in a short period of intense interaction, there are repeated cycles consisting of acceleration from initiation to greetings and then deceleration to disengagement. The pattern is smooth and rhythmical, whereas with objects there is the jaggedness of intense periods of attention interrupted by brief bursts of inattention and of activity. This performance indicates that the infant —as young as two or three weeks of age—is able to differentiate inanimate as opposed to animate events, and that he can appropriately pattern his attention and actions in relation to their unique qualities. With the object, the goal is the exploration of its qualities through vision and prehension. With people, the goal is the achievement of affective synchrony. In both, the infant would be acting intentionally and modifying his behaviour in response to the feedback from the environment.

An experimental distortion of the normal interaction

To explore further the possibility that the infant is acting intentionally, we are studying interactions in which we experimentally distort the normal feedback the infant receives. In one condition, we asked the mother to become completely unresponsive to the infant by sitting before him and looking at him silently with a still face for three minutes.

The baby's characteristic pattern of behaviour to his 'still-faced' mother is shown in the following description:

> Baby is looking contemplatively down at his hands, fingering fingers of one hand with the other. As mother comes up, his finger movements stop. He looks up with a half smile, eyes lidded but looking into her eyes. Her still, mask-like face greets him. He looks off quickly to one side, but remains completely quiet. After 20 seconds, he looks back again in her face, his eyebrows and lids raised now, and as he looks into her eyes, his hands and arms startle slightly. He looks down quickly at his hands, waits about 8 seconds, then checks her face once more, yawns and turns his eyes and face up just over her hair. His fingers now pull at the fingers of the other hand, the rest of his body is motionless. His yawn and head-stretch lasts 5 seconds, he throws out one arm in a slight startle, quickly brings his hand to his clothing to 'place-hold' as he looks in her face briefly once more (for the fourth time). His arm movements are jerky now, his mouth curves downward, his eyes narrow and he turns his face so that he keeps her in peripheral vision with his semi-lidded eyes. He fingers his fingers again, his legs stretch out toward her, but jerk back again. He arches forward, slumping over, head on chest, and looks up at her face from under his brow as if expecting her to straighten him up. For over a minute, he stays in this helpless position checking up at her with his eyes about once every 10 seconds. He grimaces briefly as his eyes and face look very serious. He finally collapses in a curled-up ball looking helpless and does not check her again. He fingers his mouth with one hand, inserting one finger to suck at intervals, rocking his head gently. He looks utterly helpless and hopeless. As she walks away, he remains curled up and motionless, looks up halfway in her direction, but seems to expect no response from her.

This is a typical example of the kind of response to the mother's still face we have seen in babies in this 2–20-week period. There is an initial check which is brief, and the infant begins to sense that the normal interaction is not being fulfilled. As he continues to 'check', his attitude becomes that of both waiting and of trying to elicit her usual behaviour. When that fails after two (long) minutes of repeated attempts, he withdraws and turns to self-comforting behaviour. These long repeated attempts to get the interaction back on track, and his withdrawal, both reflect his attempts to cope with this rejection. It reminds one all too easily of Bowlby's (1969) second stage of acceptance and withdrawal in hospitalized separated children.

A naturally occurring distortion of the normal interaction

Another dramatic illustration of how adaptively an infant can behave in a distorted interaction was seen during the interaction of a sighted infant and her non-sighted parents. The mother had been blind since birth (see Fig. 5), and often had a mask-like face as she talked. The father had not lost his vision until he was eight years of age and did talk 'with his face'. At four weeks of age, the infant was visually very alert. Yet, she would glance only briefly at her mother's eyes and then avert her eyes and face from the mother as the mother leaned over to talk to her. But she watched her father's face and sightless eyes carefully for long periods as he talked to her. With us, she greedily watched our eyes and faces and followed every move. The mother was sensitive to this and asked us why she didn't look at her. When we asked how she knew this, she displayed her remarkable sensitivity to this baby with her reply: 'I can tell from the direction the sound of her breathing is coming'. Her sensitivity to the infant was also demonstrated by her instructions to her husband as to how to

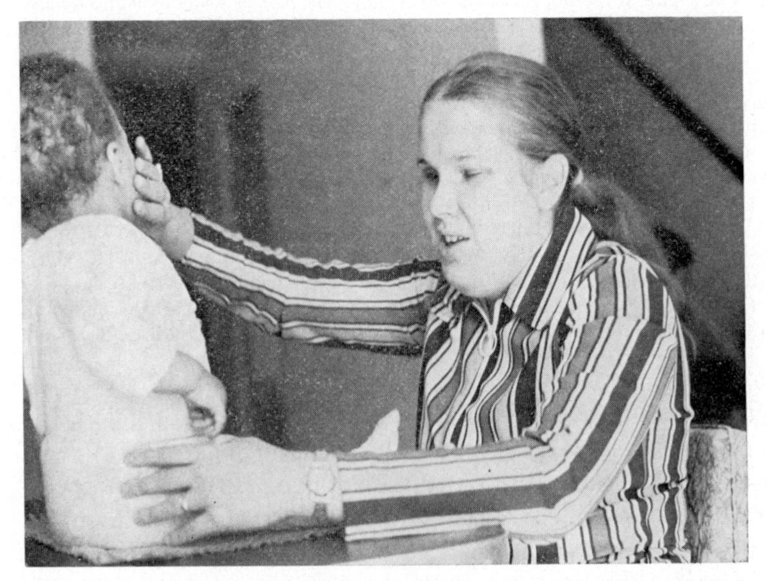

FIG. 5. A blind mother with mask-like appearance interacting with her sighted infant.

get her to vocalize to him: 'Slow down, wait for her, pitch your voice higher'.

At four weeks, the baby would check on her mother's face and eyes from time to time as she talked, but her face remained averted. Their communication seemed to be heightened in the vocal and auditory areas. By eight weeks, when cooing and smiling had become locked into rhythmic cycling with us, it had not done so with her mother. Instead, the infant still demonstrated longer periods of searching, looking into her mother's motionless face and sightless eyes, and averting her face after these periods in the same fashion. When the father replaced the mother, she latched onto his eyes with hers and maintained the cyclical pattern of looking–not looking, evidencing the same build-up of excitement as is typical in her interactions with sighted adults. After eight weeks, she engaged in a mutually satisfying interaction with her mother even though it still appeared distorted. We felt that the pair had overcome the initial violation caused by the mother's distorted use of the visual mode of communication by successfully using other modes, such as the auditory, in its place.

DISCUSSION

Our observations of the normal interaction and the distortions of normal indicate that interaction is a mutually regulated system in which both partners modify their actions in response to the feedback provided by their partner. It is surprising how early the infant plays an active role. In the still-face condition, the mother produces a distorted response to the infant's initiations and greetings. By her entrance and continued *en face* position she is initiating the infant's interest but with her lack of response she is disengaging and violating the normal interactional sequence. For the infant, she is part of a feedback loop for his own actions, and he alternates between initiation-greetings and disengagement. His goal is affective synchrony. He makes repeated attempts to achieve it before he gives up, and first becomes wary, then dejected.

In the interaction of the sighted child and her blind parents, the mother's response to her infant's actions are distortions of the normal homeostatic system, since the mother fails to respond to the visual displays of her daughter and does not provide the baby with appropriate visual feedback. This is less true in the case of the father. These distortions are disturbing to the infant. She is pre-set for visual input such as face-to-face postures and facial displays. Fortunately neither the parents nor the infant are tied to particular stimuli or modalities for the achievement of mutually satisfying interactions. Just as in the interactions between sighted persons where no particular behaviour defines a phase, this infant and her parents found other modes for achieving affective synchrony and, eventually, a normal cycling of phases.

Even in his earliest interactions with his environment, social and non-social, the infant is impressively self-regulated and intentional. His capacity to differentiate and set his pattern of attention in one kind of pathway for objects and another for interaction seemed particularly adaptive and economical, and we felt that this accounted for the infant's focused and intense short-term exploration of the limited amount of information from objects, whereas the more cyclical pattern provided an opportunity for heightened and prolonged investment in the social situation where he could learn important affective and cognitive information from his caregiver. If it weren't for an economical homeostatic model and his ability to regulate the input, he might easily be overwhelmed by the amount of information which is available in a short period of interaction with another human being. Moreover, when the social environment is distorted, either artificially or by natural accidents, his remarkable ability to regulate the deviation of his attentional cycle and to modify his behaviour is even more strikingly evidenced. These capabilities for self-regulation allow him to prolong his engagement in the world around him in the face of immaturity and its physiological demands. We are convinced that in a 'good' interaction, mother and baby synchronize with each other from the beginning, and that pathways may be set up in intrauterine life, ready to be entrained, especially by the mother, immediately after birth. Intrauterine experience with other maternal cues, such as auditory or kinesthetic, may well set the stage for enhancing the meaning of the synchronous rhythms. Rhythmic interaction seems to be basic to human affect (Condon & Sander 1974). We are pretty sure that a mother who is sensitive to her infant's needs can enhance his capacity for attending to her important cues within a few weeks. We feel that messages which are communicated to the infant via the mother's face and movement seem to be at the root of their communication.

In clinical paediatrics, infant–mother pairs who have failed to thrive demonstrate a chaotic non-synchrony, with evidence in the infant of how painful facial communication, eye-to-eye contact and asynchrony of rhythms have become. It would be vitally important if we could see how such a failure in interaction evolved, for it seems that it embodies a basic violation of complex, expected and necessary rules for interaction.

ACKNOWLEDGEMENT

This research was conducted with the help of a grant (No. 4180) from The Grant Foundation, Inc. New York, N.Y.

References

BRAZELTON, T.B., KOSLOWSKI, B. & MAIN, M. (1974) The origins of reciprocity in mother–infant interaction, in *The Effect of the Infant on its Caregiver* (Lewis, M. and Rosenblum, L.A., eds.), pp. 49–76, Wiley-Interscience, New York

BOWLBY, J. (1973) *Attachment and Loss*, Basic Books, New York

CONDON, W.S. & SANDER, L.W. (1974) Speech: interactional participation and language acquisition. *Science (Wash. D.C.) 183*, 99–101

STERN, D.N. (1974) The goal and structure of mother infant play. *J. Am. Acad. Child Psychiatr. 13*, 402

TRONICK, E., ADAMSON, L., WISE, S., ALS, H. & BRAZELTON, T.B. (1975). Mother–infant face to face interaction, in *Biology and Language* (Gosh, S., ed.), Academic Press, London

Discussion

Bell: A more intense form of the response to the non-smiling and non-mobile face has been reported by several people investigating vocalization in infants aged three to four months. These workers conditioned vocalization and smiles by making their cooing, talking, or touching contingent on a smile or vocalization from the baby. In the extinction phase, when the observers were not smiling or vocalizing and had sometimes looked away, many of the babies became upset and, apparently, even more disturbed than the babies you saw, Dr Brazelton. One way of interpreting that is, again, as a violation of expectations.

Carpenter: Distress from violation of expectation in the first *weeks* of life is referred to in papers by Carpenter *et al.* (1970) and Carpenter (1974)! It was interesting that you could 'hold' the babies for three minutes without their becoming disturbed, Dr Brazelton. Some of the babies we saw cried and showed real distress within 30 seconds. They were younger than yours—one to seven weeks of age.

Brazelton: The effect we see seems even more distressful to watch than crying. With a stranger or with the father they may cry, but with the mother they act as if they are even more distressed, and even hopeless. Our violations are carried out so that we can define the limits of the normal interaction.

Carpenter: What is the evidence that the cyclical response pattern is the 'normal' one? The turning away might reflect some process of matching the current input of information against an expectation which has been violated by the still face. That is, turning away might be a time-out period for information processing rather than evidence of a cyclic interactional phenomenon.

Brazelton: I have reported this work on the cyclical aspects of mother–infant interaction in a previous paper (Brazelton *et al.* 1974). The behaviours which the baby added while he was looking at his mother formed the positive part of the curve, and the behaviours he used to maintain a period of not looking formed the rest. In this way, looking and not looking became a homeostatic curve of attention as the baby interacted with this mother. When she overloaded him with too much information he turned her off and added three or four behaviours to the turning off, as if it were a very active process. These negative parts of the curve seem to be necessary to information processing or to physiological recovery, or both, as well as the parts of the curve representing attention. After he looks away, the baby begins to attend to the mother again. Over a three-minute period the cycles of looking and not-looking seem to average about four a minute.

Carpenter: Within 30-second periods, we found that the time spent looking away from the mother was greater when she was stationary and silent than when she was speaking. Yet the infant looked back to the unresponsive mother more often, which suggests active involvement. This makes me wonder whether the infant behaviour you see reflects primarily interactional synchrony or a cognitive process.

Dunn: You suggested that with an insensitive mother the baby checked briefly and then looked away for a longer period than if the mother was sensitive. What evidence have you that it was the mother who created this pattern rather than the baby? Have you any longitudinal data?

Brazelton: In the earlier study we observed five normal mothers from my practice. The children are now about five or six years old. Within this normal group, two mothers seemed to be extremely sensitive, from the beginning, to the rhythmic needs of their babies, and these babies would look longer and check away for shorter periods by about three or four months of age. Mothers in our experimental situation were tense and eager to please us. As a result they tried too hard to stimulate their babies, and as the baby looked away the mother got more intense rather than less. Over the four months the baby began to spend less and less time in face-to-face interaction with the mother. I have always been impressed with Lipton *et al.*'s (1961–1962) ideas about how psychophysiological mechanisms can be regulated by attentional ones. My idea is that the baby's homeostatic mechanisms for controlling respiratory, cardiovascular and other systems are being shaped by such an interactional system. An attentional level may dominate the psychophysiological mechanisms. After watching this level of interaction one becomes more aware of the importance of synchrony. Katherine Barnard showed us a film (1973, University of Washington, Seattle) of a six-month-old baby with cerebral palsy whom the mother could not teach. The baby had a jerky kind of movement pattern which put the mother off. A very sensitive physiotherapist came to show the mother how to work with him. When the physiotherapist began to get into a jerky rhythm with the baby, the baby quieted down and began to watch the therapist, and they began to work with each other. The mother watched this successful interaction, began to imitate the therapist and finally began to work with the baby in the same way. From then on therapeutic interaction began to work between the mother and the baby. I thought it was necessary for the mother to become locked into this kind of interaction if she was to meet the baby's needs, and it was necessary for the baby to shape the mother rather than vice versa.

Papoušek: We have been observing dyads where the mother is psychotic. The situation is comparable to your observations on the blind mother, except that the psychotic mother does not respond to the baby. One young mother whose baby was around six weeks old had a transient psychosis only, and when she recovered, about three weeks later, she was able to explain that during the observation session she was responding to environmental changes which had disturbed her tremendously. She was fantasizing about having the baby in a sort of laboratory where they were going to break his bones, to poison him, and so on. She was responding to such ideas when we asked her to interact with her infant. In her infant we saw something very similar to what you described, Dr Brazelton. The onset of the mother's whole disturbance preceded our experimental session by two or three days. The baby was not only responding to the mother's incomprehensible behaviour but was also making attempts to get into contact with the mother, as in the 'frozen face' situation. Here the mother was responding and her face was not frozen or blind, but her responses showed no synchrony with the baby's behaviour.

Did you monitor any of the physiological functions of the baby during interaction sessions, Dr Brazelton?

Brazelton: No. I wish we had been able to do that.

Oppé: Some barbaric institutions still require mothers and nurses to wear surgical masks when they are with infants. Of course this preserves eye contact but gives a strange appearance. Have you watched babies in this situation?

Brazelton: I think babies are disturbed by masks, particularly on their mothers. If the mother is giving out all the usual cues of smell, speech and so on, the mask is a violation. L. Sander (1973, personal communication) asked mothers of seven-day-old babies to put on a mask but to feed and treat the babies normally otherwise. He found that for 24 hours the rhythms of sleep, feeding and all the rest were completely disturbed, just from the mother having worn a mask. I think that a very powerful set of expectations are set up. The entrainment of interactional rhythms is only one of them.

Oppé: Deprivation and battering are at opposite ends of the spectrum of disturbed interaction. Ounsted *et al.* (1974) described the frozen watchfulness of battered babies, who latch on with their eyes. Have you seen this?

Brazelton: I see latching on to an object as the opposite side of the same coin as turning away. Frozen attention is one way of keeping visual input under control, just as turning away might be. The frozen look on a non-thriving baby is as disturbing to me as a baby who curls up in a ball and looks away. We are following up babies who fail to thrive and one of my associates, Dr Daniel Rosenn, has been carefully monitoring their hospital course daily, using a seven-point approach–withdrawal scale. Many of the infants who for environmental reasons initially fail to thrive respond very little either to objects or people. Early in their recovery, they tend to be much more responsive to inanimate as opposed to animate stimuli. As the frozen look, the averted face and the inability to accept interpersonal approaches start to diminish, the capacity for rhythmic, cyclical social interaction slowly emerges. Using the approach–withdrawal scale, we have begun to gather characteristic behavioural profiles which seem to distinguish infants whose failure to thrive is organically caused from those in whom it is environmental.

Simpson: When two strange individuals of some species of fish meet, they take it in turns to face each other. Your description of the mother and her baby could almost be these two fish, each spending about five seconds facing the other and discovering by their interaction whether they should then go on to a courtship or a fight. This underlines how very general the phenomenon may be in the animal kingdom.

This kind of interaction is hard to study and few detailed reports have appeared. Just because it is mothers and babies we are looking at, we find it easy to feel that there is a dance-like rhythm in what they are doing—indeed Mary Middlemore (1941) described mother–infant interactions as being dance-like or not dance-like—but we must remember that we still have the methodological problem of showing this statistically.

Brazelton: We have spent three years finding a computer program which will document this. We are trying to discover which partner leads the other.

Simpson: Do you think who is leading whom is the wrong question? Don't they reach a stage in this 'dance' of theirs at which neither needs to lead the other, but when each uses minimal cues from the other to keep in step?

Brazelton: I think that the most important phase is when they get locked and the two of them are dancing to the same tune.

Curtis-Jenkins: When I test vision in babies aged seven months I get a bit irritated because some of the children 'face-fix' so strongly that I cannot get them to follow a rolling ball. Even if I hide my face, they still watch to see where it has gone. How should I be interpreting this? Is face-fixing different from interaction? Is it a phase that only some babies go through?

Brazelton: We find the same thing in newborn babies. Some just won't lock onto an object after they have had the experience of locking onto a face. They will follow the face back and forth and even in circles. If we show them the object after that, we have impossible competition. Most newborn babies are not quite so hooked on human faces as this. By seven months the interaction between human stimuli and objects is so complex that I can't really answer your question.

Hinde: In this phase of discovering exciting new things about what goes on between mother and baby, we tend to talk about their consequences in a Newtonian way, too easily implying that the more the mother shows the behaviour in question, the better it is. The conspicuous thing about development is its regulatory property. We may be dealing with step functions: if the mother deviates a little, it doesn't matter, but if she deviates a lot, development will set off along a different course. I think we have to find a non-Newtonian or 'systems' way of talking about it. This is important because of what is said to mothers before or during such studies. Listening to you, Dr Brazelton —and absolutely fascinated by what you were saying—I was thinking that in any dealings with an infant I would have to make sure that I behaved in the way you described. It would be easy to make parents hyperanxious about what they do.

Brazelton: I thoroughly agree. This is a dangerous kind of research, in a way. We let mothers watch the videotapes and they certainly do get more sensitized to the laboratory situation at first. But as they get over the sensitivity, they begin to be able to profit by their ability to see themselves with their babies. They begin to be involved with us as well as with their babies. The way we get them entrained might interest you. We show them the neonatal scale (Brazelton 1974) in the lying-in hospital, as part of our research study. We become locked into their attachment to their babies as a result. They feel that we are showing them behaviour in the babies which they value, and they feel that we are crediting them for valuing this behaviour. By that time they are over the anxiety about the laboratory that Dr Papoušek mentioned. They begin to feel that we are all trying to produce the best baby we can. As a paediatrician I am perhaps hypersensitive about the anxiety they feel about creating the best baby they can. Young mothers in the US are so hungry for support, so hungry for anybody to get teamed up with them, that we become more of a support to them than a danger. They bring us all sorts of reports about their babies, with their interactions—the rhythms and the violations described in detail.

References

BRAZELTON, T. B. (1974) *Neonatal Behavioural Assessment Scale* (Clinics in Developmental Medicine, No. 50), Spastics International Medical Publications/Heinemann, London

BRAZELTON, T.B., KOSLOWSKI, B. & MAIN, M. (1974) The origins of reciprocity: the early mother–infant interaction, in *The Effect of the Infant on its Caregiver* (Lewis, M. & Rosenblum, L., eds.), Wiley-Interscience, New York

CARPENTER, G.C. (1974) Visual regard of moving and stationary faces in early infancy. *Merrill-Palmer Q. 20*, 181–194

CARPENTER, G.C., TECCE, J.J., STECHLER, G. & FRIEDMAN, S. (1970) Differential visual behaviour to human and humanoid faces in early infancy. *Merrill-Palmer Q. 16*, 91–108

LIPTON, E.L., STEINSCHNEIDER, A. & RICHMOND, J.B. (1961–1962) Autonomic function in the neonate. *Psychosom. Med. 23*, 472–484

MIDDLEMORE, M.P. (1941) *The Nursing Couple*, Cassell, London

OUNSTED, C., OPPENHEIMER, R. & LINDSEY, J. (1975) The psychopathology and psychotherapy of the families; aspects of bonding failure, in *Concerning Child Abuse* (Franklin, A.W., ed.), Churchill Livingstone, Edinburgh

Consistency and change in styles of mothering

JUDITH F. DUNN

MRC Unit on the Development and Integration of Behaviour, University Sub-Department of Animal Behaviour, Cambridge

Abstract The idea that the immediate postpartum period is particularly important for the developing relationship between mother and child is being increasingly discussed; however, little is known of the long-term significance of the individual differences in adjustment found in this period. A longitudinal study of 70 mother–baby pairs showed that difficulties during feeds were related to longer labour and to measures of the baby's state at birth. Differences between babies in the latency with which they responded by crying to interruption of sucking (in tests of non-nutritive sucking) were also related to the smoothness of the feed. Measures of affectionate maternal behaviour were associated with differences between babies in sucking rate, and were not influenced by labour and delivery. During later observations (8–30 weeks), strong consistency in individual differences across age was found in the levels of maternal touching, vocalizing, and responsiveness to baby's vocalizing. Maternal affectionate contact during early feeds (babies up to 10 days old) was related to these later maternal measures for breast-fed babies. Other aspects of coordination and warmth in the early feeds did not correlate with later measures, which suggested that predictions based on observations early in the neonatal period should be made with caution. Measures of maternal response to crying showed little consistency across the first seven months and were influenced by how much the baby cried at earlier ages.

The idea that the immediate postpartum period is particularly important for the developing relationship between mother and child has been increasingly discussed since Klaus & Kennell (1970) described the long-term effects of separating baby and mother at this time. Several different explanations have been put forward for these findings. One suggestion is that the immediate postpartum period is a 'sensitive' period in which the mother is particularly responsive, ready to adapt to the baby in a way that will not recur. Another interpretation, not incompatible with this one, is that mothers who handle and care for their babies immediately after birth develop different expectations and styles of handling—a different 'model' for mothering—to those developed by mothers who are separated from their babies at this time. Both interpretations suggest that qualitative differences in the early adjustment and interaction may have important consequences for the developing relationship, even where mother and baby are not separated. In itself, however, the evidence from studies of separation is not sufficient to establish the point. For this, one would need information about the long-term significance of the individual differences in adjustment and coordination which occur in mother and baby pairs who remain together from birth on.

People who care for or study mothers and babies in the early postnatal days cannot fail to be struck by the great range of individual differences in coordination and smoothness of interaction. But there have been few studies of the long-term implications of these early differences. Sander (1969*a*) has shown that differences in caretaking during the first 10 days can have effects detectable several weeks later in the infant's behaviour, and there are clinical studies showing the long-term consequences, for successful breast-feeding, of difficulties and differences in feeding patterns in the first two weeks (Gunther 1955; Illingworth *et al.* 1952).

There is also not much information about the factors contributing to these early differences in interaction. In a detailed study, Levy (1958) found that the state of arousal of the baby was particularly important; neonatal characteristics (Osofsky & Danzger 1974) and parity (Thoman *et al.* 1972) have also been shown to be relevant.

In the descriptions of differences in quality of mothering given in studies of early feeding interactions, particular attention has been paid to smoothness of interaction during the feed, with the suggestion that this reflects underlying sensitivity to the baby's signals on the mother's part; to the mother's timing and pacing of the feed; to the interest the mother shows in the baby in terms of looking, talking and caressing; and to the way in which she responds to his crying. But how closely are these different qualities related? How far are they influenced by differences between babies, and how much consistency do they show over later weeks? There has been much recent concern over finding indices of 'good' mothering in the early postpartum period, so that possible later disturbances in the mother–child relationship might be predicted. Do the early differences in coordination provide this sort of measure?

In this paper these questions will be discussed on the basis of material from a longitudinal study of 70 mother–child pairs (Richards & Bernal 1972). An outline of the procedures used and the information gathered is given in Table 1. Our findings from the first 10 days will be briefly described first, so that both the relationship between maternal variables during this period and the influences

TABLE 1

Procedures used in first 7 months of the infant's life

Time	*Procedure*
2–6 weeks before delivery	Interview with mother
Delivery	Precoded medical information collected by midwife. (Observation of first mother–infant interaction in a few cases)
Days 2, 3; 8, 9, 10	Observation of a feeding session on each day. Interview
Days 0–10	Continuous diary kept by mother of baby's time spent in cot, feeding, crying, bathing, out of cot
Day 8 or 9	Neurological examination, sucking test (Waldrop & Bell 1966)
8 weeks (2 visits)	One feeding session observed, and two periods with baby awake, not feeding. 48-hour diary kept by mother
14 weeks, 20 weeks, 30 weeks	2 visits at each age, with observations at each visit of 2 periods with baby awake, not feeding. 48-hour diary kept by mother

on them can be assessed. The early patterns will then be compared with later observations and the significance of the early period will be discussed.

RELATIONSHIP BETWEEN MATERNAL VARIABLES IN THE FIRST 10 DAYS

The measure of the mother's affectionate talking to the baby (defined as any talking except that directly concerned with the course of the feed, such as urging the baby to suck or to bring up the wind) during a feed showed a low positive correlation with smiling at the baby (Kendall $\rho = 0.18$, $n = 70$, $P < 0.02$). The affectionate talking and smiling measures correlated with a measure of the baby's sucking behaviour, the sucking rate, from the sucking test made on the eighth day (Table 2). In this test, developed by Waldrop & Bell (1966), individual differences in sucking behaviour were maintained from day to day over the neonatal period.

It seemed possible that the baby's sucking behaviour would be more strongly associated with the mother's behaviour during breast-feeding than during

TABLE 2

Relationship between infant's sucking rate, from sucking test on day 8, and variables from observations of the first 10 days, and from mothers' diaries (Kendall's ρ; $n = 68$)

	Mother talks affectionately	*Mother smiles at baby*	*Mother touches baby*	*Time held out of cot (diary measure)*
Rate of sucking in sucking test	0.34[b]	0.35[b]	0.19[a]	0.20[a]

[a] $P < 0.05$
[b] $P < 0.01$

bottle-feeding, but when the analysis for each type of feeding was done separately for breast-fed and bottle-fed babies, the relation between suck rate and affectionate talk was found to be significant for both feeding situations, though it was stronger with the breast-fed babies (Spearman rank correlation [rs] for breast-fed $=0.61$, $n=27$, $P<0.001$; bottle-fed rs $=0.60$, $n=19$, $P<0.01$).

A multiple regression analysis was done for each of the observation variables from feeds during the first 10 days and the 'background' variables such as parity, sex, delivery factors, and neurological and sucking test measures. The suck rate measure was associated with 18 % of the variance in the 'affectionate talk' variable, while feed type contributed a negligible amount of the variance.

But we cannot interpret this association as showing that differences in babies' sucking behaviour lead directly to differences in mothers' affectionate talking and smiling during the feed. For that, we would have to assume that the sucking test differences were congenital characteristics of the baby which were not influenced by the interaction between mother and baby. Even though the sucking test measures are made so early in life, and change little from day to day, this assumption is clearly not justified. We have for example found differences in sucking test measures between breast-fed and bottle-fed babies (Dunn & Richards 1975).

Interpretation of the association between the mother's affectionate behaviour and the suck rate measure presents us with a problem of central importance in studies of maternal or infant behaviour: that is that no measures of the behaviour of either mothers or infants can be assumed to be independent of the course of previous interaction between the two since birth.

Interestingly, the 'affectionate' measures of talking and smiling were not closely related to two other aspects of mothering we looked at next: touching (defined as including any contact not directly concerned with getting the baby to suck, or with bringing the wind up) and responsiveness to crying. The touching variable showed important differences in pattern and amount between breast-feeding and bottle-feeding, and these are discussed below (p. 161). The measures of the mother's responsiveness to crying (mean length of baby's crying bout, probability of crying leading to a feed) were obtained from the diaries kept by the mothers (Table 1)—possibly an unreliable source of information. (Measures of response to crying at later ages are derived from our own observations.) There was a low correlation between affectionate talking and mean length of crying in the first 10 days (Kendall $\rho=0.18$, $n=68$, $P<0.05$) but no significant association with the 'probability fed if crying'. The other 'affectionate variables' showed no relationship with these measures. An earlier analysis of responses to crying in the first 10 days had shown that the way in which a mother responded to crying in the first 10 days was influenced by the time since the baby was last fed, the advice she was given, and her attitude to that advice; these factors influenced the mothers differently, according to how many babies they had had (Bernal 1972*a*). The lack of a close association between the 'response to cry' measures and the 'affectionate variables' held between mothers of the same parity.

There was also no relation between mothers' attitudes to scheduling of feeds, as expressed in prenatal interviews, or in their actual scheduling of feeds after birth, and these affectionate variables.

This lack of a close relationship between the mother's feeding in response to crying and the affectionate variables is interesting in view of the association that Ainsworth & Bell (1969) reported between the ratings of mothers' feeding patterns, their physical contact with the baby and their responsiveness to the baby's crying. The difference in the results from the two studies may be explained in part by the age differences in the babies studied. Ainsworth & Bell's ratings were based on observations on infants aged between three weeks and three months. Our study, as we shall see, suggests that the interaction patterns in the first 10 days reflected special features of this early period and do not show strong continuity with the patterns of mothering seen from two months on. In a longitudinal study of mother–child pairs, Sander reported case histories

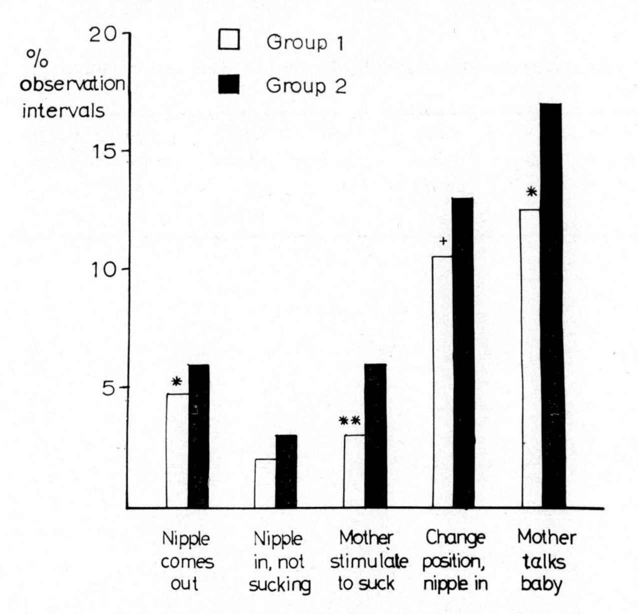

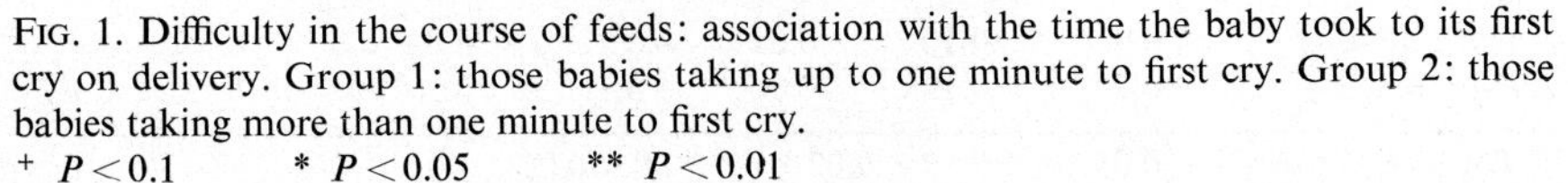

FIG. 1. Difficulty in the course of feeds: association with the time the baby took to its first cry on delivery. Group 1: those babies taking up to one minute to first cry. Group 2: those babies taking more than one minute to first cry.
$^{+}$ $P<0.1$ * $P<0.05$ ** $P<0.01$

which certainly suggest that it may take at least three weeks before the adaptation of mother and baby stabilizes to a 'characteristic' pattern (Sander 1969*b*).

Next, on the issue of smoothness of coordination during the feed, the question is raised of how closely the 'affectionate mothering' variables are related to the course of the feed, and how far—within a sample selected to be normal on strict criteria (Richards & Bernal 1972)—events during labour and delivery affect the early interaction.

Several indices of whether the feeds were going well were examined: the number of observation intervals during which the nipple is in the baby's mouth when he is not sucking, the ratio of number of times the nipple comes out of the baby's mouth to the number of intervals it remains in, the total sucking time, and the number of intervals in which the mother stimulated the baby to get him to suck. The close relationship between these measures is indicated in Table 3. In fact the measures that reflected difficulty during feeding showed no significant relationship with any of the affectionate variables discussed so far. There was, however, evidence that differences in the course of labour and delivery affected the smoothness of the feeds. Labour length and the time the baby took before its first cry were associated with difficulty in the feeds (e.g., Fig. 1).

TABLE 3

Kendall ρ correlations between measures reflecting difficulty during feeds and labour length (*n* varied between 60 and 70)

	M stim.	*M changes pos. B*	*Ratio nipple out/in*	*Total sucking*	*B on nipple, not sucking*	*Latency to cry*	*Labour length*
Mother (M) stimulates baby (B) to suck							
Mother changes position of baby when baby on nipple	0.15						
Ratio of times nipple comes out of baby's mouth to those when nipple in	0.16*	0.44^c					
Total sucking during feeds	0.10	−0.40^c	−0.38^c				
Baby on nipple, not sucking	0.42^c	0.36^c	0.34^c	−0.20^b			
Latency to cry on removal of teat (sucking test)	0.02	0.10	0.01	−0.22^b	0.09		
Labour length	0.26^b	0.19^a	0.06	0.11	0.20^b	0.07	

* $P<0.06$ ^{a} $P<0.05$ ^{b} $P<0.02$ ^{c} $P<0.01$

There was also a negative correlation between total sucking time (a measure which Levy takes as success in feeds) (Levy 1958) and the sucking test measure of latency to cry on removal of the nipple—a measure with which the baby's reaction to removal of a standard pacifying situation can be compared.

BREAST/BOTTLE DIFFERENCES

A different aspect of coordination between mother and baby was highlighted by the analysis of feed-type differences. With breast-fed babies not only did we see the mothers touching, smiling and rocking more often, but the patterning of the mother's actions was also more influenced by the baby's activity. This is illustrated in Table 4, which shows that talking to the baby and touching are importantly influenced by the baby's sucking—talking being more likely to take place during gaps between sucking bouts and touching during sucking. With bottle-fed babies the mothers touched and talked more randomly during the observation periods. A particularly interesting point was the difference in responsibility for ending sucking bouts: in bottle-feeding it was overwhelmingly the mother who ended the bout, while with breast-feeders it was equally likely to be mother or baby (Fig. 2). These differences were still significant when socioeconomic class differences in the two groups were controlled; the differences were more marked on days 8 to 10 than earlier in the first week (Table 4).

CONTINUITY BEYOND THE EARLY DAYS

Measures of maternal behaviour do not, it seems, co-vary in any simple way during the early days, and are not related to the same infant variables or delivery factors. The measures of looking at, smiling and talking affectionately to the

TABLE 4

Breast-fed/bottle-fed differences (second babies) (Mann-Whitney U-test)

	Days 2 & 3 (n = 35)				*Days 8–10 (n = 49)*			
	Bottle-fed	*Breast-fed*	*U*	*P*	*Bottle-fed*	*Breast-fed*	*U*	*P*
Probability mother touches if baby sucking	0.02	0.09	108	<0.1	0.02	0.12	131	<0.01
Probability mother talks if gap between sucking bouts	0.30	0.47	84	<0.05	0.36	0.49	178	<0.05

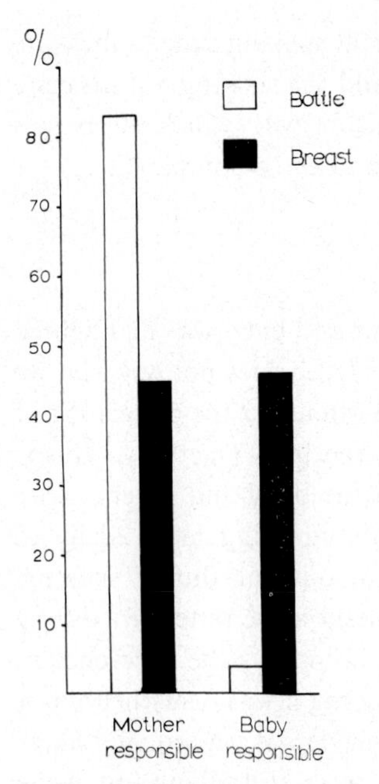

FIG. 2. Responsibility for ending bouts of sucking: differences between breast-feeding and bottle-feeding pairs.

baby were not closely related to the success and coordination of the feed, nor to affectionately touching the baby. The important question is, what is the long-term significance of these different aspects of the relationship? Which of them show continuity with patterns of interaction later, and which reflect special features of the early feeding situation that are unrelated to later behavioural measures? These early feeds are dominated for most mothers by their concern with getting enough food into the baby, and with 'getting the wind up'. A mother who felt strongly about her responsibilities in this respect might in other situations be relaxed and enjoying the baby. Although it is usually assumed that a mother's style of interacting with her baby during the feed is in important ways representative of her whole relationship with him (e.g. Brody 1956; Ainsworth & Bell 1969), there are few data on which to base such a view.

It is certainly clear that coordination can improve quickly as mother and baby get to know each other. The speed of this adjustment is illustrated by the separate analyses that we did for the feeds on days 2 and 3, and those on days 8, 9 and 10. As Fig. 3 shows, smoothness and coordination increased significantly within the 10-day period. Parity differences were interesting in this respect: on days 2 and 3 we found differences between mothers according to whether they were interacting with first or second babies; these differences were similar to those seen by Thoman *et al.* (1972) in a study of a feed on the s cond day, but by days 8–10 the differences we saw had disappeared, suggesting that it would have been a mistake to relate the early parity differences in the feeding situation too directly to parity differences in later handling or behaviour of the baby (Dunn & Richards 1975).

Analysis of the later observations has shown that there was considerable continuity in the maternal variables of touching, vocalization to the baby, and responsiveness to the baby's vocalization from eight weeks through to seven months, and that these variables were correlated with each other. Table 5 shows the correlations between touch and maternal vocalization to the baby. There was not a simple positive relationship between these measures and measures of responsiveness to crying.

Table 6 shows the relationship between two variables from the first 10 days,

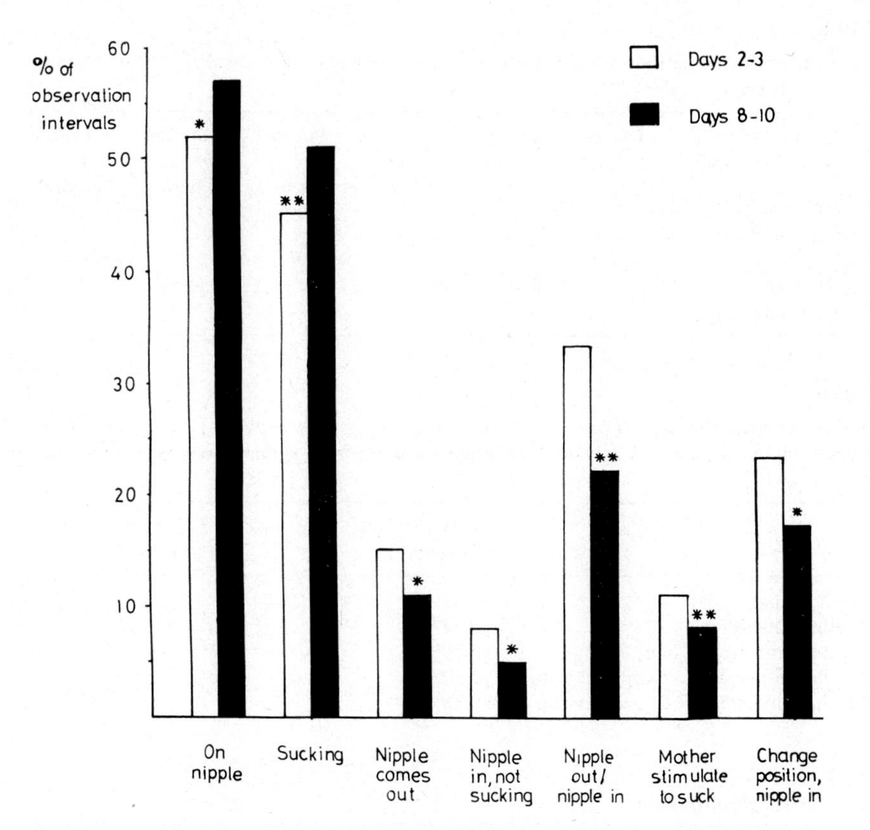

FIG. 3. Changes in the course of feeds over the first 10 days.

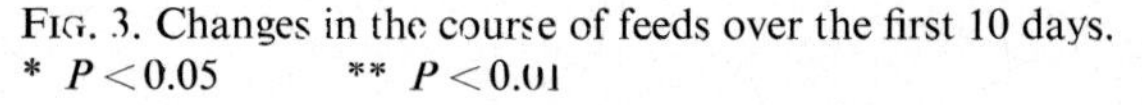
* $P<0.05$ ** $P<0.01$

and later aspects of maternal response. 'Factor 2' is derived from the factor analysis of material from the first 10 days; its major loading variables were the measures of affectionate talk, sucking rate and smile. This factor was correlated with the amount of maternal vocalization, affectionate contact, responsiveness to baby's vocalization, and unresponsiveness to crying (here a measure from the observations rather than the diaries—Bell & Ainsworth's [1972] measure—is used) at 8 weeks. At 14 weeks there was a correlation with maternal vocalization (14 weeks: $rs = 0.31$, $n = 56$, $P < 0.05$). This factor was more strongly correlated with the later maternal measures than any of the individual variables from the first 10 days that contributed to it.

The relationship between the measures of affectionate touching during feeds in the first 10 days, and later maternal contact and vocalization, was a little complicated: there were positive correlations for the sample as a whole between

TABLE 5

Spearman rank correlation between maternal touch and maternal vocalization at different ages *($n = 60$–68, $P < 0.01$)*

	Touch (14 wk)	*Touch (20 wk)*	*Touch (30 wk)*	*Vocalization (8 wk)*	*Vocalization (14 wk)*	*Vocalization (20 wk)*	*Vocalization (30 wk)*
Touch (8 wk)	0.50			0.53			
Touch (14 wk)		0.58			0.59		
Touch (20 wk)			0.48			0.56	
Touch (30 wk)							0.63

TABLE 6

Continuities from the first 10 days: Spearman rank correlations between two variables from observations on the first 10 days and maternal variables from observations at 8 weeks and 30 weeks ($n = 55$–59)

	First 10 days (Factor 2)	*First 10 days (Mother touches)*
8 weeks		
Mother touches	0.22*	0.46[b]
Mother vocalizes to baby	0.26[a]	0.23*
Mother responsive to baby vocalizing	0.30[a]	0.30[a]
Mother unresponsive to baby crying	– 0.36[b]	n.s.
30 weeks		
Mother touches		0.37[b]
Mother vocalizes to baby		0.23[a]

* $P < 0.1$ [a] $P < 0.05$ [b] $P < 0.01$
n.s.: not significant

the early measures right through to seven months. However, when the analysis was done separately for bottle-feeding and breast-feeding mothers, we found that the relationship was strong for the breast-feeders but was not significant for the bottle-feeders. That is, the amount of affectionate touching shown by a bottle-feeding mother in the early feeds bore no relation to the amount she showed outside the feeding time in later weeks. In this later affectionate contact, outside the feeds, individual differences between the bottle-feeding mothers were as consistent across age as were the individual differences between the breast-feeders. The continuity in this contact variable from the early days is particularly interesting in view of Kennell and Klaus's evidence that levels of later affectionate contact are influenced by early separation (Kennell *et al.* 1974). Their findings raise the question of whether the relationship found by Moss (1967) between prenatal attitude and later maternal affectionate contact is dependent on continuous contact between mother and baby since birth. Moss commented that the amount of affectionate contact may be a more sensitive indicator of 'enduring maternal attitude' than the absolute time spent on physical activities like feeding; the study by Kennell *et al.* (1974) suggests that this particular maternal attitude may not be 'enduring' in circumstances where mother and baby are separated.

Although we found consistency in amounts of affectionate contact over age for the sample as a whole, there was a complicated association between contact and the irritability of the babies. For instance, analysis of affectionate contact and earlier crying showed that long crying times and a high frequency of crying bouts at one age were associated with decreased contact at later ages (Table 7).

Total crying score is, of course, a measure that depends on the mother's response to crying: it might be thought that a negative correlation between total crying at one age and affectionate contact at the next was a reflection of the same underlying trait in the mother, rather than an effect of the baby on subsequent maternal handling. If this were the case, at least as strong a negative correlation between contact and amount of crying would be expected within any observation period, that is, at 10 days, eight weeks or 14 weeks. However, there were no significant correlations between the maternal touch measures and the crying measures within any observation period.

Measures of maternal affectionate contact at the later ages were also found to be associated with a measure of baby behaviour from the early postnatal period, that is, with the sucking test measure of latency to cry on removal of teat, which was related to difficulty with feeds (and also with characteristics of sleeping behaviour showing strong continuity throughout the first 14 months: Bernal 1973). The more quickly reactive babies had more maternal contact and vocalization at 14 and 20 weeks (Table 8). The correlations were not high,

TABLE 7

Spearman rank correlations (rs) between crying measures and mother's touch at later ages (second babies only)

	rs	*n*	*P*
First 10-day crying total and mother's touch, 8 weeks	−0.33	41	<0.05
14-week crying total and mother's touch, 20 weeks	−0.34	49	<0.05
14-week frequency of crying bouts and mother's touch, 20 weeks	−0.43	49	<0.01

but the possibility is raised that continuity in individual differences in reactivity between babies, reflected in this measure, contributes to the continuity found in the maternal measures. The interpretation could well be the other way round: that the correlations reflect a *maternal* influence on the babies' behaviour in the sucking test. One would have to assume that a shorter latency to cry on removal of the pacifier was related to the experience of a more responsive or attentive mother during the first eight days of life.

When patterns of consistency from the first 10 days were looked for in responsiveness to crying, the story that emerged was one of change rather than stability. For instance, the mean length of bouts of crying at 10 days correlated negatively with both the mean length of bouts at eight weeks (rs $= -0.37$, $n = 55$, $P < 0.01$) and with total crying at eight weeks (rs $= -0.28$, $n = 53$, $P < 0.05$). Those mothers who were responding most quickly in the first 10 days were responding least quickly at eight weeks, or had babies who cried for longer before settling if the mother did not intervene. There was also a correlation between the probability of the baby being fed if he cried in the first 10 days, and total crying (rs $= 0.38$, $P < 0.02$) at eight weeks; and this effect carries through to 14 weeks, where there was a significant correlation between 'probability fed if crying' in the first 10 days and frequency of crying at 14 weeks (rs $= 0.36$, $n = 45$, $P < 0.02$).

We found that it was particularly important to take account of the amount of crying when we were assessing responsiveness to crying or examining the interrelations of different measures of maternal affectionate behaviour at these

TABLE 8

Spearman rank correlations of latency to cry measure (sucking test, day 8) with later maternal measures ($n = 60$)

	Mother vocalizes if present	*Mother touches if present*	*Mother touches if baby vocalizes*
14 weeks	-0.30^{a}	-0.37^{b}	-0.36^{b}
20 weeks	−0.16	−0.22*	-0.29^{a}

* $P < 0.1$ [a] $P < 0.05$ [b] $P < 0.01$

later ages. With the considerable range of crying shown by the babies in this sample (and in other reports, e.g. Rebelsky & Black 1972) we thought it would be useful to analyse separately those mothers whose babies cried a great deal and those whose babies cried very little. If a mother is unresponsive to a baby's crying even when he cries rather little, this may mean something rather different about her general responsiveness to the baby than does the unresponsiveness to crying shown by a mother whose baby cries a great deal. This suggestion was supported by the results obtained when we analysed separately those 20 mothers whose babies cried the least, and the 20 mothers whose babies cried the most. For the mothers whose babies cried the least, there was a correlation at 14 weeks between the mother's level of responsiveness to crying and touching the baby ($rs = 0.42$, $n = 20$, $P < 0.10$), and again at 20 weeks ($rs = 0.58$, $n = 20$, $P < 0.01$). For the 20 mothers whose babies cried the most, there was no such relationship. The complexities of these interrelations will be discussed in a further publication.

The relative smoothness or difficulty of feeds did show some continuity with later success in breast-feeding: there was a significant association between successful breast-feeding for more than two weeks and the number of intervals the nipple was in the mouth but the baby was not sucking (mean number of intervals: 2.2 successful, 3.3 those giving up; Mann-Whitney $U = 167$, $n = 47$, $P < 0.05$). Again, a relationship was found between a combined score for length of labour plus drug (used for comparison with the study by Jackson *et al.* 1956), and the duration of breast-feeding. On the basis of these correlations we cannot of course decide how far a relatively short duration of breast-feeding is a *direct* result of feeding not going well at the start of lactation, and how far both reflect a common causal factor such as anxiety or distaste on the mother's part for the breast-feeding experience. The correlations between success in breast-feeding and mother's prenatal enthusiasm for breast-feeding, and educational level, were far more striking (Bernal 1972*b*), and these correlations suggest that the course of early feeds, while it may present problems for breast-feeding success, is of much less importance than the mother's determination to persevere, and the support she receives.

We looked with interest to see whether there were differences in interaction patterns between breast-feeders and bottle-feeders later on, outside the feeding situation, since the differences in pattern in the early feeds were intriguing: it is sometimes suggested that the type of interaction in which the mother times her responses to fit the baby's actions, and allows the baby an important part in patterning the interaction, provides the best groundwork on which communication can build up. Although we found no later differences in interaction patterns between breast-feeders and bottle-feeders, this could well be an area where a finer level of analysis, sensitive to the details of synchrony—such as the analysis used by Stern (1974)—might be appropriate for looking for continuities. The pattern differences apparent in feeds during the first 10 days were even more marked in the feed at eight weeks.

DISCUSSION AND CONCLUSIONS

The importance of finding ways of assessing the early mother–child relationship for potential difficulties is often emphasized when problems such as battering are discussed. The methodology and level of analysis in this study may well be inappropriate for the identification of the fine-grained synchrony and asynchrony that is needed: the 'event' recording may well have masked important differences in interactions and missed the subtleties of reciprocity; no attempt was made to measure qualitative differences in intensity and tempo, and the correlation technique made causal analysis speculative. Nevertheless several points have emerged which are relevant to the problem of how important the early period is and the extent to which one can usefully predict from it, and more generally to the problems of describing and assessing maternal affectionate and responsive behaviour.

First, a number of the relationships described here seem to reflect particular aspects of the early postnatal feeds rather than reveal important predictors of qualitative differences in the mother–child relationship. The 'affectionate' variables which were associated with the babies' suck rate and which formed Factor 2 (p. 164) could well relate rather specifically to the early feeding situation. Factor 2 did not correlate with interaction variables beyond eight weeks. Measures of smoothness and difficulty in the feeds were influenced by events during labour and delivery and by differences in the babies' behaviour; such measures were unrelated to the various aspects of maternal behaviour described, and did not provide useful indices for prediction.

On the other hand substantial continuities were traced, for breast-feeding mothers, from the mother's affectionate contact in the early feeds through to seven months. The early feeds for bottle-feeding mothers were not so revealing with respect to affectionate contact. Indeed, in attempts to assess long-term qualities of mothering, an emphasis on interaction during the early feeds for the bottle-feeding mothers could well be misleading. Analysis of the amount of affectionate contact at the different ages we observed raised the possibility that stable characteristics of the baby might have contributed to the continuity in the maternal measure. When we traced continuity in responsiveness to crying from the early period we saw a changing picture, with the relative responsiveness of mothers in the sample altering from age to age; there was no simple relationship between measures of responsiveness to crying and the other maternal measures, and the amount of crying strongly influenced the response to crying.

Although these results underline the difficulty of basing predictions of future relationships on the early mother–infant interaction, the sample we studied was strictly selected to be medically 'normal' and socially secure. We should be cautious about generalizing from this group: if a sample included mothers and babies with more extreme or pathological patterns of interaction, prediction might indeed be possible.

Finally, the lack of correlation between coordination measures from the early feeds and the later consistent maternal measures suggests that the postpartum period, rather than being a sensitive period, may be a time when the relationship between mother and baby is buffered against difficulties of adjustment. It would make good adaptive sense, in biological terms, if problems of adjustment at this time did *not* have long-term effects. It may take three or four weeks for mother and baby to settle to a characteristic pattern, and it may be more useful if indices of adjustment are looked for at this later stage.

ACKNOWLEDGEMENTS

This study was supported by a grant from the Nuffield Foundation. I would like to thank Martin Richards who initiated the project, and with whom all observations were planned and carried out. Robert Hinde gave invaluable critical help with this paper.

References

AINSWORTH, M.D.S. & BELL, S.M. (1969) Some contemporary patterns of mother–infant interactions in the feeding situation, in *Stimulation in Early Infancy* (Ambrose, A., ed.), pp. 133–163, Academic Press, London

BELL, S.M. & AINSWORTH, M.D.S. (1972) Infant crying and maternal responsiveness. *Child Dev. 43*, 1171–1190

BERNAL, J.F. (1972*a*) Crying during the first 10 days of life, and maternal responses. *Dev. Med. Child Neurol. 14*, 362–372

BERNAL, J.F. (1972*b*) Breast feeding and bottle feeding, and the mother–child relationship, in *Proceedings of Symposium on Infant Feeding*, Department of Child Health, University of Manchester

BERNAL, J. F. (1973) Night waking in the first 14 months. *Dev. Med. Child Neurol. 15*, 760–769

BRODY, S. (1956) *Patterns of Mothering*, International Universities Press, New York

DUNN, J.F. (formerly BERNAL) & RICHARDS, M.P.M. (1975) Observations on the developing relationship between mother and baby in the neonatal period. Submitted for publication.

GUNTHER, M. (1955) Instinct and the nursing couple. *Lancet* 575–578

ILLINGWORTH, R.S., STONE, D.G.H., HOWETT, G.H. & SCOTT, J.F. (1952) Self-demand feeding in a maternity unit. *Lancet 1*, 683

JACKSON, E.B., WILKIN, L.C. & AUERBACH, H. (1956) Statistical report on incidence and duration of breast-feeding in relation to personal-social and hospital maternity factors. *Pediatrics, 17*, 700

KLAUS, M. & KENNELL, J. (1970) Mothers separated from their newborn infants. *Pediatr. Clin. N. Am. 17*, 1015

KENNELL, J.K., JERAULD, R., WOLFE, H., CHENER, D., KREGER, N., MCALPINE, W., STAFFER, M. & KLAUS, M.H. (1974) Maternal behaviour one year after early and extended post-partum contact. *Dev. Med. Child Neurol. 16*, 172–179

LEVY, D.M. (1958) *Behavioural Analysis*, Thomas, Springfield, Ill.

MOSS, H.A. (1967) Sex, age, and state as determinants of mother–infant interaction. *Merrill-Palmer Q. 13*, 19–36

OSOFSKY, J.D. & DANZGER, B. (1974) Relationships between neonatal characteristics and mother–infant interaction. *Dev. Psychol. 10*, 124–130

REBELSKY, F. & BLACK, R. (1972) Crying in infancy. *J. Genet. Psychol. 121*, 49–57

RICHARDS, M.P.M. & BERNAL, J.F. (1972) An observational study of mother–infant interaction, in *Ethological Studies of Child Behaviour* (Blurton-Jones, N., ed.), pp. 175–197, Cambridge University Press, London

SANDER, L.W. (1969*a*) Regulation and organization in the early infant–caretaker system, in *Brain and Early Behaviour* (Robinson, R.J., ed.), pp. 311–332, Academic Press, London

SANDER, L.W. (1969*b*) The longitudinal course of early mother–child interaction: cross-case comparison in a sample of mother–child pairs, in *Determinants of Infant Behaviour* (Foss, B.M., ed.), vol. 4, pp. 189–227, Methuen, London

THOMAN, E.B., LEIDERMAN, H.P. & OLSON, J.P. (1972) Neonate–mother interaction during breast-feeding. *Dev. Psychol. 6*, 110–118

STERN, D.N. (1974) Mother and infant at play: the dyadic interaction involving facial, vocal and gaze behaviours, in *The Effect of the Infant on its Caregiver* (Lewis, M. & Rosenblum, L., eds.), pp. 187–213, Wiley, New York

WALDROP, M. & BELL, R.Q. (1966) Effects of family size and density on newborn characteristics. *Am. J. Orthopsychiatr. 36*, 544–550

Discussion

Thoman: You said that early caressing and patting did not correlate well with later caressing and stimulation of bottle-fed babies, although there was good correlation for breast-fed babies. This may therefore be a good measure for breast-feeders only. There may be other measures that indicate sensitivity of the bottle-feeder. Of course, a mother feeding her baby with a bottle has one hand busy holding the bottle.

Dunn: We did not record which hand was touching the baby but Levy (1958) records that since the breast-feeding mother often uses the free hand to hold her breast back from occluding the baby's nostrils, it is frequently the hand that is holding the baby that is caressing it.

Thoman: But there may be other indices of sensitivity. K. Kaye & T.B. Brazelton (1971, unpublished) reported that some mothers were more sensitive than others about stimulating their babies to suck at the right time in the suck-pulse pattern.

Dunn: Even after a baby had sucked consistently for 15 minutes, which in these early feeds is quite long, a few mothers persistently tried to get their babies to go on sucking. This sort of persistence was negatively related to the measure of affectionate talking and touching.

Klaus: Did the touching that you saw at 10 days relate to whether the baby was planned or unplanned, wanted or unwanted?

Dunn: Nearly all these babies were planned and wanted. They were very secure families.

Klaus: We have not observed touching with the free hand in mothers of premature babies who are bottle-fed, even in those who come into the nursery early. What is your experience?

Dunn: I wish we had more observations of the mothers and the babies outside the feeding time, but the babies nearly always fall asleep at the end of a feed. If we had included observations in the middle of the night when most of the babies were awake maybe we would have had better measures to compare this with.

Klaus: What is the relationship between touching and talking to the children as they grow?

Dunn: The data have not been analysed. Touching and talking are closely correlated at seven months, and talking certainly correlates well with what we get at 14 months. That is, the mother who is talking and touching a lot at seven months is the mother who is talking a lot to her baby at 14 months, and her baby is talking a great deal to her, with close interaction.

Papoušek: You dealt with the breast-feeders as a homogeneous group, which surprises me a little. When we were analysing adjustment to sucking, we always had to differentiate a group of skilful breast-feeding mothers and mothers who had difficulties, particularly from soreness of the nipples (e.g. rhagades: Papoušek & Jungmannová 1967). We found that this depended on the behavioural components, not hormonal or bacteriological ones. Rhagades could be prevented if mothers were instructed adequately, and the mutual adjustment between mothers and infants then went much more smoothly. The nipple should always be inserted centrally in the neonate's mouth, and not displaced when the mother pushes her engorged breast away from the baby's nose in order to prevent obstruction of his air passage. An eccentrically inserted nipple can easily be damaged by the baby's jaws. The resulting rhagades or mastitis complicates the mutual adjustment during breast-feeding. Were there any such cases among your breast-feeding mothers, Mrs Dunn?

Dunn: Yes, and we were interested in how this related to success in breast-feeding. We found a relationship between some of the measures of coordination and success in breast-feeding, but much more powerful correlations were found between measures of the mother's enthusiasm for and interest in breast-feeding and the support she was given by the people around her than with the minutiae of adjustment during the early feeds. What happened to these babies in the first 10 days bore, in important respects, not much relation to the consistent patterns that we found in later months. The mothers in our sample were getting varied advice and support because they were being visited by different nurses, some of whom were extremely skilled in showing them how to breast-feed successfully.

Bowlby: You said that your initial measures of maternal sensitivity to crying were obtained from a diary, which you explained was not very reliable. What about the later measures?

Dunn: The later measures of responsiveness to crying were derived from observations made for two hours at each of the ages. To make the work directly comparable with Mary Ainsworth's I used a measure of latency between the babies crying and the mothers responding. We found, first, that how the mothers responded to crying was not stable across the ages of 8, 14, 20 and 30 weeks. Secondly, there was not a close relationship between how the mother responded to crying and these other maternal measures which did not show very good consistency. Thirdly, these measures of responsiveness to crying were affected by the level of irritability that the baby had shown at the previous age. That is, the amount of crying that the baby had done at eight weeks had a negative relationship with the mother's response to his crying at the next stage of 14 weeks. No correlations went in the direction that the more responsive the mother was, the less crying the baby did at the next stage. They were all in the other direction.

Kennell: Have you compared mothers who had their babies in a hospital with those who delivered at home?

Dunn: Nine out of 70 babies were delivered in hospital and stayed there for 48 hours. It is not really enough for comparing them on these measures.

Richards: We did some pilot observations in hospital at the beginning of our project. My general impression is that there are big differences. The social situations in which all these things happen are crucial. One specific difference was that virtually all the mothers in hospital cried during a feed. That occurred so rarely after home deliveries that we dropped the category of 'mother cry' from the check sheet. This alone should alert us to the point that things may be rather different in the two situations.

I think that when we compare breast feeds and bottle feeds, we may need to think about the social meaning of breast-feeding or bottle-feeding to the mother. The lack of correlation across ages with the bottle-feeding might mean that the mother defined the bottle feed in some sense as not being part of social interaction, whereas a breast-feeding mother may see this as social interaction as well as feeding. We should think much more in terms of social definitions, in terms of both the environment and of what is going on in the mother's head.

Cooper: Your work touches on the question of trying to predict which families are at risk of child abuse, Mrs Dunn, but those who respond to research of this kind are probably not likely to include families with this problem. The incidence of abuse is something like 6/1000.

Dunn: People who are setting up research programmes to pick out mother–infant pairs who are likely to be at risk are anxious to learn what they could look for in the first 10 days that would indicate which mother–infant pairs are at risk.

Cooper: The way a baby behaves in a particular situation may be totally different from the way it behaves if it changes mothers. In fostering or adoption this is very relevant. One extremely good mother who had a grown-up family had also had 41 foster-children. The 42nd child was one that she took at five days of age, to care for until the mother decided whether she would have the baby adopted or whether she would take her back to care for her at home. Over the period from five days to four months when she was referred to me, the child had an increasing crescendo of crying, screaming and refusing to feed. When she came in we thought that she must have cerebral palsy because she was almost rigid with tension and extremely restless. A fortnight's observation in the ward revealed to our astonishment that she was a perfectly normal baby. I could not understand how this extremely good foster-mother, who had never had any trouble with her children before, had done this to her foster-baby. The foster-mother lived 40 miles away yet she visited the baby for three hours every day she was in hospital. The foster-mother had plenty of other things to do, but she felt guilty about this child that she couldn't care for. She afterwards admitted that on seeing the child at five days she had thought she was a mongol. She had a mongol niece whom she didn't like, and she never related well to this baby. The type of mothering the child is getting, and what the mother feels about what the child does, seem to be relevant and perhaps wouldn't be revealed in these observations.

D'Souza: The 'abnormality' of that baby may well have been that she did not want close mothering contact, but was prepared to be 'normal' in a hospital environment.

Cooper: But immediately the baby was placed in an adoptive home she enjoyed close mothering and became happy and responsive. She has continued to do very well.

Oppé: I want to comment on your speculation that the first 10 days might be a buffer period, Mrs Dunn. We tend to forget that with modern obstetric procedures, a woman who has had a baby is a great deal fitter rather sooner than many women used to be. They were then often worn out by long labours, exsanguinated by haemorrhages or had infections, and many of them were just not fit to care for their babies in the first 10 days. It would make a lot of biological sense if you were right.

Dunn: Cross-cultural anthropological descriptions of labour and delivery suggest that it would not make biological sense if difficulties of adjustment during those first few days had long-term consequences. Although no medical technology or medication are interfering, it is not true that labour and delivery are easy and quick in all cases. Some cultures also have taboos on helping the mother immediately after birth.

Rosenblatt: You concluded that what happens in feeding may not be predictive for what happens at any other time. Could you speculate further on that? Many studies are oriented around the feeding situation. Daniel Stern (unpublished work, 1974) also concluded that feeding is not a good time to make observations.

Dunn: Mothers are very anxious about getting food into the baby in the first 10 days. They are really concerned about their responsibility for making sure that he gets enough. They are told that he should sleep for four hours after his feed. They know that if he does not get enough food he is going to be awake in two hours. Observations slightly later, when the mother is perhaps more relaxed about feeding, might bear a closer relationship to the consistent patterns of mothering we found from eight weeks on, outside the feeding situation.

Mary Ainsworth and Sylvia Bell (1969) did one study using rating scales of what was happening during the feed. They found good correlations between ratings of the mother's sensitivity and competence in adjusting to a baby of three to six weeks during feeds and her responsiveness to the baby's crying outside the feeding situation, general attitude to flexibility of schedules, and so on. One explanation of the difference between our findings and theirs might be that this early period is one where particular anxiety is invested in feeding.

Bell: Our observers think that in the first few months, although there are certainly individual differences in the feeding situation, and in the performance of the baby and the mother, feeding is a much more stereotyped situation, and much more endogenously regulated than other situations. So our investigators are looking at other situations, such as the short periods when the baby is awake and active, to see how the mother and baby interact and how she handles the fussing and crying.

A useful method for estimating the direction of influence between mother and baby is the cross-lagged correlation technique. It is quite useful in developmental studies, particularly in shorter-term studies where one can be fairly certain of having the same infant and the same maternal behaviours over the time span of the study. Events such as the infant's crying and the mother's responsiveness at, say, 12 weeks and 17 weeks (Time 1 and Time 2) can be correlated on a cross-lagged plot. The situation is not an experimental one so it isn't really possible to talk about cause and effect, but an estimate of the direction of influence can be made by comparing the two correlations involving early infant to later maternal behaviours, and vice versa, against the background of the other correlations within and across time.

The best description of this is in a developmental study by Clarke-Stewart (1973). She obtained a different direction of influence in the two areas (see Figs. 1 and 2, based on Clarke-Stewart 1973). One area was the effect of the mother's stimulation on the baby's later developmental scores. There the mother's early behaviour appeared to be influencing the change. The strength of the attachment between the mother and the infant, on the other hand, appeared to be influenced primarily by the infant's earlier behaviour. So different results appear, depending on the area. There is no single direction of influence. It should be kept in mind that all of the foregoing involves the rank order of individuals, not change in their absolute standing.

In addition to the necessity of having relatively similar measures at the two time periods, it is necessary to find out the capabilities of one's measures for producing correlations over time, because the measures have certain psychometric properties. Some might be defective. This is discussed in the well-known study by Eron *et al.* (1972) on whether aggressive television programmes produce later peer aggression. There are various ways of estimating what the cross-lagged correlations, and the difference between them, should be to be significant, and these are referred to in the study by Eron *et al.* There is an

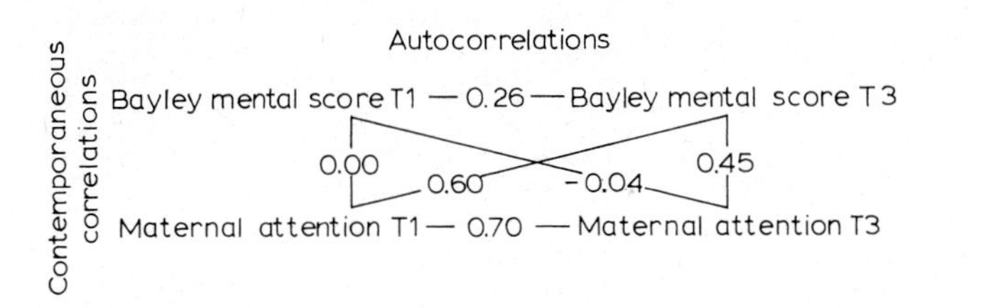

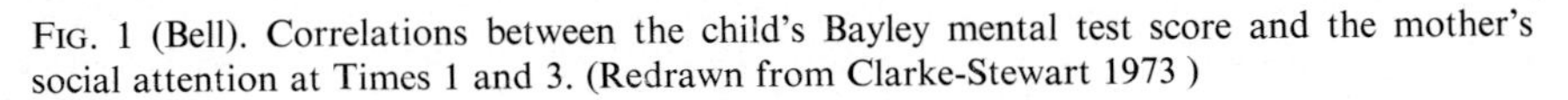
FIG. 1 (Bell). Correlations between the child's Bayley mental test score and the mother's social attention at Times 1 and 3. (Redrawn from Clarke-Stewart 1973.)

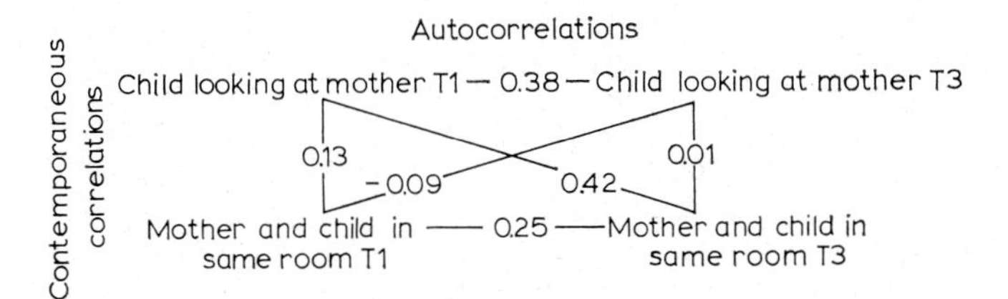

FIG. 2 (Bell). Correlations between the frequency with which the child looks at his mother and the amount of time they spend together, at Times 1 and 3. (Redrawn from Clarke-Stewart 1973.)

ongoing discussion amongst statisticians on just how to do this, but the general technique of cross-lagged correlations had been used by social psychologists for some time before developmental psychologists became interested.

References

AINSWORTH, M.D.S. & BELL, S.M. (1969) Some contemporary patterns of mother–infant interaction in the feeding situation, in *Stimulation in Early Infancy* (Ambrose, A., ed.), Academic Press, London

CLARKE-STEWART, K.A. (1973) Interactions between mothers and their children: characteristics and consequences. *Monogr. Soc. Res. Child Dev. 38*, No. 6–7

ERON, L.D., HUESMANN, L.R., LEFKOWITZ, M.M. & WALDER, L.O. (1972) Does television violence cause aggression? *Am. Psychol. 27*, 253–263

LEVY, D.M. (1958) *Behavioural Analysis*, Thomas, Springfield

PAPOUŠEK, H. & JUNGMANNOVÁ, Č. (1967) Nutrition, in *The Neonatal Care* (Kubát, K., ed.), pp. 50–83 [in Czech], Statni zdravotnické Nakladatelstvi, Prague

How a rejecting baby affects mother-infant synchrony

EVELYN B. THOMAN

Department of Biobehavioral Sciences, University of Connecticut, Storrs

Abstract In any mother–infant relationship, characteristics of both the mother and infant contribute to an ongoing process of mutual modification of behaviour. With intensive observation and objective recording of behaviours, it is possible to describe individual infants, depict patterns of interaction with their mothers, and identify some of the consequences of interaction for both the mother's and the infant's developing behaviours.

Even a normal infant can have behaviour patterns that play a disruptive role in the relationship. For example, an infant has been observed who, from birth through the first weeks of life, showed avoidance responses to being picked up and held. The infant's behaviour was a source of frustration and confusion to the unsuspecting parents. It is obviously difficult for the parents to respond appropriately to the needs of such an infant. And, in turn, the resulting interaction affects the infant's developing behaviours.

The theme of this paper is to emphasize, though each relationship is unique, that observations made from the first days of life can permit the infant's contribution to the mother–infant relationship, and the manner in which that relationship influences his development, to be assessed.

The role of the mother–infant relationship in facilitating the child's development is a central concept in developmental theories. Studies of the interactive aspects of that relationship are, however, relatively new, and procedures for them have not yet been fully developed. Much of the early research was devoted to identifying ways in which specific kinds of parental caretaking affected the infant's development. These studies are notable for having contributed little to our understanding of the development of behaviour. It is now recognized that the nature of parental behaviour is in large measure a function of the child's characteristics, including his precipitating behaviour as well as his response to the parents' activity. Thus, an understanding of the interactive process is needed before the influence of a parent on the child can be depicted.

The significant role of the infant in the interactive process has been recognized in recent research, for example in the studies reported in *The Effect of the Infant on its Caregiver* (Lewis & Rosenblum 1974). These studies are typical of many now being published in that they are concerned primarily with the probable *implications* of observed infant behaviours for the mother–infant relationship rather than with the characteristics of the interaction itself.

Very few studies of mother–infant interaction give attention to the relationship during the earliest days after the infant's birth. Consequently, little is known about the early stages of interaction or about how these early patterns may lead to more stable ones that become established over time. Our studies of mother–infant interaction suggest that very early interactive patterns may be responsible for later interactional patterns as well as for the behaviour characteristics that develop in the child. For example, in studies of mothers feeding their newborn infants, we found marked differences in the mother–infant interaction as a function of the parity of the mother (Thoman *et al.* 1970, 1971, 1972). Inexperienced, primiparous mothers take longer to feed their infants, they change their feeding activity more often, and they stimulate their infants more than multiparous mothers do. Yet the infants of primiparous mothers consume less if they are bottle-fed and suck less if breast-fed than infants of multiparous mothers. Differences in sucking patterns were not apparent when infants were fed by an experienced nurse. These studies suggest that primiparous mothers were less sensitive or less responsive than multiparous mothers to their infant's cues during feeding interaction.

There may be more than a coincidental relationship between the interactive patterns that we have reported and the patterns found in studies concerned with birth-order (parity) differences in mothering of older children: mothers of first-born children are much more persistent, more demanding, more inconsistent, and more attentive than mothers with second or subsequent children (Stout 1960; Lasko 1954; Hilton 1967; Sutton-Smith & Rosenberg 1965). Accordingly, first-born children differ from those of greater birth order in that they are more motivated for achievement (Altus 1966), more anxious (Schachter 1959), more susceptible to social pressure (Warren 1966), more dependent (Sears 1950), and less physically aggressive (Dean 1947) than later-born children.

These studies of feeding interaction also support the notion that the sex of the infant is important from the earliest interactions: among primiparous mothers, if the infant is female, the mother will stimulate the infant more, talk to her more and smile at her a great deal more than the mother with a male infant. These differences do not reflect any apparent differences in the infants' behaviour, but they may provide some of the antecedents for differences observed in mother–infant interaction with male and female children at a later stage (Moss & Robson 1968; J. Levine *et al.* 1967, unpublished). Thus, our studies suggest that some patterns of mother–infant interaction, including those that have been associated with birth order and sex of the infant, may have their inception in the interactions of mothers with their newborn babies.

Mother and infant each possess characteristics that developed before the infant's birth, and their interaction afterwards develops as a function of ongoing changes in the behaviour of each of them. Ideally, the interaction thrives and develops as a consequence of the synchrony or dovetailing of behaviours, which might occur as depicted in this sequence: the infant's behaviour gives cues to the mother, she responds to these cues, and her responses may then affect the infant's behaviour. Her responses are most appropriate if they facilitate the infant's behavioural organization. For example, if the infant is crying and the mother picks the baby up, the baby is likely not only to stop crying but also to become alert. This is a highly probable sequence (Korner & Thoman 1972). When alert, the infant is more capable of receiving environmental stimuli than when he is crying. It is therefore meaningful to say that, in such an interaction sequence, the baby's more organized or receptive state is a function of the mother's intervention.

There are sequences of mother and infant behaviours in which the interaction can have a significant but more subtle organizing effect. This happens especially during feeding. K. Kaye & T.B. Brazelton (1971, unpublished) have demonstrated that maternal stimulation may either elicit or inhibit sucking. The effect of the mother's stimulation is primarily a function of her timing within the infant's suck–pause sequence. Stimulation too early in the pause period is more likely to prolong the pause rather than induce sucking. Thus, the mother may either facilitate or impede the infant's feeding organization according to how appropriately she responds to the infant's cues of cessation of sucking. This may be relevant to the observation reported above which indicated that primiparas stimulated their infants more and yet their infants sucked less during feeding.

These examples of interactional effects suggest the general rule that the earliest organization of the mother–infant system occurs as a function of the capacities of both the mother and her infant: the infant's capabilities for indicating its status, signalling its needs and responding to maternal interventions, and the mother's ability to perceive cues provided by her infant and to respond appropriately to these cues. To the extent that they are mutually responsive, the relationship of the pair should develop in such a way as to facilitate the infant's development. In summary, our approach to mother–infant interaction is based on the notion that the mother and infant constitute a system which is psychobiological in nature and characterized by mutual modification of behaviour.

A MODEL FOR THE STUDY OF MOTHER-INFANT INTERACTION

On the basis of the viewpoint described, the model for our research can be depicted by the following triadic sequence:

Infant behaviour → Maternal behaviour → Infant behaviour

If an infant is behaving in a particular way before the mother intervenes, the behaviour of the infant after the intervention will indicate the effectiveness of the mother's response. The behaviour of the infant may include the states of sleep and wakefulness, as well as activities such as sucking, smiling, vocalizing, etc.

The ongoing reciprocal nature of the relationship is the basis for this model which guides our study of mother–infant interaction. Although the notion is a simple one, it is important in that it extends one's viewing beyond the two-step description of any series of mother–infant behaviours. If one adheres to an interactional framework for viewing the mother and infant, it becomes difficult to conceive of either as 'causing' the behaviour of the other. The baby may cry and cause the mother to pick him up; or by picking the baby up, the mother may cause him to stop crying and become alert. However, the identification of such causal relations becomes trivial within the context of an ongoing series of sequences. For this reason, it is difficult to conceive of any specific form of maternal behaviour as having an identifiable effect on the infant's development. The effect of the mother's behaviour will be a function of the infant's role and their interaction. It is necessary, of course, to identify the components of a series of sequences, such as the mother picking up the infant when he cries, etc. But clearly, it is insufficient to look at isolated two-step mother and infant behaviours as interactions. The consequences of successive con*sequences* must be analysed in some way if we are to understand the characteristics of a mother–infant relationship and its effect on the infant.

Within the framework of this interactive model, our approach is primarily a descriptive one, aimed at: (1) describing the characteristics of infants from the time of birth; (2) describing the characteristics of the mother–infant relationship; (3) identifying changes in the infant's behaviours that may be related to the mother–infant relationship.

PROCEDURES FOR STUDY OF EARLIEST MOTHER–INFANT INTERACTION

Some progress towards achieving these aims has been made by employing fairly simple and obvious strategies.

First, as indicated in the objectives listed above, study of the infant and of the mother–infant relationship is begun at its inception, that is, within 24 hours after the infant's birth. Only by observing the infant separately and with the mother from the time of birth will it be possible to identify the initial characteristics of the infant and his contribution to the mother–infant relationship. Also, only with such early observations will it be possible to infer the effect of the relationship on the infant.

Secondly, the mother and infant are observed under circumstances which are as natural as possible. That is, they are observed in the hospital immediately after the infant's birth; and they are observed in the home during their usual routine, without any interventions or contrived situations. In this way, and to the extent that the effect of the presence of an observer is minimized, it should be possible to describe real mothers and infants interacting in their real world. Infants are observed alone when they are left alone by the mother and the mother and infant are both observed when they are together.

Finally, our studies of mothers and infants involve intensive observations, in terms of total duration of observation, frequency of behaviour recording, and number of behaviours recorded. For a current project, each mother and infant pair is observed for approximately 32 hours during the infant's first five weeks of life. The infants are observed throughout this time, and any maternal behaviour directed towards the infant is recorded. The complete list of mother and infant behaviours that are recorded is given in Table 1. These behaviours come under the general headings of: proximity of the mother to the infant, her general activity with respect to the infant, such as feeding or bathing or changing the baby, and the forms of stimulation which she may give to the infant; and the infant's location (in cot or elsewhere), position, behavioural state, and other kinds of behaviour.

The infant's behavioural states include categories of sleep and wakefulness, which were originally suggested by Anders *et al.* (1971) and Wolff (1966). Subsequently we refined some of their behavioural categories, and these discriminate infant behaviours in a meaningful way, as indicated by individual differences which persist over the first five weeks of life (Thoman 1975).

Our procedure consists of recording, at a signal given through an ear microphone every 10 seconds, any of the 90 variables listed in Table 1. The observer watches throughout the 10 seconds and, at the signal, records the behaviours seen during that time. Recording the observation takes no more than one or two seconds. Reliability between observers ranges from 0.65 to 0.99; and reliability checks are made frequently.

In addition to behavioural states and sleep behaviours, whenever the infant is in the cot an analogue recording of respiration is obtained on a portable chart recorder connected to a small sensor placed under the infant's mattress

TABLE 1

Mother and infant observations

Mother's location
- Out
- Far
- Near
- In contact
- Holding infant
- Carrying infant

Infant's location
- Crib
- Cradle board
- Other

Infant's position
- Prone
- Supine
- Up

Mother–infant activity
- Changing infant
- Feeding infant
- Bathing infant
- None of these

Feeding inputs
- Breast or bottle
- Water
- Solids

Maternal stimulation
- Pacifier
- Suck-stimulation (during feeding)
- Positioning infant *en face* (when infant's eyes open)
- Looking at infant (other than during feeding, changing, bathing)
- Talking to infant
- Smiling or laughing at infant
- Patting
- Caressing
- Moving
- Rocking

Infant behaviours
- Not attached to nipple (during feeding)
- Not sucking (during feeding)
- Mouth
- Rhythmic mouthing
- Suck
- Smile
- Frown
- Grimace
- Vocalize (not fuss or cry)
- Burp
- Gag
- Hiccup
- Bowel movement
- Small movement
- Large movement
- Startle
- Jerk
- Spit up

Infant states
- Asleep
  - Quiet (2 categories)
  - Active (3 categories)
- Awake
  - Drowse
  - Daze
  - Alert
  - Active
  - Fuss
  - Cry

pad. From this recording, it is possible to obtain measures of regularity of respiration, rate of respiration and the occurrence of apnoea.

INFANT–MOTHER–INFANT SEQUENCE ANALYSIS

Results from a preliminary study (Thoman *et al.* 1973, unpublished) for the major project show how interaction data from infant–mother–infant sequences can be analysed. The triadic sequence here was:

Duration of infant vocalization before maternal intervention → maternal intervention → Duration of infant vocalization after intervention

Subjects

The subjects for the study were six mothers and their infants (normal full-term newborns). Three infants were female, two of these born to primiparous mothers; the male infants were all born to multiparous mothers.

Procedure

While the mother and infant were in the hospital, they were observed together during one feeding; and the infant was observed alone for one interfeeding period. Home observations were then made once a week for the next four weeks. We intended to observe an hour of mother–infant interaction before a feed, then a feeding period, and finally an hour of state behaviours without maternal intervention. However, because mother and infant behaviours varied greatly, it was often not possible to do this in a continuous $2\frac{1}{2}$ hour sequence. The length of individual observations therefore ranged from $2\frac{1}{2}$ to 7 hours. The average length of all home observations was $3\frac{1}{2}$ hours per day, or 14 hours per subject.

Analysis of triadic sequences

Since mothers and infants are both variable, one way of depicting triadic sequences involving the infant's crying is to indicate the range of latencies involved. Fig. 1 presents the range of latencies before the mother intervened when the infant cried, for each of the six mothers. Since infants may cry for varying periods, and may in some instances soothe themselves without maternal intervention, the range of durations of crying where the infants spontaneously ended crying episodes is shown, for each infant, in Fig. 1. Since there was no evidence of change over weeks for these subjects, the figure reflects all instances of crying throughout the four weeks of observation.

Maternal delay in responding to the infant's vocalization and consistency in the length of her delay are important forms of feedback reaching the crying infant. For example, Fig. 1 shows that mother *M* sometimes responded to her infant almost immediately after the onset of crying, while at other times the

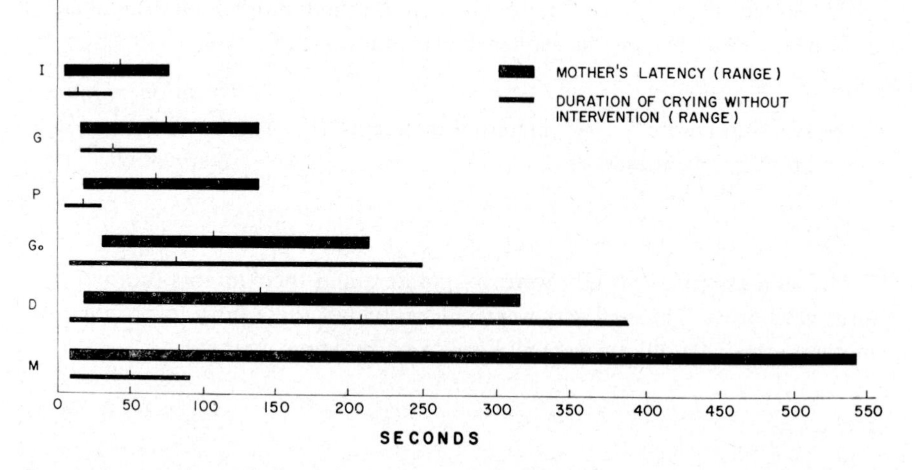

FIG. 1. Latency (range in seconds) before mothers intervened after infant started crying' and length of crying (range, in seconds) when there was no intervention, for six mother–infant pairs during home observations.

infant cried for almost 10 minutes before eliciting a response from the mother. However, the feedback to the infant from this interaction is somewhat more certain than in the interaction between mother–infant pairs *Go* and *D*. These mothers provided no signal as to how long their infants must cry to elicit intervention, as the spontaneous soothing times of the infants ranged well beyond the longest latencies for maternal intervention.

In contrast to the feedback given to infants *M*, *Go* and *D*, the three infants *I*, *P* and *G* received definite information from their mothers. Brief periods of crying elicited an intervention from each of these mothers. The consequences of such consistency, or lack thereof, should have implications for the development of communication in the mother–infant relationship.

The 'infant-consequent' side of this triadic sequence is expressed in the infant's readiness to be soothed. Fig. 2 summarizes the soothing latency of the six infants over the four weeks of observation. It should be noted that interventions which consisted of the mother changing the infant are not included in this figure. In those circumstances, caretaking activities were almost invariably associated with continued crying by the infant. Fig. 2 strongly suggests that the length of time an infant cried before the mother intervened was related to his crying time after intervention. Such a relationship should not be surprising —the longer an infant cries, the more aroused he becomes, and the longer it should take to soothe him. The lower data point for mother–infant *D*, however, suggests that the relationship is not necessarily a linear one.

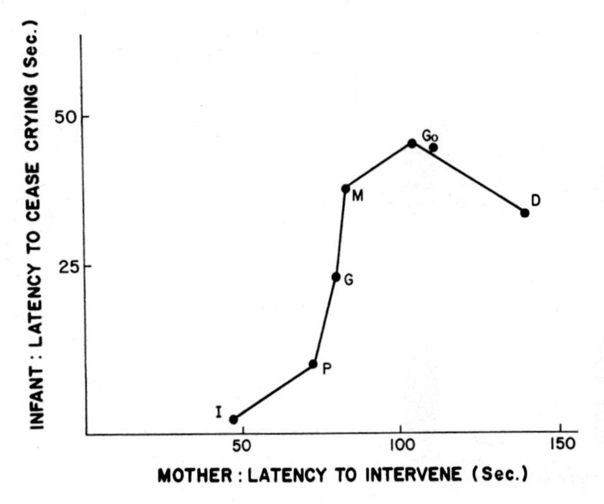

FIG. 2. Mean time before infant stopped crying as a function of the delay before mother intervened.

The results from this sample suggested an interesting phenomenon with respect to soothing latency. Fig. 3 shows the mean latency before the infants were soothed when the mothers intervened with a delay of either less or more than 90 seconds. Visual inspection of the data had suggested this 90-second cut-off point. There is clearly a dramatic difference in the speed with which a crying infant is soothed if he is picked up or stimulated before 90 seconds has

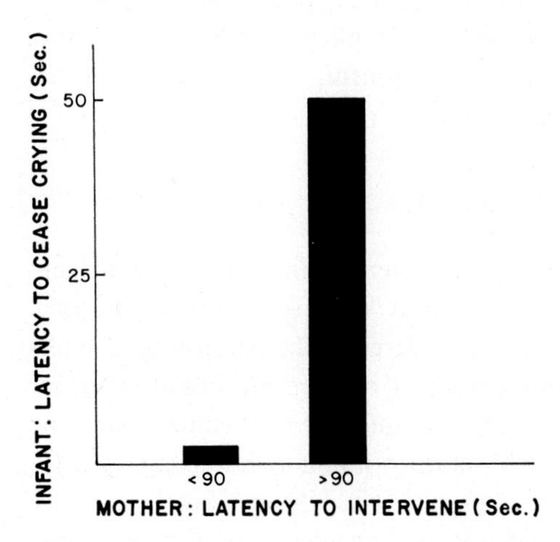

FIG. 3. Mean time before infant stopped crying when mother intervened before and after 90 seconds.

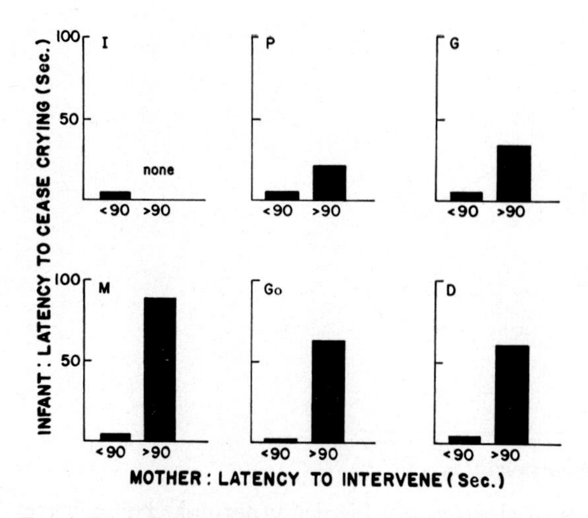

FIG. 4. For individual infants, mean time before infant stopped crying when mother intervened before and after 90 seconds.

elapsed. Fig. 4 shows the same measures for each of the six infants in our preliminary study. In every case, the time of intervention made a dramatic difference in the duration of crying after the mother's intervention.

We could find no relationship between this measure of soothability and any of the variables measured in this study, with the exception of the sex of the infant. The three infants showing the shortest latencies before being soothed (infants *I*, *P* and *M*) were females. The three males (*G*, *D* and *Go*) showed much longer latencies. The reliability and significance of this sex difference remains to be explored in a larger sample. If mothers are, in fact, more effective in soothing female infants, this phenomenon should have implications for the infant's behavioural development, the mother's maternal behaviours, and their subsequent interaction.

Consistency in sequence patterning for one mother–infant pair

Any mother–infant relationship can be characterized in terms of the infant–mother–infant sequences that occur consistently over some period of time. To illustrate that consistency, I should like to describe the patterning of interaction of one mother–infant pair. This particular mother and infant from our major project were chosen because: (*a*) the infant's behaviour would be expected to play a disruptive role in the mother–infant relationship, and (*b*) the infant's behaviours affected the mother–infant synchrony, but in a rather subtle way. The infant's behaviours did not play an obviously disruptive role in the relationship, possibly because of the responsiveness of the mother.

When this infant was in the cot, most mother–infant interaction sequences were initiated by mild vocalization on the part of the infant. The most notable characteristic of their interaction, however, was that any time he was picked up and held, the infant became drowsy, dazed or fussy. Whether the mother was feeding or just holding the baby, he continued to be drowsy except when fussing or crying. This mother was judged by the observers to be relatively gentle; the observations indicate that her stimulation was neither continuous nor vigorous. Nevertheless, there was a consistent sequence of social interaction leading to a dazed stare or drowsiness on the part of the infant.

What was apparent to the observers, and seemingly was not apparent to the mother during the early weeks, was that the baby spent a great deal of time in the cot being wide-eyed and quietly alert, scanning the floral decorations on the lining of the cot. It is not unusual for infants to spend some of their time in the cot being alert and awake—if the infant awakens and the mother is out of the room, she may miss such periods. However, in this infant alertness was very common, which was even more remarkable in view of his lack of attentiveness during social interaction, a time when most infants are most likely to be alert (Korner & Thoman 1972).

An example of this interaction during our home observation when the baby was one month of age, was that the mother tried waving her hand in front of his drowsy face and then tried showing him a rattle while she held him. In neither instance could she raise the baby's visual level from drowsing. She complained to him about his lack of attentiveness. While she was feeding him, she looked directly at his face less often over the weeks, and instead kept her gaze beyond him. During our first home observation, when the baby was 10 days old, mother and baby spent 16% of the feeding time *vis-à-vis*, but at five weeks only 8% of the time. Clearly, their interaction was being affected by the baby's aberrant state behaviour. However, the picture is not a simple one. This mother still watched the infant throughout the feedings; and when she was holding the baby during non-feeding periods, she positioned him face to face in markedly increasing amounts over successive weeks. She also spent increasing amounts of time holding the baby despite his 'rejecting response'.

This description of this baby's reaction to social stimulation is supported by various observations, first on the distribution of his states as a function of his location. Fig. 5 shows, for a group of six infants, the mean percentage of time they spent in an alert state while the mothers were holding them, and the mean percentage of time they were alert while awake in their cots. Although the absolute times differed in these two locations, the percentage figures are very close for each week. Fig. 6 shows the same measures for the 'rejecting' baby described above. First, it should be noted that the mean percentage of time

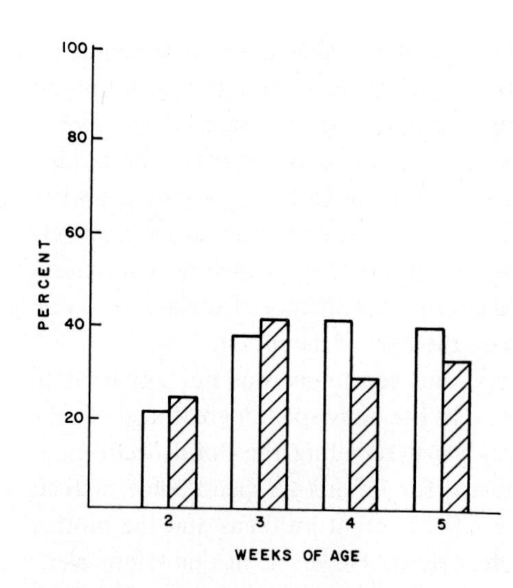

FIG. 5. Mean percentage of time spent in an alert state by six infants either being held by the mother (□), or when they were awake and in the cot (▨), during successive weekly observations.

this baby spent alert while being held was generally lower than that for the group of babies. His overall mean alert time over the four weeks was 22%, whereas the mean for the group of six infants was 33%. The overall mean percentage of time he spent alert and awake in the cot over the four weeks was

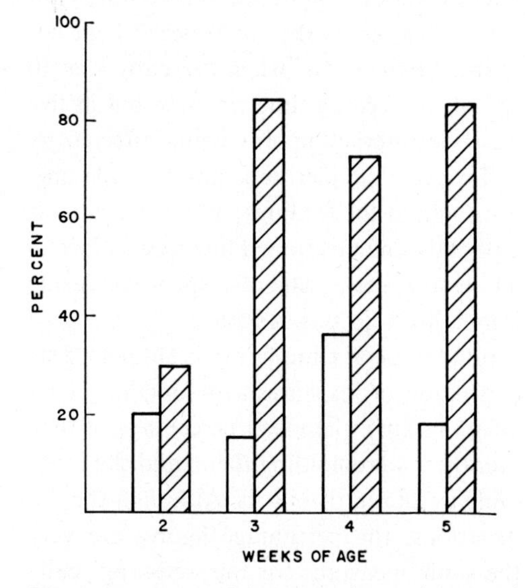

FIG. 6. Percentage of time spent in an alert state by a 'rejecting' held by the mother (□) or awake and in his cot (▨) during successive weekly observations.

67%, compared with 31% for the group of infants—a striking difference, especially as this infant spent a mean of only 46 minutes per week awake in his cot during the four weeks of home observations, whereas the mean for the six infants was 61 minutes.

For this baby, the mother–infant interaction could not be a source of facilitation for perceptual learning. In fact, on the contrary, when given social stimulation he withdrew from perceptual access to environmental stimuli.

A great deal of sensitivity would be needed by any parents before they perceived that holding and cuddling their infant actually reduced his attentiveness to his world. The parents of the infant described were no exception. Although they expressed concern about his inattentiveness during social interaction, they apparently were not aware of the sequential relationship between their holding him and his state until our six-weeks interview with them. At that time we pointed out the infant's reaction tendency and suggested more frequent use of a cradle board for the baby so that he could view family activity without being held. The family was visited when the baby was four months old. His state of deviance persisted, but it was not as striking as when he was younger. The family had adapted very well to his idiosyncratic responsiveness. He was now often placed on a cradle board and moved around the house so that he could watch his father and mother. The mother expressed recognition of the fact that the baby does not like to be held, and she indicated that she now mainly holds him for only brief periods. There is a time during the day that he regularly enjoys being held in her lap, provided his head is on her knees and away from her body; so she plays with him each evening holding him in this manner. When she has to carry the baby, she does so by holding him with his back towards her so that he faces away from her. In this position, the infant may become quite alert. Otherwise, he seems to be developing normally. Developmental tests at six months confirm this impression.

The infant's interaction with his parents appears to be developing as well as possible in the circumstances. In our judgement, this is because both parents are sensitive to the infant's communication that he does not 'like' to be held and cuddled. Although unexpected in their nature, the infant's cues are responded to, and synchrony in the interaction is developing.

INFANT–MOTHER–INFANT INTERACTION: CONCLUSIONS

It is clear that from the time of birth infants can signal information about their status or their needs. If their signals are accurately perceived and appropriately responded to, the resulting mother–infant relationship is characterized by synchrony and is such that it would be expected to facilitate an infant's development. This should happen not only because the infant's needs are met but also because the feedback given to the infant communicates to him that his signals are perceived. An environment responsive to an infant's signals should facilitate the development of his use of signalling efforts.

Throughout this paper I have emphasized that an infant's behaviour will reflect the effects of caretaking activities as a function of the circumstances in which those caretaking activities occur. A mother's behaviour and her infant's behaviour are interdependent. This interactive principle is illustrated by the findings from our studies.

Synchrony in any mother–infant relationship depends on the ability of the infant to emit cues as to his status or his needs, on the sensitivity and responsiveness of the mother to the baby's cues, and on the responsiveness of the infant to the mother's intervention. Thus, each member of the pair may either facilitate or impede the progress of synchrony. For example, numerous studies have documented the disruptive effects of a child's abnormal behaviours on the parent–child relationship (Milowe & Lourie 1964; Prechtl 1963; Morse & Sahler 1970; Kogan & Wimberger 1969; Brazelton *et al* 1971; Stott 1962; Moss 1967).

The rejecting infant in our story is faring better than prediction would allow if the mother's role were not taken into account, namely her early acceptance and later understanding and adjustment to the baby's behaviour. This example shows clearly that aberrant behaviour by the infant makes it very difficult for a good mother–infant interaction to be established, but that such behaviour does not necessarily preclude the development of synchrony in the mother–infant relationship.

ACKNOWLEDGEMENTS

The research described in this paper was supported by the Grant Foundation. The project described is being carried out with the collaboration of Patricia T. Becker and Margaret Poindexter, and with invaluable assistance from Victor Miano, Carol Suhaney, Margaret Becker and Margo Gerber.

References

ALTUS, W.D. (1966) Birth order and its sequelae. *Science (Wash. D.C.) 151*, 44–49

ANDERS, T.F., EMDE, R. & PARMELEE, A. (eds.) (1971) *A Manual of Standardized Terminology Techniques and Criteria for Scoring States of Sleep and Wakefulness in Newborn Infants*, UCLA Brain Information Service, NINDS Neurological Information, Los Angeles

BRAZELTON, T.B., YOUNG, G. & GULLOWA, M. (1971) Inception and resolution of early developmental pathology. *J. Am. Acad. Child Psychiatr. 10*, 124-135

DEAN, D.A. (1947) The relation of ordinal position to personality in young children. Master's thesis, State University of Iowa

HILTON, I. (1967) Differences in behavior of mothers toward first and later-born children. *J. Pers. Soc. Psychol. 7*, 282–290

KOGAN, K. & WIMBERGER, H. (1969) Interaction patterns in disadvantaged families. *J. Clin. Psychol. 25*, 347–352

KORNER, A. F. & THOMAN, E. (1970) Visual alertness in neonates as evoked by maternal care, *J. Exp. Child Psychol. 10*, 67-68

LASKO, J. (1954) Parent behavior toward first and second children. *Genet. Psychol. Monogr. 49*, 97–137

LEWIS, M. & ROSENBLUM, L. A. (eds.) (1974) *The Effect of The Infant on Its Caregiver*, Wiley-Interscience, New York

MILOWE, I. D. & LOURIE, R. S. (1964) The child's role in the battered chlid syndrome. *J. Pediatr. 65*, 1079

MORSE, C. W. & SAHLER, O. J. Z. (1970) A three-year follow-up study of abused and neglected children. *Am. J. Dis. Child. 120*, 439–446

MOSS, H. A. (1967) Sex, age, and state as determinants of mother-infant interaction. *Merrill-Palmer Q. 13*, 19–36

MOSS, H. & ROBSON, K. (1968) Maternal influences in early social visual behavior. *Child Dev. 39*, 401–408

PRECHTL, H. F. R. (1963) Mother–child interaction in babies with minimal brain damage, in *Determinants of Infant Behavior* (Foss, B. M., ed.), vol. 2, pp. 53–59, Methuen, London

SCHACHTER, S. (1959) *Psychology of Affiliation*, Stanford University Press, Stanford, Calif.

SEARS, R. (1950) Ordinal position in family as a psychological variable. *Am. Soc. Rev. 15*, 397–401

STOTT, D. H. (1962) Abnormal mothering as a cause of mental subnormality—I. A critique of some classic studies of maternal deprivation in the light of possible congenital factors. *J. Child Psychol. Psychiatr. Allied Disciplines 3*, 79–91

STOUT, A. M. (1960) Parent behavior toward children of differing ordinal position and sibling status. Doctoral dissertation, University of California

SUTTON-SMITH, B. & ROSENBERG, B. G. (1965) Age changes in the effects of original position on sex-role identification. *J. Genet. Psychol. 107*, 61–73

THOMAN, E. B. (1975) Sleep and wake behaviors in neonates: consistencies and consequences. *Merrill-Palmer Q.*, in press

THOMAN, E., BARNETT, C., LEIDERMAN, H. & TURNER, A. (1970) Neonate–mother interaction: Effects of parity on feeding behavior. *Child Dev. 41*, 1103–1111

THOMAN, E., BARNETT, C. & LEIDERMAN, P. (1971) Feeding behaviors of newborn infants as a function of parity of the mother. *Child Dev. 42*, 1471–1483

THOMAN, E., LEIDERMAN, P. & OLSON, J. (1972) Neonate–mother interaction during breast feeding. *Dev. Psychol. 6*, 110–118

WARREN, J. B. (1966) Birth order and social behavior. *Psychol. Bull. 65*, 38–49

WOLFF, P. H. (1966) The causes, control and organization of behaviour in the neonate, in *Psychological Issues*, International Universities Press, New York

Discussion

Bell: Bell & Ainsworth (1972) reported that the more responsive the mother is, the less the infant cries. In contradiction to this, in experimental procedures Etzel & Gewirtz (1967) reduced crying by not responding to the infant's crying and by reinforcing competing behaviours. Moss & Robson (1968) have observations indicating that the more quickly the mothers respond to their infants and the more attentive they are, the more likely they are to have babies who cry a great deal.

Dunn: We find that the more likely the mother is to feed the baby when he cries in the first ten days the more frequently he will be crying at 14 weeks. Moss was looking at babies aged 3–12 weeks. We find that some babies cry a great deal and some never cry, and separate analyses of the two groups give different pictures of how the mother's responsiveness to crying relates to other aspects of her responsiveness. The finding that a mother was a non-responder to crying even when her child cried very little correlated well with some of the other measures of her responsiveness. But if a mother didn't respond to an extremely irritable baby that told us little about other aspects of her responsiveness.

Bell: Then we have to add the infant's contribution: if fussing and crying get above a certain level they turn the mother off.

Thoman: So many relationships between behavioural variables are based on U-shaped functions. The mothers we see who are super-responders are not necessarily the mothers who are really dovetailing with their babies, and the mothers who are slow responders are also not dovetailing. The mother who scoops her infant up and puts him to the breast the moment he utters a cry may not be in synchrony with him. A more synchronous relationship might be reflected by a mother who may watch the baby when he begins to vocalize until she is assured that it is a sincere cry before she does something about it. For instance, the baby may be crying in his sleep, and he may become quiescent again without awakening. Thus, instead of interfering at once, the mother in the second instance allows the baby to maintain his sleep state. It has been clearly demonstrated that a baby who is fed while asleep or sleepy does not feed as well as a baby who is thoroughly awake. So the mother who is making the most immediate response to her baby is not necessarily the one who is making the most appropriate response.

Dunn: That makes the measure of latency a little difficult.

Bowlby: Mary Ainsworth's measure is sensitivity to crying, not solely latency, so her measure is not the same as yours.

Dunn: Her measure in her crying study (Bell & Ainsworth 1972) is duration of maternal unresponsiveness to crying and that is the length of time before she responds to crying. Using her measure of duration of maternal unresponsiveness to crying, we found some consistency between 8 and 14 weeks. However, some babies didn't cry at all during our observations and of course on that measure the mothers are described as being optimally responsive to crying. When the non-criers were excluded, the stability in the maternal unresponsiveness measure disappeared.

Brazelton: What intrigues me most is what you said about the last baby you described contributing to the interaction in such a negative way, Dr Thoman. What sort of index do you have of that? I could see it as the mother contributing a sort of tension to the baby that makes him turn away.

Thoman: Perhaps you are right. I had assumed that the data contrasting the baby's alertness with the mother and in the cot, from the first home observation, clearly indicated that the infant's reaction was a characteristic of the infant. If this is not sufficiently convincing, we have further evidence which suggests, first, that the baby's aversive response to being held was present from the time of birth; and secondly that the nature of the response was not unique to his interaction with the mother alone.

Our observations of the babies and of the mother–infant interaction begin on the second day of the baby's life. At this time we make two feeding observations, at 09.30 and at 13.30. The baby discussed in the last part of my paper spent only 10% of the total time during these observations in an alert state (noted by the observer to be ambiguous alertness, because the baby's eyes were never fully opened). Thus, the patterning of state behaviours during interaction was apparent from the baby's second day of life.

Further, the baby's response was the same with the father as with the mother. The father held the baby only during the first home observation; and during this interaction the baby was alert only 14% of the time—a figure even lower than when the baby was observed with the mother.

Regardless of the nature of the infant's sensitivity that may have accounted for the lack of alertness, or dazing, along with the drowsing or fussing that occurred during interaction, the baby's form of response was his contribution to the interaction. The point to be made from these observations is that we cannot look only at maternal behaviours but we must look at patterns of interaction which include the baby's eliciting behaviours and the baby's response to maternal interventions if we are to have clues to the nature of their synchrony. This means a concern for individual differences in infants and their responsiveness to forms of stimulation, along with the maternal caretaking activities; and from their combined behaviours we can describe the interactions in terms of patterns of mother and infant behaviours.

It seems that one is vastly oversimplifying the issue by trying to talk about the immediacy of crying interventions on the part of the mother as being a major index of the nature of the mother–infant relationship.

Brazelton: Did that particular baby have a disturbed sleep/wake state?

Thoman: Except for the negative state responses when he was being held, as I reported them, the baby did not show any marked disorganization in sleep/wake states.

Hinde: With respect to the U-shaped function and our tendencies to make value judgements about what is good in maternal responsiveness, we should remember that the infant has to become sensitive to the mother's states, and an infant can't learn to become sensitive if a mother is always either equally responsive to it or equally unresponsive to it. There has to be some variation in the mother's responsiveness for the infant to learn to discriminate her states of responsiveness and to behave with sensitivity to her.

Thoman: That is a complex matter. An infant can tolerate a certain amount of mismatch, but when it becomes too great there is asynchrony. By asynchrony I mean that the feedback the infant receives does not provide him with clues about how his behaviour can affect his environment.

Macfarlane: Do you assess mothers before they have a child and predict how they might react to their child?

Thoman: We have three interviews with the mothers in their third trimester of pregnancy. After they have agreed to take part in the study we describe in detail what is involved, and then we have a special interview to explore their attitudes towards pregnancy, their expectations of what a baby will be like, how they expect a baby to change their lives, and so forth. We have not yet analysed whether these prenatal attitudes are related to our postnatal observations of their attitudes expressed during an equally intensive postnatal interview given when the infant is six weeks old.

Dunn: I was interested that you wrote up the clinical reports, because we tried using Sylvia Brody's general scale (Brody 1956) after the feeding observations. One problem was that we found we disagreed about how particular mothers should be rated.

Thoman: For our description made by the observers immediately after each home visit, we have no formal outline. Without conferring with one another, we write independent reports, ranging freely with our subjective descriptions. These reports are not designed to provide data. On the contrary, they are specifically aimed at giving us a rich source for hypotheses. Since one of our main interests is in individual differences, it is important for us to have questions suggested by these reports from which we go into the data. For example, three of us independently noted the dazing and drowsy response of the baby I described in the paper. On the basis of these subjective suggestions, we examined the data to see whether the hypothesis concerning the consistency of his response to interaction was confirmed. And in fact it was.

Leiderman: We interviewed mothers postnatally. We too found that typescript reports of interviews can direct the observers' thinking and raise interesting hypotheses. However, we have found that it is important to use non-interviewers as raters, in order to be certain that we are not 'reading' ourselves rather than the patient. It would be ideal if raters were to disagree about the hypotheses and then compare their observations of the mother–infant pair. Otherwise, I believe one is likely to come out with something similar to what was put in.

Thoman: As I have indicated, the descriptive reports that we write after the observations are not intended to provide a data base, nor in any way to be used as evidence for any conclusions we might draw about our observations. They are only the source of hypotheses.

On the other hand, the prenatal and postnatal (six weeks) interviews are specifically intended to provide information which will be compared with the findings from the direct observations made in the hospital and in the home. I did not discuss these interviews in detail in the paper because they were not directly relevant there. A clinical psychologist interviews the mother, the interview is recorded, and the recordings are transcribed. The transcription and the recordings are converted into scale ratings by two independent raters (clinical psychologists) who are completely naive about the research, the procedures for collecting data, and our hypotheses. Each rater listens to the recording and simultaneously reads the protocols. Then each scores the mother on nine scales which are relevant to maternal characteristics of interest for our study. No rating for any mother will be used if the two raters are in disagreement by more than one point on a seven-point scale. We assume then that the resulting ratings are obtained in as objective a way as possible. The scale ratings will be related to information obtained during the postnatal behavioural observations made at the hospital and in the home.

Hofer: So you are talking about two sets of clinical observations. The prenatal observations are rated by people who are totally disconnected from the studies, whereas the postnatal ones are used by you as a way of going back and forth between results and hypotheses.

Thoman: Yes. Our observation procedures provide information from 10-second periods—this is definitely a molecular description of the baby and of the mother–infant interaction. We assume that the 10-second periods combine to provide a picture of the interactive pattern that we see. The subjective descriptions are designed to help provide us with a framework which can guide our data analysis.

Bentovim: The direction of power and control in relationships seems a complex problem. The last baby described appeared to have a strong influence on the situation; the mother appeared to be doing the correct thing in being able to adapt to this particular baby. This problem can be seen clinically: a baby I saw seemed to have a marked 'anti-social' response. She was cured when she was put in an ordinary paediatric ward where she had so much stimulation from so many people that in the end she 'gave up' and accepted people—including her parents' attention. Temperamental factors must be powerful factors.

Certain mothers will exert a powerful influence by contrast. A psychotic mother driven by her own perceptions of the baby can violate and control the situation extremely, ignoring the signals from the baby and his attempt to alter the situation to his needs.

In studies of synchrony, an infant's blindness, deafness or cerebral palsy may well have a powerful distorting influence, just as a blind parent shapes the situation in a certain way. Sometimes these handicaps can have such a powerful effect that ordinary responsiveness is insufficient and some special responsiveness may be necessary then, such as the example given of the physiotherapist who did the abnormal yet right procedure of following the infant's jerkiness. The question of direction of power may be even more complicated in these instances.

Thoman: It certainly is terribly complex. The mother I described earlier, who responded immediately to her baby's first fretting, picked the baby up often and put him to the breast while he was, in fact, still asleep. Under these circumstances he would eat poorly and briefly; then, keeping his eyes closed, he would refuse to suck any more. The mother expressed concern that the baby ate poorly and she likewise expressed concern that he would wake up and cry and she would have to feed him again shortly afterwards. The difficulties in their interaction were functions of both of them. The baby was not well organized, cried frequently and opened his eyes during sleep; the mother was apparently insensitive to the infant's states, and it was clear that there was an asynchrony in the relationship. It is not always possible to identify the contribution of the mother and of the infant to such an interaction. You can only look at the behaviours of each and the consequent pattern of their mutual behaviours.

Papoušek: Did you check the sight of the parents and of the baby whom you showed having eye-to-eye contact? An important determinant of eye-to-eye contact seems to be the infant's capacity to converge, and this changes with age. The mother intuitively finds the focusing capacity of the baby and holds him at an adequate distance, as one can see by looking at the pair of them looking at each other. This is true if a mother believes that infants do not see anything during the first months of life. If you change the distance you can see that the infant loses his mother and shows it by a certain annoyance, re-orientation, and so on.

Similarly, you can find out a lot about the regulation of attention. Without being able to put it into words, mothers will show how much they are aware of a change in the infant's attention.

This leads to the question of whether you are thinking of both aspects of the regulation of behavioural states. Usually we take it for granted that the preceding behavioural state determines the response that follows. But we have enough information, from learning studies, and from studies of social interaction, to show that it also goes the other way. That is, the outcome of the cognitive processes influences the following behavioural state. Thus, if the baby cannot easily interlock with the mother, he can either increase his alertness, mobilizing all his powers of orientation, exploration and so on; or if he is still unable to adjust he may start switching off those mechanisms and reduce his alertness. Tests show that his responses may decrease dramatically. In his first two months of life he may actually have short periods of a sleep-like state (Papoušek & Bernstein 1969).

Thoman: We record all changes in state throughout each seven-hour home-observation period, so at least it is possible to identify the various kinds of sequences. That is, it is possible to relate the baby's states before, during and after a maternal intervention.

Richards: When we are discussing the latencies of mothers going to babies when they cry, it is essential to know what the crying means to the mother. In Cambridge, in the first few days of life, crying to a mother seems to mean that the baby is hungry. If the latency of responding is plotted as a function of when the baby has been fed, you get a U-shaped curve. Crying immediately after a feed is usually interpreted as a sign that the baby hasn't had enough food, so he is fed again. Crying in the middle of the interfeed period is seldom interpreted as hunger, as feeding is least likely to follow crying. As the time for the next feed approaches, crying is more and more often followed by feeding. So if very variable latencies are found for a particular mother, one might be able to understand what is happening by asking the mother what she was thinking at these different times.

This brings me to a more general point. I think we should all be careful about the language we use to describe mothers, and particularly about words like 'sensitive', 'insensitive' or the phrase you used, Dr Thoman: 'capability of responding to cues'. We are talking about social meanings in a culture, not constitutional differences between individual mothers. A mother who is called insensitive is merely responding to her infant in a different way from the way the observer who so describes her thinks she should. It is a value judgement imposed by the observer. But by using the word 'insensitive' the observer suggests that his value judgement is an attribute of the mother. The real danger is that other people may accept the observer's suggestion as reality.

Thoman: I really should clarify how I use the word 'sensitivity'. If a mother who is listening to her baby crying says the baby is hungry or uncomfortable, it is generally said that she is sensitive and knows what her baby's crying means. For our research, we have a slightly narrower view. I am really talking about the mother's perception of the baby's status in terms of his behavioural states. For example, the mother who picks up the baby who is asleep is 'insensitive' to the baby's state, and I think that that is a fairly objective statement. She indicates by her words or her behaviour that she thinks the baby is awake.

Richards: That is only objective if you believe there is one possible system that the mother must move towards. It is perfectly possible to build an interaction sequence where the mother would intervene every time the baby's eyes opened. And objectivity has nothing to do with it. It is a clash between *your* culture, *your* social meaning, and that of the mother.

Thoman: I think that across cultures one could say that a mother, regardless of her language or culture, could be labelled as sensitive or insensitive in so far as she can determine whether her baby is awake or asleep, or crying. If the baby is vocalizing, we call that crying. It is simply a matter of perception, and the mother who is sensitive is capable of perceiving her baby's behaviours more accurately.

Richards: She may perceive it, but what she does about it is a different matter. We all have different ideas about what ought to be done, and I think the word objectivity really can't be used.

Thoman: I agree that it can't be used for interpretation. I think we do get into trouble if we start saying that mothers ought to pick the babies up when they cry, or that they ought not to pick the babies up.

Richards: I don't think you can observe without interpretation.

Thoman: But you can say that a sequence of: 'baby cries, mother picks up, mother puts to breast, baby refuses to feed' is a different kind of sequence from: 'baby cries, mother picks up, mother puts baby to breast, baby feeds'.

You can place whatever kind of judgements you want on those events, and any sequence has to begin somewhere. The last infant behaviour in any identifiable sequence is the first one in the next sequence.

Richards: That is just where value judgements, subjectivity and cultural expectations come into it.

Dunn: Did you say that you were going to use your subjective reports to decide where to go and look for your hypotheses?

Thoman: My judgement enters into the data analysis in the sense that our model for mother–infant interaction is based on the notion that it is possible to depict sequences of infant–mother–infant behaviours. Our approach involves describing the status of the infant before there is any maternal caretaking activity, so that we can identify the infant's response to that maternal activity as a function of the baby's prior status.

Hofer: The disagreement seems to be over the word 'objective', a word that you let slip out and which you are now retracting. You seem to be saying that in practice you form hypotheses about the nature and meaning of relationships which you subject to further analysis and to presentation to other people who might disagree.

Richards: My objection isn't a quibble over words but over something fundamental to all that we are doing. Scientists have assumptions that run through everything they do, but which are often not shared by the people who are being watched. So there is a culture clash and it happens everywhere —whether we are in Africa, or in Cambridge, England, or in Boston, Massachusetts. That wouldn't matter if we spent all our time in meetings like this swopping our stories. But some of what we do gets out and is used in ways that may change people's lives. People are told that they have to be sensitive to their babies, and that their behaviour may have particular consequences for their children. If we are honest, we have to say that we have no idea of what are the long-term implications of particular fine details of early interactions. Yet there are people who are trying to get mothers to conform to these ideas, and who make the mothers feel guilty if they don't conform.

Hofer: Shifting away from a search for objectivity and towards hypotheses is the only way we can deal with the argument you are raising. And yet at some point we have to deal with something more than hypotheses. Hypotheses will gradually become principles, and then perhaps they can be applied. We can't back away from that issue entirely.

Leiderman: It is one thing to express something in terms of hypotheses, as you said, but it is quite different to elevate hypotheses to points of principle, where they become policy statements. The term 'sensitive' elevates itself very rapidly.

Curtis-Jenkins: In this particular piece of research there is a hypothesis in front of your hypothesis, because every time the mother hears her child cry she hypothesizes what the cry means. It is not just hunger. There are many ways the mother may interpret crying—the baby may be hungry, wet, cold, or just wanting attention. This I suspect complicates interpretation of these simple observations about 'crying'.

References

BELL, S. M. & AINSWORTH, M. D. S. (1972) Infant crying and maternal responsiveness. *Child Dev. 43*, 1171–1190

BRODY, S. (1956) *Patterns of Mothering: Maternal Influences during Infancy*, International Universities Press, New York

ETZEL, B. C. & GEWIRTZ, J. L. (1967) Experimental modification of caretaker-maintained high-rate operant crying in a 6- and a 20-week-old infant (Infans tyrannotearus): extinction of crying with reinforcement of eye contact and smiling. *J. Exp. Child Psychol. 5*, 303–317

MOSS, H. A. & ROBSON, K. S. (1968) The role of protest behaviour in the development of the mother–infant attachment. *Proc. Annu. Conv. Am. Psychol. Assoc. 76*

PAPOUŠEK, H. & BERNSTEIN, P. (1969) The function of conditioning stimulation in human neonates and infants, in *Stimulation in Early Infancy* (Ambrose, A., ed.), pp. 229–252, Academic Press, London

A congenital contribution to emotional response in early infancy and the preschool period

RICHARD Q. BELL

*Child Research Branch, National Institute of Mental Health, National Institutes of Health, Bethesda, Maryland**

Abstract Four follow-up studies carried out from the newborn period in three different laboratories have shown that a slow, low-magnitude reaction of the newborn to interruption of sucking is associated in later infancy and the preschool period with the expression of pleasurable emotional response. The basic test of the newborn's response varied slightly in the four studies, but essentially it consisted of establishing a baseline of infant behaviour during 30 to 120 seconds of sucking on a pacifier, then recording amount of (*a*) bodily activity, (*b*) crying, (*c*) the latency to either or both, in the 30- to 135-second period after removal of the nipple. The three aspects of the reaction are consistently intercorrelated, even when allowances are made for artifactual interdependence. Newborns who respond quickly to interruption of sucking also continue to cry and move a lot.

Up to the first month a slow, low-magnitude reaction of the newborn is associated with a later low rate of smiling, but beyond the third month there is an inversion and the association is consistently with various manifestations of positive emotional expression.

If a nipple is eased out of the mouth of a sucking neonate in such a way that no startle is produced, the infant will be relatively still at first, perhaps extend the legs or an arm very slowly, then show vigorous movements of all limbs by approximately 15 seconds, and full crying 15 seconds later. The components of the response are highly intercorrelated, so that if one or another component can be recorded reliably, there is a reasonable likelihood that the general pattern of response will be tapped. Infants who respond quickly move and cry a great deal. The interrelations of the various components make it possible for findings from several studies that measured different components to be linked together in this paper.

The observation of the response to interruption of sucking (RIS) has considerable practical value for investigators interested in the screening and

* Present address: Dept. of Psychology, University of Virginia, Charlottesville.

assessment of young infants, since extensive clinical training is not necessary to evaluate the meaning of the response, the procedure can be quickly administered just before any feeding, and it requires nothing more elaborate in the way of equipment than a pacifier, a hand counter, and a stop watch. Technical details of the test procedure, reliabilities and intercorrelations are provided in Bell *et al.* (1971, pp. 17, 22–24).

Theoretical interest in the RIS was first shown over 30 years ago by Sears & Sears (1940), who saw in it an opportunity to study formulations concerning the relationship of frustration and aggression, and by Fries (1941), whose clinical psychoanalytic interest led her to speculate that the infant's reaction to this brief deprivation might be comparable to reactions in later life to new situations, or to obstacles. Despite the intriguing comparisons to adult reactions, nothing other than Fries's clinical reports of follow-up studies on individual children was published until the late 1960s. Recently, we (Bell *et al.* 1971) reported findings indicating that the relationship of the response to later development was quite out of line with the early, imaginative interpretations of its meaning, and that it seemed to be a part of a larger pattern of neonatal behaviours that showed a curious inversion of intensity between earlier and later assessments—high magnitude, high frequency, and quick reactions in the earlier period being associated with low magnitude, low frequency of behaviour on later follow-up. The present paper will report findings from this study and three others that throw light on the developmental course of behaviours linked to the RIS. Findings from some of the studies have been available for some time but have not been seen as forming a pattern until recently. A review of the four studies should provide us with empirical data from which we can improve our hypotheses about the meaning of the response.

HOME OBSERVATION STUDY

The relation between the newborn RIS and the emotional response at the third week and third month was seen in a new analysis of findings from a longitudinal study of mother–infant interaction over the first three months of life (Moss 1967). Out of a sample of 30 first-borns and their mothers for whom home observations were available, subsamples of 12 females and 11 males were available who had also been studied during the newborn period.

Two two-minute trials of non-nutritive sucking were administered just before a scheduled feeding on each of two occasions, usually separated by one or more complete sleep–awake cycles, on the third and fourth days *post partum*. After 15 seconds had been allowed for recording aspects of sucking, and to prepare for the RIS, the nipple was eased out of the infant's mouth at the jaw-dropping phase of the sucking cycle closest to the end of the 15-second period, and two timers were started. One was stopped at the first cry that showed a full waxing and waning of pitch and volume, the other at the first time when all four limbs were moving actively and simultaneously. A 45-second period after nipple removal was allowed for accurate recording of latencies, and cries were then counted in six successive 15-second intervals, each consisting of 10 seconds for counts and five seconds for recording.

The latencies were transformed and combined with the count of cries so that the reliability could be increased. Long latencies tend to show low test–retest stability. Standardized square root transformation of the two cry latencies and the two movement latencies were combined into a single standardized measure of latency. The cry count (on one of the trials only movements were recorded) was standardized and subtracted from the standardized measure of latency, so providing a latency–cries composite; a high score for this would indicate a long latency and few cries, a low score a short latency and many cries.

Counts of smiles were available from time-sampling during an eight-hour home observation at the third week and third month. The findings from the home observation study were that correlation of the latency–cry composite with the count of smiles was -0.60 ($P<0.001$) at three weeks, but 0.23 with the count at three months. The change in correlation was significant ($t=3.5$, $P<0.01$). Since these Pearson r values did not adequately represent the scatter diagram (which was over-influenced by a few extreme cases), the two longitudinal relations were recomputed with fourfold point r's. The values were -0.45 for the relationship to three weeks, 0.45 to three months ($P<0.05$).

Thus, there is a significant shift in the correlation between the newborn RIS and later behaviour. Long latencies and few cries were associated with few smiles initially, but the pattern shifted in the direction of a relationship to a high number of smiles by the third month.

An examination of the interrelations of sleep and measures of other states indicated that at the third week smiling stood quite separately from clusters of the other measures, but that by the third month smiling had shifted to a cluster consisting of vocalization, the awake–active state, and the awake–passive state. The correlation between the third week and third month count of smiles was not significant. Thus, there was a substantial change in the contextual meaning of smiles, paralleling the change in the relationship of RIS to smiles.

LABORATORY STUDY

Birns *et al.* (1969) have reported a follow-up study to the first month, and to the third to fourth month, for a sample of 24 cases out of an original group of 49 studied on the second and third postnatal day. The sex and parity composition of the sample is not specified. In the newborn period, two minutes of sucking on a pacifier, followed by 60 seconds when latency to first cry was recorded, formed part of a general assessment of the response to visual and tactile stimulation. With age-appropriate revisions, the assessment was repeated at the first month and the third to fourth month, including a composite rating by several observers of 'pleasurable affect', based on such behaviours as cooing to toys or pictures. The longitudinal relations to be reported here are the observations from the third to fourth month.

Although the procedure they used for the RIS was not included by Birns *et al.* (1969) in their description of other procedures carried out at the newborn period, I wrote to them to obtain the information after noting that a significant correlation of 0.54 was reported in their Table 2 between latency to cry at nipple loss, from the newborn period, and the measure of pleasurable affect at three to four months. This correlation indicates—if one refers to only one area of the underlying scatter diagram—that a long latency to cry at the newborn period is associated with the high ratings of pleasurable affect recorded in later development. The finding is in line with the longitudinal relationship reported to the third month by Moss (1967), but it is opposite in sign to the relationship to the first month.

DEVELOPMENTAL TEST FOLLOW-UP

Longitudinal relations between the newborn RIS and emotional response are available, from a still later point in infancy, from a study of 13 male and 11 female infants observed from the newborn period through to an eight-month assessment with the Bayley Infant Behavior Profile at the time of a developmental test (McGrade 1968). At the newborn period the procedure consisted of 30 seconds of non-nutritive sucking followed by removal of the nipple and a count of hand and foot movements in the ensuing 30 seconds. The general ratings of the infant's characteristics in the testing situation, by an examiner who had no knowledge of the newborn behaviour, showed interesting relationships to the RIS that are in line with those from previous reports of follow-ups to the third month. A score representing the difference between activity during the nipple removal period, and during the unstimulated base period, correlated significantly with activity (—0.45), tension (0.40), and happiness (—0.51) from the Infant Behavior Profile. The latter was rated from facial expression, cooing and other non-crying vocalizations. In the published study (McGrade 1958, p. 1250) the description in the text of the nature of the relationship to happiness is in error, although the material in Table 3 is correct.

PRESCHOOL FOLLOW-UP

We have reported follow-up findings from the newborn period to the early preschool period for 30 male and 25 female infants (Bell *et al.* 1971). Test procedures at the newborn period were the same as those used in the Home Observation Study by Moss (1967) but, instead of transforming the latency measures to offset the low reliability of long latencies, we used a different scoring procedure. From the two trials of non-nutritive sucking and nipple removal carried out in each study session, the number of seconds to first cry for the shortest of the two cry latencies was added to the number of seconds to first movement of all four limbs for the shortest of the two movement latencies.

Over 70 observational, experimental and rating measures were obtained from the one-month studies of children in a research nursery school when they reached the age range 27–33 months. The longitudinal relations of the individual preschool measures were studied, as well as the relations of nine composite scores representing cluster-based classes of behaviour.

Unlike other measures of behaviour in the newborn, which showed a relationship to specific preschool composite scores, the longitudinal correlates of latency and cries came from a variety of composite measures. It appeared that these two measures 'selected' later correlates without regard to their organization in terms of shared variance at the preschool period. Latency correlated with 11 individual preschool measures, and cries with eight, where three to four would be expected by chance for a newborn measure. Generally, the preschool measures that were associated with RIS showed a common element of interest and active involvement in the games and routines of the nursery school, and susceptibility to the teacher's influence in encouraging the children to carry out these procedures. The significant longitudinal relations were only found for males, and the following recapitulation of the overall results was provided (Bell *et al.* 1971, p. 86).

> The correlations...indicate that a male newborn who waited for a long time to react following interruption of sucking, and cried very little even when he did react, watched the teacher intensely during story and refreshment time...modeled the teacher's words and gestures closely during the game period; showed great interest in obtaining bells from the rack for one of the games while being urged on by the teacher and peers, and thus pulled very hard when he encountered a stuck bell; and tore down boards rapidly in the corral barrier situation, orienting toward the toy objectives pointed out by the teachers; he played with water at the sink; and did not watch the play of others during free play indoors; reached high levels of

exuberance during outdoor play, and again, seldom just watched the play of others; was rated by the teachers as generally interested in attending school, and from the report of his mother, appeared disappointed when school was terminated.

One of the most interesting relationships contained in the list of longitudinal correlates is that with a count of squeals during outdoor play. Latency to cry and the count of cries from the newborn period correlated 0.40 and −0.28, respectively, with squeals. It is this particular preschool measure that seems to capture the essence of positive emotional expression, and which thus suggests that the results from all the longitudinal studies of the third month or later are in alignment with each other.

RELATIONS OF RIS TO BACKGROUND MEASURES

At the newborn period, the RIS has shown no relation to sex, parity, feeding, anthropometric indices or drugs administered to the mother during labour, but it has shown a negative relation to length of labour (McGrade 1968) and a consistent but low relation to socioeconomic level (Bell *et al.* 1971). A newborn from a home with a high level of education and occupation, and/or delivered after a long labour, reacted slowly and with few cries or movements to nipple removal. For the present paper, an index of gestational maturity (Ounsted & Ounsted 1973) was computed on the data from our preschool follow-up, but no relation was found to the RIS.

Although no sex differences have been found in the newborn period, some of the longitudinal data showed sex differences. Scatter-plots furnished by McGrade (1968) showed that relations between the newborn measures and those up to eight months were stronger for males, and the longitudinal relations in our preschool follow-up (Bell *et al.* 1971) only emerged in the male sample. In the home observation study (Moss 1967), longitudinal relations did not differ appreciably for the sexes. It was not possible to check sex differences in the longitudinal relations of the laboratory follow-up (Birns *et al.* 1969). If anything can be inferred from the two studies that show sex differences and the one that doesn't, it would be that the later the cases are followed the more likely it is that sex differences will appear in the longitudinal relations.

Since the RIS shows a relation to socioeconomic level, it is possible that the latter mediated the longitudinal relations. This could be checked from findings from one other home observation study (Moss & Jones 1975) and from the preschool follow-up (Bell *et al.* 1971). Neither smiles in early infancy nor the various preschool measures showed a relation to socioeconomic level.

DISCUSSION

The present findings can be interpreted against the background of other longitudinal relations in which an inversion of intensity has been uncovered, or an inversion of what is regarded as 'optimal', when value judgements are attached to newborn and later behaviours. We have pointed out (Bell *et al.* 1971) that there is a tendency for high amplitude, speed, or frequency of response in the newborn (high respiration rates, high sensitivity, short latency and many cries in the RIS) to be associated with low intensity behaviours later in the preschool period (low interest, participation, assertiveness, gregariousness and communicativeness).

In terms of 'optimals' many observers would also see an inversion. A quick, vigorous response to interruption of sucking would seem to indicate optimal functioning at the newborn period, while exuberance at the preschool period would also seem optimal. Unfortunately for such an expectation, the optimals are negatively related. Such violations of expectations are not limited to our preschool follow-up. One of the few longitudinal correlates of newborn behaviour in the study by Corah *et al.* (1965) involved an association between poor performance on the Graham Neonatal Assessment Battery and good perceptual motor performance on the seven-year follow-up. The Berkeley growth study (Schaefer & Bayley 1963) showed that quick-moving and active male infants were unfriendly, uncooperative and inattentive in the age range $4\frac{1}{2}$–8 years.

A review of the studies described here is particularly helpful because it gives an indication of the approximate point in development at which intensity may be inverted. The fact that the longitudinal relations of the RIS showed a significant shift in direction between the third week and the third month indicates that there may be a developmental shift that deserves attention, particularly in the light of the importance we attach to the development of emotional expression.

One conclusion can be drawn from the inversion of intensity and optimal performance observed in the several follow-up studies from early infancy. This is that checks should be carried out on actual longitudinal relations before too much effort is devoted to theories or clinical expectations based on the meaning of the early behaviours. Furthermore, items in developmental assessment scales should not be summarized into scales or composite indices before being related to later behaviour, lest very complex relations be overlooked that would not be expected on the logical or clinical grounds that led to the construction of the composite.

References

BELL, R.Q., WELLFR, G.M. & WALDROP, M.F. (1971) Newborn and preschooler: organization of behavior and relations between periods. *Monogr. Soc. Res. Child Dev. 36* (Nos 1, 2, Serial No. 142)

BIRNS, V., BARTEN, S. & BRIDGER, W.H. (1969) Individual differences in temperamental characteristics of infants. *Trans. N.Y. Acad. Sci. 31*, 1071–1082

CORAH, N.L., ANTHONY, E.J., PAINTER, P., STERN, J.A. & THURSTON, D.L. (1965) Effects of perinatal anoxia after seven years. *Psychol. Monogr.* No. 596

FRIES, M.E. (1941) Mental hygiene in pregnancy, delivery, and the puerperium. *Ment. Hyg. 25*, 221–236

MCGRADE, B.J. (1968) Newborn activity and emotional response at eight months. *Child Dev. 39*, 1247–1252

MOSS, H.A. (1967) Sex, age, and state as determinants of mother–infant interaction. *Merrill-Palmer Q. 13*, 19–36

MOSS, H.A. & JONES, S.J. (1975) Relations between maternal attitudes and maternal behavior as a function of social class, in *Cultural and Social Influences on Behavior in Infancy and Early Childhood* (Leiderman, P.H. & Tulkin, S.R., eds.), Stanford University Press, Stanford, Calif.

OUNSTED, M. & OUNSTED, C. (1973) *On Fetal Growth Rate* (Clinics in Developmental Medicine No. 46), Spastics International Medical Publications/Lippincott, Philadelphia

SCHAEFER, E.S. & BAYLEY, N. (1963) Maternal behavior, child behavior, and their intercorrelations from infancy through adolescence. *Monogr. Soc. Res. Child Dev. 28*, No. 3, 1–127

SEARS, R.R. & SEARS, P.S. (1940) Minor studies of aggression: V. Strength of frustration-reaction as a function of strength of drive. *J. Psychol.* 9, 297–300

Discussion

Hofer: When did you test the response to interruption of sucking in relation to the time of waking and feeding?

Bell: When the baby came out of the sleep cycle, about 30 minutes before the scheduled feeding time.

Hofer: The RIS measures were all done in the newborn period and then correlated with other measures at later ages. Did you repeat the RIS at three months, for instance, to see how that correlated with smiling?

Bell: By six weeks the reaction looked so different that I did not repeat that test at later ages.

Dunn: We found a negative correlation between 'latency to cry' when sucking was interrupted and maternal vocalizing, touching and response to baby's vocalizing at 14 and 20 weeks. It is difficult to see how this maternal behaviour could relate to the behaviour you found in the babies, correlated with the RIS. Perhaps our short-latency RIS babies were being more active later, and this is why they were getting more attention.

Bell: In this paper I have not reported relationships between the newborn behaviour and later maternal behaviour, since most of the relationships were complicated and depended on the sex of the infant. This particular sample was too small to yield stable results separately for the sexes.

Dunn: It is difficult to see how the maternal behaviour we found related to the RIS behaviour you saw in babies. One might expect more touching with a smiling baby. This would fit with your three-week measures.

Bell: Yes; however, the infants' smiling and maternal contact showed a non-significant negative correlation (−0.27) in our findings at three weeks.

Dunn: These were just the measures where we found strong continuity in the mother's behaviour over this age period. This raised the possibility that continuity in the baby's behaviour may be contributing to the continuity in the mother's behaviour. But we cannot assume that the RIS is a *congenital* contributor—that the baby's response is independent of the mother's way of handling. My doubts about that are influenced by your finding that the prenatal characteristics of the mother are related to the later differences.

Bell: It is congenital in the sense that we assess them at a time when there has been relatively little interaction, that is on the third and fourth days, whereas you are looking at eight days or older. Of course, there has been physiological interaction of mother and infant during the fetal period. That is why I was talking primarily in terms of behavioural interaction.

Papoušek: Was sucking interrupted during sucking bursts or during intervals between bursts? The infant's responses would be completely different in the two situations. We found that if we interrupted in the interval between bursts adjustment was fast and the babies did not object. But if we interrupted during the bursts of sucking movements, we always had trouble because they started crying.

Hofer: This would be a source of variability in all such studies, but few have paid sufficient attention to it before.

Richards: One thing that might be related to prenatal differences in the fetus, for which data are available, is maternal blood pressure. Our results suggest that mothers who have longer labours and babies with short latencies-to-cry after the teat is removed have higher blood pressures during pregnancy (Barnes 1974). This is a further suggestion that things are different before the baby is born. The longer labour may well be an indication of the kind of mother and of the kind of baby she has before birth.

Hofer: How would you tie together high blood pressure, long labour and short latency?

Richards: They could well be anxious mothers, and anxiety might affect blood flow to the fetus and so the baby's behaviour after birth. Or blood pressure itself may be quite irrelevant except as an indicator of anxiety. Long labour may follow anxiety and be the origin of the changed behaviour of the baby after birth. A study by Ottinger & Simmons (1964) shows that mothers rated as anxious during pregnancy have babies that cry more and are more active. One would expect these babies to have a short latency-to-cry in a sucking test.

Dunn: Those we saw had a short latency, with more crying in the newborn period, shorter periods of uninterrupted sleep in the first 10 days, and shorter sleep at 14 months, all after a long labour.

Hofer: How do you think long labour leads to these short latency responses of crying and so on?

Richards: The longer labours might not in themselves be the origin of the behavioural differences in the infants. The mother's emotional state might lead to constitutional differences in the fetus, perhaps mediated by blood flow to the fetus during pregnancy. The same emotional state might lead to a longer labour. Or alternatively, the fetus might have acquired characteristics that lead to a longer labour. After all the fetus is known to play a role in initiating labour, so it is possible that it could influence its duration. Of course, these processes would be quite different in situations where midwives or obstetricians control the length of labour.

Bell: There are at least three studies showing a relationship between anxiety or negative emotional states in pregnancy and irritability in the infant (Ferreira 1960; Davids *et al.* 1963; Ottinger & Simmons 1964).

Hofer: I am trying to get from statistical relationships to biological relationships. We are all making conceptual leaps and inferences for which we have very little or no cause-and-effect data, no knowledge about the mediating processes or mechanisms.

Richards: They are suggestions of where we can look.

Rosenblatt: The measures that you have later on, between 3½ and 4 months are mostly measures of 'positive' or approach behaviours. One aspect of an 'approach' behaviour is focusing on something and remaining focused on it, with all the positive emotions which go along with that.

The RIS test measures how long an infant can continue with sucking even though it is being interrupted. Some infants are able to continue despite the fact that an interruptive stimulus has been introduced. If we look at the latency and at how long a positive action can continue, rather than at how soon a negative response can be aroused, there is a nice relationship. The infant who can sustain a positive direction of activity, continuing to suck or at least not be strongly perturbed as a result of this interruptive stimulus, is capable at the later age of showing a similarly positive approach with more complex systems.

In looking for correlations between mother and child it must be kept in mind that a dependent mother may be anxious and so on at the time she gives birth. A person remains dependent, however, by being very obedient and not developing any rebellious activity. She is generally orientated towards peaceful activity and she is imposing this probably on her own child: 'Don't do anything that is disruptive but remain very obedient to me'. You may have that direction of correlation or of influence between maternal dependency and the child's behaviour. You are measuring how well an infant can resist the interruption. From that point of view, your results show a good deal of continuity from the early to the later dates.

Bowlby: Perhaps you could extend this work by observing not only how the infant responds to the interruption of sucking but how he responds to the opportunity to resume it. Mary Ainsworth has found a child's response to reunion with the mother after a three-minute separation an extremely revealing measure in her strange-situation test (Ainsworth *et al.* 1971).

Bell: We have a lot of trouble getting the babies to start sucking again if they show a strong reaction to interruption.

Salisbury: The infant sucking non-nutritively may have a certain periodicity for his sucking bursts. One of the two babies that we saw on the film you showed, Dr Bell, sucked for long bursts, whereas the other sucked for fairly short intervals and then paused. Would it be worth recording at which point in a stream of sucks the baby was interrupted? Interruptions at the start of a sucking episode may produce differences in the latent period before the infant responds to interruptions at the end of a sucking burst.

Bell: The important thing is to remove the nipple gently so as not to startle the infant. If they startle they may cry immediately. However, it would probably be an improvement if we waited to measure this response between bursts of sucking, and I will suggest this to new investigators starting work on the response.

Bentovim: One interesting point is the relationship of your studies to studies of temperament, Dr Bell. Sameroff (1974) finds that in a group of psychiatrically disturbed women anxiety and 'poor attitudes' during pregnancy correlate 0.37 and 0.33 respectively with the baby being difficult temperamentally at four months, and this in turn has a relationship to 'competence' at 30 months —similar to the continuity of behaviour in the first years noted by Thomas *et al.* (1963).

Bell: The early assessments by Thomas *et al.* were made at around three months—not very early. They have continuity of characteristics from early infancy but not continuity of congenital characteristics.

Bentovim: The extension Sameroff describes is interesting, where mood and temperament in infancy are related to the state in pregnancy, and not just the psychiatric disorder itself.

Bell: Whatever the basis for genetic transmission of schizophrenia, they found that there is an environmental contributor too—schizophrenic mothers tend to have bad pregnancies.

Thoman: Over what period of time do you observe smiling at three weeks and three months?

Bell: During eight-hour observations at home.

Thoman: Did you observe smiling while the babies were awake as well as asleep? At three weeks there wouldn't be many smiles while they were awake. At three months they would smile much more while they were awake. So there is a difference in the two measures and I think one would expect a negative correlation between the three-month and the three-week frequencies. The baby who is reacting with a greater number of smiles during sleep is possibly not as mature.

Bell: That is a good point. It may explain the shift I reported, from a negative correlation between the newborn RIS and smiles at three weeks, to a positive correlation with smiles at three months. It would also explain the non-significant correlation of the smile-count between three weeks and three months.

References

AINSWORTH, M.D.S., BELL, S.M. & STAYTON, D.J. (1971) Individual differences in strange-situation behavior of one-year olds, in *The Origins of Human Social Relations* (Schaffer, H.R., ed.), Academic Press, New York

BARNES, F. (1974) On having a relatively poor status at birth: some characteristics of the children and their mothers. Paper presented at the 9th International Study Group on Child Neurology, Oxford

DAVIDS, A., HOLDEN, R.H. & GRAY, G.B. (1963) Maternal anxiety during pregnancy and adequacy of mother and child adjustment eight months following childbirth. *Child Dev. 34*, 993–1002

FERREIRA, A.J. (1960) The pregnant woman's emotional attitude and its reflection on the newborn. *Am. J. Orthopsychiatr. 30*, 553–561

OTTINGER, D.R. & SIMMONS, J.E. (1964) Behavior of human neonates and prenatal maternal anxiety. *Psychol. Rep. 15*, 391–394

SAMEROFF, A.J. (1974) Infant risks in developmental deviancy. Paper presented to International Association Child Psychiatry and Allied Professions, Philadelphia

THOMAS, A.,CHESS, S., BIRCH, H.G., HERTZIG, M.E. & KORN, S. (1963) *Behavioural Individuality in Early Childhood*, University of London Press, London

Mother-infant neonatal separation: Some delayed consequences

P. HERBERT LEIDERMAN and MARJORIE J. SEASHORE

Stanford University School of Medicine, Stanford, California

Abstract An earlier study of mothers of premature and full-term infants showed that the type and amount of social interaction between a human mother and her infant in the immediate postpartum period can influence the mother's subsequent behaviour and attitude towards the infant. Separation of a mother from her infant for as short a time as three weeks in the immediate postpartum period can lead to lowered feelings of maternal competency and decreased amounts of attachment behaviour, sometimes continuing for as long as one month after the pair have been reunited. Follow-up of these mothers and infants at 11, 12 and 15 months after discharge from the hospital showed that the effects of separation on maternal attitude and behaviour had disappeared, except that non-separated mothers continued to touch their infants more than separated mothers. Differences in maternal behaviour varied with birth order and sex of the infant and social class membership of the family. These findings are discussed in terms of ethological and social learning theories as they apply to maternal 'social attachment' in the neonatal period. The importance of considering the consequences of neonatal separation for the entire family rather than mother alone is emphasized.

The influence of early separation on the subsequent relationship between a human mother and her infant has been demonstrated in several studies (Klaus & Kennell 1970; Klaus *et al.* 1970; Leifer *et al.* 1972; Seashore *et al.* 1973). Our own research has convinced us that this experience of early separation indeed influences attitudes and behaviour in the mother, at least for the short-term, and that it may have long-term consequences, as demonstrated in the recent work of Kennell *et al.* (1974). There is, however, a danger of the influence of this early, relatively brief, period of separation being over-emphasized, while the influence of other potentially important variables, such as parity of the mother, sex of the infant and family social class, is neglected. It is to this issue that we address ourselves in this paper, using information gathered from the mothers and infants in our original study (Leifer *et al.* 1972) 11 to 15 months after the end of the period of separation.

Most previous studies, including ours, have either assumed or attempted to demonstrate the primacy of the neonatal period in the establishment of appropriate attachment between a mother and her infant. Bowlby (1969), in his formulation of the development of the mother–infant bond in humans, utilizes a developmental–ethological approach. Based on observations in animals, this approach strongly implies that there is a 'critical' or 'optimal' period for the development of social relationships, at least for the infant. Whatever the utility of this concept for infants, human or mammalian, the question remains of whether the concept applies to the maternal side of the mother–infant equation. The danger inherent in stretching this concept to include the mother should be clear enough. The mother is an adult with previous experiences, acquired expectations and, for humans, a value orientation; whereas the infant, while not a *tabula rasa*, is more likely to be influenced by environmental events. Thus, although the use of the concept of an 'optimal' or 'critical' period when we look at the neonatal encounters between the mother and infant may have heuristic value in directing our research endeavours, we should be prepared to accept that what may be critical for one member of the dyad may not be critical for the other.

Human mothers, embedded in a social system with well-delineated roles, have varying cultural values placed upon the maternal role which would certainly influence their behaviour. We would anticipate that previous experience with child-rearing, the sex of the infant, and the social or cultural interpretation of the maternal role, as indicated perhaps by a mother's membership of a certain social class, would provide important variations in the mother's subsequent behaviour. By looking into these factors, we hope to ascertain more clearly whether mother–infant separation in the neonatal period makes a measurable difference in later social interaction between the mother and her child.

METHOD

The findings reported in this paper cover one segment of a comprehensive longitudinal study of families of young infants, from the birth of the infant up to two years of age. Included here is information on maternal attitudes 12 months after discharge, caretaking behaviour 11 months after discharge, and the infant's mental and motor development 15 months after discharge from the hospital. Throughout the two-year period, we conducted observations, interviews and testing at staggered intervals. This schedule permitted us to maintain contact with the families at frequent intervals without burdening mothers with many simultaneous demands for gathering information.

Subjects

Three groups were studied, two consisting of mothers and their prematurely born infants and one of mothers and their full-term infants. The dyads included in the study met the following criteria: (1) the mother had not previously borne a premature infant or one of low birth weight; (2) the infant was free from obvious congenital abnormalities; (3) the infant was not one of a multiple birth; (4) if premature, the infant weighed from 890 to 1899 g (2.0 to 4.2 lb) at birth; and (5) the father was living at home. Over the two-year period several families were dropped from the study when the father left home.

The mothers of premature infants meeting these criteria were randomly assigned to one of two treatment groups. The first group of 20 mothers (*separated* group) could view their infants from the nursery window during the 3 to 12 weeks the infants were in the intensive care nursery but they had no other contact with their infants during this time. This experience has been the standard procedure of premature nurseries, the duration of separation depending on the infant's initial weight, weight gain and health. The 22 mothers in the second group (*contact* group) were permitted to enter the intensive care nursery to interact directly with their infants throughout the period of hospitalization. This caretaking included handling, changing, and feeding the infant when he was able to suck from a bottle.

When an infant reached the weight of 2100 g (4.6 lb) he was taken out of the incubator in the intensive care nursery and transferred to a discharge nursery where he remained for 7 to 10 days until his weight reached 2500 g (5.5 lb). During these 7 to 10 days, the mothers in both the separated and contact groups were permitted to come in and care for their infants, initially under the supervision of a nurse and later independently. When the infant reached 2500 g, he was discharged to the mother's care at home. The separated and contact phases of the study were alternated in blocks of three to six months so that at any given time all mothers with infants in the nursery had the same experience—either separation or contact. The 11–15-month follow-up study included 18 families in the separated group and 17 in the contact group.

Twenty-four mothers of full-term infants served as a comparison group. All delivered without complications, bottle-fed their infants, experienced full sensory contact with their infants in the hospital during the four or five feedings per day, and were discharged to their homes within three days after parturition. As far as was feasible, the full-term group was comparable to the two groups of premature infants with respect to parity of mother, sex of infant, and social class. Twenty-one of these mothers and their full-term infants were included in the 11–15-month follow-up study.

Participation in the study was voluntary. All families were told that we were doing a study of families with newborn infants during the first two years of life and were interested both in how parents manage with young infants during this period and in the development of infants up to two years of age.

The demographic characteristics of the three groups are presented in Table 1. The separated and contact groups are quite similar, although the full-term group had a slightly higher family income and social class. The lowest socio-economic group in our sample was suburban working class and therefore 'lower class' in our study should not be directly compared to lower-class samples in other studies where urban minority groups have been observed. Further, the differences between the full-term and premature groups may be mitigated in part by their very inclusion in our study, which for all the individuals studied focused parental attention on the growth and development of the child. The ethnicity of the three groups differed only in that there were three black families in both the separated and the contact groups, but no black families in the full-term group.

TABLE 1

Description of socioeconomic status of patents included in 11–15-month study

Status	*Separated (n = 18)*	*Contact (n = 17)*	*Full-term (n = 21)*
Age (median)			
Mothers	24	22	23
Fathers	28	26	26
Family income (median)	$8600	$7200	$11 500
Education (median)			
Mothers	Some college	Some college	Some college
Fathers	Some college	Some college	Some college
Social class (median)[a]	Middle	Middle	Middle to upper middle
Ethnicity of parents (frequency distribution)			
Caucasian	15[b]	13[b]	20
Black	3	3	0
Oriental	0	1[c]	1

[a] Based on Warner's classification of husband's occupation.
[b] One family, mother Caucasian, father Oriental.
[c] One family, mother Polynesian, father Black.

Primiparous and multiparous mothers of male and female infants were included in each of the three groups, although they were not equally distributed among them. The numerical distribution of mother–infant dyads by parity and by sex is included in each of the figures.

Procedures

The 11–15-month follow-up study included the same measures of maternal attitude and behaviour and infant development as had been used during hospitalization and in the follow-up studies at 1–3 and 6–9 months.

Maternal attitude

A mother's confidence in her ability to care for her infant was measured with a paired comparison questionnaire administered during an interview 12 months after the infant had been discharged from the hospital. In it, the mother compared herself with five other possible caretakers: father, grandmother, experienced mother, paediatric nurse, and doctor. Comparisons were made for each of the six caretaking tasks classified as being either social or instrumental. Calming the baby, understanding what the baby wants, and showing affection to the baby were classified as social tasks; whereas changing, feeding and bathing were classified as instrumental tasks. The percentage of instances in which the mother chose herself as the more able caretaker was calculated. A more complete analysis of the early self-confidence data appears in a paper by Seashore *et al.* (1973).

Measures of maternal commitment and dyadization were obtained from blind ratings made by two independent coders of the information contained in interview transcripts. Each mother was rated on a five-point scale from low to high for each variable. Commitment consists of a global assessment of the extent to which the mother expresses pleasure rather than displeasure with her infant, her desire to spend time with her infant, her interest in the infant's development, and her sensitivity to the infant's needs. Dyadization is the extent to which the mother expresses a desire to and does spend time with the infant beyond that necessary for caretaking.

Maternal behaviour

Eleven months after discharge each mother and infant was observed in their own home for one to two hours. Selected mother and infant behaviours were noted during and after caretaking. Trained observers used a point-sampling

TABLE 2

Comparison of maternal behaviour and infant performance over time by experimental condition

	Time after discharge from hospital			
Mother:	*1 week*	*1 month*	*6 months*	*11–12 months*
Infant:	—	*3 months*	*9 months*	*15 months*
Behaviour				
Proximal attachment	$FT > CON > SEP^{b}$			
Ventral contact	$FT > CON > SEP^{d}$	$FT > SEP > CON$	$CON > FT > SEP^{*}$	
Smile	$FT > CON > SEP^{c}$	$FT \gg CON > SEP^{c}$		$FT \gg CON = SEP^{a}$
Hold	$CON > SEP > FT^{a}$			
Touch				$CON > SEP^{*}$
Infant performance				
Mental	—	$FT \gg CON = SEP^{d}$	$FT > CON = SEP^{c}$	$FT > CON > SEP^{c}$
Motor	—	$FT \gg CON > SEP^{d}$	$FT > CON = SEP^{c}$	$FT > SEP > CON^{c}$

* $P < 0.10$ ^{c} $P < 0.01$ FT: full-term
^{a} $P < 0.05$ ^{d} $P < 0.001$ CON: contact
^{b} $P < 0.025$ SEP: separated

TABLE 3

Comparison of maternal behaviour and infant performance over time by birth order of infant

	Time after discharge from hospital			
Mother:	*1 week*	*1 month*	*6 months*	*11–12 months*
Infant:	—	*3 months*	*9 months*	*15 months*
Behaviour				
Distal attachment	1st > Later[d]	1st > Later*	1st > Later[b]	1st > Later*
Talk	1st > Later[a]	1st > Later*	1st > Later[c]	1st > Later*
Laugh	1st > Later*			1st > Later*
Look	1st > Later[d]			1st > Later*
Attention				1st > Later[a]
Attitude				
Commitment	—	Later > 1st[d]		
Dyadization	—	—	—	1st > Later*
Social competence	—			Later > 1st*
Instrumental competence	—	Later > 1st*		

* $P<0.10$ [a] $P<0.05$ [b] $P<0.025$ [c] $P<0.01$ [d] $P<0.001$

technique to record selected behaviours of both mother and infant at 15-second intervals. Frequencies of observed behaviours were converted to percentage scores, to control for the length of the observation. Although many behaviours were observed, only those related to the mother's attachment behaviour towards the infant are included in this paper. Summary measures were devised for both distal and proximal attachment behaviours. Distal attachment included looking, talking, laughing and smiling at the infant; whereas holding, affectionate touching and ventral contact during holding were included in proximal attachment behaviours. The findings were analysed as individual as well as summary scores. These findings are considered more extensively by Leifer *et al.* (1972).

Infant development

Infant development was tested at 15 months, using the Bayley tests of mental and motor development (Bayley 1969). Raw scores, rather than standardized scores, were used in the analysis because of the difficulty of using norms based on full-term infants to convert the scores of premature infants.

Data analysis

The small sample precluded us from considering the variables of treatment group, parity, sex and social class of the infant simultaneously for most analyses.

TABLE 4

Comparison of maternal behaviour and infant performance over time by sex of infant

	Time after discharge from hospital			
Mother:	*1 week*	*1 month*	*6 months*	*11–12 months*
Infant:	—	*3 months*	*9 months*	*15 months*
Behaviour				
Distal attachment			Male > Female[a]	
Touch		Male > Female[b]	Male > Female[c]	Male > Female[c]
Ventral contact	Female > Male[a]	Female > Male[a]	Female > Male[a]	
Talk			Male > Female*	
Attention			Male > Female[c]	Male > Female[a]
Attitude				
Dyadization	—	—	—	Male > Female[b]

* $P < 0.10$ [b] $P < 0.025$
[a] $P < 0.05$ [c] $P < 0.01$

Where it was not possible to take account of all of them together, the effects of treatment group, parity, sex of infant and social class were analysed separately. Two-way analyses of variance were used to assess the effects of parity and separation, both individually and in interaction. Additional two-way analyses of variance were done to assess the effects of sex of the infant and treatment group, individually and in interaction.

The effects of both maternal attitudes and behaviour, as well as other pertinent variables, such as treatment group, parity, infant's sex and birth weight, on the infant's motor and mental development were tested using multiple regression and correlational analyses. Multiple regression analyses were also used to assess the effects of treatment group, parity, sex of the infant, infant's behaviour and social class on maternal behaviour.

RESULTS

The findings on selected maternal attitudes, maternal behaviour and infant performance are shown in Figs. 1–7. Each graph depicts the mean scores for subgroups of males and females and for first and later-born infants within each treatment group. Attitudes and behaviours that were significantly related to treatment group, parity and/or sex in these and earlier observations are indicated in Tables 2, 3 and 4.

By 11 months after discharge the only maternal behaviours that were differentiated by the initial experimental condition (that is, separated, contact and full-term) were smiling and touching. Full-term mothers smiled at their infants more than mothers of prematures. Mothers in the contact group touched their infants more than mothers in the separated group. There were no significant differences in maternal attitude scores. The differences present between full-

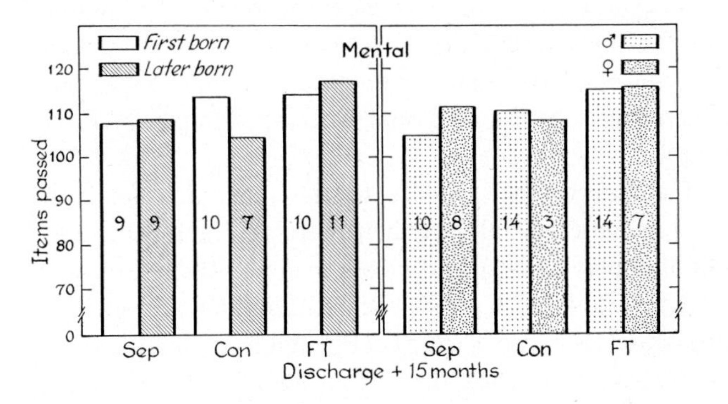

FIG. 1. Infant mental test performance (Bayley test) by parity and by sex.

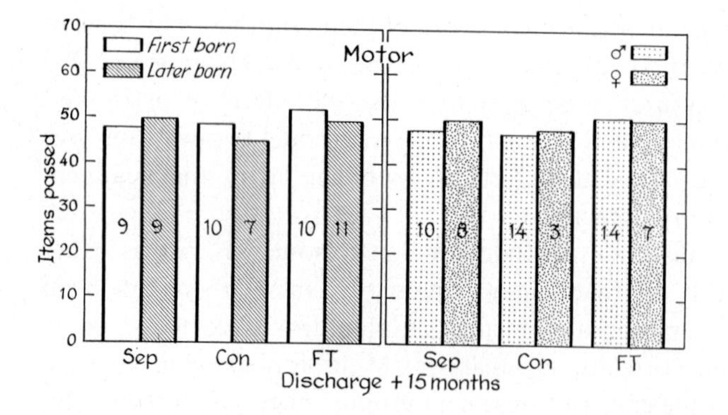

FIG. 2. Infant motor test performance (Bayley test) by parity and by sex.

term and premature infants in scores for mental and motor performance at three and nine months persisted at 15 months. Full-term infants scored higher than the infants in the contact and separated groups, which were similar to one another. The differences between the premature and full-term infants have decreased over time.

We accounted for some of the antecedents of the mother's behaviour by doing a multiple regression analysis (see Table 5), using as independent variables the classification of the initial group, the sex and birth order of the infant, infant behaviours, and two measures of family social class—one based on the father's occupation and the second on the occupation of the maternal grandfather. For maternal touching, the sex of the infant (males greater than females) was the only statistically significant independent predictor. All the variables included, however, accounted for only 30% of the total variance, which is a relatively low predictive power. For smiling behaviour, the largest independent predictor was mobility of the infant. However, several other variables (see Table 5, Pearson r) were positively, although not independently, related to smiling. These included several infant behaviours, the group membership (i.e. contact, separated and full-term) and socioeconomic class status. Smiling behaviour, as recorded in this study, seems to be the behaviour with the strongest relationship to many of the variables.

The relationship of the antecedent variables to the remaining maternal behaviours is less clear. For maternal talking, there were no significant independent predictors, although play activity and noises made by the infant were positively related to maternal talking. Current socioeconomic status was the only variable that came close to being a statistically significant predictor of holding behaviour. Lower-class mothers held their infants more than did mothers in higher socioeconomic classes. Again, the total variance accounted for was

TABLE 5

Prediction of maternal behaviours at 11-month observation: individual correlations[1] with variables included in multiple regression analysis[2]

Independent variables	$n = 56$					
	Dependent variables					
	Touch	*Talk*	*Hold*	*Look*	*Smile*	*Attention*
Initial condition						
Group	−0.13	0.02	−0.14	−0.08	0.31	0.03
Birth order	−0.12	−0.25	0.18	−0.28	0.08	−0.27
Sex	0.42[c]	0.03	−0.15	0.03	−0.04	0.24*
Infant behaviour						
Looking at no one	−0.05	0.22	0.17	0.23	0.25	0.22
Looking at mother	0.05	—	−0.28	—	−0.25	−0.18
Silent	0.15	−0.35	−0.05	−0.24	0.04	−0.20
Noises	—	0.34	0.02	0.26	−0.05	0.17
Play	0.15	0.21	−0.16	0.06	0.25	0.35[a]
Mobility	0.13	0.23	−0.05	0.16	0.40[c]	0.28
Family socioeconomic status						
Current	0.16	0.10	−0.04	−0.21	0.31	0.32[a]
Mother's background	0.11	0.04	−0.30*	−0.11	0.23	0.21
Variation accounted for by all variables (%)	30	23	27	21	40	39

[1] Pearson r values: $\geqslant 0.22$, significance of $P < 0.05$
$\geqslant 0.31$, significance of $P < 0.01$
$\geqslant 0.34$, significance of $P < 0.005$

[2] F values included when significant.
Significance of F: * $P < 0.10$
[a] $P < 0.05$
[c] $P < 0.01$

low (27%), but the correlations were suggestive. Lower-class mothers also tended to look at their infants more than other mothers, although there was a stronger relationship between birth order and looking, with first-born infants being looked at more often than later-born infants. Furthermore, the infant's play activities and the current socioeconomic status were significantly related to the mother's attention to her infant, other than when caring for him. Finally, maternal attention was related to the mobility of the infant and to the infant being a first-born or male, or both.

We concluded from these observations that the differences in maternal attitudes and behaviour reported in our previous papers (Leiderman *et al.* 1973; Leifer *et al.* 1972; Seashore *et al.* 1973) at one week and one month after discharge from the hospital were evanescent, suggesting that circumstances other than the initial separation condition determined to a large degree the behaviour of mothers at the 11-month observation. Nonetheless, the smiling and touching behaviours of mothers which differentiate the groups have interesting implications. 'Touch' was the one maternal behaviour strongly reinforced for the contact group during the infant's hospital stay. Mothers were told to go to the nursery to 'touch' their babies; furthermore, they observed the nurses 'touching' their babies in the course of caretaking.

In the earlier nursery phase there was little else for the mothers to do, beyond relatively simple acts. Feeding and more complex caretaking of infants were not possible until the infants approached the discharge weight of 2500 g, generally after 3 to 12 weeks' stay in the hospital. It seems that mothers in our contact group *learned* to touch their infants, and that this behaviour, acquired under conditions of relatively high saliency in the postpartum period, persisted for one year after discharge from the nursery. As one might anticipate, touching behaviour was particularly prominent in primiparous mothers. Mothers in the full-term and separated groups, who did not receive this emphasis on touching during their initial contact with their infants, do not emphasize this type of behaviour with them. Whether one should account for this early learned behaviour by the ethologically derived concept of imprinting is debatable. The important fact is that touching behaviour is relatively resistant to extinction for the contact group of mothers. However, this touching behaviour cannot be considered equivalent to the Bowlby–Ainsworth concept of 'attachment', since mothers in the separated and full-term groups were surely 'attached' to their infants in ways not reflected by touching behaviour.

The smiling behaviour which differentiated the premature and full-term groups also has interesting implications. This finding suggests that either the behaviour of the premature infant during his first year does not elicit smiling

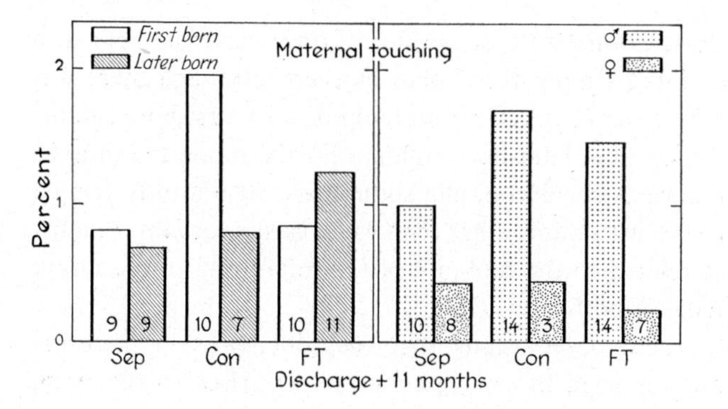

FIG. 3. Maternal touching behaviour by parity and by sex (home observation).

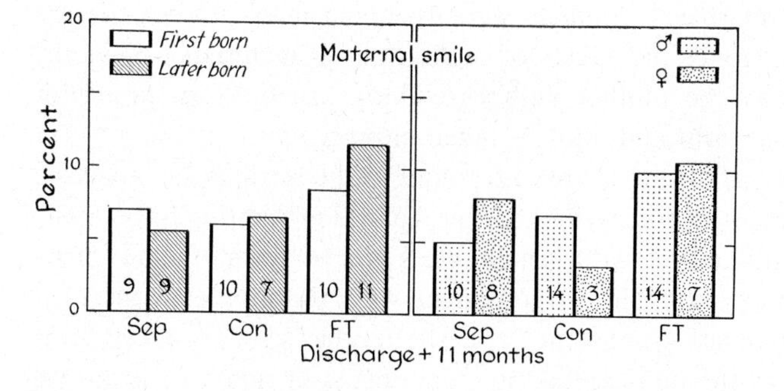

FIG. 4. Maternal smiling behaviour by parity and by sex (home observation).

from the mother, or that the mothers of premature infants experience greater anxiety or for other reasons derive less pleasure from their infants than do mothers of full-term infants. Although, as mentioned above, infant mobility is the only statistically significant predictor of maternal smiling behaviour, father's socioeconomic status and treatment group as well as other infant behaviours were positively, though not independently, related to mother's behaviour.

Since smiling behaviour can be reasonably assumed to be one of the important behavioural elements in an index of an infant's social attachment, the finding of a lower score in the mothers of premature infants may be ominous. It is well known from the work of Drillien (1959) that lower-class premature children as a group do not develop as rapidly as full-term children, at least in the early years of infancy. The observation of less smiling by lower-class mothers of premature infants provides one possible explanation for the slower development of lower-class premature children: that is, decreased bonding or attachment of mothers may result in slower psychological development of infants. The findings relating social class and development in our study are consistent with those of Drillien and will be reported elsewhere.

We turn next to the analysis of data according to the birth order of the infant. As indicated in Table 4, by 11 months after discharge maternal behaviours of mothers of first-born infants differ from the maternal behaviours towards later-born infants, specifically for distal attachment (talking, laughing, looking and smiling), and attention paid to the infant during non-caretaking periods. Some of these differences (talking, laughing and looking), as well as the combined measure of distal attachment, were found at one week of age. The differences in distal attachment and talking between the first-born and later-born infants persisted throughout all observations of mother–infant interaction. The results suggest that the motivational components found in the primiparous mothers play important roles in influencing subsequent maternal behaviours. Therefore, in assessments of the effects of separation on maternal behaviour, the prior experience of the mother with caretaking becomes an important determinant of her behaviour and must be taken into account.

Differences in maternal attitudes are also found in the birth order analysis. Dyadization, a self-report of the mother on her feelings of wanting to be alone with and, in fact, spending time with her infant, is greater for mothers of first-born than later-born infants. This is consistent with the mother's observed behaviour. Only with social competency (i.e. the mother's sense of her competence in dealing with the non-caretaking components of infant care) do we find that multiparous mothers score higher than primiparous mothers. This is not a particularly surprising finding, in that we might expect more experienced mothers to feel more competent.

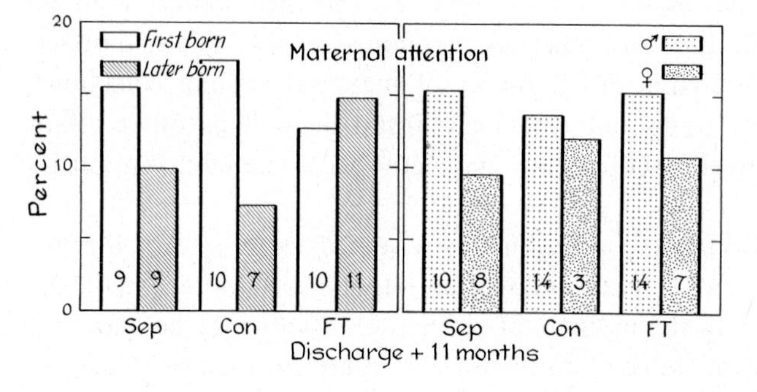

FIG. 5. Maternal attention (non-caretaking) by parity and by sex (home observation).

The findings on birth order are particularly interesting, since available sociological and psychological information on first-born infants suggests that they have higher need-achievement, higher success, and higher neuroticism when compared to later-born infants (Sutton-Smith & Rosenberg 1970). To the extent that the maternal–infant interaction in the first year has some effect on later psychological development, the findings reported here suggest some mechanisms which might account for the development of these psychological characteristics.

Maternal behaviour was also found to vary according to the sex of the infant. The mothers of male infants were observed to touch and give more attention to their infants than mothers of female infants. As for maternal attitudes, the expressed dyadization and self-evaluation of competence were also greater for mothers of male infants. Although others (Goldberg & Lewis 1969; Moss 1967) have reported that mothers varied in their behaviours according to the sex of the infant, the details are not always consistent. There is, however, agreement

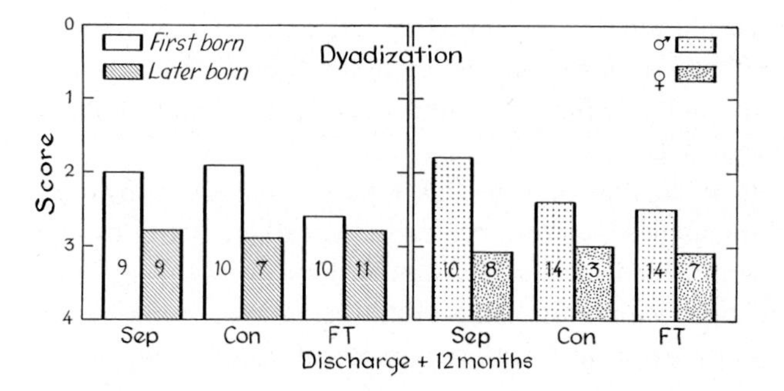

FIG. 6. Dyadization by parity and by sex (12 months after discharge)

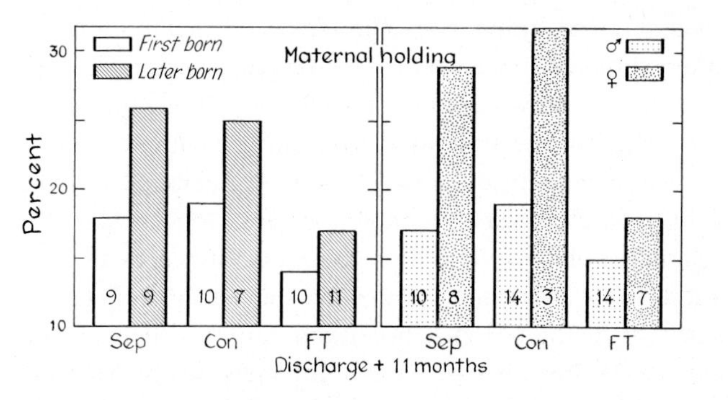

FIG. 7. Maternal holding behaviour by parity and by sex (home observation).

that differences occur, and this suggests that details may depend on the varying types of observations. The extent and significance of these differences over time bear further investigation.

The explanation of our finding on sex differences is not clear from these data, but most certainly it is confounded by behaviours derived from the mother's value system towards infants of each sex, and the finding may be in part due to differences in the behaviour of male and female infants towards the mother. The mothers of females appeared to 'cuddle' their infants more than mothers of males, whereas the mothers of males 'attended to' them and 'touched' them more, quite possibly on the basis of differences in the activity levels of male and female infants, although we do not have adequate data to support or refute this argument.

If the mother's handling of the infant has any particular effect on the subsequent cognitive and social growth of the infant, then from our observations we might conclude that first-born males are a particularly favoured group and later-born females a less favoured group. Obviously, these intriguing findings need to be confirmed by other studies, but they emphasize the complexity of attempting to account for maternal behaviour. Certainly, simple explanations of maternal behaviours that are based on one or a series of experiences immediately after birth are not adequate for understanding complex human behaviours observed one year later.

The major conclusion to be drawn from this type of analysis, consistent with findings based on the analysis of variance reported earlier, is an obvious one. Maternal behaviours, under the relatively standardized conditions of this study (i.e. a 50-minute observation at home with the mother doing some caretaking and playing), are associated with a number of mother and infant characteristics and situational factors. Therefore, behaviours at one year cannot be attributed merely to one type of maternal experience in the nursery. This is not particularly surprising, but it emphasizes the need for methodological clarity and the use of more sophisticated statistical techniques, covering a wide range of factors, before one can draw definitive conclusions about the effect of any single experimental manipulation on later maternal behaviour.

Regardless of the absence of differences caused by the originally postulated main effect, inclusion in separated versus contact groups, the substantive findings of this study should not be overlooked. Besides differences due to sex and birth order, there were differences related to socioeconomic status. This finding is particularly intriguing not only because it confirms the work of others (Tulkin & Kagan 1972), but also because it provides a link between infant behaviour and social class, mediated through mother behaviour. This analysis of mother–infant behaviour is incomplete, however, because it omits the father's interaction with the mother and infant, which is probably also related to social class membership. It should be emphasized that membership in a social class is important not because it 'explains' the social development but because it provides sufficient variation in family structure and function to help us to understand the underlying socialization processes at work in the course of an infant's development.

DISCUSSION

We conclude from the findings that the manipulation of the premature nursery has little long-term effect on the mother's subsequent behaviour and attitudes, and almost no effect on the infant's behaviour and test performance. Although mothers who are allowed early contact with their infants touch their infants more when evaluated one year later, the sex of the infant, parity, the socioeconomic status of the family and the infant's behaviour are even more powerful influences on maternal behaviour. But even when all these variables are taken into account, only 40%, and in many cases much less, of the total variance in the mother's behaviour is accounted for, leaving considerable leeway for the effect of other variables not included in this study.

The finding that first-born male infants are favoured by mothers is consistent with a Western-derived psychoanalytic orientation. Irrespective of the psychodynamics of the mother, this same maternal orientation towards first-born male infants is to be expected in a patrilineal society which values male achievement and power differentially over female achievement. A sociocultural explanation could also be applied to the finding that, compared to mothers in lower socioeconomic groups, mothers in the middle and upper classes both smile and talk to their infants more, as well as allowing them more freedom. On the one hand, the greater education of these mothers may make them believe in the importance of providing stimulation for young children. On the other hand, the greater stress of daily living for the lower socioeconomic families may impinge upon the mothers in this group so much that they are more grim or preoccupied, feel more restricted in their options, and are more concerned with coping with the present than building for the future.

These observations would seem to argue against the likelihood that a simple ethological perspective could be used to account for the development of the attachment bond of a human mother for her infant. The ethological explanation would describe bonding behaviour as species-specific and relatively uninfluenced by either the prior experience of the mother, or her expectations or cultural values. Cultural and maternal experiential factors are powerful, and in a complex study, as presented here, we find that these influences have a measurable effect on maternal behaviour, in addition to the effects of prematurity and type and amount of early mother–infant contact.

In interpreting the findings so far, we have de-emphasized the effect of early interactive experience of mother and infant on subsequent behaviour. The question might be asked 'What is the effect, if any, of separation, even for a brief period, of a mother from her newborn infant?' There is a hint in the clinical evidence that we gleaned during interviews with mothers and fathers that separation of a mother from her infant in the newborn period does not affect only the mother. Table 6 presents the information obtained when the marital status of the families was followed up when the infants were 21 months old. By this time, seven divorces had occurred in the original sample of 66 families (families were not included in analyses after being divorced). Five divorces occurred in families of the separated group, two in the contact group and none in the full-term group. When we examined the demographic data for these divorced families, neonatal separation of the mother from her infant stood out as the major critical variable. Thus, we suggest that separation in the newborn period does have an effect, albeit non-specific, by acting through

TABLE 6

Description of discovered families

Group	*Sex of infant*	*Birth order*	*Father's socioeconomic status*
Separated	M	Later	Mid
Separated	M	Later	Low
Separated	F	First	High
Separated	F	First	Mid
Separated	F	Later	Mid
Contact	M	First	Low
Contact	F	First	Mid

the family as a stress that creates disequilibrium in the nuclear family structure. Home observations of the mother–father relationship and the father's relationship to the infant would undoubtedly supply additional useful information about the mechanism by which the stress of neonatal separation becomes a stress on family relationships.

This study raises questions about whether the concept of attachment derived from ethological theories can be used in accounting for a mother's behaviour towards her infant. We cannot conceive of a species-specific biological principle that could account for the variations in maternal behaviour related to sex and birth order of the infant that we have found in this study. Rather than an ethological model for the mother's relationship with her infant, we believe that the variations in the mother's behaviour can best be understood by a learning theory model modulated by the culturally conditioned expectancies involving mother–infant roles. Such a model would postulate that a primiparous mother, valuing the first-born male infant highly, expects more gratification from this child and modulates her behaviour to encourage or achieve this gratification. The specific behaviours that are acquired in the newborn period under conditions of high saliency, such as those in the newborn nursery, are, over time, supplemented and amended by the usual principles of learning. Thus, we would suggest that the most reasonable explanation for the maternal behaviours observed in this study is one that emphasizes cultural, social and experiential influences on the mother—influences that are modified according to well-known principles of social learning. Whether an ethological model can be used in explaining the development of the infant's relationship with his mother remains an open issue.

Regardless of whether one adopts a learning theory or an ethological model, it should be apparent that an opportunity exists for rapid learning in the nursery during the newborn period. The nursery situation can therefore be utilized to encourage specific kinds of behaviour, in both mothers and fathers, that might serve to enhance subsequent familial relationships and the cognitive development of the infant. One could conceive of mothers and fathers of 'at-risk' infants learning to 'talk to', 'play with', and 'laugh at' their infants, with appropriate kinds of reinforcements provided by the hospital nursing staff and physicians. This would be especially valuable when the rewards provided by the infant's responsiveness are, as happens with prematures, extremely rudimentary.

The inclusion of both parents in this enterprise might encourage new relationships between the mother and father, as well as between each of them and the infant. Although we did not study paternal behaviour, we did interview the fathers in our study. From these interviews, we substantiated our impression that the effects of early separation should not be sought solely in the mother–infant relationship, but in all aspects of family life. We conclude that the discontinuity in the neonatal mother–infant relationship has ramifications for the equilibrium of the family unit

We believe that influences such as social class, sex of the infant and birth order, as well as parental attitudes and expectancies, are only a few of the elements which affect the relationship between a mother and infant in addition to the immediate experiential ones in the newborn nursery. While the newborn period does not, of course, tell the whole story, the relationships of all family members during this period may be exceedingly important in the determination of later social relationships. A more enlightened view of the importance of these early parent–infant interactions should lead to an attempt to enrich the socially sterile atmosphere in today's hospitals, thereby permitting the development of reasonable mother–father–infant relationships in the early postpartum days.

ACKNOWLEDGEMENTS

This research was supported by funds from the Grant Foundation, New York, the National Institute of Child Health and Human Development (grant number HD 02636) and the National Institute of Mental Health (grant number MH 20162-05/A1). We wish to acknowledge the collaborations of our colleagues, Dr Clifford R. Barnett, Mrs Rose Grobstein and Dr Aimee Leifer, in the earlier phases of this project. We especially thank Mrs Ellen K. Curtis for her research assistance and Miss Tome Tanisawa for secretarial assistance.

References

BAYLEY, N. (1969) *Bayley Scales of Infant Development*, Psychological Corporation, New York
BOWLBY, J. (1969) *Attachment and Loss*, Hogarth Press, London
DRILLIEN, C. M. (1959) *Arch. Dis. Child. 34*, 37–45
GOLDBERG, S. & LEWIS, M. (1969) *Child Dev. 40*, 21–31

KENNELL, J.H., JERAULD, R., WOLFE, H., CHESLER, D., KREGER, N.C., MCALPINE, W., STEFFA, M. & KLAUS, M.H. (1974) *Dev. Med. Child Neurol. 16*, 172–179

KLAUS, M.H. & KENNELL, J.H. (1970) *Pediatr. Clin. North Am. 17*, 1015

KLAUS, M.H., PLUMP, N. & ZUEHLKE, S. (1970) *Pediatrics 46*, 187

LEIDERMAN, P.H., LEIFER, A.D., SEASHORE, M.J., BARNETT, C.R. & GROBSTEIN, R. (1973) in *Biological and Environmental Determinants of Early Development* (Nurnberger, J.I., ed.) (Assoc. Res. Nerv. Ment. Dis. vol. 51), pp. 154–173, Williams & Wilkins, Baltimore

LEIFER, A.D., LEIDERMAN, P.H., BARNETT, C.R. & WILLIAMS, J.A. (1972) *Child Dev. 43*, 1203–1218

MOSS, H.A. (1967) *Merrill-Palmer Q. 13*, 19–36

SEASHORE, M.J., LEIFER, A.D., BARNETT, C.R. & LEIDERMAN, P.H. (1973) *J. Pers. Soc. Psychol. 26*, 369–378

SUTTON-SMITH, B. & ROSENBERG, B.G. (1970) *The Sibling*, Holt, Rinehart & Winston, New York

TULKIN, S.R. & KAGAN, J. (1972) *Child Dev. 43*, 31–41

Discussion

Stewart: What was the gestational age of the premature babies in your study? Did you allow for the number of weeks of prematurity when you calculated the results of your developmental assessments?

Leiderman: The babies were from about 32 to 37 weeks of gestational age. We studied only those infants who could stay in the nursery for at least three weeks before the mother would be admitted to the discharge nursery for a six to eight-day period of caretaking before discharge. The infants' weight at this time would be about 2000 grams. Of course, mothers in the contact group would be in the nursery shortly after the infants' births. All the age data presented measure age from the time of discharge from the hospital.

Stewart: So the difference between date of birth and date of discharge would roughly approximate to the number of weeks that the child was born preterm, but not absolutely.

Leiderman: We did additional data analysis using actual date of birth but found the artificially contrived date to be the more useful in our analyses. It certainly enabled us to directly compare premature and full-term groups.

Richards: You use Bayley scores for rate of change over time, and the difference between the groups depends entirely on when you think life begins. You make an implicit assumption that experience up to discharge is not important for the premature babies. That may or may not be correct. Bayley scores do not correlate with much else. To call them a mental age suggests IQ and that may be a mistake.

Leiderman: I would agree that the sub-tests of Bayley tests should not be labelled mental and motor, although this usage is common in the US. More descriptive would be the terms perceptual–sensory, and psychomotor. As for the lack of correlation with later tests, this is unimportant, since we use the test only to assess current psychological developmental status, and not to make a prediction about later performance.

Kennell: When non-medical people other than the mothers and fathers of patients come into our premature nursery and see the small babies, they sometimes ask whether this or that little premature baby can actually grow up to become a normal-sized adult with the usual adult proportions and features. We believe that this is one of the big questions a mother may be considering as she sees her own premature.

In the observations we have made in our long-term study of prematures, the difference between the ways mothers treat boys and girls has not shown up as strikingly as in your study, Professor Leiderman. The only difference we have found is that at the time of discharge from the nursery, mothers of girls were significantly more likely to keep their eyes on the baby during a filmed feeding.

Leiderman: I believe these differences between subgroups are real and potentially important for later infant development. Your sample consisted of urban black mothers, ours mainly of suburban white mothers.

Kennell: At the time we were enrolling patients in our premature study most of the premature babies in our urban centre came from lower socioeconomic class black families, but there were also black middle income and white low, middle and upper income families so it is difficult to generalize about the racial and income characteristics of our population.

Leiderman: I would agree. My only point here is that one needs to analyse the data to take behaviour characteristic of subpopulations into account. Otherwise when the data are reported for all subjects, one may miss some important component of the variation between subgroups.

Kennell: You asked whether we should call this a bond or an attachment. Starting with the bias that there is a maternal sensitive period, we were impressed with the attraction or the magnetism the baby exerted on the mother and everyone present at the time of delivery. Dr Bowlby used the term monotropy in describing one quality of attachment in the other direction, that is infant to mother. He has written (Bowlby 1969, p. 309): 'Because the bias of a child to attach himself especially to one figure seems to be well established and also to have far-reaching implications for psychopathology, I believe it merits a special term ... I referred to it as "monotropy".' For similar reasons we thought some name should be given to this important period. We wondered if we might call this the sensitive period of neonatropy in the human mother. Evidence has been presented which appears to show differences between the behaviour of groups of mothers who have early and those who have late contact with their full-term babies in the first minutes or first few hours of life and to a lesser degree, at least in our studies, with their prematures. Does this mean that the sensitive period in the human—if there is a sensitive period—lasts for just a few hours or one or two days? Or is it that coming into a nursery and touching a baby is not enough to bring about the attachment that is achieved with the wide array of interactions that are available to a mother who is lying comfortably in bed with an alert and responsive full-term baby?

Leiderman: There is an effect of separation but it is not to be seen in the mother–infant interaction in our research. Unfortunately, much research on neonatal separation has been confined to the mother and infant but really should include the mother and father relationship, father–infant relationship and mother–infant relationship. For example, in our study, a major effect of neonatal separation was on family dynamics. Seven families were divorced by the time of the 12-month follow-up. Birth order, father's socioeconomic class, and sex of infant, seem to make no difference, but neonatal separation does. On the basis of our clinical findings I believe it is important to bring families into the premature nursery early. The non-specific stresses of parental exclusion potentially can ramify through the entire family unit. To summarize my point, I believe it is necessary to take into account the culture of the family, the dynamics of the family group, the organization of the family and its current equilibrium, and the expectancies of the mother and the father, before we can draw any definite conclusions about a 'sensitive' period for attachment of human adults to their infants.

Klaus: You underplayed the two mothers in the separated group who abandoned the babies. Did you do that for a reason?

Leiderman: As a research clinician in psychiatry I am perhaps over-reacting against my clinical colleagues who sometimes need only one case in order to develop a theory. We did have two mothers who gave up their infants to the fathers, a rather rare event even in California, although probably increasing in frequency even with full-term infants. In our area, shared infant caretaking is becoming more frequent. We now have married faculty members at the university who share a single position, half-time at home and half-time at work. There is a new *Zeitgeist* developing so the 'abandonment' of infants by two mothers may just reflect this new arrangement. Nonetheless I agree it is an important lead, but not yet sufficiently convincing to support a theory of adult–infant attachment.

Klaus: You are saying that when a mother is brought into the nursery, we (doctors) affect her social learning?

Leiderman: The background conditions for learning in the nursery are high saliency or high arousal, whichever term you like to use. It is well known that rapid learning can take place under these conditions. Thus one can manipulate learning quite well by manipulating the degree of arousal. However, learning under high arousal is relatively difficult to extinguish. Novel or initial experiences are long remembered even when what is experienced is quite trivial. For example, patients will tell you about the 'high' of their first sexual experience, whether in love with the individual or not, and even after they fall in love with someone else. I have used the term learning to describe the fact that their experience will extinguish over time. In other words the experience of the mother with her infant in the neonatal period follows learning principles, depending on the proximate association of stimuli, and it can be reinforced or extinguished. A critical test of what I am suggesting may be to get parents of premature babies to smile and not touch their infants. If smiling behaviour of the parent is reinforced perhaps it could be enhanced to the level of the full-term mothers. In sum, I do not think that complex explanations are needed when simpler explanations can suffice.

Klaus: You are saying that the quality of this connection, without calling it either bond or attachment, is different under different conditions?

Leiderman: Yes, it is different. We would like to compare fathers with mothers in the neonatal period.

Klaus: When you use the word ethology, are you suggesting that we should not raise the question in the human of a sensitive period or species-specific behaviour?

Leiderman: I see no need to postulate a species-specific kind of behaviour. Some of our data showed the kind of variability that depended on the previous experience of the mother. Perhaps others here, more conversant with an ethological theoretical orientation, could elaborate on it. I do not believe that ethological theories are needed for the mother–infant side of attachment. The fact that human beings may be different from other animals, even higher primates, should be recognized. Values, expectations and language are very powerful channels for making changes in behaviour. Thus we may be able to teach and give therapy to mothers (and fathers) in nurseries so that they change their expectations and their behaviour towards their infants. That is what I think you do so well.

Klaus: Though many qualities of the bond from the mother to her infant differ from the bond from infant to mother, some of the properties and principles that go into their formation appear to be remarkably similar and cannot be explained solely by learning theory. For example, when the bond is broken, mourning and grief occur in both cases. Secondly, with both bonds there is evidence that there is a time when the bond or the attachment is more easily developed (sensitive period), followed by a less optimal time. Thirdly, the innate mechanisms operative for both bonds predispose the individual to a one-to-one attachment. We first noticed this property in S. Doxiadis's nursery in Athens where infants wait for four to five months before they can be legally adopted. The nurse caretakers or mother substitutes who live with the infants become closely attached to one baby at a time. They like the other infants but a special bond is formed to only one infant. As evidence, there is prolonged mourning when that infant leaves the unit. In our own and other premature nurseries, we have noted that the nurses like many babies they care for, but again they have a single favourite, never two at the same time. Also if you send one of a pair of premature twins home before the other, the mother appears not to become as closely attached to the second twin. In 1958, John Bowlby described this property for the infant-to-mother bond, and he used the term monotropy then. Thus, I suggest that innate mechanisms are operative in the formation of both of these attachments. The more we understand these principles, the more appropriate our clinical interventions will be.

Hinde: I agree that we are not sheep or lambs or other animals, but I don't understand most of the other words that have been used, including the difference between involvement, attachment and relationship. Nor do I understand the meaning of the word ethology. We now know, largely through the work of Bateson, a great deal about how the bond is formed between a chicken and a hen (Bateson 1973; and see other references in Hinde 1974). It is a complicated process in which many different types of learning are involved. One important issue is that each partner directs towards the other a number of different types of response, each of which is initially elicited by relatively generalized stimulus characters, but which come to be confined to the particular stimulus characters provided by the partner. And because all those stimulus characters come from one partner, that partner acquires status as an individual rather than as a collection of different stimuli. It seems to me that these sorts of principles, at that level, are equally applicable to both bonds. What you are talking about, because the parent is told to smile or touch, doesn't make much difference. The important issue is still the learning involved in the direction of *these* responses to *that* subject.

Bowlby: I agree with both of you. A further point for your list, Dr Klaus, is how a woman tells you she feels about the baby. Not infrequently, as we heard earlier (p. 100), she will say that up to a certain moment it just seemed like another baby but then she suddenly 'fell in love with it', or some phrase of that sort. And women who have had two or three full-term babies which they have taken home in the usual way, and who have then had a premature baby which they have had to leave in hospital, describe how they have always felt quite differently towards that one. In talking about 'bonds' we are talking about relationships which have strong feelings connected with them—enjoyment, grief, anxiety, anger and so on.

Dreyfus-Brisac: Do you know anything about why a mother smiles or looks at the baby for a long time?

Leiderman: Mothers of premature babies, by virtue of being fearful about the health of their infants, feel more apprehensive and in fact smile less at their infants. The mothers tell us this and we observe it.

Oppé: Do enough people really watch mothers of premature babies carefully? How many studies are based on a few minutes of observations or asking questions later? Recently I was looking at a mother carefully and even though she was an inexperienced mother she didn't have to be told to touch her premature baby. The baby was connected to monitoring devices and had several catheters inserted, and I felt that she was reassuring him in the sort of way a mother reassures her child when she wants to protect him from the gross interference of doctors and nurses.

James Robertson (1970) makes the point that one of the things parents can do for their children in hospital is protect them from environmental assaults and reassure them when they are being made.

A recent paper by Bidder *et al.* (1974) again reports little difference between mothers of premature babies and mothers of normal babies during the follow-up period, but mothers of premature babies go on perceiving their baby as 'the weak little one'. What implications this long-continued view of a premature baby has in terms of behaviour, I don't know.

Leiderman: I agree that touching in the nursery is not enough. The amount and type of social support given beyond 'touching' is important. Many other factors operate, and that is the thrust of what I was trying to show empirically. I would agree completely that the kind of social network a mother has is a critical factor. Divorce in the families in our study illustrates this. It was a stressor without adequate social support for the families.

Rosenblatt: Professor Hinde has made the distinction in his early work that one can talk about that early period either in terms of its consequences or in terms of what is going on in the early period—that is, what the processes of attachment are. Dr Klaus may tend to talk mainly in terms of consequences: because of an early contact he expects certain consequences to be present later. That gives an impression of a kind of momentary action which has some amazing effect 12 months later. But in fact that action may really start something which then snowballs into something much more elaborate. Perhaps the disagreement may be less sharp than Dr Klaus implied. Not everything that happens in the early critical period results in consequences that may become specific months later.

Brazelton: We should include ourselves as physicians in a triad of what is going on around the whole process of birth. In the last part of pregnancy a woman is going through a lot of emotional work which is primarily centred around her own self-image and her own integrity. The paediatricians who are working with young mothers at this time find that the mother in her last trimester forgets what the paediatrician's role is and turns to him as a supportive figure for herself. In the last trimester, when she is doing her work for changing roles, protecting herself for the last push and afraid of being destroyed by her labour and the delivery, a mother of a premature baby has her work suddenly interrupted by the premature birth. As a result, she ends up with a damaged image of herself, quite different from her fantasies. She has to create a new image of herself as a person who produces a damaged child, and she also has to make an attachment to this child. She is particularly vulnerable as she tries to deal with a new kind of image of herself and the baby. We must set ourselves up to give her permission to look at the baby in a new way, to get attached to the baby, to touch the baby—all of these become important symbolic measures on our part. I was particularly impressed with what was said earlier (p. 100) about there first being a kind of general attachment to all babies, in a normal mothering process, and then a more specific attachment. I feel that what we are really doing in this initial period is giving her permission to become a mother in a hurry, and to deal with some of her grief over having given up the old image of herself before she was quite ready, as well as that of the idealized baby. We are also giving her some instrumental as well as some psychologically important ways of attaching herself to this baby, at a time when probably she hasn't much energy for that. We become terribly important symbolic people to her at this particular time.

We are now trying to reconstruct my neonatal scale (Brazelton 1974) for premature babies. These babies are difficult babies to relate to, to bring into a social interaction system. Touching becomes important to the mother because it contains the baby and holding him helps him to contain himself. It quickly becomes an important modality for interaction. It may be a more important modality with these babies than looking or vocalizing or any of the things that we normally do with a full-term baby who responds in kind. We don't find these responses in premature babies until we have touched and handled and jazzed them up, if you will. Then we may get into a kind of 'locked looking' that we see in premature babies. But this may not be a very rewarding system. We are really talking about a fairly disordered system in which we superimpose ourselves as manipulators. A mother is sensitive to how distorted these other modes of interaction may be with premature babies.

References

BATESON, P.P.G. (1973) Internal influences on early learning in birds, in *Constraints on Learning: Limitations and Predispositions* (Hinde, R.A. & Stevenson-Hinde, J., eds.), Academic Press, London & New York

BIDDER, R.T., CROWE, E.A. & GRAY, O.P. (1974) Mother's attitudes to preterm infants. *Arch. Dis. Child 49*, 766–770

BOWLBY, J. (1958) The nature of the child's tie to his mother. *Int. J. Psycho-Anal. 39*, 350–373

BOWLBY, J. (1969) *Attachment and Loss, vol. 1: Attachment*, Basic Books, New York

HINDE, R.A. (1974) *Biological Bases of Human Social Behavior*, McGraw-Hill, New York

ROBERTSON, J. (1970) in *Young Children in Hospital*, 2nd edn, Tavistock, London

Cognitive aspects of preverbal social interaction between human infants and adults

HANUŠ PAPOUŠEK and MECHTHILD PAPOUŠEK

Max-Planck Institute for Psychiatry, Munich, and Department of Neurology and Psychiatry, University of Munich

Abstract Our previous studies on learning and on cognitive development in preverbal human infants indicated that motor activity and social interaction played particularly important roles in the cognitive development of infants. Closer analysis has revealed that motor activity and social interaction have some underlying common regulatory mechanisms. These mechanisms can be detected more easily in infants than in older subjects. An attempt to synthesize our observations led us to the concept that there is a fundamental cognitive process in the integration of adaptive behaviour. This concept may help to elucidate the motivational and emotional aspects of social interaction, the role of mothers or other caretakers in their interactions with infants, and the unfavourable effects of early social deprivation of different types on cognitive development. Some of the assumptions on which this concept is based have been corroborated by analyses of adult–infant interaction.

Interest in the early development of human social interaction has grown in different scientific fields and has been influenced by several theoretical sources. The relevant data have also been diverse and we usually categorize them according to the approaches or methodological tools familiar to students of social interaction. As Ciba Foundation symposia traditionally aim to provide cross-disciplinary syntheses of different views, we want to attempt here to synthesize different categories of our own observations and view them from one central point, i.e. the infant's fundamental adaptive response system, which underlies much human behaviour.

In doing this we may violate certain principles of behaviouristic approaches, although we hope that we were not violating them in the way we obtained our results. In fact, our first attempt to enter the infant's 'black box' and look from there at the environmental changes he experiences, both in experimental situations and in everyday life, soon seemed to shed light on discrepancies we had previously found confusing.

A simple rationale for such an attempt can be deduced from the basic equations of the statistical theory of information (Shannon & Weaver 1949), according to which the information content of a system is defined as a function of probability of the information-carrying process, i.e. as a function of the probability that a given number of signals will appear, and of the probability distributions of these signals in time and in space. It follows from this that not only the physical parameters of a stimulus but also the probability with which the structure of the whole stimulation can be perceived and processed by the infant will determine the outcome of his response.

Although it may seem difficult to describe the complex structure of the informational input at any point in time, we hope we were justified in attempting to do this, since it helped us to focus on some little-known aspects of early social interactions.

First, we realized that a single response system might be hypothesized as underlying all the other response systems, such as food intake, defence, reproduction or socialization. This fundamental system is the one controlling, activating or inhibiting different mechanisms connected with the input and processing of information as well as with the organization of adaptive responses, and it may be viewed as a *fundamental cognitive response system*.

Second, it became obvious that, in looking at the structure of the complex informational input, we ought to pay much more attention than usual to the information coming from the infant's internal milieu. Here we have in mind the three major categories which are so difficult to bring under experimental control: the autonomic system, the memory, and both proprioceptive and kinesthetic information about the infant's own motor activities. If we disregard these categories of information we will hardly understand the roles of some highly relevant biological determinants—e.g. of the biorhythmical changes in the behavioural state, we will neglect the effects of past experience resulting from both the evolution of species and the ontogenesis of the individual, and we will underestimate the interrelations between cognitive development and motor activities.

Third, while paying more attention to the fundamental cognitive response system, we also realized its connections with the regulation of general behavioural states as well as with intrinsic motivation.

From these views, the problems of preverbal social interaction appeared in a new light, and we were able to conceptualize even the role of social interaction in cognitive development in children more easily. To elucidate our approach, it may be useful if we first survey our earlier studies of learning abilities and cognitive processes in infants, and then describe some analyses of social interaction which we designed to test our hypothetical models.

EARLY DEVELOPMENT OF COGNITIVE PROCESSES IN THE CHILD

In earlier studies of the human neonates and infants we tried to elucidate the early development of habituation, and classical or instrumental conditioning. From one point of view these studies could be characterized as learning experiments, and from another they represent problem-solving situations. Although these two characterizations of the experimental situation may appear contradictory, they both tap the same underlying adaptive processes. The earlier studies can be referred to for detailed descriptions of the procedures (Papoušek 1967*b*, 1969).

In the studies of neonates and infants aged three and five months we were confronted with the practical problem of selecting a convenient and versatile behavioural response. We wanted to observe a large set of behavioural parameters which might provide evidence about psychobiological adaptation and development, but at the same time we had to be careful to avoid undue strain on our infant subjects in the daily experiments.

Careful selection of our infants and standardization of their general living conditions allowed us to minimize the influence of otherwise uncontrolled factors. Our research facility collaborated closely with an allied obstetrical department, which meant that we had reliable information on conceptual age, the course of intrauterine development, and parturition. Since our facility offered mothers and their children a six-month cost-free stay, a child's daily regimen could be programmed without neglecting his individual needs. For example, we were able to monitor systematically the sleep–waking rhythms of the infants and control the sleep–feeding–waking sequence. The controlled state of waking and satiation meant not only that we could compare results from different investigations but also that the infants were in optimal mood during our observations.

For our investigations, we chose head movement as a suitable motor behaviour. As a simple reflex, head movement is well coordinated in the neonate and soon develops into a differentiated response, e.g. for food intake, attention during orientation or social interaction, avoidance during protective reactions, and so on. Head movements are easily measured polygraphically, and their latency, intensity and form are also readily quantifiable, as Fig. 1 shows. They also facilitate the analysis of eye contact because they regularly accompany eye movement during the first year of life. For these reasons head-turning offers numerous experimental possibilities. For example, polygraphic analysis of head movements together with respiration and total motor activity readily allows various forms and states of behaviour to be detected and differentiated. Fig. 1 shows some typical patterns.

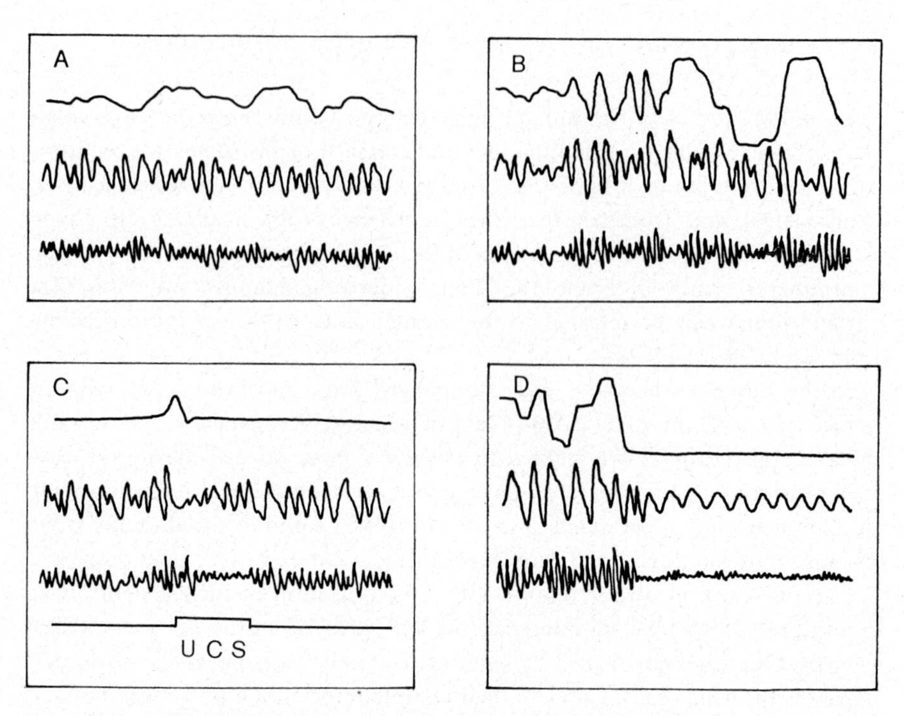

FIG. 1. Polygraphic records of typical head movements, respiration and total motor activity in infants. A: quiet orientation; B: intensified orientation; C: conditioned 'switching-on movement' (UCS = visual reward); D: avoiding movement with sudden change in behavioural state.

During the experiments reported here, coded protocols of the type of vocalization, total motor activity, and eye movements were also taken. The list of observed parameters was not long, but it allowed us to analyse basic adaptive processes as well as to detect emotional components and general behavioural state through further analysis of characteristic combinations of individual parameters.

Early observations suggested that some differentiation of the infant's waking states is fundamental to learning studies. Consequently we defined four different levels of the waking state:

Waking state I: regular respiration, open eyes, otherwise no other movements or vocalizations

Waking state II: irregular respiration, slight movements of the distal limbs, head and eye movements, no vocalization

Waking state III: active movements of all limbs and torso and vocalization without crying, moaning, or similar sounds of distress

Waking state IV: irregular respiration, agitated and poorly coordinated movement of the limbs and/or torso, and crying or other vocalizations of distress

The subtle electromyographic and electroencephalographic parameters of behavioural state were rejected because daily preparations which were longer or unpleasant for the infants might have jeopardized the entire course of these studies.

Because these studies looked at the total course and individual phase of adaptive processes as well as at interindividual differences, the usual comparisons based on time blocks were rejected; instead, relatively rigorous final criteria for the various categories of experiments were selected and the experiments ended only after the infant had reached the prescribed criterion.

Simple conditioning experiments were the point of departure in these studies of learning and cognitive processes. To some extent, these experiments encompassed elements of both principal learning theories—classical Pavlovian as well as operant conditioning. Conditioning experiments were then transformed into more complex problem situations, and the order of presentation to each infant followed a scale of increasing complexity:

(A) Acquisition of a simple conditioned response to an auditory conditioned signal, i.e. rotation of the head away from the mid-line towards the left, was reinforced by milk presentation.

(B) Extinction and reinstatement of the conditioned response learned in (A).

(C) Conditioned discrimination of two auditory signals from the mid-line position; one signalled milk presentation from the right side, the other from the left side.

(D) Discrimination reversal of the conditioned responses learned in (C) after interchange of the referents of the signals.

(E) Acquisition of a new 'switching-on response' (i.e. a rotation of the head was regularly followed by a 5-second presentation of a reward of multicoloured lights, above the mid-line), and introduction of more complex conditions for attaining the reward. For example, the infant might repeat this response two or three times or he might alternate between a right and a left turn according to some pattern in order to attain the reward. The infant had to discover these reward contingencies on his own, of course.

Experiments from (A) to (D) were begun with three different age groups: three days, and three and five months. Experiments were run five times a week during the usual morning feeding-time; 10 trials constituted a session with the child's normal quantity of milk subdivided into ten reinforcement doses (for details see Papoušek 1967*b*).

The learning curves in neonates are of special interest, as they do not correspond well with the older ideas about the immature and still unmyelinized brain. Moreover, our results differ somewhat from results in previous experiments on conditioning in human neonates. The difference is apparently due to the method of conditioning. Earlier investigations in which classical Pavlovian conditioning techniques were used produced either negative results (Wickens & Wickens 1940) or scarcely convincing results since they failed to control for pseudoconditioning (e.g. Marquis 1931).

By contrast, studies with operant methods have demonstrated learning in the neonate (Papoušek 1961; Siqueland & Lipsitt 1966; Sameroff 1968). Habituation, which is also regarded as one of the basic learning mechanisms, functions in the human neonate even during deep sleep (Martinius & Papoušek 1970). According to our interpretation, learning in the neonate is possible when reinforcement is contingent on the child's own behaviour and when the nature of the reinforcement corresponds to the biological motivation of the neonatal organism, e.g. when the neonate can satisfy his hunger through learned behaviour.

Among our subjects, prominent individual differences were manifest in the speed and course of learning as well as in the latencies and the form of individual responses (Papoušek 1967*a*). By standard criteria, a statistically significant learning effect was shown on day 7. In general, neonates need more trials than the older infants, hence the various phases of learning can be detected unusually clearly, as if projected in slow motion; in older infants, these phases pass too rapidly to be immediately identifiable. As soon as a neonate had detected that the delivery of milk was contingent upon his correct response, he intensified his orienting and total motor activity. This first phase of adaptation was often associated with signs of distress but he gradually integrated his smooth, fast and economical movements until he grew quieter. Finally, the infant performed these movements with a positive affect whose components, e.g. relaxation and smiling, were still rather rudimentary (Papoušek & Bernstein 1969).

It should be stressed that all aspects of the learning process, except extinction (see point B), develop rapidly during the first months of life. In simple conditioning and conditioned discrimination alike, rate of acquisition increases significantly, response latencies decrease, and the learning curve becomes steeper and smoother. While correct responses are being made in the successful adaptation phase concomitant components of positive affect—e.g. smiling and vocalization—also become more prominent.

We were somewhat surprised to discover that during the average session of conditioning or conditioned discrimination we saw no relation between the course of responding and the level of satiation. This implied that hunger played no role in motivation. So that we could examine the phenomenon more precisely, the influence of maximal satiation in a group of four-month-old infants was analysed in sessions immediately after the original learning experiments. An example is presented in Fig. 2.

It is clear that performance of the correct response plays a larger role in motivating the child than reinforcement with milk. Even after complete satiation, at a time when the infants could not drink another drop and even turned their heads away at the offer of milk, succeeding conditioning signals were followed by quick and intensive correct head rotations and were accompanied by smiling and vocalization, independent of any social contact.

A second observation was that during simple conditioning the phase of distress at the beginning of adaptation shortened with age. However, signs of distress became frequent again when the infant was exposed to more complex situations (e.g. those described in C and D above). In these situations, infants were observed first to intensify their orienting, total motor activity and autonomic reactions, then to lose coordination of responses if they proved to be ineffective, and finally to turn away from the experimental situation. The

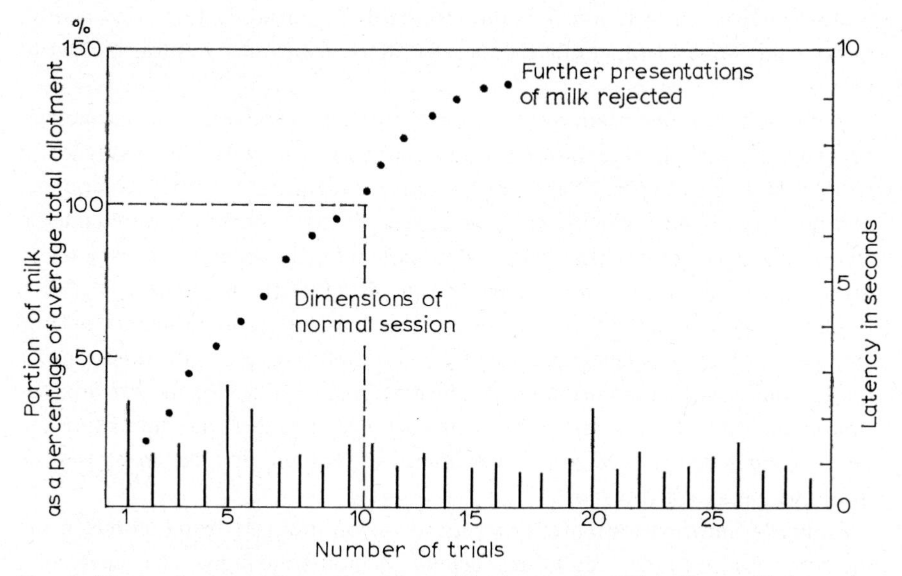

FIG. 2. Temporal course of a prolonged conditioning session with milk provided as reinforcement. Thick vertical lines: latencies of the conditioned head movements. Dots: milk portion as a percentage of average milk quantity per session.

dynamics of this particular reaction clearly differentiated this form of turning away from random or otherwise directed types of head movement. Reactivity and total motor activity decreased over this period, and even reinforcement with milk was rejected. A sudden change in general behavioural state sometimes characterized reactivity in the first two months of life: the eyes remained open but stared without converging, respiration became slow and regular as in sleep, and all other movements and vocalizations ceased. Such an avoidance response has been observed as early as the first days of life in neonates (Papoušek 1967*b*).

A closer look at the general behavioural state also reveals that an infant's functions are not just a product of circadian and other chronobiological factors but also depend on the type of environmental stimulation and the course of adaptation (Papoušek 1969). Not only does the general behavioural state influence learning, but the course of conditioning may also influence the infant's behavioural state.

THE RELATIONSHIP BETWEEN COGNITIVE PROCESSES AND MOTOR ACTIVITY

Studying the thought processes of children without interfering grossly with their natural conditions or physical integrity restricts research to the external manifestations of somatic or autonomic processes—in practice to changes in motor activity and secretion. It is only for heuristic purposes, then, that neural, motor and humoral functions can be abstracted from their natural biological unity.

A physiological perspective of the motor system and its hierarchical organization suggests that the integration of muscular activity may well be analogous to or may be one of the real bases for cognitive integration of single experiences and perceptions. At the level of motor activity, a vast number of simple muscle elements are integrated into functional units of a higher order and subsequently grouped in various ways into the behaviour of the whole organism.

This integrative activity, as suggested, proceeds on various levels: from the simplest reflexes of single muscles up to the more complex coordinations of many synergists, antagonists and concurrent positional or locomotor adaptations; and from the shortest of reactions up to extremely long and exhaustive performances which necessitate multilateral autonomic adaptation as well as intensive metabolic transport.

Similarly, information on motor activity is continuously being stored in the memory; for example, adults can usually demonstrate how they acted at a certain moment if someone unexpectedly asks about this. The storage and processing of such information may be independent of language: adults often find it easier to repeat a motor sequence directly than to describe it in words. There is therefore no reason to suppose that processing of information about motor reactions could not be one of the functions that start to develop very early in infants.

Unfortunately, psychology at present has at its disposal no methods for the investigation of proprioceptive or kinesthetic perception that are nearly as simple as the methods usually used for the study of auditory and visual perception. Otherwise this area would not have been neglected for so long, and psychologists would now be much better informed about the relations between cognitive processes and motor reactions. Nevertheless, integration of motor activity potentially involves the simplest types of early cognitive functions, perhaps even those occurring during intrauterine development.

There is a second feature of motor activity which is important for the development of cognitive capacities. Daily observations of children who spent their first six months in our research ward suggested that the quantitative and physical aspects of environmental stimulation were not as important as the relationship between environmental change and the child's own activity. An external change which is directly contingent on the neonate's behaviour is most effective. Only social stimulation, to be discussed below (p. 254), has a comparable effect.

Various types of external changes and responses to them can be enumerated and elaborated from this point of view:

(1) Random external change which occurs once or repeatedly, but which is completely independent of the infant's activity and does not signal any other relevant change (e.g. nutritional supply or social contact), elicits attention or orientation which tends to habituate quickly.

(2) External change which is also independent of the infant's activity but which is regularly associated with another relevant change may function as a signal for the latter change and facilitate the infant's adaptation to his environment. As soon as regularity of this type is detected, the infant shows intensive orienting reactions and begins to adapt to the new circumstances, e.g. by learning a conditioned reaction to a conditioned signal.

(3) External change which is contingent on the infant's own activity elicits the most intensive of orienting reactions: approach and manipulatory explorations of various types. These reactions all tend to be remarkably resistant to habituation and usually cease only after trial and error or other operant forms of learning have shown the infant how to get the relevant environmental change repeated.

(4) External change which depends on the infant's activity but where the dependency is difficult to perceive represents a problem situation. Problems

may also arise when correct information processing and behavioural adaptation reach the limits of efficiency of the nervous system. This often happens in immature and inexperienced infants and may occur in situations which more mature and experienced beings (e.g. older children) might otherwise solve easily and rapidly. In these situations, the person may be confronted with a complexly-structured environment or set of events which he must differentiate, for which he has to categorize a vast assembly of information units, within which he has to discover temporal or spatial regularities, and to which he must adapt his own behaviour.

It is evident, therefore, that successful problem-solving in such situations presupposes basic modes of thought and obviates the simplified stimulus–response scheme (S → R), which represents the physical qualities of stimulation rather than the structural relations inherent in interactions between the environment and the person's own activity.

One of the reasons why learning theories have paid little attention to the relation between environment and bodily activity is probably that for a long time no neurophysiological mechanism for detecting the contingency of environmental change on behaviour was available. However, the discovery of so-called 're-afference' (von Holst & Mittelstaedt 1950) or 'corollary discharge' (Teuber 1961), in addition to efferent motor pathways and direct feedback, now substantiates the existence of a neurological basis for learning. According to current

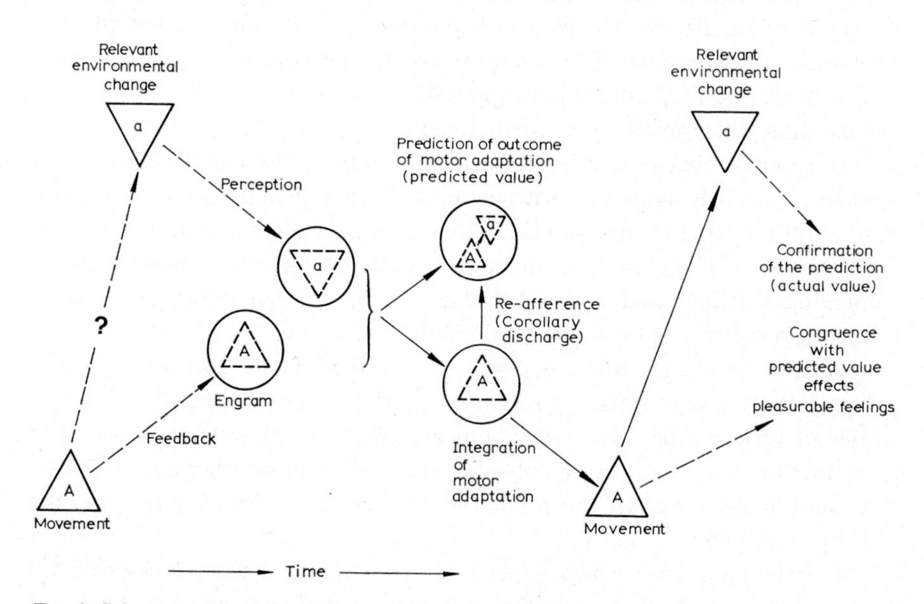

FIG. 3. Schematic progression of successful motor adaptation in infants.

theory, the scheme of intended reaction is projected into the association areas of the brain through re-afferent pathways before behaviour is manifest. This allows a conceptualized prediction of the success of the particular reaction (the 'predicted value') to be made. The feedback mechanism makes it possible for this prediction to be compared with the course of the actual reaction (the 'actual value'). Fig. 3 shows the simplest temporal course that this adaptive process can take.

The correct estimation of the predicted value tends to be associated with a positive 'feeling'. Independent of the extent to which contingent external change itself may be a reinforcement, the confirmation of the prediction—a successful solution of the problem—may also function as an 'intrinsic reward'. As observed, this type of motivation plays a highly effective role in many types of behaviour during human infancy.

If the infant cannot discover the correct solution in a problem situation, he usually continues to intensify his efforts, but his reactions soon become uncoordinated and signs of distress appear in his facial expression and vocalization. At the same time, intensified respiration, heightened pulse frequency, increased blood flow to the epidermis, or increased perspiration, all indicate that the autonomic system is active. This activity may easily be enough to exhaust the infant.

In such a dangerous situation, a sudden behavioural change in infants may occur which reminds one of Pavlov's protective inhibition (1953) or of a biological 'playing 'possum': the infant lies motionless with non-converging, staring eyes and sleep-like respiration (cf. Fig. 1D). This passive behavioural state, which may be characterized as a sort of 'total inner separation from the environment', may appear more frequently during the first two months of life than later on. In similar situations, infants older than three months tend much more often to avoid actively everything connected with the unsolvable problem. Active avoidance and passive unresponsiveness may both be regarded as opposite poles to attention and orientation.

The relation between fundamental forms of thought and regulation of movement became clearest in the most complex experiments when 'switching-on responses' were acquired (see E, p. 245). There, no instruction and no conditioning signals were used. The four-month-old infants taking part in this experiment had to find out by themselves, at first by chance, that a head rotation of at least 30 degrees to a predetermined side would switch on 5 seconds of multicoloured stimulation from a blinking light. Before the experiments began, the light stimulation itself, regardless of the infant's activity at the time, proved to be an attractive source of stimulation and generated distinct orienting reactions. After it had been repeated several times, orientation decreased, a reaction which is typical of habituation. But during experimental sessions, as soon as the infant had discovered that light presentation was contingent on his own head movements, his behaviour changed dramatically. Orientation reactions increased in intensity, and the infant continuously made all possible types of movements to try to switch on the visual stimulation again. If successful, he repeated his feat so many times and with such joyful affect in his gestures and vocalization that it seemed more like attachment than habituation. Before an infant discovered the movement or additional conditions needed for switching on the visual stimulation, he often repeated a chain of other inessential movements similar to the so-called 'superstitious behaviour' of rats in operant conditioning experiments.

Although social interactions played no role in these experiments, under certain conditions infants reacted regularly with typical social signals in facial expression and vocalization. Roughly speaking, these were always situations in which the child discovered something new or relevant, in which his expectations were fulfilled, in which an unexpected outcome of his own behaviour took him by surprise, or in which he could not find the solution by himself. Our impression is that the child may experience as unpleasant the difficulties of adaptation and as pleasant successful adaptation. However, there is no direct evidence for such an impression. Behavioural changes of this type are usually denoted as emotional behaviour, and this is a difficult category to define. Most emotional behaviour may be thought of—at least operationally—as a combination of motor and autonomic manifestations during behavioural adaptation, with communication signals going out to the social environment about important experiences.

The adaptive process engendered in these experiments appears to be only a simple form of operant learning. However, to understand its true complexity the observer himself would have to pose as an experimental subject. How easy is it to discover that 'reinforcement' is contingent on head movements, or that head movement has to be performed three times successively in a given time interval, with rotations of at least 30 degrees each time? It is equally difficult to program a cybernetic model to perform in such a manner. Hence it is surprising that a child can behave so adaptively at a preverbal age. This state of affairs can best be understood if we assume that basic modes of information-processing and motor adaptation already function at a preverbal stage of development. Infants are apparently capable of discovering certain regularities in and categories of combinations of environmental stimuli, as well as recognizing that their own activities can influence events.

The fundamental cognitive response system

In our conceptualization, orientation mechanisms play an exceptionally important role in the relation between thought and motor activity during adaptation to environmental conditions. Pavlov (1953) was the first to describe these mechanisms, but only in the context of reactions to environmental novelty. Subsequent extensive analysis, e.g. by Sokolov (1963), revealed their more general nature. The various components of the orientation reaction not only direct the sensory organs towards the source of novel stimulation but also facilitate perception through inner mechanisms (increasing nerve conduction velocity, decreasing thresholds and so on). On the autonomic level, they prepare the organism for an increase in motor activity. According to Sokolov, switching on the orientation mechanisms depends on the discrepancy between the novel stimulation and already-existing concepts stored in the memory.

Orientation mechanisms have been regarded by Sokolov and others as being exclusively 'on-off' mechanisms. Attentive activity in the infant's social behaviour is similarly conceptualized by Bowlby (1969). However, our recent alternative conceptualization (Papoušek & Papoušek 1974) suggests that the orientation and avoidance mechanisms represent only parts of a more general and fundamental regulatory system (Fig. 4) in which orientation and avoidance

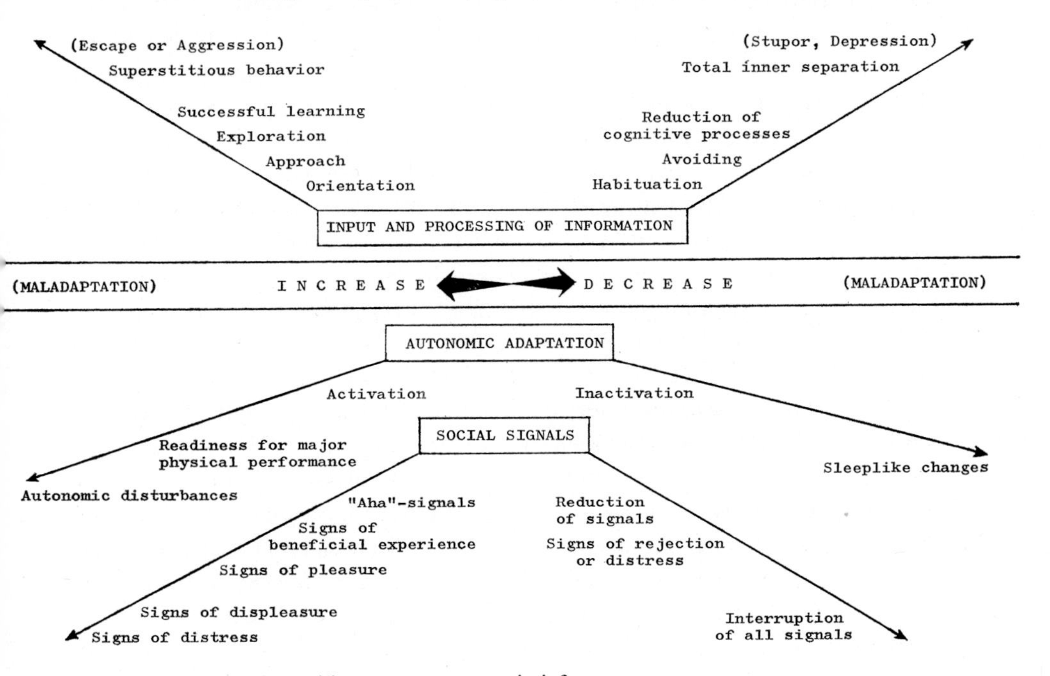

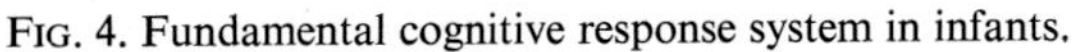
FIG. 4. Fundamental cognitive response system in infants.

control the supply and processing of information as well as the organization of adaptation.

By eliciting active avoidance or general protective inhibition, this adaptation protects the infant from overstrain in problem situations. The regulatory system contains very simple motor reflexes, such as head-turning towards the source of stimulation or away from dangerous stimuli; it also includes highly complex behavioural and cognitive modes essential for discovering the more complex dependencies of relevant environmental change, for organizing optimal adaptation or for switching off from such circumstances, and for inhibiting all unsuccessful efforts at adaptation. All these mechanisms appear distinctly in infancy because infants do not inhibit or disguise this general behaviour for social reasons, as adults commonly do. The basic modes of this fundamental cognitive response system may be found in the human organism at the beginning of postnatal life, as mentioned in our analysis (pp. 244–248) of the early development of learning capacity.

SOCIAL INTERACTIONS BETWEEN INFANTS AND ADULTS

Analysis of adult–child interactions is also vital to an understanding of the early development of learning capacity and cognitive processes. Although we report only studies of the infant's interactions with his mother here, several of our studies have also looked at child–father and child–stranger interactions. The mother's role is a particularly important one during the first months of the child's life, and she is optimally prepared for it—biologically (hormonally) as well as socially (motivationally) (Papoušek & Papoušek 1974).

The most impressive feature of the interaction between infant and mother is the continuous sequence of short scenes in which the two members *mutually* stimulate and reinforce one another. Thus, the mother is not just a source of rich external stimulation or a selective reinforcing agent of behavioural expressions of her child. The child's spontaneous behaviour engages her too, and sets the occasion for her responding. The interaction of these two, therefore, tends to be reciprocal. Besides mutual stimulation and reinforcement, both members also learn how each can influence the other with his or her own behaviour. In sum, it is not simply the quantitative aspects of stimulation, but the structure, sequence and causal relations between individual components of behaviour which play the decisive roles. The discovery and mastery of the active and adaptive manipulation of a partner is a more decisive feature of mother–infant interaction than passive behavioural modification which is acquired through external reinforcement.

This situation is analogous with the relationship between cognitive functions and motor activity, as emphasized in the earlier sections of this paper. Also, it is clear that a type of social environment in which infants commonly develop represents essentially a learning situation in which fundamental cognitive functions are necessarily acquired: the child samples his mother's behaviour widely, a process which quickly enables him to differentiate meaningful changes; at the same time, he samples his own behaviour and learns about its effects on his mother's behaviour.

In cognitive terms, the child simultaneously attains two sources of pleasure with this mastery: one source of pleasure derives from his own power over environmental changes (cf. Fig. 3), the second from the contingent characteristics of maternal behaviour.

In both motor coordination and social interaction, the balance between stability and variability of environmental stimulation, between repetition and modification of movements, is important. Relevant examples of this connection are familiar to all adults, such as when one hears well-known songs, or in dancing. Psychological investigations (McCall & Kagan 1967) have shown that maximum attention can be generated in infants by repeated and only slightly modified stimulation. Similarly Lewis & Goldberg (1969) stressed the roles of novelty and familiarity in their 'response decrement' theory of early social interactions.

Our analysis of the learning process during infancy (pp. 244–248) suggests that more repetition helps the infant—who at this period is still learning at a relatively slow rate—to discover essential and regular forms in the stable components of stimulation generated by an otherwise continuously changing environment. The more variable components may by contrast keep his attention aroused. And, as noted, even newly acquired responses have to be performed and repeated a certain number of times before they release concomitant signs of pleasure in the infant's facial expression and vocalization. The morphological aspects of the human face, composed of stable parts (the triangle of eyes and nose) and variable parts (eyebrows, mouth and facial muscles), as well as the characteristic modes of maternal behaviour, again substantiate this point. For these reasons, a certain continuity and consistency in the mother's behaviour towards her child tends to be particularly important.

Analyses of filmed spontaneous interactions between mother and child reveal a number of maternal reactions which convey specific intended meaning. Some are emitted so quickly and directly that without a detailed structural analysis the observer misses them. Indeed, they also escape the conscious control of the mother—a good thing, for she would soon be exasperated if she had to reflect and decide on every step during the course of an interaction with her child.

During spontaneous interaction, the mother continuously attempts to stay within her child's visual field and also to maintain an optimal distance from him. This is especially important in the first two months of life, during which the child's capacity to converge is still relatively weak. Mothers usually modulate their voices and behaviour into simple and repetitive patterns which they modify if the child's attention wanders. Mothers are often seen to stimulate their children through a number of perceptual channels, e.g. by combining visual and auditory with tactile and vestibulary stimulation. Mothers may also facilitate coordination of the child's motor and visual systems, e.g. by moving the hand of the child rhythmically in his visual field. Such a list could be elaborated to demonstrate how important maternal behaviour is for the infant's acquisition of cognitive mechanisms. Mothers stimulate intensively, reinforce efficiently, and also allow themselves to be manipulated; this informs children about the consequences of their own activity at a very early age. Here again, intimate and now familiar relations between social behaviour, motor coordination, and cognitive processes stand out. Some time before a child has developed a capacity for manual manipulation of his objective world, he may have learned the skills needed for manipulating and predicting events in his social world.

Unfortunately, communication between mother and child does not always attain an optimal level; instead it may be disturbed in various ways. The mother may be living in adverse conditions which can result in disturbances; she may simply be physically exhausted by her job; she may have an ambivalent attitude towards her child after an undesired pregnancy; marital conflicts may be redirected towards the child; she may lack an adequate model from her own childhood; or she may suffer from various psychic disorders or physical illnesses, etc. The child himself also precipitates a number of adverse conditions which can complicate the communication process (a latent inflammation of the middle ear causing an auditory defect in chronically vomiting infants, or perinatal brain damage, just to mention two). Hence, we should not overlook the possibility that, even under seemingly normal conditions in 'good families', the social interaction between the infant and his partner or social agent can be disturbed and may eventually turn into the 'deprivation situation' which has often been described recently.

To sum up: inexperience, uncertainty or strongly preferred private interests on the part of the mother, and physical irritation or illness on the part of the child, can often lead to a situation in which mother–child interaction becomes erratic and thus 'incomprehensible' for the child.

The effects of one such situation were investigated in studies we carried out at Harvard University in 1968 (Papoušek & Papoušek 1974). In these studies, the capacity of four-month-old infants for 'comprehending' their mothers' behaviour was analysed. The specific question was asked: how do infants react to the deliberate omission from a behaviour chain of an important segment containing key information?

Experimentally induced mother–infant detachment

In the first experiment, the mother was asked to leave her child six times for 15 seconds each time and to act in the same way she would act at home when leaving her child for a short time. All mothers tended to employ similar routines on leaving (stepwise separation under control of eye contact, verbal repetitions, etc.), and on returning they experienced no difficulties in renewing happy contact with their children.

In the next experiment, with a different group of infants, the mother was required to leave her child without any preparations when overhead lights were turned off for 3 seconds, and then to return under the same conditions after 15 seconds. This 'incomprehensible' disappearance and reappearance of the mother produced rather conspicuous changes in the child's behaviour, as illustrated in Figs. 5, 6 and 7. At first the infant reacted cheerfully to his mother on her return (Fig. 5). Although still rather quiet during her absence

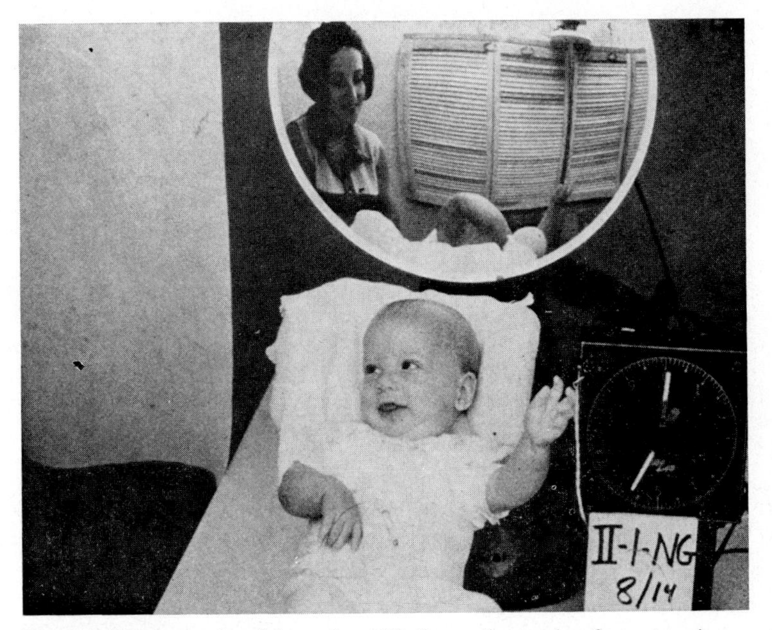

FIG. 5. Infant has a cheerful reunion with the mother on her first return in experiments with repeated short separations.

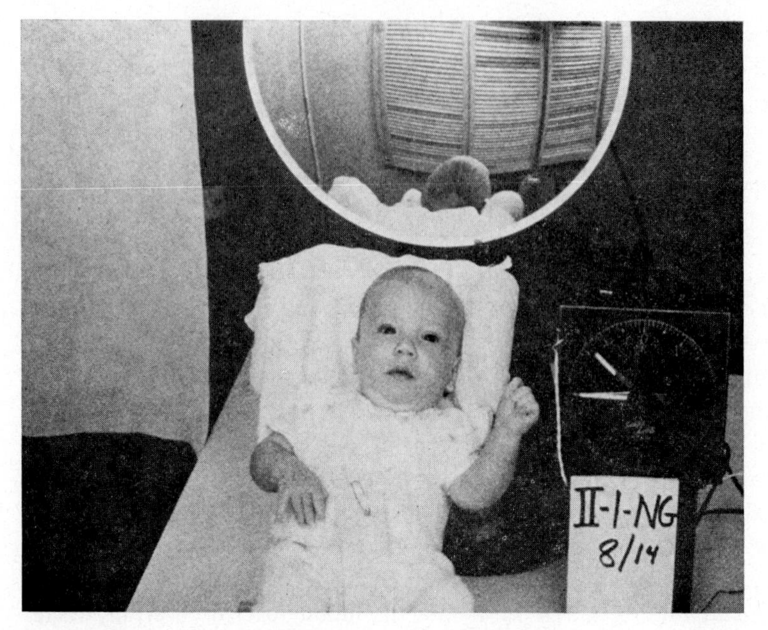

FIG. 6. Infant's behaviour during short separation.

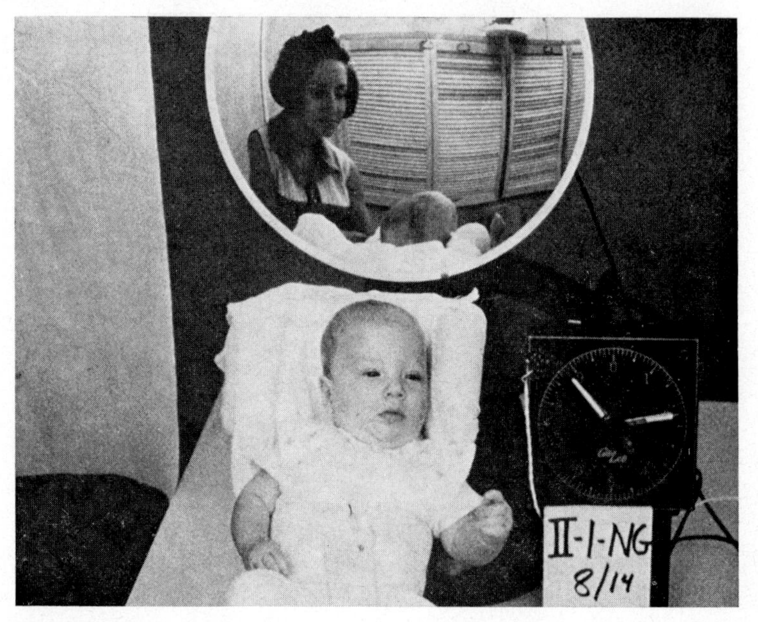

FIG. 7. Infant rejects his mother when she returns after later absences in experiments with repeated separations.

(Fig. 6), after her later reappearances the child gradually rejected the renewal of contact with his mother more and more strongly (Fig. 7). Thereafter, the mother's efforts to renew contact only intensified the baby's turning away; in some of these infants such renewals even led to listless or whining rejection of the mother. Control experiments in yet another study showed that the short periods of darkness as such did not produce changes of this type. These experiences surprised the mothers as well as the observers, and we noted with some relief that the children's relationship with their mothers recovered quickly after the experiments ended! Again, one might consider these reactions to be analogous to the behaviour of infants in the experimental problem situations. However, more penetrating experiments with children are out of the question. Such observations warn us that unnatural disturbances of the interaction between the infant and his mother or any other social agent may entail unhappy consequences.

CONCLUDING REMARKS

Using results from learning experiments and from analyses of social interactions, we have attempted here to explain our methodological approach to problems in child development. We have also attempted to conceptualize our data by emphasizing the relations between the coordination of movements, regulation of behavioural states, basic cognitive functions, and social interactions. At the same time, we have tried to concentrate on important aspects of the mother–infant relationship, e.g. maternal love, from the perspective of the child's further cognitive development. We believe that this relationship offers a very important opportunity to the child at this age, one which may perhaps never appear again: namely, the opportunity to acquire and develop their capacity for cognition and communication. These capacities may represent an incomparably decisive step in the development of highly complex cognitive and social functions, e.g. language. Thus, neither they nor their social implications should be underestimated or neglected in future research.

ACKNOWLEDGEMENTS

The studies carried out at Harvard University were supported in part by Grant B 3233 from the Carnegie Foundation to the Center for Cognitive Studies. The generosity of Professor Jerome S. Bruner in making this possible is very much appreciated. The authors also express their gratitude to Dr Marc H. Bornstein and Helen Bornstein for their contributions.

References

Bowlby, J.A. (1969) *Attachment and Loss, vol. 1: Attachment*, Hogarth Press, London

Lewis, M. & Goldberg, S. (1969) Perceptual-cognitive development in infancy: A generalized expectancy model as a function of mother–infant interaction. *Merrill-Palmer Q. 15*, 81–100

Marquis, D.P. (1931) Can conditioned reflexes be established in the newborn infant? *J. Genet. Psychol. 39*, 479–492

Martinius, J.W. & Papoušek, H. (1970) Response to optic and exteroceptive stimuli in relation to state in the human newborn: habituation of the blink reflex. *Neuropädiatrie 1*, 452–460

McCall, R.B. & Kagan, J. (1967) Attention in the infant: effects of complexity, contour, perimeter, and familiarity. *Child Dev. 38*, 939–952

Papoušek, H. (1961) A physiological view of early ontogenesis of so-called voluntary movements. *Plzeň. Lék. Sb. Suppl. 3*, 195–198

Papoušek, H. (1967*a*) Genetics and child development, in *Genetic Diversity and Human Behavior* (Spuhler, J.N., ed.), pp. 171–186, Aldine, Chicago

Papoušek H. (1967*b*) Experimental studies of appetitional behavior in human newborns and infants, in *Early Behavior: Comparative and Developmental Approaches* (Stevenson, H.W. *et al.*, eds.), pp. 249–277, Wiley, New York

Papoušek, H. (1969) Individual variability in learned responses in human infants, in *Brain and Early Behavior* (Robinson, R.J., ed.), pp. 251–266, Academic Press, London

Papoušek, H. & Bernstein, P. (1969) The functions of conditioning stimulation in human neonates and infants, in *Stimulation in Early Infancy* (Ambrose, A., ed.), pp. 229–252, Academic Press, London

Papoušek, H. & Papoušek, M. (1974) Die Mutter–Kind-Beziehung und die kognitive Entwicklung des Kindes, in *Seelische Fehlentwicklung im Kindesalter und Gesellschaftsstruktur* (Nissen, R. & Strunk, P., eds.), pp. 83–100, Luchterhand, Neuwied

Pavlov, I.P. (1953) *Sämtliche Werke*, Band III/2, Akademie-Verlag, Berlin

Sameroff, A.J. (1968) The components of sucking in the human newborn. *J. Exp. Child Psychol. 6*, 607–623

Shannon, C. & Weaver, W. (1949) *The Mathematical Theory of Communication*, University of Illinois Press, Urbana, Ill.

Siqueland, E.R. & Lipsitt, L.P. (1966) Conditioned head-turning behavior in newborns. *J. Exp. Child Psychol. 3*, 356–376

Sokolov, E.N. (1963) *Perception and the Conditioned Reflex*, Pergamon Press, Oxford

Teuber, H.L. (1961) Sensory deprivation, sensory suppression and agnosia: notes for a neurological theory. *J. Nerv. Ment. Dis. 132*, 32–40

von Holst, E. & Mittelstaedt, H. (1950) Das Reafferenz-prinzip. *Naturwissenschaften 37*, 464–476

Wickens, D.D. & Wickens, C. (1940) A study of conditioning in the neonates. *J. Exp. Psychol. 25*, 94–102

Discussion

Brazelton: Did the baby reject the mother's image even if the mother sat there and the screen came down between them?

Papoušek: She had to move away behind the screen. Darkness alone didn't affect the baby's behaviour, but moving away during darkness is very different from the way a mother normally moves away from her baby. In everyday life that is really a stepwise detachment, with the mother talking as she leaves and the baby picking up various cues which make the mother's behaviour predictable.

Hofer: The process of despair and detachment that Dr Bowlby has described (1973) usually takes several days to evolve, but here it seems to have been compressed into a few minutes, through the intervention of darkness and the mother's mysterious disappearance. Have you looked at children older than four months, in the same situation, to see when this kind of reaction ceases to occur as a sense of 'object constancy' develops?

Papoušek: When we saw what happened, we didn't feel like repeating it with another age group. Instead, we have begun to use minor interventions and pay closer attention to certain behavioural patterns, such as eye-to-eye contact and turning towards or away from the mother. Here we can see part of the behaviours, and we can repeat the minor interventions without violating the interaction between mother and infant. Because of the convergent capacity it is better to analyse babies aged three months or older in this kind of test. Even a glass shield with transparent horizontal stripes makes the infant lose interest in the mother, although he can still see her eyes and mouth.

Brazelton: Is it just lack of interest then, or a real aversion?

Papoušek: The baby loses eye-to-eye contact and turns away from the mother as soon as the striped screen is placed between them while they are interacting normally.

Rosenblatt: Some of that behaviour must be laboratory-produced. I suggest that the child has a priority order of things which make him feel comfortable. The mother comes first, but at home, if the mother leaves to answer the phone, the infant can turn to something else. The room itself may be a comforting place, or other things may act as stop-gaps until he can regain a sense of orientation. If a cat leaves its kittens, the kittens are comforted by the familiar smells and warmth of the floor for a time. The severe reaction you see may be because the infant depends totally on his mother for his sense of security and orientation—then you take her away without giving him anything else in her place.

You are also suggesting that there is an early form of reinforcement to which we haven't paid much attention. This has to do simply with the performance of an action which coincides with what the infant 'intended' to do. The reward is not food or anything like that, but simply the fact that something works out as planned. This provides a kind of reinforcement which fixes certain patterns of behaviour.

Papoušek: It is not the external reward alone—for example, the mother's smile—but also the confirmation of prediction which works as an intrinsic reward and is crucial for the intrinsic motivation. This aspect has probably been neglected because we had no plausible explanation of how this takes place in the nervous system.

Thoman: If someone plays peek-a-boo with a baby, covering their face and then quickly exposing it, the infant laughs, partly because of the built-up tension. If the person holds their hands over their face too long, the infant becomes agitated and begins to pull at the hands. For your observations, in a sense you may have intuitively selected time parameters which were long enough for the anxiety level to build up to a peak, so that the passage of time until the mother's reappearance required another adjustment by the baby. If you used different times of disappearance, you might get different effects. If the mother stayed away longer and then reappeared, as in Dr Brazelton's situation, the baby would possibly greet the mother without the accentuated telescoping of the response that you see.

Papoušek: Our situation was certainly abnormal compared with everyday life, but we did that on purpose. Interestingly, all these deviations from everyday life seemed to be relevant, and it was difficult to say which one led to the change in behaviour of the infant and finally to his rejection of the mother. This pilot experience led us to further concepts, including the idea that the child has a regulatory system for either paying more attention to something or turning away from things. We will probably need to analyse this for a couple of years before we understand enough to know whether it is a useful concept or not. I certainly agree about the time parameters. The 'biorhythms' which we see and the rhythms which Dr Brazelton mentioned may also depend on the processing of information. The baby may need a certain time for conceptualizing the environmental change and adapting to it. This basic period of 'cognitive latency' may represent one of the pacemakers.

Carpenter: I am interested that you put so much emphasis on the problem of convergence at the age of four months. The pictures you showed and your ideas apply perfectly to behaviour and data that can be obtained on the ocular response of the two-week-old infants to a stranger's still face, in the absence of any other patterned input. Emphasizing Dr Rosenblatt's point about the abnormal situation, avoidance responses from these very young infants seem specific to conditions where a face appears. In my work, during the inter-trial interval babies are very happy looking at blinking lights even in an abnormal environment—in an infant seat within a chamber lined with dark green felt. It is only when the stimulus door opens (removing the lights) and a face appears under certain conditions that they turn away and show what is being called rejection.

Rosenblatt: Blinking lights are one of the best and most effective ways of imprinting young chicks.

Hinde: Why didn't you say that earlier when you were expressing surprise that the young infant should show operant conditioning to get a stimulus change? It is well established in the imprinting context that a day-old chick will show an operant response more frequently if that response produces a stimulus change such as a blinking light or something of that sort (Bateson & Reese 1969).

In your conceptual scheme, Dr Papoušek, an increase in information input was associated with increased activity, and a decrease in information input was associated with increasing stages of inactivity and rejection. As it is well known that stimulus input can soothe, aren't there important limitations to the generality of that scheme?

Papoušek: Soothing is a regular part of the orienting response. While he is orienting towards a novel stimulus the infant reduces his other activities. Thus the activation of selective attention may be accompanied by a decrease in the general motility. However, if the stimulus appears to be relevant and contingent upon the infant's activity, then the general motility increases again because new patterns of approaching, exploring or manipulating behaviours are activated together with increased processing of information. You can see evidence for it in human infants who do not yet try to control or mask such behaviour, but you can also see many analogies in your own adult behaviour if you pay attention to what triggers or inhibits your exploratory thinking and acting.

We don't want to explain every change in behaviour with one concept. There are different particular categories of behaviour, such as sexual, appetitional or aversive ones, in which particular stimuli elicit particular responses. We have been interested in the regulation of common adaptive mechanisms which participate in all these particular categories. In all of them, it is necessary to process the incoming or stored information, make decisions, and organize some adaptive sets of responses. We assume that even these common cognitive steps depend on a set of general auxiliary mechanisms, and we try to explain their general regulation in our concept. However, in particular categories of behaviour, the outcome will also be determined by their particular features.

Klaus: Babies show all sorts of body movements—changes in respiration, head and leg movements in response to some change in the environment. Our observations of the baby have in the past related to what we can see with our eyes. Yet the baby is often covered. We have possibly been prejudiced as investigators since we receive so much of our own information through vision. Perhaps, for example, a much more important mode of communication from baby to mother during feeding is through slight changes in respiration, or body movements undetectable even with the fine-grained measurements described by Mrs Dunn and by Dr Thoman (this volume). One way of explaining the effect of the striped glass is that a much greater amount of information is coming to the baby from the body than through the eyes, even though he is interested in the eyes. We as observers may not be observing the most significant communications. In countries where mothers carry naked babies, the mother knows when the baby is going to urinate through slight changes in body movements. How much information do you believe comes from body-to-body interaction and how much do you think comes through the visual system?

Papoušek: Unfortunately, we cannot learn enough about the information coming through the kinesthetic and proprioceptive pathways, compared to what we can learn about the visual and auditory systems. We can only speculate on its crucial importance. We certainly process and store a lot of it, mostly unconsciously, but even then we can recall and repeat past body postures or movements in surprising detail. I do not doubt that a lot of mother–infant communication goes through these pathways. If we find better access to them we shall probably find important cues for cognitive development, too.

Brazelton: Dr Papoušek, you said that if the mother said goodbye to the baby, then the baby didn't have to go through the pattern of self-defence and self-protection after she came back. I was also interested in Dr Rosenblatt's idea that the baby would have compensatory ways of dealing with things as early as four months, with which I would certainly agree. We saw this when we were using Ainsworth's paradigm for studying separation in year-old babies (Ainsworth & Bell 1970). Ainsworth's suggested routine was for the mother to interrupt the interaction without saying goodbye. If we let her say goodbye the results were quite different from what Ainsworth described. How early can a baby internalize a cue from the mother and not have to go through the defensive withdrawal manoeuvres when the mother returns after an interruption?

Papoušek: Infants aged one or two months are quite different from those aged three or four months. If his expectations are violated, the younger infant more typically changes his behavioural state: he goes into a general state of inhibition, a sleep-like state in which he stops responding. At about three months of age, he more typically changes the strategy of his behaviour: he stays alert and actively turns away, eventually rejecting attempts to bring him back to his original position. This complicates the comparability of developmental studies.

In our conditioning studies with fully controlled acoustic signals and appetitional reinforcements, we saw deliberate turning away of this kind even in the neonates. The problem is more complex, of course, when we talk about the social interactions. They may occur on the basis of the experience coming from vestibular, tactile, thermic, olfactory or proprioceptive information, and we cannot control all of them. What we know so far has been based on interventions affecting visual and auditory communication.

Macfarlane: Familiarity with the surrounding smells and so on is important to the baby, and the laboratory must certainly be abnormal for them.

Richards: There is a danger of missing an important point here. Talking about familiarity and unfamiliarity implies that we think the infant has a passive view of the world. Dr Papoušek has shown us, very elegantly, the importance of the infant's intentions and his active way of dealing with the world. What is crucial is that when a mother leaves without preparing the infant for her departure, the infant's expectations are violated.

Papoušek: We have filmed the mother–infant interaction both in the laboratory and in the homes. In infants up to three or four months of age, even in the laboratory, it is surprising how little a good interaction can be disturbed by the observer and his equipment. Neither the mother nor the baby pay attention to the environment while they are enjoying each other. On the other hand, they both respond sensitively to deviations in the behaviour of the other. An intervention in the interlocking mechanisms on one side of the dyad may have a powerful effect on the other side.

Bentovim: One question is when disturbances of the interlocking procedure actually happen in practice. As suggested, disturbances may be contributed to by the baby's physical state, e.g. conditions such as the hypertonic baby, or by the mother if she is psychotic. How much violation can the infant adapt to normally, and when does initial perfect and later good-enough adaptation have to lessen so that separation and independence can occur?

Papoušek: For ethical reasons we cannot design experiments which push children to the functional limits of their capacities. In very young infants, these limits are so narrow that they can be reached rather easily even in everyday life. Unintentionally we reached them in our experiments, too; however, in older infants where the limits are much broader we would not feel justified in testing their resistance. Perhaps you could do it in animals.

Macfarlane: Do you think there is a hierarchy in the sensitivity of the different sensory systems used in the interlocking systems between mothers and infants to such notation? Interference with some things is obviously going to be worse than others. Dr Rosenblatt, in animal studies can you differentiate whether some such systems are more important than others?

Rosenblatt: In some studies of kittens we are beginning to get some idea of how the sensory systems get related to one another successively during development. For example, the kitten at first seems to use thermal stimulation in gradients to find its way around the world, as I said earlier. But apparently that is a difficult sensory system to work in, so the kitten quickly switches over to the olfactory gradients. How the kitten knows where it is is determined by the warmth or cold, but how it gets from one place to another is determined by an olfactory gradient. Shortly after that, it gives up olfaction and uses vision, but whether it moves into an area to which it seems to be visually attracted depends on whether the background smells are right. So a sensory system which is in the foreground functionally seems to sink into the background and another one takes over, and then another. Yet the background condition also seems essential. The sensory systems build themselves up in a nest of cubes but they are all functioning at once.

Hofer: Are there examples in lower animals of the inhibitory behavioural state that Dr Papoušek saw when interaction was violated in the human mother–infant pairs?

Rosenblatt: If you put a kitten in a strange place it draws itself up into a little ball and cries, and moves its head very slowly from side to side. It is completely inhibited. Monkeys do that too.

Hofer: Have you seen this in rats?

Thoman: Eighteen-day-old rats freeze in response to a sudden stimulus.

Hofer: They are practically adolescent then.

Hinde: Infant rats give at least two kinds of ultrasonic cries.

Thoman: But this occurs when they are in the freezing posture.

Hofer: If a two-week-old rat is separated from its mother, it will remain active only if its temperature is kept up artificially, but otherwise it becomes *less* active as its body temperature falls towards the temperature of the environment (Hofer 1973). There seems to be a thermoregulatory-dependent process in this species, rather than the phenomenon we are talking about in the human, which seems to be capable of rapid shifts which are unlikely to depend on changed body temperature.

Curtis-Jenkins: There is an anecdotal evidence that the child who fails to thrive has colder extremities than the child who is loved. D. MacCarthy (MacCarthy & Booth 1970), who has done a lot of work with deprived children, says he can tell by feeling the warmth of their limbs whether a child is loved or deprived.

Cooper: You can see it too, because their hands, noses and feet are red.

Brazelton: I think there is cardiovascular instability as well as other kinds of unstable mechanisms. As they begin to get into affective interaction with objects their cardiovascular mechanisms begin to stabilize.

Thoman: Another response in immature animals is tonic immobility if they are turned on their backs.

Richards: But rats in a freezing posture and babies who are deprived cannot necessarily be regarded as being in the same category. They may be totally different phenomena.

Hess-Haeser: In apes the importance of the physical and social environment seems clear. If we try, for instance, to introduce a hand-raised infant into a social unit, most of these experiments fail if the infant has had no previous experience with the room or with individuals of the group. Such a situation may lead after a certain time to inactivity, to a rigid posture and averted head, and to failure of initiative in making any sort of contacts.

Dreyfus-Brisac: Do any infants fall asleep when you do this test, Dr Papoušek? And if they fall asleep, what stage of sleep do they reach? Have you compared any premature babies of the same age to the full-term newborn infants?

Papoušek: All the work I described was done in full-term babies. In the conditioning experiments we used a schedule which guaranteed that the infant would be fully awake for the experiments. Yet in certain typical situations, younger infants showed a sleep-like state. This state differs from the usual sleep cycle because it occurs rather suddenly, without the typical transitional stages, and doesn't last long. We can elicit it through repeated application of inhibitory stimuli. We couldn't prolong it because it might be bad for the infants. It occurs in everyday life, too, yet we don't feel like doing experiments of this kind. Our experience was that in deprived infants this sleep-like situation occurred more often. We think it may be induced by deprivation, too, and is unfavourable for the child, particularly if it takes up most of his waking time.

Brazelton: We were able to put neonates to sleep with aversive stimuli (Brazelton 1962).

Papoušek: One can induce sleep through other mechanisms. Any repeated stimulation could lead to a change in behavioural state. The regulation of behavioural states is a completely different aspect. We are looking at these things from the point of view of the regulation of adaptive behaviour, and that is one of our limitations.

Kennell: Frequently mothers who breast-feed in the US are criticized by their own mothers and by others because they can't wind or burp their baby as well as other mothers. During our 12–14 weeks in Guatemala we never saw a mother wind her baby at all, whereas in the US investigators have reported that some mothers give their babies as many as several thousand pats on the back in the course of one feeding (S. Brody and S. Axelrad, unpublished findings, 1967).

D'Souza: We urgently need cross-cultural studies to understand what mothering means in different cultural contexts. It is also vitally important to pay attention to variations within one culture. Dr Thoman's example of a 'non-responsive' or 'rejecting' baby (this volume, p. 186) perhaps emphasizes the need for more knowledge. Although this was, in a sense, a non-positive interaction between mother and baby, the pair were still meshing. They were interacting by allowing each other to *be*. We must always be aware of these so-called anomalies, simply so that we do not arrive too soon at fixed ideas of what constitutes 'good' mothering.

We should also remember that making simple analogies between human and non-human behaviour can be, to say the least, misleading. However, the *methods* and ideas developed in non-human behaviour studies can probably be applied to the human context and show more clearly what we ought to be looking for.

Hofer: We keep coming back to the interaction between cultural and biological factors in attempting to understand how mothers respond.

Bentovim: Winnicott (1971) stated that from the first moment a mother has to use her imagination to put herself where her baby can find her and find just what he is looking for, without her really knowing anything at first about that baby's needs, so that there is a sort of illusion created that baby did it for himself! In the kind of interaction Dr Papoušek described the two became so interlocked that it is not possible to separate them or see where one begins or ends except by some violation of the situation. Out of the shared 'illusion'—the transitional state (Winnicott 1971)—something grows between the two which becomes two individuals. The interlocking or intermeshing clearly has many different factors entering, such as the cultural ones that have been mentioned, and our help and understanding are needed if it is going wrong.

Hinde: None of the work we are doing is of prime importance unless we can show that the facets of mother–infant interaction that we are studying have long-term effects. It is so easy for us to get fascinated by the complicated things that go on between mother and infant, and to assume that small changes in those interactions will have long-term effects on the relationship just because we find them so fascinating. Whereas the fact is that the organism has a lot of buffering in it—it is a self-regulating thing to a very large extent. Small changes in these processes of interaction probably have negligible long-term consequences, if any, and the relation between the changes in the interactions and the long-term effects is probably a threshold relationship rather than a continuous one.

Thoman: Observations on animals show that apparently minor early experiences can have lasting effects. In humans we don't know which experiences have a long-term effect, but we do know that whatever happens earlier at least foreshadows what happens later. One problem is that people keep telling us it doesn't matter how the mother is treated prenatally, or what happens early on to the baby, because it doesn't affect their behaviour later on anyhow. We can do something about this by studying the earlier period and finding out what happens and whether there is any continuity between early experiences and later behaviour. But we must first get refined measures of the early behaviour. If we can measure the effect of early experience on later behaviour, even though some effects may be apparently trivial, we may eventually find ways of identifying continuities between behaviour over time.

Hinde: This is one of those areas where the precise loading you give to what you say has to be tempered to some extent by the prevailing social climate. The issue is knowing exactly where to put the balance.

References

AINSWORTH, M.D.S. & BELL, S.M. (1970) Attachment, exploration and separation. *Child Dev. 41*, 49

BATESON, P.P.G. & REESE, E.P. (1969) The reinforcing properties of conspicuous stimuli in the imprinting situation. *Anim. Behav. 17*, 692–699

BOWLBY, J. (1973) *Attachment and Loss, vol. 2: Separation; Anxiety and Anger*, Basic Books, New York

BRAZELTON, T.B. (1962) Observations of the neonate. *J. Child Psychol. Allied Disciplines 1*, 38

HOFER, M.A. (1973) The effects of brief maternal separations on behavior and heart rate of two-week-old rat pups. *Physiol. Behav. 10*, 423–427

MACCARTHY, D. & BOOTH, E.M. (1970) Parental rejection and stunting of growth. *J. Psychosom. Res. 14*, 259–265

WINNICOTT, D.W. (1971) Transition objects and transitional phenomena, in *Playing and Reality*, pp. 1–25, Tavistock, London

Parents of babies of very low birth weight: long-term follow-up

ANTHEA BLAKE, ANN STEWART and DIANE TURCAN

Department of Paediatrics, University College Hospital and Medical School, London, and Medical Research Council Human Biochemical Genetics Unit, University College London

Abstract One hundred and sixty babies of birth weight ⩽ 1500 g who survived after perinatal intensive care have been followed up and observations have been made on their parents. In spite of attempts to minimize maternal separation and the distressing aspects of the birth and management of a baby of very low birth weight, an emotional crisis was observed in the mothers which was not fully resolved until the parents had been looking after the baby at home. The duration and degree of the crisis varied but the mothers who received sympathy and support from the baby's father appeared to have least difficulty. A rigid maternal personality and circumstances surrounding the birth which predisposed to feelings of failure and guilt appeared to prolong the crisis. Nevertheless, most of these parents subsequently formed satisfactory relationships with their children, although they tended to be over-protective and anxious. Failure to establish an adequate relationship was rare and occurred only among mothers with personality or psychiatric disorders. Although serious behaviour disorders among the children were rare, more children than would be expected were mildly over-dependent, shy and anxious at follow-up.

In recent years, modern methods of perinatal care have improved the chance of survival for high-risk newborns, particularly those of very low birth weight (LBW) (Schlesinger 1973; Reynolds & Stewart 1975). In addition, it has been shown that specialist perinatal intensive care units save more lives than those which are less specialized (Usher 1971). The incidence of serious handicap among very LBW babies (⩽1500 g) has also fallen. (Stewart & Reynolds 1975). These improvements have been achieved by admitting the babies from birth to incubators in special units, sometimes many miles from the place of delivery; in consequence, the babies have been separated from their mothers for days or even weeks.

Because early separation may adversely affect the formation of a satisfactory relationship between mother and child (Klaus & Kennell 1970) we, like other workers in perinatal intensive care units, are concerned that these methods, although efficient at saving lives and preventing serious handicap, may cause disordered mothering with consequent long-term disability in the survivors. High incidences of battering and of failure to thrive among LBW survivors have been suggested as evidence of this effect (Klaus & Kennell 1973).

Like others (Kaplan & Mason 1960; Oppé 1960; Klaus & Kennell 1970), we have observed the intense emotional distress of the parents at the birth and management of a very LBW baby, and their sometimes inappropriate attitudes to much-wanted babies. Since we introduced intensive care in University College Hospital in 1965 we have therefore gradually begun using measures designed to minimize separation of the parents from their children and to help these parents to overcome their distress. In 1974 a pilot study was carried out, using tape-recorded interviews in the home, of mothers selected from the earliest year of intensive care, an intermediate year and the most recent year, in an attempt to find out whether these measures had achieved their objective. The numbers were too small to allow conclusions to be made about the changes in management, but the results gave us a considerable insight into the problems which the mothers had had. They also showed that, in spite of the changes in management, the mothers still undergo an emotional crisis similar to that described by Kaplan & Mason (1960).

As we have followed up all the very LBW survivors treated in the Neonatal Unit at University College Hospital since 1966, we decided to examine our data for evidence of long-term effects of these experiences on the children and on their parents, so that we could plan a prospective study. In this paper, we describe these preliminary observations and our attempts to interpret them.

MATERIAL AND METHODS

Study population

One hundred and sixty-three babies weighing 1500 g or less survived after intensive care in University College Hospital during the years 1966–1973. Two babies returned to Ghana and Germany shortly after birth and have been lost to follow-up and one child died aged 2 years after a traffic accident. The remaining 160 babies, 66 boys and 94 girls, have been followed up for periods of 10 months to 8 years, including a child who died aged 4 years from burns resulting from an accident in the home. Ninety-eight of these 160 children were born in University College Hospital and 62 were admitted from hospitals in and around London. One hundred and thirty children were aged more than two years (range two to eight years) in 1974, and were old enough for major physical or mental handicap likely to prevent them from functioning normally in society to be detected. Among these 130 children the incidence of mental handicap was 3.1% (four cases), that of physical handicap was 3.8% (five cases), and that of combined mental and physical handicap was 3.1% (four cases), giving an overall incidence of major handicap of 10% (13 cases). In addition 19 children had been reassessed at age seven to eight years. Four of these older children (20.0%) had minor handicaps, including minimal cerebral damage and deafness, and one had learning difficulties due to a behaviour disorder. The Developmental Quotients of all the 30 younger children born in 1973 were over 80 and are considered to be within the normal range.

Management of parents of very LBW babies in hospital

Our management of the parents of very LBW babies has changed gradually since we introduced perinatal intensive care facilities in 1966. Three phases can, however, be defined.

1966–1969. Both parents were allowed to view their infants in incubators through a glass partition at specified times. Mothers, only, were allowed into the unit to handle their babies once they were out of the intensive care area and in a cot; and they were taught to feed and bathe them.

In 1969, a visitors' room became available and the mothers were allowed to take the older babies into this room in their cots so that the fathers could see them.

1970–1972. Unlimited visiting was introduced in 1970, for both parents of babies who were out of the intensive care area and in cots. Both parents were encouraged to handle the baby, at this stage. Mothers were also allowed into the intensive care area to see their babies. As there was no change in the infection rate, the following year both parents were allowed into the intensive care area to see their baby as soon as the mother was fit enough; and she was encouraged to touch the baby in the incubator.

1973, onwards. Fathers are now encouraged to go into the intensive care area to see their babies in the incubator on their first visit after the birth and then to 'report' to the mothers, We give each father a Polaroid photograph of the baby to take to the mother.

Mothers are encouraged to visit as soon as possible after delivery, accompanied by the father. They are encouraged to hold their baby for a few moments, from the first visit, if the baby's clinical condition permits; even the tiniest babies and those on prolonged mechanical ventilation are taken out of their incubators for their mothers to cuddle briefly. Subsequently the mothers and fathers are encouraged to visit and handle their babies as much as possible; and siblings are allowed to come into the Neonatal Unit to see their baby once survival is reasonably certain.

Throughout all three phases, both medical and nursing staff have been freely available for discussion with the parents. However, we believe that we have become more willing to talk as we gained confidence in the efficiency of intensive care methods. The more we have talked to the parents, the more apparent has become their need for discussion, and we suspect that the time we have spent talking to them has increased considerably in the past two years.

Management after babies leave hospital

All parents are asked to bring their babies back to the follow-up clinic, including those whose babies have been transferred back to their referring hospital. We see the children frequently in the first three months after discharge for clinical examination and discussion of management. Once satisfactory management has been established, the intervals between visits are increased to three months and development is assessed using the developmental screening inventory devised by Knobloch *et al.* (1966). After 18 months of age, if progress is satisfactory, the intervals are increased to six months. We are, however, prepared to see the children at any time at the parents' request. Local arrangements are made with colleagues for children living too far away to attend our own clinic. We also invite these parents to come to our clinic, if and when they wish, even if they live abroad.

At age three years six months and seven or eight years, a detailed psychological and behavioural assessment is made by a clinical psychologist. Tests used include the Stanford Binet Scale of Intelligence (Form L. M.) (Terman & Merrill 1961), selected items from the Merrill Palmer Scale (Stutsman 1931) and the Reynell Expressive Language Scale (Reynell 1969) at three years six months, and the Wechsler Intelligence Scale for Children (Wechsler 1949), the Bender-Gestalt test (Koppitz 1963), the Bristol Social Adjustment Guide (Scott & Marston 1971) and a selection of educational tests at seven or eight years. Audiometry and ophthalmic examinations are also carried out.

OBSERVATIONS

The first six months after discharge from hospital

In the follow-up clinic we have noticed a particular pattern of behaviour in the mothers of the very LBW infants in the weeks immediately after the child is taken home from hospital. This resembles the third stage of the emotional disorder described by Kaplan & Mason (1960) although it is not seen until the child has gone home. The intensity and the duration of this experience vary widely, and there are other factors which appear to affect both of these variables in a predictable manner. We recognize three phases:

(1) The 'honeymoon phase' when the parents first take the baby home. Although they may be apprehensive about their ability to manage, and many of them telephone the Unit for guidance on minor matters, excitement prevails and they are usually euphoric at the first visit to the clinic, 7–10 days later. This phase lasts 7–21 days. (2) A 'phase of exhaustion' follows, when the euphoria has waned and the mother complains of many minor problems with the management of the baby. In particular, she may complain of feeding difficulties and has often reverted to feeding the baby every three hours or even more often. She is—and looks—exhausted and is inefficient; hence the feeding difficulties are often genuine. This phase may last only a few days or it may continue for several weeks until the baby begins to smile and be responsive—which for a baby born at 28 weeks of gestation is not until 18 weeks after birth. Then (3), relatively suddenly, the problems disappear. The mother looks better and handles the baby with pleasure and confidence. At this stage, the mothers often wish to talk about their experiences both in the perinatal period and since taking the baby home, and they appear particularly anxious to tell us of their feelings towards their baby.

For example, Joanna's mother, Mrs S., a 33-year-old teacher of mentally retarded children, developed hypertension during her fourth pregnancy after a normal first pregnancy and two abortions. The hypertension did not respond to treatment and an elective Caesarean section was performed at 29 weeks of gestation. Mrs S. was told that the baby would be very small and would need to be in the Neonatal Unit in an incubator but that chances of survival were 'good'. Joanna weighed 915 g. Her newborn period was uneventful and her subsequent progress at home during her first year has been completely normal. Mrs S. was euphoric when Joanna first went home. This was followed by a period, lasting many weeks, when she was clearly not managing either the baby or her own affairs. She was miserable, looked ill and tired, and complained of clinging behaviour of her three-year-old boy and of Joanna. She told us she was sure Joanna was autistic because the infant related only to herself. Mrs S. was unable to accept any explanation or reassurance to the contrary. Then one day, when Joanna was five months of real age ($5\frac{1}{2}$ months after discharge from hospital), Mrs S. came in to see us, transformed. She was delighted with Joanna's progress and no longer complained about Joanna's physical or emotional well-being. She then told us, quite spontaneously and extremely vividly, of her experience after Joanna's birth. She had been appalled by Joanna's appearance when she first saw her and wished she would die. When Joanna did not die, she felt she wanted to kill her. This feeling was so strong that she did not dare to go to see the baby unless her husband was with her. These 'horrible' feelings gradually waned and she became ashamed and intensely guilty. She spent the first few weeks that Joanna was at home trying to make amends for her early hostility to the baby, but afraid that it would in some way have permanently affected the child's ability to relate to her. By the time Mrs S. told us of her feelings, she had established a good relationship with the child, although she appeared rather over-protective and anxious. She herself says that she will always feel guilty and wish to make amends to Joanna.

We presume that Joanna's mother used the word 'autistic' to express her concern for her child because of her personal experience. Other mothers of less intelligence and with no knowledge of how babies behave and no experience of handicapped children have described similar feelings, and we believe that almost all mothers of very LBW babies experience them to a varying degree. Several have expressed concern or guilt at the possible harm they may have done to their child by failing to love, or even hate, the child at first. Those with a history of a psychiatric disorder, infertility, pregnancy failure or abnormal pregnancy appeared to suffer most, especially if they had been delivered in another hospital so that visiting was impossible in the early days and difficult subsequently. On the other hand, when the women showed little evidence of disturbance, we always found that the fathers were sympathetic and supporting.

Fathers

Since we have allowed fathers to come into the Neonatal Unit, and particularly since they have been encouraged to participate in the care of their babies, most of them have visited frequently. Many are regular attenders at the follow-up clinic, including a few who bring the baby regularly without the mother. They ask many questions and are clearly involved in day-to-day care. They express similar anxieties and are as over-protective as the mothers. We have the impression that these fathers are exceptionally well orientated towards their children by the time they go home, and we wonder whether very low birth weight may actually be advantageous to the formation of paternal relationships in some cases! Several weeks of visiting the child in the Neonatal Unit may allow the father time to gradually accept both the child and the inevitable change in his relationship with his wife.

From six months of age to eight years

The parents of our group of very LBW children have continued to need a lot of reassurance while their children are growing up. All the more tiresome aspects of normal development have tended to be presented as problems. For example, variations in appetite, temper tantrums, and fighting with siblings have caused a lot of concern; and, at least among the first parents we observed, some appeared to be waiting for the signs of the brain damage which they assumed must have occurred. In addition, a few parents have given the impression that they would not be satisfied until some abnormality had been found. Others have been very protective—to the extent that they sometimes denied their children the experience necessary for the normal development of, for example, interrelationships with other children or motor skills. Since about 1970, however, over-protective attitudes have been less prominent and the parents have been more easily reassured, although in general they continue to be over-anxious.

During the pre-school period we have observed several children with mild behaviour problems, usually either attention-seeking behaviour or excessive shyness. Most of these problems appeared to result from chronic mishandling; discussion with and counselling of the parents, attendance at nursery school, or amelioration of disturbing influences at home, produced improvements. Among the 19 children aged seven and eight years on whom we have done cognitive and behavioural assessments, one is both of low intellect and severely maladjusted, and six are mildly over-dependent, anxious and shy. Four of these six children are performing satisfactorily in school and are not handicapped by their behaviour. Although the fifth child is only making slow progress at school this is due to a number of factors other than her behaviour. The sixth child has a serious learning problem. She is of dull/normal intellect and as far as we can judge at present she has no evidence of brain damage or cognitive dysfunction. Her mother is phobic, and is particularly anxious about travelling. We consider that it is the mother's psychiatric disorder which is mainly responsible for the child's behaviour. Nevertheless, it is interesting to speculate how much this behaviour may be due to the disturbances in the family which result from the mother's disorder, and how much to the complete infant–mother separation, for which the mother's phobia about travelling was almost certainly responsible.

Among our 160 very LBW survivors, there are just two children—apart from five who were adopted—who were rejected by their mothers. One of these rejected children was born at 26 weeks of gestation and weighed approximately 800 g. Her mother, aged 35, was an obsessional woman who was liable to depression. She had had three previous late abortions and regarded this most recent pregnancy as yet another abortion. When the child survived after six weeks on a mechanical ventilator, she could not accept the child as a person, but despised her as a freak. The child had a language-learning difficulty in addition to a cleft soft palate, a hearing loss of 40 decibels, and minimal cerebral damage. The child's progress since entering school has been remarkable and we believe, with hindsight, that the language-learning difficulty was largely behavioural in origin.

The other rejected child was the tiny (1200 g) member of a rubella-infected monozygous twin pair. Both girls were transferred to our Neonatal Unit after birth in another hospital in Outer London. The smaller twin was very ill for three weeks and probably had a subarachnoid haemorrhage. The mother, a 28-year-old undemonstrative, obsessional woman, rejected the child from birth because she was 'too small, too ill and too ugly to be normal'. We suspect that the father also rejected the child at birth, although he 'covered up' for his wife and actually looked after the child during the months that she was at home. At the parents' insistence, the child is now 'in care' and is very retarded at two years six months of age. Because of the perinatal history, we assume that the child is brain-damaged, although emotional deprivation is probably responsible for some of her disability.

DISCUSSION

In spite of our attempts to minimize the separation of very LBW babies from their parents during perinatal intensive care, we continue to observe that in the weeks after delivery the mothers undergo a form of emotional crisis similar to the first three parts of the disorder originally described by Kaplan & Mason (1960). We also observe an equally specific pattern of behaviour among mothers during the first few weeks that the children are at home, which suggests that the emotional conflicts are not completely resolved until the parents have their children at home to care for themselves. Because these mothers are inefficient at recognizing signals from the baby immediately after the baby goes home, they are anxious and probably react indiscriminately to everything, consequently becoming exhausted. Rigid mothers, in particular, find it difficult and are slow to learn to respond appropriately. Exhaustion leads both to inefficiency in practical matters such as feeding the baby or domestic duties, and to resentment; and then the mothers feel guilty at their resentment. Most of them have already suffered feelings of failure and guilt, in addition to anticipating the baby's death. The delivery of a very LBW baby is itself sufficient to induce such emotions; and previous infertility, pregnancy failure or termination, abnormalities of pregnancy, denial of pregnancy and unwanted pregnancy, particularly when there have been attempts to terminate it, all tend to intensify these feelings. In addition, many of the mothers experience horror and hate at the sight of their babies, which must lead to even more guilt, especially as our culture dictates that babies are 'beautiful' and that mothers automatically love them on sight. The mothers, however, cannot rationalize sufficiently to explain their problems. Instead, they complain of physical difficulties in the baby, such as feeding, vomiting or constipation. The problem ends, usually suddenly, when the mother gains insight and learns to respond appropriately to her baby's signals.

As the mother's confidence in her ability to care for the child grows, and the child becomes responsive, she discovers that 'concerned caring' produces results. We believe that it is out of this 'concerned caring' that a relationship between the mother and child grows. The time taken for this to happen varies greatly, and probably depends on the emotional stability of the mother, the amount of support she receives from the father, and the amount of guilt or sense of failure which she has had to overcome, as well as on both the degree of anticipatory grief and the duration of early separation. Almost all the mothers of our group of very LBW babies have eventually established a satisfactory relationship with the children, and for some of the fathers premature birth and a prolonged stay in the intensive care unit with frequent visiting appeared advantageous to the formation of a good relationship with their children. Nevertheless, particularly among the families we observed first, the relationship has been characterized by over-protectiveness and persistent anxiety in the parents. This may be reflected in the high number of mildly over-dependent, anxious and shy children whom we have detected among the older members of the group. However, the incidence of serious behaviour problems as the children grow older is not nearly as high as the 22% reported by Drillien (1969) among children weighing 2000 g or less, who were born and cared for in the 1950s when parents were banned from premature baby nurseries.

We think it is significant that in our group of 160 very LBW survivors the two mothers who completely failed to relate to their children and the mother whose child had a serious behaviour disorder had all had a psychiatric or personality disorder before pregnancy. Caution, however, is needed in interpreting and applying this and our other observations. Intensive care is used exclusively in highly abnormal situations, including very low birth weight, and we have experience only of looking after the parents of such babies. We do not know, for example, how parents of normal-term babies born after an uneventful pregnancy would react if they were given the same intensive and prolonged contact with the nursing, medical and psychological staff both in the newborn unit and the follow-up clinic. It must be emphasized also that these are observations which we originally assembled in order to plan future research; they are not the results of prospectively-planned studies, and the number of babies is small.

In spite of these limitations, it seems reasonable to infer from our observations that many factors influence the formation and the quality of the relationship between parents and their very LBW children. These factors include the emotional and psychiatric well-being of the mother, circumstances surrounding the birth of a very LBW baby that are likely to induce feelings of failure or guilt, the amount of anticipatory grief experienced by the mother, and the duration of mother–baby separation. We consider that equal attention should be paid to all four aspects when intensive perinatal care is being planned. Thus, separation of the baby from its parents needs to be minimized, and we think that fathers need to be considered in this respect too, if only because their support is invaluable to the mother; all those concerned with the parents of babies of very low birth weight should understand the emotional problems which such parents are likely to have and be prepared to listen or talk to the parents whenever necessary; and mothers with a history of personality or psychiatric disorder should be regarded as likely to have more difficulty than other mothers in forming a relationship with their child. In addition, we consider that long-term support should be available for these parents in order to help them to minimize, if not overcome, their anxieties.

ACKNOWLEDGEMENTS

We should like to express our thanks for all the help and encouragement with this study which we have received, both from the parents and from our medical, nursing and psychological colleagues in University College Hospital Neonatal Unit and Out-patients Department and in the Department of Child Psychology, University College London. In particular we should like to thank: the parents for taking part in the pilot study and for making so many helpful suggestions; the Research and Statistics Department of the Inner London Education Authority and the Chief Education Officers of many Outer London boroughs for permission to examine children in their schools; Dr E. O. R. Reynolds, Miss Linda Collins and Miss Grace Rawlings for their inspiration and guidance; and Professor L. B. Strang for his unfailing support and encouragement throughout the study. Dr A. Stewart was a member of the Medical Research Council's scientific staff (Human Biochemical Genetics Unit) during the early part of this study, and is now supported by a grant from the Department of Health and Social Security. Miss D. Turcan was supported by a grant from Birthright.

References

Drillien, C. M. (1969) School disposal and performance for children of different birthweight born 1953–1960. *Arch. Dis. Child. 44*, 562–570

Kaplan, D. M. & Mason, E. A. (1960) Maternal reactions to premature birth viewed as an acute emotional disorder. *Am. J. Orthopsychiatr. 30*, 539–552

KLAUS, M. & KENNELL, J. (1970) Mothers separated from their newborn infants. *Pediat. Clin. North Am. 17*, 1015–1037

KLAUS, M. & KENNELL, J. (1973) Care of the mother, in *Care of the High-Risk Neonate* (Klaus, M.H. & Faneroff, A.A., eds.), p. 98–118, W.B. Saunders, Philadelphia

KNOBLOCH, H., PASAMANICK, B. & SHERARD, E.S. (1966). A developmental screening inventory for infants. *Pediatrics 38* (Suppl.), 1095–1108

KOPPITZ, E.M. (1963) *The Bender Gestalt Test for Young Children*, Grune & Stratton, New York

OPPÉ, T. (1960) The emotional aspects of prematurity. *Cereb. Palsy Bull. 2*, 233–237

REYNELL, J. (1969) Reynell Developmental Language Scales (R.D.L.S.), National Foundation for Educational Research, London

REYNOLDS, E.O.R. & STEWART, A.L. (1975) Intensive care and follow-up of infants of very low birth weight, in *Proceedings of the N.I.H. Conference on Perinatal Intensive Care, Bethesda, 1974* (Dancis, J., ed.), National Institutes of Health, Bethesda, Md., in press

SCHLESINGER, E.R. (1973) Neonatal intensive care: planning for services and outcomes following care. *J. Pediatr. 82*, 916–920

STEWART, A.L. & REYNOLDS, E.O.R. (1974) Improved prognosis for infants of very low birth weight. *Pediatrics, 54*, 724–733

STOTT, D.H. & MARSTON, N.C. (1971) *Bristol Social Adjustment Guide No. 2: The Child in School*, University of London Press, London

STUTSMAN, R. (1931) *Mental Measurement of Pre-School Children*, Harcourt Brace & World, New York

TERMAN, L.M. & MERRILL, M.A. (1961) *Stanford–Binet Intelligence Scale*, Harrap, London

USHER, R.H. (1971) Clinical implications of perinatal mortality statistics. *Clin. Obstet. Gynec. 14*, 885–925

WECHSLER, D. (1949) *Wechsler Intelligence Scale for Children*, Psychological Corporation, New York

Discussion

Bentovim: The effect of having a baby of low birth weight is in many ways similar to that of having a child with some sort of malformation (Bentovim 1972). The same events in the responses of parents occur, in the same sequence of mourning responses, grief, despair, rejection, anger and guilt at the loss of the expected 'normal' child. The staff in the premature unit play an important part in helping parents towards acceptance by the way they have adapted to coping with tiny babies who are not at all responsive in the normal way. The hospital staff act as a sort of 'extended family' to the parents; usually the real family has no experience of tiny babies and cannot give 'mothering' and proper support to the parents. The parents therefore use the nurses and medical staff as surrogate parents, and clearly continue to do so afterwards. The question is whether this should be capitalized on by systematically trying to do what Caplan (1960) would describe as crisis intervention, either in groups or individually. This would entail getting the parents to express and work through the angry rejecting thoughts that they have at the loss of the perfect child expected, and then begin to readjust and accept contact with the particular infant that they have got.

Stewart: Should we try to prevent these feelings or should we accept that this state should occur and try to help the parents to get through it quickly?

Bentovim: Group methods might help to shorten the response. The sharing of these sorts of feeling by parents might be a tremendous relief to them, and enable them to deal with them earlier. These families have the common stress of having a very small baby. They are all attending the ward regularly and this could well be capitalized on, especially as use is already being made of staff in this way.

Stewart: The mothers certainly appear to be happier if we tell them that others have told us that they experienced the same feelings; practically all the mothers have said this at one stage or another.

Leiderman: We have had some experience with follow-up needs of our families. From 1967 to 1972 we asked parents of babies of low birth weight what kind of help they thought they needed or wanted. We asked that they choose between doctors, social workers, psychologists, family, friends. The first choice of the women in our area was other parents, then nursing staff, then doctors, and finally family and friends. Geography plays a part, too. They wanted help in their own districts (we cover a district of about a 30-mile radius). When we asked whether they would come in if we offered group sessions once a week or once a month at our hospital, they said they would attend about once a month, but in their own area, with other parents who had experienced the birth of a premature baby. In fact, when we pursued it further, we discovered that some parents themselves had organized these sessions without our help. They were alerted to the presence of one another through their contact at Stanford Medical Center and utilized these contacts. We have no follow-up about whether this works but certainly it seems to reduce the amount of anxiety. I would suggest that if you can get a few of the parents to take the lead, providing them with the usual kind of support, they probably can do a great deal on their own.

Stewart: One woman, Joanna's mother, actually volunteered that she was quite prepared to talk to the current mothers, if I thought it would help. We haven't taken her up on this yet, and I don't know whether we should.

Oppé: Is there a general urge to destroy an infant who looks abnormal, or behaves abnormally, throughout the animal kingdom, or in various human races? Some human societies destroy twins, while others value them extremely highly.

Hinde: Animal comparisons ought not to be made here, and they are really of little use. But if we are making comparisons, there are many cases of monkey mothers carrying dead babies around for days and weeks, until they are decayed masses of fur.

Rosenblatt: On the other hand, the aggression may be a distortion of something very useful. Most animals protect their young and are aggressive if anyone comes to attack them. As rats become more maternal they also get more aggressive. They attack anything that is any different from their young.

Oppé: Why do you say that this is a particular area where we mustn't make animal comparisons, Professor Hinde? Who selects the animal comparisons which we should or should not make?

Hinde: You yourself have just emphasized the different attitudes to infanticide in human cultures, with the emphasis on higher level cultures. That is why animal comparisons would probably be superficial.

Curtis-Jenkins: As an alternative to aggression, some parents say that the child they have been given is not theirs, particularly when an anaesthetic has been given at the time of delivery and they were not physically present or conscious at the time the baby arrived. It is sometimes as long as eight months or a year before those mothers say they accept the baby as theirs.

Stewart: Our mothers say: 'I don't think I have had a baby', rather than saying it is the wrong one.

Curtis-Jenkins: That is because they have at least been presented with the baby, and they have to make an excuse for it being in their arms.

Richards: We come from a culture that has ideas about life that are rather different from some other cultures. Kalahari Bushmen are alleged to have a list of categories of babies that the mother herself must bury at birth. They include twins, breech deliveries and babies who are slow to breathe. Other cultures have similar lists. In our own culture, a mother taking the life of her own child within the first year is regarded quite differently from anyone else taking life at any other time. Infanticide is not the same offence as murder or manslaughter. It is a rare offence, and in practice women don't even go to prison for it but get put on probation.

Brazelton: Included in the Kalahari list are babies who are slow to show attachment behaviour, and they are selected for being left in the desert.

Leiderman: It depends on the kind of economic resources that are available. Nomadic people are less inclined to maintain damaged babies, whereas agricultural people who have a more stable kind of environment are more willing to tolerate greater deviance, which they can take care of within the family unit. There is a tremendous variation.

Cooper: One so-called primitive tribe that I worked with in West Africa used to choose a particularly big cotton tree and make a pit in the ground at its base. There the mother had to leave her abnormal baby to die. Food 'to last it' was put in the hole too, only it couldn't eat the food because it was too young. That was a form of ritual killing of the abnormal child, who was considered to be a devil. The varieties of practice from area to area are so enormous that it is hard to generalize, but killing abnormal children by some form of exposure seems not uncommon.

Hofer: We mustn't lose sight of the fact that if the infant is sick and is a source of worry and anxiety to the mother, he is also going to elicit feelings of anger, simply because he is causing the mother pain. The emotional anguish of parents who have a child with leukaemia, for example, is such that almost everybody at some point reacts with resentment and anger, and the feeling that they wish the child was dead and that they were out of the dreadful period they are going through. This driving force is not a cultural one but an internal psychological ambivalence. Almost every parent of a sick or a threatened child must have to deal with this. And it happens even with a normal baby, to the extent that every mother worries about even a normal baby being all right.

Klaus: One way to exaggerate the question is to ask whether the major problem for the mother of a premature baby is one of being deprived of her baby or, at the other end of the scale, a problem of having a malformed baby far from the mental image she had before its delivery. The intervention might be quite different for the two cases. In one case, the mother and premature would be put together; in the other case, the mother has to be helped to mourn the loss of her perfect image of the baby and then helped to take over the care of the actual baby. Kaplan & Mason's earlier work (1960) suggests the latter. When we first started this kind of work, we believed that if we gave the mother the baby early, there would be much less grief. The more Dr Kennell and I work in this area, the more we agree with you, Dr Stewart. But a second element cuts across this in a complex manner. If, because the maternity unit cannot manage the problem, a full-term baby is transported away from the mother for a minor illness such as jaundice, the mother often unrealistically believes that the baby is going to die. The bond between the mother and infant is present at birth, for there is grief for a long period even when the baby dies at one minute of age, but the quality of the bond is such that when the baby is taken to another hospital away from the mother, she thinks he may die. One can decrease this grief by simply transporting the mother and baby together. If the mother is going to have a premature baby, which can be predicted in 50–60% of the cases, the mother can be taken into the premature unit and delivered there, so that she can be with the baby immediately. Thus, if the major problem for the mother of a premature is separation, the time can be shortened, and if the problem is similar to having a baby with a malformation, the mother can more quickly see the actual baby. We agree with you that if the mother is in the unit it is much easier than if the baby has to be brought in alone.

Dr B. Craemer in Lausanne has interviewed a group of 13 mothers intensively and found what you reported. He also helped me to realize how the nurse can act like the mother's mother if she allows and encourages the mother to do a number of tasks with her small infant, such as cleaning, fondling, etc. Acceptance by the nurse can be very helpful.

Brazelton: I agree with you, Dr Klaus. When you expect a grief reaction from the mothers and accept it, this enables the parent to have a grief reaction under cover, in a premature unit, rather than having to have it with the baby afterwards. Without the expectation which gives them this permission, a grieving mother cannot allow herself to talk to doctors. My own explanation of this is that the mother's anger and guilty feelings are first directed towards herself, but she can't tolerate them. The next projection would be onto the baby, but she can't tolerate that either, so the next projection is onto the person who is being aggressive to her baby. It is obvious to me that a mother needs to become aggressive or angry or hostile to us as physicians. A nurse can become the good mother, and gradually we can help them to overcome their negative reactions to us. The most important thing becomes to allow them to express these feelings, and to let them feel that these *are* normal feelings which they can share, first with their peers, then with the nurses, and finally with us, the physicians. Then they have done the work and the magic of attachment to their infants takes place.

Stewart: We were absolutely staggered at the spontaneity with which the mothers spoke to us. Those of us who work in the follow-up clinic have nothing to do with day-to-day care in the premature unit. We go in to see them but we don't decide when they need a drip, or more or less oxygen, so possibly the mothers feel that they do not need to be aggressive with us—or maybe they have already been aggressive with the resident doctor.

Macfarlane: I am interested in trying to assess what is done to babies in intensive care units and how this alters their behaviour when they come out of hospital. If the child is in hospital in an incubator and has to undergo a large number of different medical procedures, he doesn't go through all the interactional processes we are talking about. One might therefore expect strange things to happen to the baby if in his first weeks people keep sticking umbilical catheters and so on into him. When he gets home, how long does he take to reorientate towards the kind of interactional processes which the mother is offering him instead of the kind he was getting in hospital?

Stewart: The group we are looking at is possibly an unusual one because they have almost all had interventions such as umbilical catheters and intravenous drips and many have been intubated or mechanically ventilated. When they come out of the incubators they spend quite a lot of time simply growing and fattening up in a cot, with the parents themselves handling them perhaps two or three times a day. Obviously there is some change when they go home, but we have stopped interfering with them, in the strict sense of the term, some weeks previously.

Macfarlane: But for how long is the experience they had in the intensive care unit going to upset future interaction?

Stewart: There is also the question of gestational age and what interaction they are able to offer. A lot of variables are operating in the perinatal period and if we subdivide them into different groups, we will end up with unmanageably small numbers in each group.

Salisbury: Dr Marfarlane is painting a somewhat black and white picture of an infant who has been attacked and violated and given many painful stimuli, then is suddenly transported home, where he has to relate to his mother. But this bridging period in between surely allows them to adjust to each other before they go home.

Stewart: For a baby of very low birth weight it is quite a long period, usually six weeks or more.

Bentovim: The intensive care unit at Northwick Park Hospital now has what they call a 'nesting unit' where mothers stay for several days before they take the baby home. The period after the initial euphoria of having the baby is the most difficult time.

Stewart: We tell the mothers, when they take the baby home, that they can come and talk to us whenever they feel like it. I agree that it might help if they could live in for a while but there still comes the time when they must take the baby home and feel they are on their own, in their own place.

Kennell: The anxiety and concern of a mother which persist long after the baby is doing well are also encountered in mothers of full-term babies who have a number of conditions that are perceived as life-threatening in the first days of life, such as jaundice. As an experienced physician I would have to say that the organization of our hospital services and the behaviour of doctors and nurses may play an important part in this phenomenon. We used to be taught that almost all small premature babies would die and that we should prepare the parents for that. It is difficult for us to alter our buildings and our programmes, yet minor changes might produce a great improvement in the outcome. In the UK certain aspects of hospital care are under much better regional control than in the cost-conscious private hospital system of the United States. If a baby is premature in some hospitals in the UK, the mother is delivered in hospital and may stay in hospital near her baby. If the baby has to be transferred to another hospital for care, she and the baby may go there together—and efforts will be made to keep mother and baby within sight of each other. In the

US the mother may be put to sleep after a Caesarean section before she hears that first crucial cry from the baby, and she may not see the baby until many hours later. Many practices followed in caring for mothers and babies have been established because they are more convenient for the doctor, yet with slight modification they could be satisfactory for all three.

I hope the Northwick Park experience is carried on longer. We have tried 'nesting' for one group of mothers. Each mother lived in the hospital in a private room with her own infant for three days, caring for her baby as much as possible as she would at home. It was difficult to arrange this in our hospital, but we did see phenomenal things happening during the nesting period. The mothers quickly told us that they had to have their husbands there, although we had not planned for that. Then we found that the mothers were invariably awake for the entire first night, whether the baby made any noise or not. They changed the pattern of feeding and fed the babies more often than the nurses had and each mother set up the room differently, though it had little furniture in it. She made her own nest, if you like. All of this seemed to be helpful to the mothers. After the three days all of them were confident and strong in their desire to take the babies home. Many of them objected to our research routine of sending the baby back to the nursery for a day of discharge studies. The control group of mothers were not ready to take their babies out; they felt that the babies ought to be a little larger and so forth.

This may be difficult to arrange in most US hospitals but it would be possible in new hospitals. Maybe three days is all the average family can tolerate, but perhaps there would have been a stronger effect if the period had been longer. The nesting period usually occurred a month or more after birth.

Brazelton: How did you get the mothers to come in?

Kennell: The nesting was arranged in a room in a government-supported Clinical Research Center, and the beds were free, which was extremely important. Most of the mothers that we asked to take part in this study agreed to come for three days, though we often had to arrange it at a time like the weekend when the father or someone else could care for the other children.

Dreyfus-Brisac: Was life at home a lot easier for the mothers after these three days?

Kennell: They told us that the experience was helpful. They were often tired after three days in hospital but they did have another day before the baby went home. To test the effects of this experience, we did not use their verbal reports but looked at their behaviour a month later, during a standardized office visit with a filmed feeding. We did not find any significant differences compared with the control group, but the numbers were small. In retrospect we wish we had made our observations earlier.

Cooper: We do admit mothers of the small babies before they go home in some British maternity units, but perhaps they are not so thoroughly studied and helped. Admission alone is not enough. Cherishing and explanations about every small detail of their baby's behaviour are what they seem to need. Dr Stewart said that the crisis of having a premature baby perhaps enhances the relationship of the parents with each other, and the total family relationship. I would suggest that every birth in every family is a crisis, and that we should pay more attention during every pregnancy and in the newborn period to the whole family situation, with explanations and support. It is within the power, not necessarily of doctors alone, but of the total medical caring team, to do this for every family at every birth. I believe we would have to change attitudes, hospital routines and staff training to achieve success. Some voluntary bodies provide excellent extra support, and they are attempting to fill some of the gaps left by the medical profession. This is something that we should bear in mind and perhaps we should try to forge closer links between the two, and learn from each other.

References

BENTOVIM, A. (1972) Handicapped pre-school children and their families: effects on the child's early emotional development and family attitudes. *Br. Med. J. 3*, 579–581, 634–663

CAPLAN, G. (1960) Patterns of parental response to the crisis of premature birth: a preliminary approach to modifying the mental health outcome. *Psychiatry 23*, 365–374

KAPLAN, D. & MASON, E. (1960) Maternal reactions to premature birth viewed as an acute emotional disorder. *Am. J. Orthopsychiatr. 30*, 539–552

Speculations on the relevance of developmental psychology to paediatrics

T. E. OPPÉ

Paediatric Unit, St Mary's Hospital Medical School, London

Abstract Many paediatricians are now interested in applying the concepts, theories and methods of developmental psychology to clinical practice. The new understanding so obtained should enable abnormalities of clinical importance to be detected earlier; it should also provide means for evaluating the outcome of some disease processes and medical procedures more fully than was hitherto possible. The genesis of the nurturing failure or deficiency which underlies many paediatric problems becomes explicable as the nature of the maternal bond is unravelled. New ways may thus be opened for the more effective prevention and treatment of child abuse, neglect and deprivation. Developmental psychology also promises to provide for the first time a framework on which child-rearing methods which will positively promote healthy psychological development can be based. However, some caution and critical interpretation, as well as much collaborative investigation, will be needed before the full relevance of developmental psychology to paediatrics is established with certainty.

Investigation of the development of behaviour in human infancy and early childhood is of interest to several scientific disciplines, and the practical application of knowledge obtained from, and methods used in, such studies is relevant to the practice of several clinical specialties. It is not helpful, when speculating about the relevance of this academic area to clinical practice, to attempt to delineate too closely the boundaries between developmental psychology and the more entrenched disciplines of clinical and educational psychology, nor to make sharp distinctions between the contributions being made by anthropologists, ethologists, physiologists and sociologists. It is also unprofitable to particularize the clinical responsibilities of anaesthetists, obstetricians, paediatricians, family doctors, and others who provide medical care to mothers and their infants.

However, paediatrics (in particular neonatology) and developmental psychology share two important attributes. Being young, they are less committed to conventional wisdom, established authority, and traditional methods than older disciplines, and, in consequence, they have approached child development from the standpoint of contemporary observation and prospective study rather than from the retrospective viewpoint (downward projection from adulthood) which marked the older psychology of development and the early practice of children's medicine.

In common with other clinical specialties dealing with outstandingly dangerous periods of life, paediatrics tends to be preoccupied with the preservation of life, and with the prevention, amelioration and cure of disease. These objectives may seem at variance with those who espouse such causes as population control, the rights of women to determine their reproductive function, the conservation of the old, or the elimination of the allegedly 'unfit'. But it would be wrong to suppose that those responsible for perinatal care are concerned only with the immediate events which threaten life or which might produce permanent brain damage; they are also interested in the long-term sequelae of those events and with the promotion of healthy growth and development.

Developmental psychology, unlike traditional psychoanalysis and educational psychology, participates in the immediate happenings of perinatal and neonatal life and their subsequent outcome, not simply because these events may explain pathological phenomena encountered in later life, but also because intervention at the time offers promise of great benefit.

Now that many of the former hazards to successful child-bearing, such as gross trauma, infection and neonatal asphyxia, have been reduced or eliminated it is right to examine carefully some less serious but possibly more widespread problems, and also to enquire whether the means necessarily adopted for minimizing maternal and infant mortality and morbidity succeed in meeting all the criteria for optimal medical care.

Until developmental psychology provided the impetus little was done to establish the outcome of pregnancy in terms other than survival of, or the exclusion of gross defect or disease in, the newborn infant. Success, or failure, of new methods of obstetric care were measured by their effect on perinatal mortality and on the incidence of pathological effects such as neonatal asphyxia. In recent years, refinement of the 'neurological' examination of the newborn has led to increasing accuracy in the determination of gestational age, and has given a somewhat more reliable prediction of future development than hitherto. However, neurological examination concentrates mainly on locomotor function and leaves largely unexplored the sensory, perceptual and cognitive functions which are of greater importance in human development. The conventional view that the nervous system at birth is so poorly developed that only gross lesions disturb the primitive level of functioning enough to provide elicitable physical signs went unchallenged by most clinicians, as did the generalization which asserted that the immature nervous system was sufficiently 'plastic' to overcome damage to its cells and connections by effective anatomical rearrangement.

Developmental psychology has forced reconsideration of these views and provided methods which can be used clinically for investigating the revised concepts. Paediatricians can no longer regard the newly born as primitive simpletons but must accept that they are individuals with well-organized and developed neural mechanisms which subserve not only survival but active participation in their new environment. In theory and increasingly in practice paediatricians have been given the capability for:

(*a*) A far more comprehensive screening of newborn infants into normal and abnormal groups.

(*b*) The earlier detection and diagnosis of many neurodevelopmental disorders.

(*c*) The more precise evaluation of the effect, beneficial or adverse, of medical procedures related to the perinatal period.

(*d*) The more accurate prediction in individual infants and in groups of infants of their future developmental progress and of the success or otherwise of anticipatory or prophylactic interventions based on the predictions.

It is unlikely that a simple battery of tests fulfilling these aims will soon be available or that personnel will exist to apply them. It is therefore important to allocate some priorities to the desirable (to the clinician) immediate objectives. I rank highly work which will (*a*) increase the specificity and sensitivity of the examination of the newborn, mainly because in the UK 90% of the total newborn population is accessible to medical examination, a situation which does not recur until school entry, and (*b*) identify with greater precision the practices in obstetric and neonatal care which adversely affect the normal function of the neonate either transiently or permanently.

Obstetricians and paediatricians may with some justice be accused of emphasizing unduly, if not unreasonably, the consideration given to one of the mother–infant pair to the detriment of the other. Developmental psychology is relatively free of such bias because of its primary concern with the mother–infant dyad. The clinical specialties have been preoccupied with the caretaker–infant relationship rather than the mother–infant relationship, largely because in the past the puerperal mother was often herself in need of medical and nursing care, and her child was nursed by others. Studies by ethologists and developmental psychologists of animals other than man have avoided this pitfall but may have led some developmental psychologists to a too-ready extrapolation of their findings to the condition of human mothering.

Recently there have been changes in these attitudes which are extremely promising not only for the better understanding of the human mother–child relationship but also for the beneficial application of this knowledge in medical practice.

Paediatricians now generally accept the advantages of maternal participation in the management of the sick child in hospital, and have found that unrestricted visiting is neither disruptive of ward routines nor an infection hazard. However, what is now common practice in children's wards has not yet become universally accepted in maternity departments or special-care baby units. This is surprising in view of the mounting evidence of the desire of mothers to take an active part in the handling of their babies in the first few days of life, and of the possible importance of this in securing bonding between mother and child.

The real significance of the immediate postnatal period to the development of mother–infant attachment and the effects subsequently of its success or failure is as yet uncertain. Nevertheless there is now evidence that the lying-in period is of much greater importance than has hitherto been recognized.

A number of conditions in the first year of life that were previously inadequately explained are now recognized as being manifestations of 'mothering-failure'. They include: some feeding and sleeping problems, frequent avoidable illness and injury, non-accidental violence, and disturbances of growth and development. Clearly mothering failure is the end-result of many contributory factors and it is unlikely that the quality and quantity of postnatal mother–baby interaction is exclusively responsible—but it seems important enough for those looking after mothers and infants to examine their arrangements critically, so that they can effect optimal contact between mother and child and amend procedures which disturb it.

Greater awareness of the significance of bonding failure should also lead to opportunities for therapeutic and anticipatory intervention when disturbed mother–infant relationships are detected or elicited. Some progress has been made in this area but the number of intervening variables is large, and there is little evidence that intervention is effective, whether it is personal—from health visitors, social workers or doctors—or by environmental manipulation.

Developmental psychology has not answered the important questions of whether human mothering ability is largely inherent (instinctive), conditioned by early experiences, or can be learned. The assumption of many clinicians is that if cognitive knowledge of child-bearing and child-rearing (mothercraft, parentcraft) is instilled, a real benefit is conferred. There are clear limitations to this approach, in that emotional and social factors are disregarded or underemphasized, while the authority of the professional view is magnified.

Paediatrics, partly because of the way it is practised in the USA, has become identified with the health care of the well individual in a way which is not the case with general (adult) medicine. Neither experience with sick children nor the body of knowledge assembled by clinical and educational psychologists has been of much help to paediatricians in their role as expert advisers on child-rearing. In the main they have followed rather than led the social, cultural and political pressures which determine family life and the upbringing of children.

Developmental psychology may in due course provide a framework which will place child-rearing practices on a more scientific basis but there is a long way to go before we can be convinced that intervention based on existing studies is beneficial; and this is of special difficulty in regard to predictive or prophylactic interventions which are unsolicited by parents.

Discussion

Macfarlane: I am concerned about the data base of the new information that we as physicians are using. How we collect and use this information and the things that influence our decisions depend mainly on our memories of our medical training. One problem is that we get a series of criteria for babies who may be battered and we intervene on that basis. Yet of 100 babies who fulfil these criteria, only 20 may be battered and in 80 cases we have intervened unnecessarily. That seems to be the way that medicine works, but are we justified in making such a decision?

Oppé: Probably the most difficult change to make is that of attitude, and the attitudes of doctors certainly depend very much on what is slotted into their minds during training. With battered babies the problem is really one of predicting exactly which babies are going to be battered. If we could do that, we could evaluate whether the intervention helped. But we are nowhere near that.

Macfarlane: I still feel that much medicine, especially in obstetrics, works on the kind of basis for intervention that we are trying to avoid here. For example, if the second stage of labour takes more than 45 minutes or so, perhaps 10% of babies or more might become anoxic, so forceps are used; yet maybe 90 out of 100 babies on whom forceps are used don't actually need that.

Klaus: The trouble is that the system has already been changed. The delivery of a baby was within a family for centuries. In the United States in 1930, mothers with toxaemia were brought into the hospital for treatment and delivery. They did well and on that basis most mothers then came into the hospital to deliver. The present system in obstetrical units may be in many ways compared to the situation 20 years ago in paediatric units where parents were only allowed to visit their sick children in the hospital for half-an-hour once a week.

Oppé: We come into this scheme at all sorts of levels. Our new information from developmental psychology that puffy eyes are not a good thing is going to force us to evaluate the procedure of putting silver nitrate in the eyes at birth.

Klaus: The problem is that this has now become part of the culture.

Rosenblatt: The women who were delivering babies in the Santa Cruz community said that they had to contend with the idea that giving birth was a disease, an illness for which some treatment would be used. I get the same feeling from Dr Oppé, that life is a disease. Many of these studies are directed by this idea about life. Extreme conditions certainly need attention but they are conditions which interfere with the full development of life, not the way it should normally be. We are interested in infants and in their lives being pleasant, even if adults' lives are not. The world is not a hospital, with doctors at the top, running the whole thing.

Oppé: The fact is that doctors are in the disease business, rightly or wrongly, just as bankers are in the money business. On the whole, this is how doctors do their business but I thoroughly agree with you.

Hofer: Certainly doctors are in the health business as well as in the disease business, and there are really two issues here. One is the happiness and satisfaction of the woman who is giving birth and the family who is taking part at the time, without any relevance to long-range issues. That is probably going to be dealt with by 'the consumer', namely the people who go to hospitals or health care units. The other issue which we as scientists or doctors have to consider is what we can do to predict and intervene. I am not sure that we should even try to deal with the first issue here.

Rosenblatt: I don't think we can *not* deal with it. That is the larger context.

Brazelton: Both issues form the context within which this symposium has been brought to fruition. I don't think they ought to be ignored. At least in our culture in the US, and I suspect in England too, one of the givens is that the family is at risk. The fragility of the mother–father–infant relationship is uppermost in all our minds as a result. People at this conference believe in the importance of those bonds and in reinforcing them for young parents. Many problems are indeed generated by the physicians. Many of us have been trained with a negative model, a pathological model. This comes across both in the way we have treated childbirth and in the way we have lost opportunities for early bonding of mothers, fathers and children. We treat this period as if it was a pathological situation. As such we might well produce a Hawthorn effect on peoples' images of themselves as they enter this situation. Perhaps it has created something that we can now look on as an opportunity for intervention. That is, we have made people feel so dependent and so incapable of forming these bonds that they look to other people like ourselves and Dr Stewart's group for support at this tough moment of birth. This makes it absolutely necessary for us to get on with the business of seeing what we can offer in the way of support. We have information now about what infants are like, how powerful they are, and how powerfully they can perform their part of the bonding. We have also been talking about how parents can do this in the face of real interference in the pathological situation of an at-risk baby. Dr Stewart's paper was a beautiful example of what we could look forward to in the way of an atmosphere, in the way of energy, in the way of a positive model rather than a negative one, if we are willing to put our minds to it. I think we know enough, and it is time that we got on with it.

One of the warnings that you as scientists have given me as a clinician is that if we are too narrow in some of our assertions, or in some of our wishful planning, we may miss some of the marvellous strengths of human beings and their capacity to interact. I wouldn't want to fight for a too simple model, such as that presented by a critical period model or one kind of binding potential, to offer parents in a nursery for premature or at-risk babies. I would want to look for multiple models, so that we can offer parents free choices and make up for some of the damage we have done with our pathological approach to childbirth and early bonding.

Papoušek: Here again we should reconsider what Robert Hinde categorically underlined, that is that any intervention is nonsense unless we know the long-term effects. One long-term effect I believe in is that we are accumulating knowledge. That is important, but we must be careful in applying it. We have no criteria for the truth, and on the question of long-term effects on the survival of mankind I am lost. Academically speaking, we shall never know the final criteria, because we would need to observe hundreds of generations, which is impossible. Physicians, like parents and teachers, have to make concrete decisions daily, yet we don't know the right values or the right criteria for the evaluation of long-term effects.

One more problem with our trivial approaches is that we may not see any effect because we do not know enough about abnormal development. Thus, if a population at age one year is normal, and after our intervention is again normal at the age of 30 years, we can either say that there was no long-term effect or that the intervention itself guaranteed such a normal development. In the complex determination of human development, such a fine discrimination is often tremendously difficult.

How do you deal with this problematic aspect of long-term effects, Professor Hinde?

Hinde: I am not sure that I can follow that, but I want to make one point about the interaction of the scientists and the physician. It seems to me that the scientist has been too wont to sneer at the physician for being anecdotal and clinical, and for publishing single cases and so on. A lot of the scientific work at this meeting has been concerned with groups of subjects, whether patients or animals, yet clinicians *have* to apply their knowledge to individuals. In our monkey experiments on separation, some mother–infant pairs return to normal quickly. In others, the mother–infant relationship is set on a different course; it seems almost as if positive feedback is involved and the relationship diverges from there onwards. Predicting which individuals are going to be affected by an intervention or show certain symptoms is the crux of the matter. I think that scientists have given insufficient attention to individual differences. And in studying individual differences it is important to remember that the continuous distribution of a behavioural character may conceal a dichotomous response to external intervention.

Hofer: The clinicians' reply to that would be that if you can intervene in a way that would not harm those who don't need the intervention, and if you pick up the ones for whom the intervention will help, then the thing is worth doing as a preventive. After all, we nearly all have inoculations against lockjaw, and only a few of us will be exposed to it. This conflict has been well represented here by Dr Brazelton on the one hand and Dr Papoušek on the other. I don't suppose we can resolve it today.

Hinde: I thought it was the scientists who had to reply to what I was saying. I wasn't attacking the physicians.

Leiderman: You really stated the issue extremely well, Professor Hinde. The scientist is orientated towards principles and he uses groups. The physician is addressing the specific case. There is always going to be tension between those two elements. Those of us who attempt to do both, if we are not completely schizophrenic, try to reconcile these two points of view but we never achieve the complete synthesis. The tension when we move from one to the other is essential for progress, in my opinion. In his new book (1974), Dr Spock —who has had 30–40 years of experience of work in the American culture— says that parents have been too permissive. He says now that parents have to be much more certain, much more authoritarian, and not allow the permissive kind of culture. Presumably for the next generation the Spockian edict will bring about an 'experiment' in nature, hopefully within the purview of science and the individual physician. These broad changes have to be taken into account in all developmental research because they probably have large non-specific effects on our work. We may have a new developmental psychology within the next ten years.

Reference

SPOCK, B. (1974) *Raising Children in a Difficult Time*, Norton, New York

General discussion

NEONATAL CARE UNITS

Hofer: Dr Bowlby, you have had experience in trying to proceed from clinical observations to change in practice and—continuing what Robert Hinde said just now (p. 296)—I wonder if you can help to bring us from the general to the particular?

Bowlby: Although we are all interested in the long-term effects of particular practices, we know that that kind of information is extremely difficult to get. My view is that we have to use our common sense by adopting criteria which are near at hand and which seem likely to be relevant. A criterion I would give much weight to is whether a hospital-based or a home-based practice gives a mother greater confidence in her performance and greater enjoyment of her baby.

A mother who is confident and enjoying what she is doing is almost certainly going to do far better for her baby, both physiologically and psychologically, than if she is anxious and miserable. That type of criterion isn't too difficult to apply. Dr Richards is already doing so when he notes (p. 172) that in hospital women usually weep when feeding the baby and at home they don't. In terms of this type of criterion, there would probably be a consensus among us as to which are and which are not useful practices during the early weeks of life. If we could agree on that, then I wouldn't have the least hesitation in commending one practice in preference to another. I think one has to stick one's neck out.

Hofer: Can we stick our necks out now on the premature infant as a critical life event or a crisis?

Klaus: At this time, we can state that parents should be a part of every premature unit. They should be allowed to visit at any time. They should be permitted and welcome to help with the care of their infants. Already in some premature units a bed is always available for the mother and as a result breast-feeding can be easily maintained. This is especially important in developing countries where breast-feeding during the first year of life significantly reduces mortality and morbidity (Kahn *et al.* 1954). If we know that the mother has an increased chance of having a high-risk baby, it would be wise to move this mother to a special delivery unit when she goes into labour at 32 weeks.

Dreyfus-Brisac: One problem with highly sophisticated centres is that the number of premature births in such departments is small. Most of the premature babies come from outside, where intensive care for high-risk mothers is not available.

Richards: Your point clashes with Dr Bowlby's comment, Dr Klaus. A mother doesn't want to go 50 miles just because someone thinks she might have a small baby. She wants to stay at home with her other children and with her husband.

Klaus: We have to find out her medical needs and work out the decision with her.

Stewart: Isn't there an order of priorities to be observed at this stage? First, the mother has to have a baby before she can get attached to it. She may have to decide between going away and having a live baby, or staying at home and maybe not having a live baby.

Richards: There is a direct clash of values. Such evidence as we have suggests that many women would like to have their babies at home. The obstetricians say that this carries a risk which is reduced if they go to hospital. Does that mean that every mother should be in hospital, when some will be unhappy by John Bowlby's criterion?

D'Souza: Can one not treat people as adults and put before them the possibilities, risks and choices available?

Stewart: That implies being able to predict high-risk situations at an early stage. In certain circumstances we can, but at least 50% of high-risk situations cannot be predicted, so we cannot present the choice to the mother, and these are the situations when she has the stark choice of a live or a dead baby.

Bowlby: We seem to be bedevilled by the health statistics. The number of live or dead babies is a statistic that is chalked up either in favour of or against a particular hospital or a particular district. Other statistics may be just as important, but unfortunately we don't have them to chalk up. Let us consider the case of a woman who already has two children and is having her third pregnancy, which she is not enthusiastic about. If one goes to great lengths to make absolutely sure of a live baby there, one may have a most damaging effect on the family and the two children already existing. The problem is that in our technological society the pressure to utilize every possible means of ensuring a live baby outweighs all other considerations. This seems to me a most dangerous state of affairs.

D'Souza: As yet we have little real knowledge of what the physiological implications are of giving a mother the responsibility for deciding these things. For example it may well be that having such a responsibility may even affect whether it will be a high-risk baby or not. I should like to make one final and perhaps not very acceptable point. There has been heavy use in these discussions of words such as 'permit' and 'allow' when people referred to mothers' access to their babies. A newborn baby *belongs* to its mother; giving responsibility to a mother implies that she has a choice about whether or not she will visit her baby and this may be a more healthy state of affairs. I, of course, accept that there may be sound medical reasons for some kind of intervention between a mother and her newborn child but I would be happy to think that hospital staff 'enable' rather than permit the mother to be in close contact. Much of the research presented at this symposium would suggest that the earliest possible contact between a mother and her child is vital, and medical staff therefore have a most essential role to play.

Stewart: The next priority, if the baby is alive, is whether he will be normal or not. This may be even more important than the alive/dead decision. For babies of low birth weight we have to decide what care that child should have. Again, if we can predict in advance, we can make a sensible and rational judgement. But when a woman suddenly has a premature baby in the middle of the night, at 27 weeks, time spent sitting down to ask her what she wants means delay in obtaining optimum care. with consequent risk to life—or possibly more important—risk of irreversible damage to the baby.

Bentovim: The attachment or bond between mother and infant is potentially an immensely strong one, if a setting is provided in which the bond can grow without unnecessary disturbance. Dr Stewart's study indicates that useful changes can be introduced into a highly abnormal situation, if the parents' feelings are kept in mind. The family's needs can be met even in the highly abnormal situation of a premature nursery, although it is difficult to reproduce features of a 'home' in any institution!

Richards: Robert Hinde is quite right to say (p. 296) that scientists are bad at thinking about individuals, and that our techniques are based on groups. But it is a myth to suppose that medicine deals with individuals. The whole problem is that everyone gets the same: all mothers in one hospital may get 100 mg of pethidine; in another 250 mg; all babies go to special care nurseries if they weigh less than so many grams. Somehow, we must build institutions for medical care that allow for variety and for people's individuality.

Bentovim: It has to be remembered that medical institutions also have to reduce the anxieties of the people working in them, and rigidity and predictability achieve this (Menzies 1960). A system is necessary which can bear individual differences and which can listen to what staff and patients feel about their situation, rather than one that denies the existence of feelings.

Macfarlane: It is not only the medical institutions we have to build, but also the medical doctors to run them and people who can remain aware of the value of individual differences.

Stewart: Properly trained people are more important than the buildings.

Curtis-Jenkins: Does individual choice ultimately make any real difference? What was the main influence in deciding on the change in emphasis in the early treatment of spina bifida? Was it individual choice by parents, or was it a purely economic decision, made when it was pointed out that the existing burden of spina bifida children would cost this country £80 million a year by 1980? The seeds of the same problem are present in decisions about building highly specialized premature baby units. The choice may not be an individual choice but something as simple as an economic one; yet it will be accepted and then, later, many of these decisions to build such enormously expensive units may have to be reversed.

Stewart: Economic pressures in the UK may already have made their mark on decisions about how care for the newborn will be organized.

Hofer: Are you implying that the right thing will be done for the wrong reason?

Stewart: No, I am implying that, whether for the right reason or the wrong one, what finally tips the scales may well be economic factors.

Richards: Surely that is already implicit in the whole system. At the moment, we spend a great deal of money on special nurseries for the newborn, but much less on, say, the treatment of cystitis, for which many doctors send people to self-help groups. We can find endless examples of this kind which demonstrate the values of the present system. In effect, we are saying that certain things are worth spending money on and others aren't. Our present system of medical care has grown up through a long and muddled history of tradition and accidents. At last I think people are beginning to question whether these are the right values. Is it right to spend several hundreds of pounds a day on a very small baby as opposed to spending the same amount on something else? Everything we do means we cannot do something else.

Stewart: We don't have the alternative of spending a particular amount on a small baby. If we don't spend it, the baby may well *not* die but he may be damaged and so have to be supported by the state for life. The cost of keeping such an individual is fantastic, compared to the cost of resuscitating him properly.

Klaus: The decisions have to be made. There is no getting away from that.

Rosenblatt: Dr Kennell said earlier that in the State of Michigan there had been a 10-fold increase in the incidence of battering of babies who had been born by Caesarean section. Dr Ray Helfer (unpublished work, 1974) said that those mothers who by his criteria are likely to become battering parents are the ones who use contraception or abortion least. That is largely because they are having the baby in order to force some man, or some situation, to take care of them.

Bentovim: The incidence varies according to the population. About 30% of our series of abused children have been hospitalized for medical or surgical intervention as neonates (Bentovim 1974). Adequate care is not being given to the families of these neonates and the children are returning abused.

Hofer: A few minutes ago there seemed to be a feeling of powerlessness about decisions being forced on us by economic factors or something outside our control. Do we have to take such a helpless position? In the specific case of premature babies haven't we defined enough principles to be of help in this risk situation?

Thoman: It seems to me that we are really making an appeal for flexibility in terms of decision-making processes at each stage. What kind and quality of help should be given and who should get it? That is not very specific but at least it is a direction to go in.

Bowlby: Unfortunately, we have to have general principles as well. However much a physician wants to deal with his patients on an individual basis, his measures are limited by the policies adopted by the health institutions within which he is working.

Klaus: A survey (unpublished) from Stanford in 1970 of 1400 premature nurseries in the US revealed that only 34% of these institutions permitted mothers to come in to touch and handle their infants.

Leiderman: One of the most important points of that survey was that the information about parent's entry into the premature nursery was disseminated by nurses who attended workshops at various places and then went back to their community hospitals. University hospitals did not lead in the change but were followers. The changes had already taken place elsewhere when universities other than Stanford began to 'study' the idea. This is a critical point. Who are the leaders? Who are the innovators? Who are the people who permit flexibility within the rigidities of institutions? My feeling is that we have to permit many kinds of institutions to try out many different approaches. Science alone is not going to do it, and it is a special problem to get it translated into policy. I like the notion that John Bowlby stated; common sense at a particular time is one way to get an idea over to people, and then we who are wearing our scientific hats can perhaps evaluate the short- and long-term effects.

Klaus: Permitting a mother to make a choice of whether to come to the premature nursery certainly does not appear to be damaging.

Stewart: We will have to emphasize that there is a choice. We have had ladies who refused.

Klaus: It is absolutely necessary to listen to them.

Brazelton: We have to accept that all parents of at-risk babies go through a grief reaction, and that each of them is going to do it at his or her own speed, in his or her own time. Then we have to accept something which medicine really hasn't accepted yet—that we have an opportunity and perhaps even a responsibility to do something about this grief reaction on behalf of the infants for whom we are responsible and of whom we are taking optimum physical care. If those two things are really accepted, we will be able to get on with the question of how to change things for the parents, in order to fit them to provide an optimum environment for their babies.

Stewart: Less specifically, we have to try to see, from the information available, what is the optimum experience. For example, if everybody thinks and feels that the parents should be in the premature baby nursery, we should offer this to the parents. What is more, if we believe this is the optimum arrangement we should encourage it, but we must be flexible: by mistake, people have been made to come into nurseries against their will. We must give them the opportunity to come in their own time, which will vary among individuals.

Hofer: What exactly are the liabilities and difficulties if a mother is forced to come into such a nursery when it doesn't suit her?

Leiderman: The third or fourth mother to whom we gave the choice of entry said she would come in the next day but she didn't appear for three or four days. It turned out that her infant had been an 'unwanted' child. She was truly ambivalent and it went back to events in her personal life and to her relationship with her own mother. This child meant that the mother could not fulfil part of her professional life as she had intended in the past. She felt that she needed time to reconcile herself to having any child, let alone a premature child. This alerted us to the coercive aspects of our nursery, so from then on we were extremely cautious. About 10% of the women in the first year or two did not want to enter the nursery. Later, when this practice became the culture of the hospital, the percentage of refusals fell. Similarly, many fathers need time for their 'paternal' feelings to unfold. We try not to oversell what we consider to be a very salutary circumstance in the mother's and father's life, early care of their infant in the hospital. It is beneficial for most parents but not for all.

Kennell: In Cleveland, mothers have been coming into the nursery since the 1950s and there isn't quite the same aura of this being an unusual and perhaps harmful practice. It is much easier to keep mother and baby together when people around that mother agree that this is a good idea. If a woman is fearful and doesn't want to go into the nursery, early experiences in her own life may be responsible, as you mentioned; but very often an obstetrician or another paediatrician may have told her that he thinks the baby has only one chance in ten of surviving. These statements are based on statistics from several years ago; now the chances are usually nine out of ten. For a number of years in our nursery we have been telling parents that we expect things to go well and have pointed out the good features of their babies. Fortunately, the advances in the care of prematures have helped us to be correct most of the time. Of course we do not make optimistic statements if we are convinced the baby's chances are slim.

Bentovim: A grief reaction for someone that you have loved and become attached to as a real person can be worked through, but for someone never known feelings might be ignored, and might then affect the person in more hidden ways.

Stewart: This raises the question of introducing mothers to babies who are going to die. We were worried about this ourselves to begin with, and it has also been raised by parents. One mother was very aggressive, saying how wicked it was to have shown her one twin who died. She still had a baby to take home but she was obviously feeling absolutely frightful about it. In spite of this, we now feel it is better to introduce them even if the baby might die. The death of a baby is a terrible experience anyway but at least the parents are grieving over a person if they had been introduced and can grieve properly. But should the mother have a free choice about seeing such a baby?

Oppé: In these specific practices we are coming to accept that the mother or the parents should have the choice of running the show their own way. John Bowlby said that we should base our practices on common sense, whatever that may be in this context, so is it possible to have a controlled clinical trial of this kind of thing? Or are the individual variations too great?

Stewart: This is what we would have liked to do, but now we don't consider it is ethical.

Oppé: People who refuse to do clinical trials always say it isn't ethical. But here it is not ethical not to do a controlled clinical trial.

Leiderman: I agree that we should do clinical trials, but they will not give us all the answers, as I tried to point out in my paper. After one year there aren't many differences between those who enter the nursery and those who don't, although there are some differences. The clinician has to decide whether the benefits of allowing mothers into the nursery will outweigh the presumed disabilities ensuing to those few people who might be harmed.

Oppé: Can you tell us how to arrange the clinical trial—what are the measures we should look at, when should we do our follow-up and so on?

Hofer: That is precisely what we hoped would come out of this meeting. We must go away from here with our own ideas and pursue different kinds of clinical trials. Then we may learn something that will have a wide application.

Carpenter: Apart from the presence of the parents, nobody has mentioned the work suggesting that these babies benefit from patterned visual, tactile, and vestibular stimulation (e.g. D. G. Freedman, H. Boverman & N. Freedman, unpublished work, 1966; Hasselmayer 1964; Scarr-Salapatek & Williams 1973). Should these infants be exposed to the constant noise or constant light of incubators, etc.? In animals, absence of patterned sensory input is known to affect early development—the cat's visual system is a well-known example.

Dreyfus-Brisac: Barnard (1972) found that when an auditory stimulus (a heart beat, recorded on magnetic tape) was given regularly to premature babies, they slept better. Weight gain was also faster. This was just a small group but it is something worth trying.

Carpenter: There is a fair amount of information suggesting that early sensory stimulation has beneficial effects on the development of high-risk infants (Hasselmeyer 1964; Neal 1967; Scarr-Salapatek & Williams 1973; Solkoff *et al.* 1969). Scarr-Salapatek & Williams (1973) have demonstrated higher developmental status in their stimulated group over a 12-month period.

Klaus: Two long-term studies of mothers of premature babies permitted half the women to come in to handle their infants in the first days of life. The others, the control group, came in at 21–30 days. A total of 100 patients are included and the studies have lasted four to five years. The evidence supports the idea that mothers should be allowed to come into the premature nursery. I would take part in trials to determine whether we should use incubators or bassinettes with infrared warmers, etc., but not in any more clinical trials on whether the mother should come into the premature unit.

Oppé: I agree. In my nursery any change would have to be in the direction of getting the mothers out, because they have been coming in for so long. Like you, I would not run a controlled trial which would mean forbidding some mothers, on whatever basis, entry to the nursery. Nevertheless, there are still nurseries in the UK that keep mothers out and they could be compared with our kind, although it might be a very impure trial. Or, in nurseries where mothers are now forbidden, it might still be ethical for some mothers to be allowed in on a systematic basis.

Leiderman: If we are reasonably satisfied about certain conditions, this should be translated into a recommendation for hospital care. The next generation of studies will focus on cognitive studies of the infant, the role of the father, and finally on the effect on the entire family unit of a high-risk infant. I would think our concern should be about the next generation of studies rather than simply rediscovering what is already known.

Brazelton: A kind of competition exists unconsciously between 'caretakers' of small babies and their parents. This is a major barrier to change in nurseries which we don't always realize. Until we bring this out into the open we cannot talk about real change.

Bentovim: Helping nurses who deal with children to be family-focused and to share the care of children, particularly of difficult prematures, is a basic problem. Studies should be begun to test ways of helping parents to deal with the emotional crisis of coping with premature babies, and on ways to help caretakers to help on both emotional and practical levels.

Stewart: This is the one thing few parents in our unit would admit to. A few said they were jealous of nurses, but I suspect many more felt jealous without being able to tell us.

Brazelton: Did you ask the nurses if they were jealous of the parents?

Stewart: Yes. They certainly were jealous of them.

Oppé: One desirable change in England would be to stop student midwives coming to premature baby units for a couple of weeks' training. Nurses need to stay in those units for a certain time.

Stewart: I agree. People working in these nurseries need to understand what is going on, and what response to make in any particular situation, as well as how to carry out nursing procedures. Mothers notice any changes.

Brazelton: It is not just education either, but creating new roles for the caretakers in optimizing the parent–child interaction. Nurses and doctors, paediatricians particularly, go into their caretaking roles for specific reasons, and taking away their role with infants without replacing it with a fostering role of another kind is where we might go wrong.

Leiderman: In Stanford some years ago we set up a small discussion group in the premature research nursery which consisted of myself, two other members of the research team, paediatricians, the resident doctors, and the entire nursing staff. Many of these issues about competition, transient staff, family dynamics, infant malformations, and death, were usefully discussed at meetings held once a week for about three years, at times when two shifts of nurses could attend.

Richards: In the UK the Department of Health and Social Security recommends that mothers should have access to their babies in special care units. This may not be being carried out everywhere, but the policy statement has been made.

A number of procedures in premature baby nurseries are introduced on criteria that are rather narrowly medical and they need to be looked at in other ways. For example, Dr Klaus commented (p. 97) that seeing a baby having phototherapy with his eyes covered might be upsetting for the mother. I have also seen mothers upset at seeing their babies having phototherapy when the bandages had slipped so that they were staring straight into these bright lights. No one has studied the possible effects of this on a baby. Anyone without a medical background coming into this environment sees many things they immediately want to ask about. A great deal of research needs to be done on the social and psychological effects of medical practice. And of course one could ask many of the same sorts of questions about delivery units for normal mothers and babies as we have been asking here about premature baby units.

References

BARNARD, K.E. (1972) The effect of stimulation on the duration and amount of sleep and wakefulness in the premature infant. Thesis, University of Washington, Seattle

BENTOVIM, A. (1974) Medical perspectives in care of the abused child, in *The Maltreated Child* (Carter, I., ed.), Priory Press, London

HASSELMEYER, E.G. (1964) The premature neonate's response to handling. *J. Nurs. 11*, 15–24

KAHN, E., WAYBURNE, S. & FOUCHE, M. (1954) The Baragwanath premature baby unit. *S. Afr. Med. J. 28*, 453–456

MENZIES, E.P. (1960) *The Functioning of Social Systems as a Defence against Anxiety: A Study of the Nursing System of a General Hospital*, Tavistock, London

NEAL, M.D. (1967) The relationship between a regimen of vestibular stimulation and the developmental behaviour of the premature infant. Ph.D. dissertation, New York University, N.Y.

SCARR-SALAPATEK, S. & WILLIAMS, M.L. (1973) The effect of early stimulation on low-birth-weight infants. *Child Dev. 44*, 94–101

SOLKOFF, N., YAFFE, S., WEINTRAUB, D. & BLASE, B. (1969) Effects of handling on the subsequent development of premature infants. *Dev. Psychol. 1*, 765–768

Summing up

M. A. HOFER

In a new area of research, such as the early parent–infant relationship, one's sense of its exciting potential often develops together with an appreciation of its complexity. What is really remarkable is how this group of people has been neither paralysed nor discouraged by this complexity, even while confronting it directly, as we have done in the last three days. Because of our recently changed views on the roles of both parent and infant, we have been led to work with the concept of interaction, and even more importantly with interactions which change over time. This concept of interaction has returned again and again throughout the conference, with different meanings and applications.

Detailed studies of the play interaction between mother and infant over periods of time measured in microseconds and minutes by Hinde and Simpson, Brazelton, Klaus, Thoman and Papoušek have revealed the existence of a dance-like synchrony of movements, facial expressions and vocalizations. Hinde and Simpson have developed measures derived from hours of observation of rhesus monkeys which begin to give operational meaning to such words as 'warmth', 'mutuality' and 'control', concepts which we instinctively know are important but which we have not been able to use with any hope of reliability or quantification. Interestingly, another level of interaction became evident when we heard that these ratios and correlational procedures were derived by an interaction between the intuitive or emphatic hunches of the investigators and their more rigorous cognitive activities of classification, counting and abstract mathematical conceptualizations.

The identification of qualities of interactions and the ability to assign quantitative responsibility to one or the other member of a dyad for those qualities, has enabled investigators to ask the next developmental questions: how do these measures change over time measured in weeks and months? Who is primarily responsible for these changes and what is it about the responsible member which produces these changes? Professor Hinde has sharply distinguished these questions in his analysis of rhesus monkey dyads and has set an example, under these controlled conditions, which it will be a challenge to follow in human studies with their unavoidable profusion of uncontrollable intervening variables.

Dr Rosenblatt gave us a further extension of the meaning of the interactional concept which this conference has developed. He has reminded us of the effect of prenatal hormonal changes on maternal behaviour and presented evidence from his work with rats that, in the hours after birth, there is a transition to the infant as the major variable which then serves to elicit and maintain maternal behaviour. This synchrony between a change in regulatory processes and the major life event of birth represents another form of interaction which has important implications for our understanding of the establishment of the human mother–infant relationship. Clearly, the immediate postpartum period cannot be isolated from processes at work both before and afterwards. Nor can we infer similar behavioural regulatory processes for identical behaviours occurring even a few days apart on the developmental time scale.

The descriptions that Dr Klaus gave us of the behaviour of human mothers at first contact with their newborn infants in different cultures strongly suggested that this event initiates a regular series of interactions which have biological roots powerful enough to cut across divergent cultures and might thus earn the label 'species-specific'. Within this general pattern, he has also demonstrated remarkable individual differences which appear to be the result of cultural values and constraints imposed by hospital routines and regulations. In turn, Drs Kennell and Leiderman have shown that the timing and duration of the contact that hospital personnel allow between mother and infant in those first few days can have effects on the relationship lasting months and even years. In particular, more or less complete separation of a mother from her prematurely born baby by the artificial barriers of special treatment apparatus appears to have an adverse effect of the whole family unit. It is not yet clear how long lasting these effects really are. Dr Leiderman has emphasized, with detailed results, that such variables as parity of the mother, socioeconomic class, and sex of the infant may be even more powerful interacting determinants of the long-term mother–infant relationship. Professor Oppé has critically reviewed how developmental psychology may contribute to prevention of paediatric illness if it discovers the processes responsible for failure in the early parent–infant relationship.

Many questions are raised by these studies. What exactly are the behavioural and psychological processes going on during the first minutes and hours of the mother–infant interaction? To what extent can the situation be the same for the father? What are the qualities of the relationship which should be established at this time for the sake of the eventual well-being of both parents and infants? What qualities should be avoided? What, if anything, can the health professions do to promote the establishment of 'successful' relationships? Should we indeed attempt to make such value judgements? Alternatively, on the time-honoured premise that the first job of a good doctor is to do no harm, how can we avoid setting the stage for the development of an unhappy and unhealthy relationship?

The clear urgency of these questions is in obvious conflict with the uncertainty raised by the complexity of the processes which, as studies on animals have shown, underlie the formation of social relationships. This conflict has been reflected in the feelings generated at this meeting. But again, it is encouraging, even surprising, that instead of animosity we have had animation. (Except of course for those moments when our thresholds were exceeded and the 'turn-off' or 'withdrawal response' of Papoušek and Brazelton restored our homeostatic balance.)

A good beginning is being made in the effort to extend our knowledge about the processes by which the newborn infant and his/her mother may regulate their interaction during the first few days after birth. Dr Macfarlane has shown that by the sixth day of life the neonate is able to discriminate and turn towards his own mother, using olfactory cues emanating from her lactating breast. This evidence forces us to realize how sophisticated the cognitive faculties of the neonate may actually be, if only we can recognize the channels of communication. It also offers a specific suggestion to hospitals in that the application of lanolin and deodorants to mothers may not be harmless customs but may actually make the infants' task more difficult. Dr Salisbury has shown us that the chemical senses of neonates also involve specific buccal receptors by which different patterns of feeding and breathing are integrated according to the chemical composition of ingested fluids. This newly discovered capacity of the newborn allows developing regulatory systems for sucking and respiration to be shaped by the kind of food provided by the mother.

In an effort to explore further some of the important questions about the first postnatal days and their value as predictors of future qualities of the relationship, Mrs Dunn and Dr Bell presented studies which search for consistency in maternal and infant behaviours over time, and which show the correlation of those qualities in each person during the neonatal period which are predictive of future behaviours of the other member of the dyad. Dr Bell has taught us some new methodological approaches for simplifying complex data and he demonstrated a simple infant behavioural measure which may tap into a basic mechanism for the regulation of infant emotional behaviour which continues to function over years into early childhood. Mrs Dunn suggested that although there are some interesting consistencies, aspects of the interaction which seem fundamental to the early relationship do not serve as stable predictors of affectionate variables months later in life, but are most closely related to variations in labour and delivery. This might indicate that the early relationship is well buffered against difficulties of adjustment and that it contains the potential for considerable compensation. This buffering or adaptive strength was illustrated vividly by Dr Thoman who showed how a mother was able to compensate for a baby with a congenitally aberrant responsiveness to being held, and by Dr Brazelton's observations on a blind mother. Dr Thoman demonstrated how a range of differently patterned relationships can be quantitatively described, and indicated that different forms of synchrony are possible, all of which may be equally successful developmentally. This lends yet another dimension to our developing concept of interaction which cautions us not to prematurely label some patterns 'good' and others 'bad'.

In fact Drs Stewart, Bentovim, Cooper, Curtis-Jenkins and Brazelton have all emphasized the highly variable psychological tasks faced by different women in making the transition from the mental representation of the child within the womb to the reality of the newborn in their arms. Different tasks give rise to different needs for the mother, but most mothers appear to undergo an 'unhinging' or loosening of anxieties and conflicts during pregnancy which may make it possible to rebuild their personality in a new way so as to accommodate their new child. Indeed this period is an opportunity (not just a crisis) for the growth of security and trust within a family. Professor Hinde pointed out that the infants also must have some mismatch initially between their rhythms and needs and those of their mothers if they are to have any opportunity to learn to be responsive to her and to achieve the flexible mutuality which is most adaptive in the long run.

This idea of both infant and mother having a very complicated and demanding job to do in the first days after birth is illustrated by both Dr Papoušek's studies in infants and Dr Stewart's studies of mothers of premature infants. The word 'job' hardly does justice to the complex integration of cognitive and emotional adjustments which is required of mothers and infants and which is so vividly described in these papers. Even with our newly gained respect for the capacities of the very young infant, Dr Papoušek's observations on the integration possible, at the age of a few weeks, between cognitive, motivational and general behavioural states are remarkable.

The evidence presented at this conference, on both animals and humans, seems to add up to the conclusion that many factors and processes are involved in the forging of a relationship between parents and their infants. There is a transition from the general to the specific in terms of mutual elicitation of behaviours, a transition from random to organized and from independence to synchrony in the dyad. Other, more hidden processes, such as a transition from hormonal to sensory mediation of behaviour may also be involved at this time. Subjectively, the mother experiences this as a transition from anxiety, conflict and bewilderment to joy and a sense of competence. Unnecessary and unwanted separation of the newborn from its parents immediately after birth has a far more deleterious effect on these ongoing developmental processes and transitions in the mother than the same amounts of separation later on, because the postnatal period is characterized by such rapid reorganization of her behaviour, and that of her infant, in relation to each other.

We have struggled, in our final discussion, with the problems raised by attempting to move from research findings to proposals for altered medical care. It was recognized that the medical profession is too often unmindful of the fragile new relationship between mother and infant, and of the complex interlocking needs of that relationship. The more medical routines intrude during the immediate postnatal period, the more difficulties are posed for establishment of the parent–infant relationship and the greater the long-term risks to the stability of the family and to the later health of the child. But the thrust of this principle leads us sharply against a number of countervailing forces, including the life support needs of the sick newborn and early premature infant, the individual preferences of parents, economic and cultural pressures, and our own disagreements about the relative importance of different factors in long-term effects on the infant.

General agreement was reached that parents should have reasonably free access to their premature and full-term infants, beginning as soon as possible after birth, but that this should be arranged flexibly, to accommodate individual differences among parents and infants. I think we also agreed that further research along lines suggested by this conference is imperative and will be immensely useful to the future health of infants and parents alike.

This conference gives evidence of a growing body of basic work leading to concepts which are becoming generally accepted and which will stimulate both further enquiry and more effective management of the neonatal period.

Index of contributors

Entries in **bold type** *refer to papers; other entries are contributions to discussions*

Indexes compiled by William Hill

Subject index